6249

D1597081

Advanced Studies in Theoretical and Applied Econometrics

Volume 49

Giovanni Cerulli

Econometric Evaluation of Socio-Economic Programs

Theory and Applications

 Springer

Giovanni Cerulli
Research Institute on Sustainable Economic Growth
CNR-IRCrES National Research Council of Italy
Roma, Italy

ISSN 1570-5811   ISSN 2214-7977 (electronic)
Advanced Studies in Theoretical and Applied Econometrics
ISBN 978-3-662-46404-5   ISBN 978-3-662-46405-2   (eBook)
DOI 10.1007/978-3-662-46405-2

Library of Congress Control Number: 2015938330

Springer Heidelberg New York Dordrecht London

Printed on acid-free paper

Springer-Verlag GmbH Berlin Heidelberg is part of Springer Science+Business Media
(www.springer.com)

*To my wife Rossella and to my daughters
Marta and Emma, priceless gifts from God.*

Preface

This book provides readers with a set of both theoretical and applied tools in order to illustrate the correct implementation of modern micro-econometric techniques for program evaluation in the social sciences. As such, the reader is offered a comprehensive toolbox for designing rigorous and effective ex post program evaluation using the statistical software package Stata. The theoretical statistical models relating to each individual evaluation technique are discussed and followed by at least one empirical estimation of the treatment effects using both built-in and user-written Stata commands.

During the course of the discussion, readers will gradually become familiar with the most common evaluation techniques discussed in the literature, such as the Regression-adjustment, Matching, Difference-in-differences, Instrumental-variables, and Regression-discontinuity-design, and will be offered a series of practical guidelines for the selection and application of the most suitable approach to implement under differing policy contexts.

The book is organized in four chapters.

The first chapter provides an introduction to the econometrics of program evaluation, paving the way for the arguments developed in subsequent chapters, laying out the statistical setup, standard notation, and basic assumptions used in the estimation of a program's treatment effects in the socioeconomic context. The concept of selection bias, both due to observable and unobservable factors, is discussed and an overview of the econometric methods available to correct for such biases is illustrated. The chapter concludes with a brief discussion of the principle Stata commands for the estimation of the treatment effects, along with the various econometric methods for binary treatment proposed in the literature.

The second chapter focuses on the estimation of average treatment effects under the assumption of "selection on observables" (or "overt bias") and provides a systematic account of the meaning and scope of such an assumption in program evaluation analysis. A number of econometric methods (such as: Regression-adjustment, Matching, Reweighting, and the Doubly-robust estimator) are discussed, in order to ensure correct inference for casual parameters in this setting.

The chapter ends with a series of empirical applications of these methods in a comparative perspective.

The third chapter focuses on econometric methods for estimating average treatment effects under "selection on unobservables" (or "hidden bias"). This occurs when non-observable factors significantly drive the nonrandom assignment to treatment. In such a situation, the methods discussed in Chap. 2 are no longer appropriate for estimating program effects. In Chap. 3, therefore, we present three techniques for correct estimation in the presence of selection on unobservables: Instrumental-variables, Selection-models, and Difference-in-differences, the implementation of which requires either additional information or further assumptions.

The fourth chapter addresses two related subjects: the Local average treatment effect (LATE) and the Regression-discontinuity-design (RDD), both considered as nearly quasi-experimental methods. It offers a discussion of the theory underlying the LATE approach, illustrating the setting of a randomized experiment with imperfect compliance, and goes on to discuss the sample estimation of LATE. The second part of the chapter focuses on the RDD, used when a specific variable (the so-called *forcing* variable) defines a "threshold" separating—either sharply or fuzzily—treated and untreated units. After presenting the econometric background for the RDD model, the discussion focuses on both sharp RDD and fuzzy RDD methodologies. A simulation model both for sharp RDD and fuzzy RDD is also presented in order to illustrate the role played by each of the underlying assumptions of these differing approaches.

The chapters of this book can be considered as fairly self-contained units. The more interested reader will however find it useful to have a thorough understanding of the subjects singularly treated in each chapter. Finally, it should be noted that I assume the reader to be familiar with basic econometric theory and to have some prior knowledge of the use of Stata for econometric purposes.

Rome, Italy   G. Cerulli

Acknowledgements

Writing this book has been a long and demanding process. I would therefore like to take this opportunity to thank those people, who have contributed to the final product. In particular: Una-Louise for editing Chaps. 2, 3, and 4 and Christopher Baum and Paula Arnold for their useful suggestions and corrections of Chap. 1. My motivation for writing this book derives from the doctoral course in "Micro-econometric causality" I teach, in collaboration with Paolo Naticchioni, at the Doctoral School of Economics, La Sapienza, Rome. I would like to thank, therefore, both Paolo and our students, for their interest and their stimulating interventions over the past few years.

Thanks are also due to my research institute, CNR-IRCrES (former Ceris), for the assistance I received during the preparation of this book and to all my colleagues for their ongoing support. I also thank TStat, which commissioned me to write a number of course units for teaching micro-econometric courses to applied researchers. Thanks go also to all the participants to the recent Italian and the UK Stata meetings, to the Stata staff I met there, and in particular to David M. Drukker for his useful suggestions on the methods presented in Chap. 3.

Finally, a special thank you goes to my family and parents, for both their patience and understanding, without which writing this book would not have been possible.

Contents

Chapter 1
An Introduction to the Econometrics of Program Evaluation

Contents

1.1 Introduction

It is common practice for policymakers to perform ex post evaluation of the impact of economic and social programs via evidence-based statistical analysis. This effort is mainly devoted to measure the "causal effects" of an intervention on the part of an external authority (generally, a local or national government) on a set of subjects (people, companies, etc.) targeted by the program. Evidence-based evaluation is

© Springer-Verlag Berlin Heidelberg 2015
G. Cerulli, *Econometric Evaluation of Socio-Economic Programs*,
Advanced Studies in Theoretical and Applied Econometrics 49,
DOI 10.1007/978-3-662-46405-2_1

progressively becoming an integral part of many policies worldwide.[1] The main motivation resides in the fact that, when a public authority chooses to support private entities by costly interventions, a responsibility towards taxpayers is assumed. This commitment, constitutionally recognized in several countries, draws upon the principle that, since many alternative uses of the same amount of money are generally possible, any misuse of it is seen as waste, especially under severe budget constraints.

In this spirit, results from program evaluation may serve two related goals: "learning" aimed at providing improvements of various kinds for future policy programs, generally directed to managers and administrators, and "legitimation" directed to higher political levels and to participants and other stakeholders involved in the program (Moran et al. 2008).

Ex post impact evaluation is part of the so-called *cycle of policymaking*, the reference framework of public policy analysis in political science (Althaus et al. 2007). Within this framework, ex post policy assessment is performed both by qualitative and quantitative techniques. This book focuses on the quantitative (or econometric) side of the coin, although it recognizes that a comprehensive and accurate impact evaluation should integrate elements of quality assessment as well. This is in the hope of avoiding "black box" results, as it is not only important to measure the effects, but also to know the etiological mechanisms driving the eventual policy success or failure.

A proper quantitative evaluation design should take into account at least three key qualitative aspects: (1) the political, institutional, and normative context within which the policy was implemented (the environment); (2) a clear understanding of the motivations and incentive schemes underlying the behavior of the involved public and private entities; (3) a clear-cut definition of direct and potentially indirect effects generated by the intervention. Further preconditions are also important for an econometric impact evaluation to be effective, for instance: (1) an appropriate evaluation design, based on the declared policy goals; (2) detailed and well-documented data and information; (3) a broad and appropriate coverage of beneficiaries and non-beneficiaries; and (4) a broad coverage of the spatial context when policies are geographically based.

In the last two decades, the literature on the econometrics of program evaluation has evolved, with new econometric techniques becoming a fundamental tool of analysis in many research areas both in economics and in other social sciences (Millimet et al. 2008; Imbens and Wooldridge 2009). These include labor economics, industrial organization, development studies, and sociological and demographic empirical research. This book presents an exposition of the modern tools

---

[1] A wide range of literature witnesses this relevance. See reviews and books such as: Heckman (2000); Heckman et al. (2000); Blundell and Costa Dias (2002); Shadish et al. (2002); Cobb-Clark and Crossley (2003); Imbens (2004); Lee (2005); Morgan and Winship (2007); Imbens and Wooldridge (2009); Angrist and Pischke (2008); Millimet et al. (2008); Imbens and Wooldridge (2009); Cerulli (2010); Guo and Fraser (2010); Wooldridge (2002, Chap. 18); Wooldridge (2010, Chap. 21).

for an econometric evaluation of the effect of socioeconomic programs, with a primary focus on practical issues and applications in order to provide an accurate and rigorous empirical research in this field of study.

The econometrics of program evaluation has its roots in epidemiological statistics and in the so-called literature on "treatment effect" estimation (Neyman 1923; Angrist 1991; Rothman et al. 2008; Husted et al. 2000). In the simplest terms, the treatment effect is defined as the effect of a specific *treatment* variable on an *outcome* (or *target*) variable, once any potential *confounders* affecting the link between the cause and the effect are ruled out. The treatment variable may be, according to the disciplinary context, a new drug, a new type of physiotherapy method, as well as, in the economic context, a training program for unemployed workers, a subsidy to firms' capital investment, and so on.

In this literature the terms "treatment" and "causal factor" are exchangeable, thus meaning that the researcher is not looking for a mere association among phenomena, but rather a precise causal link. In doing so, the econometric approach makes use of observational data, whose character is inherently ex post (i.e., "after-the-fact"). This places econometrics within the sphere of nonexperimental statistical designs, where the analyst has no capacity to manipulate the design of the experiment. In contrast, experimental and quasi-experimental designs are characterized by a scientist's capacity of controlling the experiment. In the classical experimental setting, the scientist deliberately produces a *random assignment* of the units involved in the experiment. In contrast, in quasi-experimental designs, although assignment is nonrandom, the scientist can manage the form of this nonrandomness at least to some acceptable extent. The simplest case of a quasi-experimental setting is the so-called non-equivalent groups design (NEGD) where the control (or comparison) group is chosen beforehand to be as similar as possible to the treatment group (Trochim and Donnelly 2007).

In experimental and quasi-experimental designs, the treatment effect is generally estimated by the "counterfactual" approach, so that scientists in that field often refer to measuring "counterfactual causality" (Pearl 2000, 2009). The concept of counterfactual causality, as we will discuss, draws upon the assumption that causality takes the form of a *comparison* between the outcome of a unit when this unit is *treated* in a certain way, and the outcome of the *same* unit when it is not treated. If one observes a unit only in its treated status, the untreated status is defined as the *counterfactual status* that is—by definition—not observable.

To better clarify the concept of counterfactual causality, Fig. 1.1 shows a representation of the effect of a policy taking place between t_0 and t_1 for a representative unit. The solid line represents the unit observed performance, the dashed line the unit counterfactual performance (i.e., what the unit would have done, had it not been supported by the policy). This specific example refers to a policy aimed at increasing company patenting activity. In t_0 (i.e., before the policy), the company filed ten patents, whereas in t_1 (i.e., after the policy) it ends up with filing six patents, fewer than before. At first glance, by only focusing on the indication provided by the observed performance, one might be tempted to conclude that the policy failed in achieving its objective. Nevertheless, once taking into account the counterfactual situation, one can clearly recognize that—without the

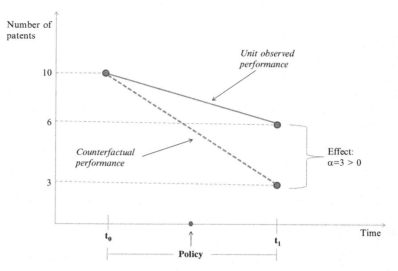

Fig. 1.1 An instructional graphical representation of "counterfactual causality"

policy—the company would have been patenting even fewer patents. It might appear surprising, but from a counterfactual point of view the policy was successful, as the final effect is positive (indeed, $\alpha = 6 - 3 = 3 > 0$). In this case, we can state that the policy "has reduced the damage."

If a public agency had only considered the observed levels, its conclusion about the usefulness of the policy would have been severely biased. This is the typical trap an agency can come across when considering just one side of the coin, the observed side. Only considering the observed performance is sometimes referred to as *policy monitoring*, whereas *policy evaluation* in the proper sense *always* needs to encompass the counterfactual comparison in order to draw reliable conclusions about the actual causal effect.

The concept of counterfactual causality is not new to economists and econometricians. For many years, however, the discipline mainly focused on macroeconomic analysis, where the main interest was in conceptualizing and measuring causality within structural econometric models (SEM). SEM involved systems of simultaneous equations, where the key issue was that of achieving parameters' identification by invoking some form of economic structure, generally driven by a given theoretical framework (Hoover 2001).

This was in the spirit of the foundation of modern econometrics, as witnessed by the famous Cowles Commission-NBER debate on "measuring without theory" of the 1940s (Koopmans 1947, 1949; Vining 1949a, b). Yet, in the next decades, quantitative macroeconomists went on to debate about identification and causality, as shown by the 1980s' Lucas-Sims debate on problems of identification under the Rational Expectations Hypothesis (Lucas 1976, 1980; Lucas and Sargent 1981; Sims 1980, 1996), or by the dispute among structuralists and empiricists in vector auto-regressive (VAR) models (Cooley and LeRoy 1985).

As microeconometrics has increased its relevance in many economic and social fields, the task of measuring causality in a counterfactual way has become increasingly appealing to economists and social scientists, especially for those involved in policy evaluation at the micro-level. Therefore, in recent years, a huge number of theoretical and applied studies for assessing the effect of policy interventions in the labor market first and then in many other policy environments, have appeared.

In the SEM tradition, as distinct from epidemiology, scholars generally refer to "probabilistic causality":

> In *probabilistic causality* one tries to find a (or the) cause for Y by checking whether the possible cause changes the probability distribution for Y where no counter-factuals are envisioned (Lee 2005, p. 196).

The difference between counterfactual and probabilistic causality is subtle and not resolved:

> Causal parameters based on counterfactuals provide statistically meaningful and operational definitions of causality that in some respects differ from the traditional Cowles foundation definition. First, in ideal settings this framework leads to considerable simplicity of econometric methods. Second, this framework typically focuses on the *fewer* causal parameters that are thought to be most relevant to policy issues that are examined. This contrasts with the traditional econometric approach that focuses simultaneously on all structural parameters. Third, the approach provides additional insights into the properties of causal parameters estimated by the standard structural methods (Cameron and Trivedi 2005, pp. 32–33).

Although taking a different perspective, the counterfactual approach to causality is not in contrast with the traditional SEM framework, of which it can be considered as a generalization.

To better shed light on this point, take the case of the traditional regression model. It is usually specified assuming that causality assumes a linear form, where the analyst is interested in assessing the effect of a (usually) continuous variable (x) on a dependent variable (Y), by adding within the regression some *control* (or *conditioning*) factors. As we are embedded in a nonexperimental framework (a social experiment, as said above), at the heart of this causal framework there is the *exogeneity* issue: the "true" causal effect of x on Y can be identified, as long as independent changes of x only produce a *direct* effect on Y, by ruling out any potential *indirect* effect of x on Y, via the relation of x with unobservable factors. This is the condition under which x can be assumed to be *exogenous*; otherwise it is said to be "endogenously determined" and traditional estimation via ordinary least squares (OLS) produces biased estimates of the causal parameter.

It is easy to show that in this case, OLS estimates the so-called "pseudo-true value" which is not the actual causal effect the analyst seeks (Cameron and Trivedi 2005, pp. 18–38). An example can better clarify this argument. Take the simple regression model $Y = \beta x + u$, where β is the causal effect of x on Y and u is an unobservable component, and differentiate by x, thus yielding:

$$dy/dx = \beta + du/dx \qquad (1.1)$$

The model is identified as long as $du/dx = 0$, as in this case $dy/dx = \beta$; otherwise, autonomous changes in x are not exogenously determined, as x has also an *indirect* effect on Y through its effect on u. As du/dx is *unobservable*, the analyst is unable to separate the direct effect (β) and the indirect effect (du/dx). The model is no longer identified as a single equation and needs further information or assumptions to recover β correctly (such as, for instance, the availability of an instrumental variable). In this example, the "pseudo-true value" is equal to the sum of the "direct" and "indirect" effect (equal in turn to the "total" effect, in the SEM language).

The counterfactual approach to causality, in its simplest form, can be reformulated in terms of the same regression model where the variable x assumes in this case a binary form (x_0 for the treated and x_1 for the untreated status) instead of a continuous form. By assuming to observe both Y_1 and Y_0 (i.e., the outcomes in the two states for the same individual), we can write that $Y_1 = \beta\, x_1 + u_1$ and $Y_0 = \beta\, x_0 + u_0$. By subtracting previous relations, we get $Y_1 - Y_0 = \beta\, (x_1 - x_0) + u_1 - u_0$, a formula that, apart from the problem of a *missing observation* (Holland 1986), is equivalent to $\Delta y = \beta\, \Delta x + \Delta u$. By dividing by Δx, we finally obtain:

$$\Delta y/\Delta x = \beta + \Delta u/\Delta x \qquad (1.2)$$

which is the discrete version of (1.1). As in (1.1), the causal parameter of interest in (1.2) is β, and if $\Delta u/\Delta x \neq 0$, a bias appears even in this case.

Yet, in many regards, the econometrics of program evaluation has opened up a series of very interesting issues that conventional econometrics was unable to address or that remained—in that tradition—substantially "hidden." These issues include a more rigorous definition of "causal parameters" and of their relations; the importance of sample generation and selection; the role of unobservable heterogeneity, as well as the relative advantage of adopting parametric and nonparametric methods have been highly developed in this field of econometrics (Angrist and Pischke 2008).

Of course, as recognized by James J. Heckman (2001) in his Nobel Prize lecture, the issue of parameters' identification still remains at the center of the scene in both traditions, so that econometric counterfactual methods should be considered just as a different angle to look at previous efforts of conceptualizing and measuring causality within structural econometrics. What is crucial is that the counterfactual approach has opened up a new perspective on traditional estimation.

As an example, deriving the parameter of a binary regression as developed above and showing that it is actually equal to the "average treatment effect" is much more informative than just defining it as a regression coefficient, although this second meaning is still correct.[2] Overall, the literature on the econometrics of program evaluation, by contributing to the development of a new perspective to

---

[2] Probably more explicit in this direction might be the recent developments in the field of "continuous treatment" where the treatment variable x assumes a continuous form. In this case, although the setting is very close to the traditional econometric regression, the counterfactual approach provides new insights on the meaning of causal parameters, as in the definition and estimation of the Average Partial Effect (Wooldridge 2001) or of the Average Potential Outcome (Hirano and Imbens 2004).

nonexperimental settings and the causality issue, is also able to shed new light on traditional econometric practice, thus widening both our technical knowledge in this field and our capacity to apply more appropriate statistical tools to a variety of old and new (micro)economic policy issues.

1.2 Statistical Setup, Notation, and Assumptions

As sketched above, from a statistical point of view, we are interested in estimating the so-called "treatment effect" of a policy program in a nonexperimental setup, where a *binary* treatment variable D—taking value 1 for treated and 0 for untreated units—is assumed to affect an *outcome* (or *target*) variable Y that can take a variety of forms: binary, count, continuous, etc. Throughout this book we will assume D to be *binary*, although recent literature has provided a generalization of the counter-factual methods both to the case of D taking more than two values (*multiple treatment*) (Angrist and Imbens 1995; Frölich 2004; Cattaneo 2010) and to the case of D taking continuous values (*continuous treatment* and *dose–response* models) (Imbens 2000; Imai and Van Dyk 2004; Hirano and Imbens 2004; Cerulli 2014b).

To begin with, we define the unit i *treatment effect* (TE) as:

$$\mathrm{TE}_i = Y_{1i} - Y_{0i} \tag{1.3}$$

TE_i is equal to the difference between the value of the target variable when the individual is treated (Y_1) and the value assumed by this variable when the *same* individual is untreated (Y_0). As TE_i refers to *the same individual at the same time*, it goes without saying that the analyst can observe just one of the two quantities in (1.3), but not both. For instance, it might be the case that we can observe the investment behavior of a subsidized company, but we cannot know what the investment of this company would have been had it not been subsidized, and vice versa. The analyst faces a fundamental *missing observation problem* (Holland 1986) that must be tackled econometrically in order to reliably recover the causal effect (Rubin 1974, 1977).

What is *observable* to the analyst is the observable status of unit i, obtained by:

$$Y_i = Y_{0i} + D_i(Y_{1i} - Y_{0i}) \tag{1.4}$$

Equation (1.4) is the so-called potential outcome model (POM), and it is the fundamental relation linking *unobservable* with *observable* outcomes.

Both Y_{1i} and Y_{0i} are assumed to be independent and identically distributed (i.i.d.) random variables, generally explained by a structural component dependent on observable factors and a nonstructural component comprised of an error term. Recovering the entire distributions of Y_{1i} and Y_{0i} (and, consequently, the distribu-tion of the TE_i) may be however too demanding without further assumptions. The

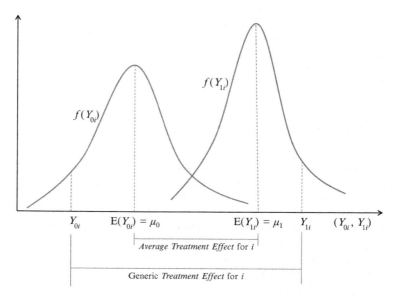

Fig. 1.2 Density distributions of Y_{1i} and Y_{0i}, treatment effect, and average treatment effect

literature has thus focused on estimating specific moments of these distributions and in particular the mean, thus defining the so-called population average treatment effect (hereinafter ATE) of a policy intervention as:

$$\text{ATE} = \text{E}(Y_{i1} - Y_{i0}) \tag{1.5}$$

where $\text{E}(\cdot)$ is the mean operator. This parameter is equal to the difference between the average of the target variable when the individual is treated (Y_1) and the average of the target variable when the same individual is untreated (Y_0). In what follows, for the sake of simplicity, we will not use the subscript referring to unit i when not strictly necessary.

Figure 1.2 provides a simple graphical representation of the density distribution of Y_{i1} and Y_{i0} by showing a generic treatment effect (TE_i) and the ATE. It is rather intuitive that for distributions poorly concentrated around the mean, the ATE might be a weak representation of the global effect of the policy. For this reason, some scholars have recently proposed to consider an alternative set of (global) causal parameters, the "quantile treatment effects,"[3] allowing the identification of the effect of a policy program in the Q-th quantile of the distribution of Y_1 and Y_0. Figure 1.3 sets out a graphical representation of the quantile treatment effect.

---

[3] For an in-depth study of this subject, see: Imbens and Wooldridge (2009, pp. 17–18); Frölich and Melly (2013); Abadie et al. (2002); Chernozhukov and Hansen (2005). See also Frölich and Melly (2010) for a Stata implementation.

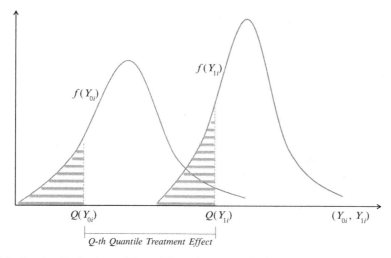

Fig. 1.3 Density distributions of Y_{1i} and Y_{0i} and Q-th quantile treatment effect

Although the quantile approach may be complementary to the analysis based on the mean, this book will focus on traditional average treatment effects, as widely developed in the literature. A possible reason why the literature has mainly focused on the mean rather than quantiles of TE_i may depend on the fact that while for the mean it holds that:

$$E(Y_{i1} - Y_{i0}) = E(Y_{i1}) - E(Y_{i0})$$

the same does not occur for quantiles. For instance, consider the 50th percentile (i.e., the median) of TE_i. In such a case we have that:

$$\text{Med}(Y_{i1} - Y_{i0}) \neq \text{Med}(Y_{i1}) - \text{Med}(Y_{i0})$$

These two median measures convey different and sometimes contrasting conclusions about policy effectiveness. Consider, for instance, a policy aimed at increasing the level of education. In such a case, it might be that:

$$\text{Med}(Y_{i1} - Y_{i0}) > 0$$

meaning that at least 50 % of the population has a positive TE_i, and at the same time:

$$\text{Med}(Y_{i1}) - \text{Med}(Y_{i0}) < 0$$

meaning that the median person's level of education has decreased.[4] This possibility has made the quantile treatment effect less appealing than that based on the mean.

---

[4] See Lee (2005, pp. 12–13) for a simple numerical example of such a situation.

By relying on the mean, however, the mainstream literature has emphasized two additional parameters as relevant to estimate. These are known as the average treatment effect on the treated (ATET) and the average treatment effect on the untreated (ATENT), defined respectively as:

$$ATET = E(Y_1 - Y_0 | D = 1) \tag{1.6}$$

$$ATENT = E(Y_1 - Y_0 | D = 0) \tag{1.7}$$

It is fairly easy to see that the ATET is the average treatment effect calculated within the subsample of treated units (those with $D = 1$), while the ATENT is the average treatment effect calculated within the subsample of untreated units (those with $D = 0$). These two parameters can provide additional information on the causal relation between D and Y. It is also useful to show the relation linking ATE, ATET, and ATENT:

$$ATE = ATET \cdot p(D = 1) + ATENT \cdot p(D = 0) \tag{1.8}$$

that is, the ATE is a weighted average of the ATET and the ATENT, with $p(D = 1)$ representing the probability of being treated and $p(D = 1)$ that of being untreated. Equation (1.8) simply follows from the law of iterated expectations (LIE).

Nevertheless, another important ingredient is necessary to proceed with the econometrics of program evaluation. For each unit, beyond the values of Y and D, researchers (normally) have access also to a number of *observable covariates* which can be collected in a row vector $\mathbf{x}$. Usually, these variables represent various individual characteristics such as age, gender, income, education and so on. The knowledge of these variables, as we will see, is of primary usefulness in the estimation of the treatment effects, as they may represent relevant *confounding factors* that must be taken into account.

It is then worth stressing that, given the knowledge of $\mathbf{x}$, we can also define the previous parameters as conditional on $\mathbf{x}$, as:

$$ATE(\mathbf{x}) = E(Y_1 - Y_0 | \mathbf{x}) \tag{1.9}$$

$$ATET(\mathbf{x}) = E(Y_1 - Y_0 | D = 1, \mathbf{x}) \tag{1.10}$$

$$ATENT(\mathbf{x}) = E(Y_1 - Y_0 | D = 0, \mathbf{x}) \tag{1.11}$$

These quantities are, by definition, no longer single values as before, but *functions* of $\mathbf{x}$. They can also be considered as "individual-specific average treatment effects" as each unit typically has specific values of $\mathbf{x}$. Furthermore, the LIE implies that:

$$ATE = E_\mathbf{x}\{ATE(\mathbf{x})\} \tag{1.12}$$

$$ATET = E_\mathbf{x}\{ATET(\mathbf{x})\} \tag{1.13}$$

$$\text{ATENT} = \mathbf{E_x}\{\text{ATENT}(\mathbf{x})\} \qquad (1.14)$$

making it clear that one can retrieve the global effects of a program by simply averaging ATE(x), ATET(x), and ATENT(x) over the support of **x**.

What is the meaning and usefulness of relying on the ATE, ATET, and ATENT measures in program evaluation? A simple example can shed light on this question. Suppose that in evaluating a program through some econometric procedure, we find a value of ATET equal to 100 and a value of ATENT equal to 200. Was this program successful? At first glance, the answer seems to be positive: the group of treated individuals received, on average, a treatment effect of 100. Thus, the policy was successful in promoting good outcome for the individuals selected for treatment. Nevertheless, the knowledge of the value of ATENT might question this conclusion. As the value of ATENT is higher than that of ATET, if the average untreated unit had been treated, then its outcome would have been raised by 200. This is higher than the increase in outcome obtained by the treated units when compared with their untreated status. If the agency had been treating those who were not selected for treatment, the performance would had been better than in the opposite case. In other words, one may conclude that the agency failed in selecting the right group to support, as they were not able to maximize the outcome. It would have been better to select those who actually were not selected.

Although we generally hold that the agency is trying to maximize the outcome measure, in many cases this might not be the prime objective of an agency. If welfare considerations are part of the policy's purposes, the agency might have been purposely aimed at supporting lower performing units. For instance, in a microcredit program, a public agency may find it consistent with its (social) objectives to support disadvantaged people living in depressed economic and social areas who are clearly in a position of weakness compared to those better off. It is not surprising that these people will ultimately perform worse than those better off. This example also reminds us that we must understand the program's direct objectives as well as select a correct comparison (counterfactual) group. Evaluation conclusions might be otherwise severely misleading.

Besides ATE, ATET, and ATENT, the knowledge of ATE(x), ATET(x), and ATENT(x) may carry additional useful information on the characteristics of program effects. In particular, an analysis of the distribution of those parameters explicitly illustrates how results are dispersed around the mean effects. Figure 1.4 reports an example where we assume that the program target is a variable Y that the program aims at increasing.

The figure shows that, as expected, the distribution of ATET(x) is localized on the right compared to that of ATE(x) and ATENT(x). It means that there is a tendency of the treated units to perform better than the untreated ones, thus proving that the selection was correct. This is confirmed by the values taken by ATE, ATET, and ATENT. But another aspect is useful to stress: the distribution of ATENT(x) is much more dispersed around its mean (ATENT) than ATE(x) and ATET(x). This implies that, while ATE and ATET are good proxies of the overall effect of the

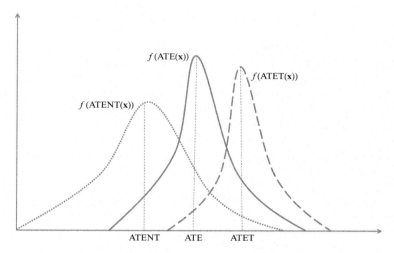

Fig. 1.4 Distribution of ATE(x), ATET(x), and ATENT(x)

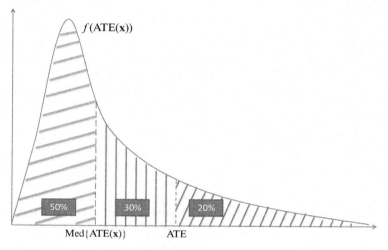

Fig. 1.5 Strong asymmetric distribution of ATE(x)

policy, the same cannot be maintained for ATENT. The larger tails in the distribution of ATENT(x) imply that untreated units are more diversified with regard to the program effect. This questions the use of the mean for very dispersed and/or asymmetric distributions of the effects. In this sense, Fig. 1.5 shows an example in which ATE(x) presents a very strong asymmetry (i.e., very long right tail).

It is immediate to see that the value of ATE is in this case poorly representative of the overall ATE(x) distribution, as indicated by the much lower value of the median of ATE(x). In such a case, relying only on the mean of ATE(x)—, i.e., ATE—to draw conclusions about policy effectiveness may be seriously misleading, as around 80 % of the population receives an idiosyncratic ATE(**x**) lower than ATE. In this sense, the knowledge of ATE(**x**), ATET(**x**), and ATENT(**x**) is an essential ingredient for drawing more accurate conclusions about the actual effect of the evaluated program.

Given these premises, the aim of the econometrician involved in program evaluation is that of recovering previous parameters from *observational* data, that is, from an i.i.d. sample of observed variables for each individual i of this type:

$$\{Y_i, D_i, \mathbf{x}_i\} \text{ with } i = 1, \ldots, N$$

Observe that, according to this specification, we exclude the possibility that the treatment of one unit affects the outcome of another unit. However, assuming that units are independent might be rather restrictive in many evaluation contexts. In the literature (Rubin 1978) this occurrence is called SUTVA—or *stable unit treatment value assumption*—and we will assume the validity of this hypothesis throughout this book. Assuming a lack of interaction among individuals might be plausible in many biomedical experiments, although even in this field there are many cases in which such "neighborhood" or "proximity" effects may be pervasive and SUTVA no more plausible. In epidemiology, for instance, when treatments are vaccines for contagious diseases, it is quite intuitive that one unit treatment can influence the outcomes of others in their neighborhood. Similarly and a fortiori, in economic applications such as the support to companies' research and development (R&D) activity, it might be hard to believe in the absence of "spillovers" from treated to untreated units activated by some form of subsidization. This rises relevant questions regarding the identification and estimation of treatment effects when interference between units is plausible.

It is worth stressing, however, that the literature on the estimation of treatment effects in the presence of interference is still a recent field of statistical and econometric study, and so far only a few papers have dealt formally with this relevant topic.[5]

1.2.1 Identification Under Random Assignment

As said above, the problem in estimating ATE (and thus ATET and ATENT) resides in the fact that for each observation we observe only one of the two states (and never both). Nonetheless, if the sample was drawn at random (i.e., under *random assignment*), it would be possible to estimate the ATE as the difference between the sample mean of treated and the sample mean of untreated units, which is the well-known "Difference-in-means" (DIM) estimator of classical statistics.

---

[5] Key references are: Manski (1993, 2013), Rosenbaum (2007), Sobel (2006), Hudgens and Halloran (2008), Tchetgen-Tchetgen and VanderWeele (2010), Cerulli (2014a).

Correct estimation is feasible because in the case of random assignment "$(Y_1; Y_0)$ are independent of D." This means that the process generating the *sample selection* and thus producing D has nothing to do with the realization of the outcome in both states of the world. We call this the *independence assumption* (IA) formally stating that:

$$(Y_1; Y_0) \perp D \tag{1.15}$$

where the symbol $\perp$ refers to *probabilistic independence*. Under randomization, D is fully exogenous without other specifications. By using the POM of (1.4) and by taking expectations under IA, we can show that:

$$
\begin{aligned}
E(Y|D=1) - E(Y|D=0) &= E(Y_1|D=1) - E(Y_0|D=0) \\
&= E(Y_1) - E(Y_0) = \text{ATE}
\end{aligned}
\tag{1.16}
$$

implying also that $\text{ATE} = \text{ATET} = \text{ATENT}$.

Thus, under random assignment, it is possible to apply the DIM estimator to recover the ATE, being it the sample equivalent of (1.16):

$$\widehat{\text{DIM}} = \frac{1}{N_1}\sum_{i=1}^{N_1} Y_{1,i} - \frac{1}{N_0}\sum_{i=1}^{N_0} Y_{0,i} \tag{1.17}$$

where N_1 is the number of treated and N_0 that of untreated units. It is well known that under the IA this estimator of ATE is consistent, asymptotically normal and efficient, and it is also worth noting that, in this case, the knowledge of $\mathbf{x}$ is unnecessary for a correct estimation of this casual effect.

1.2.2   A Bayesian Interpretation of ATE Under Randomization

In Sect. 1.2, we gave a clear-cut definition of ATE and found that under randomization:

$$\text{ATE} = E(Y|D=1) - E(Y|D=0)$$

that is equivalent to the group Difference-in-means (DIM) estimator. Since it is well known that such an estimator can be obtained by an OLS of this type:

$$Y = \mu + \text{ATE} \cdot D + error$$

we can easily conclude that:

$$\text{ATE} = \frac{\text{Cov}(Y;D)}{\text{Var}(D)} = \text{Corr}(Y;D)\sqrt{\frac{\text{Var}(Y)}{\text{Var}(D)}}$$

showing that $\text{ATE} = 0$ *if and only if* the correlation between Y and D is zero. This leads to the important conclusion that, under randomization, zero correlation implies zero causation, and vice versa. Of course, ATE will be identified as long as $\text{Var}(D) \neq 0$; indeed, since:

$$\text{Var}(D) = p(D = 1) \cdot [1 - p(D = 1)]$$

we can conclude that, for ATE to be identified, we need:

$$0 < p(D = 1) < 1$$

Although previous findings give to ATE a clear causal interpretation, it is less clear which is the relation between ATE and the typical causal reasoning that epidemiological and medical research poses between possible "causes" (treatments) and observed "effects" (consequences). As known, this is generally embedded into a Bayesian causal setting that is not apparently linked to the way in which ATE has been defined, identified, and estimated above. However, ATE and Bayesian causality do not conflict; on the contrary, ATE can have a clear Bayesian interpretation (Rubin 1978). In what follows, we briefly account for this.

Suppose there are two events, Y and D, and we are interested in the causal effect of event D on event Y. Assume that both are represented by two dichotomous variables taking value $\{0; 1\}$. For instance, D can be participation to a job training (attendant vs. non-attendant), and Y subsequent employment status (employed vs. unemployed), and so forth. The Bayes theorem states that:

$$p(Y|D) = \frac{p(Y)p(D|Y)}{p(D)}$$

where $p(Y)$ is the unconditional probability function of Y generally assumed as *prior* knowledge of the researcher; $p(D|Y)$ is the likelihood of observing the event D, given the observation of event Y, and is generally estimated on observed data; $p(D)$, the unconditional probability of D, is assumed to be a scale parameter.

To see the relation between previous formula and ATE, consider the event $\{Y = 1\}$ and write previous Bayes formula for the events $\{D = 1\}$ and $\{D = 0\}$ separately:

$$p(Y = 1|D = 1) = \frac{p(Y = 1)p(D = 1|Y = 1)}{p(D = 1)}$$

$$p(Y = 1|D = 0) = \frac{p(Y = 1)p(D = 0|Y = 1)}{p(D = 0)}$$

By subtracting the two previous expressions, we get:

$$p(Y = 1|D = 1) - p(Y = 1|D = 0) = p(Y = 1)\left[\frac{p(D = 1|Y = 1)}{p(D = 1)} - \frac{p(D = 0|Y = 1)}{p(D = 0)}\right]$$

However, having Y a Bernoulli distribution, we can rewrite previous formula as:

$$E(Y|D = 1) - E(Y|D = 1) = E(Y)\left[\frac{p(D = 1|Y = 1)}{p(D = 1)} - \frac{p(D = 0|Y = 1)}{p(D = 0)}\right]$$

or equivalently:

$$\text{ATE} = \underbrace{E(Y)\text{prior}} \cdot \underbrace{\left[\frac{p(D = 1|Y = 1)}{p(D = 1)} - \frac{p(D = 0|Y = 1)}{p(D = 0)}\right]}_{\text{likelihood}}$$

which provides a link between ATE and usual Bayesian causal inference. Indeed, we can see that, given the unconditional mean of Y, ATE is determined by the right-hand-side (RHS) difference set out in squared brackets. What does this difference refer to? And, what is its interpretation? The first term of that difference can be interpreted as the relative likelihood to observe the event $\{D = 1\}$ once the event $\{Y = 1\}$ has been observed first; as such, it returns a measure of how frequently the event $\{D = 1\}$ appears when the event $\{Y = 1\}$ appears first. For the second term of the difference, the one referring to $\{D = 0\}$, the same argument follows. As a consequence, if the first term is remarkably high compared to the second, it means that the observation of the event $\{Y = 1\}$ is highly more associated to the occurrence on the event $\{D = 1\}$ than to the occurrence of the event $\{D = 0\}$; therefore, it seems more plausible (read "likely") to consider the effect $\{Y = 1\}$ as determined by the cause $\{D = 1\}$ rather than $\{D = 0\}$; it means that a positive ATE should lead to the conclusion that the treatment $\{D = 1\}$ has been the main factor bringing about the observed outcome.

Finally, the last formula of ATE can also have a typical Bayesian learning interpretation, as ATE can be seen as an update of the population mean of Y (derived by some prior distribution of Y), where new information from observation is brought by the likelihood (i.e., the difference in brackets).

1.2.3 *Consequences of Nonrandom Assignment and* Selection Bias

Policy programs hardly select individuals to treat (and, equivalently, to not treat) at random. This nonrandomness is inherent to a policy for two distinct reasons: (1) the *self-selection* into the program operated by individuals and (2) the *selection mechanism* of the agency managing the program.

Self-selection concerns the choice of individuals to participate to a specific supporting program. This generally entails a *cost-benefit calculus*, as applying for a policy program can be costly to some reasonable extent. For instance, in industrial incentives aimed at promoting company fixed investments, firms have to bear opportunity costs, (private) information disclosure of ongoing business projects, administrative costs needed for making an application, and so forth that should be compared with the benefits of applying. As this decision is intrinsically "strategic," it should not be assumed to be done at random, as firms are "endogenously" involved into this choice.

As for the program *selection mechanism*, generally operated by a public agency, a nonrandom assignment process is even more evident, as agencies generally select units to support according to some predetermined objectives. These objectives may have a *direct* and *indirect* nature. The former refers to the main target of the policy (such as, for instance, "reducing the rate of unemployment" in a certain area); the latter may refer to collateral effects (such as alcohol abuse reduction in that area if people get hired more easily). For project-funding programs, where units are selected according to the submission of a proposal (as usual in industrial supporting programs or in educational programs), individual's and proposal's characteristics drive the selection-into-program, once specific *selection criteria* are established ex ante (*ex ante evaluation*). In order to maximize the effect of the policy, an agency could apply the principle of "picking-the-winner," i.e., choosing to support those units having the highest propensity to perform well; similarly, the agency objective might be aimed at "aiding-the-poor"—as in the case of supporting economically depressed areas or poorly educated people. This provides convincing arguments to state that in socioeconomic programs, the sample of beneficiaries are far from being randomly selected. On the contrary, they are not expected to be so at all, as they have to comply at least with agency's selection criteria that are, by definition, not randomly established.

When the selection of treated and untreated units is done not randomly, depending on either individual "observable" or "unobservable" characteristics, the DIM estimator is no longer a correct estimation for ATE. In this case, in fact, "$(Y_1; Y_0)$ are probabilistically dependent on D," so by using again the POM and the expectation operator, we obtain:

$$\begin{aligned}
\mathrm{E}(Y|D=1) - \mathrm{E}(Y|D=0) &= \mathrm{E}(Y_1|D=1) - \mathrm{E}(Y_0|D=0) \\
&\quad + [\mathrm{E}(Y_0|D=1) - \mathrm{E}(Y_0|D=1)] \\
&= [\mathrm{E}(Y_0|D=1) - \mathrm{E}(Y_0|D=0)] + \text{ATET} \quad (1.18)
\end{aligned}$$

Equation (1.18) states that a *selection bias* equal to $[\mathrm{E}(Y_0 \mid D=1) - \mathrm{E}(Y_0 \mid D=0)]$ arises using the DIM and it can be also proved that ATE $\neq$ ATET $\neq$ ATENT. To see that, suppose that $Y_1 = \mu_1 + U_1$ and $Y_0 = \mu_0 + U_0$, where μ_1 and μ_0 are scalars and $\mathrm{E}(U_1) = \mathrm{E}(U_0) = 0$. By subtracting, we have:

$$Y_1 - Y_0 = (\mu_1 - \mu_0) + (U_1 - U_0) = \text{ATE} + (U_1 - U_0) \quad (1.19)$$

By taking the expectation of this equation over $D=1$, we have:

$$\mathrm{E}(Y_1 - Y_0|D=1) = \text{ATET} = \text{ATE} + \mathrm{E}(U_1 - U_0|D=1) \quad (1.20)$$

where $\mathrm{E}(U_1 - U_0|D=1)$ can be thought of as the average "participation gain" for those who actually participated in the program. Similarly, by taking the expectation of (1.20) over $D=0$, we can show that ATE $\neq$ ATENT, since:

$$\mathrm{E}(Y_1 - Y_0|D=0) = \text{ATENT} = \text{ATE} + \mathrm{E}(U_1 - U_0|D=0) \quad (1.21)$$

As soon as $\mathrm{E}(U_1 - U_0|D=1) \neq \mathrm{E}(U_1 - U_0|D=0)$, then ATET $\neq$ ATENT. Only if Y_0 were independent of D, that is $\mathrm{E}(Y_0|D) = \mathrm{E}(Y_0)$, the selection bias does disappear so that ATE $=$ ATET $=$ ATENT. Unfortunately, this event hinges on a too strong assumption. Observe, furthermore, that the selection bias is *unobservable* since we cannot recover $\mathrm{E}(Y_0|D=1)$ from observation. This leads to looking for an additional assumption for estimating ATE, ATET, and ATENT under nonrandom selection. Before going on, however, we need to distinguish two different forms of *selection*: the "observable" and the "unobservable."

1.3   Selection on Observables and Selection on Unobservables

On the part of an analyst interested in ex post program evaluation, the factors affecting the nonrandom assignment of beneficiaries could have an *observable* or an *unobservable* nature.

In the first case, the analyst knows and can observe with precision which are the factors driving the self-selection of individuals and the selection of the agency. In this case, the knowledge of **x**, the structural variables that are supposed to drive the nonrandom assignment to treatment, are sufficient to identify—as we will see later—the actual effect of the policy in question once adequately controlled for.

Nevertheless, when other factors driving the nonrandom assignment are impossible or difficult to observe, then the only knowledge of the observable vector **x** is not sufficient to identify the effect of the policy. The nature of the unobservables can be twofold. On the one hand, there are unobservable elements due to some lack of information in the available datasets. This is more a problem of data availability than genuine incapacity of gauging specific phenomena. For convenience, we can call them *contingent* unobservables. In project-funding programs, for instance, researchers might have full access to a great bulk of information on units' characteristics, while poor data might be available on proposed projects. On the other hand, there are *genuine* unobservables that would be fairly impossible to measure, even in the case of abundant information. Examples of this kind are represented by factors, such as entrepreneurial innate ability, propensity to bear risks, ethical attitudes, and so on. This last class of unobservables could be relevant, although complex and sometimes hard to translate into feasible indicators.

These two different situations are known in the literature as the case of "selection on observable" and "selection on unobservables," respectively: they ask for different methodologies to identify the effect of a policy program, and the greatest effort of past and current econometric literature has been that of dealing with these two situations and provide suitable solutions for both cases.

1.3.1 Selection on Observables (or Overt Bias) and Conditional Independence Assumption

Under selection on observables, the knowledge of $\mathbf{x}$, the factors driving the nonrandom assignment, may be sufficient to identify the causal parameters ATEs, even in case of nonrandom assignment. Of course, since the missing observation problem still holds, we need to rely on an assumption (or hypothesis) able to overcome that problem. Rosenbaum and Rubin (1983) introduced the so-called *conditional independence assumption* (CIA), stating that "conditional on the knowledge of $\mathbf{x}$ (sometimes called *pretreatment covariates*) Y_1 and Y_0 are probabilistically independent of D." Formally:

$$(Y_1; Y_0) \perp D | \mathbf{x} \tag{1.22}$$

This assumption means that once the knowledge of the factors affecting the sample selection is taken into account (or controlled for) by the analyst, then the condition of randomization is restored. This assumption is too strong when we are interested, as we are, in *average* effects, so it is usual to rely on a weaker assumption, the so-called *conditional mean independence* (CMI), stating that:

$$E(Y_1 | \mathbf{x}, D) = E(Y_1 | \mathbf{x}) \tag{1.23}$$

$$E(Y_0 | \mathbf{x}, D) = E(Y_0 | \mathbf{x}) \tag{1.24}$$

Assumption (1.23) and (1.24) restricts the independence only over the mean. The CMI is the basis for (consistent) estimation of ATE, ATET, and ATENT by both parametric and nonparametric methods. Showing how these parameters are identified under CMI is straightforward. By considering the POM in (1.4), and taking the average of this conditional on $(\mathbf{x}, D)$, we get:

$$
\begin{aligned}
E(Y|\mathbf{x}, D) &= E(Y_0|\mathbf{x}, D) + D[E(Y_1|\mathbf{x}, D) - E(Y_0|\mathbf{x}, D)] \\
&= E(Y_0|\mathbf{x}) + D[E(Y_1|\mathbf{x}) - E(Y_0|\mathbf{x})]
\end{aligned} \tag{1.25}
$$

We can express (1.25) both for $D = 1$ and $D = 0$ as follows:

$$
\text{if } D = 1 : E(Y|\mathbf{x}, D = 1) = E(Y_1|\mathbf{x}) \tag{1.26}
$$

$$
\text{if } D = 0 : E(Y|\mathbf{x}, D = 0) = E(Y_0|\mathbf{x}) \tag{1.27}
$$

By subtracting (1.26) and (1.27) we obtain:

$$
E(Y|\mathbf{x}, D = 1) - E(Y|\mathbf{x}, D = 0) = E(Y_1|\mathbf{x}) - E(Y_0|\mathbf{x}) = \text{ATE}(\mathbf{x}) \tag{1.28}
$$

that, once rewritten, shows that:

$$
\text{ATE}(\mathbf{x}) = E(Y|\mathbf{x}, D = 1) - E(Y|\mathbf{x}, D = 0) \tag{1.29}
$$

where the RHS consists of all "observable quantities," meaning that $\text{ATE}(\mathbf{x})$ is correctly identified and no bias emerges. For the sake of simplicity, let's then define:

$$
m_1(\mathbf{x}) = E(Y|\mathbf{x}, D = 1) \tag{1.30}
$$

$$
m_0(\mathbf{x}) = E(Y|\mathbf{x}, D = 0) \tag{1.31}
$$

so that:

$$
\text{ATE}(\mathbf{x}) = m_1(\mathbf{x}) - m_0(\mathbf{x}) = m(\mathbf{x}) \tag{1.32}
$$

From (1.12) we have:

$$
\text{ATE} = E_{\mathbf{x}}\{\text{ATE}(\mathbf{x})\} = E_{\mathbf{x}}\{m(\mathbf{x})\} \tag{1.33}
$$

implying that an estimation of ATE can be obtained by the "sample equivalent" of (1.33):

$$
\widehat{\text{ATE}} = \frac{1}{N}\sum_{i=1}^{N} \widehat{m}(\mathbf{x}_i) \tag{1.34}
$$

provided that a *consistent* estimator of $m(\mathbf{x})$, indicated by $\widehat{m}(\mathbf{x})$ in (1.34), having known asymptotic variance and distribution, is available. A similar procedure can be used to obtain the estimation of ATET and ATENT. Indeed, since:

$$\text{ATET} = \text{E}_{\mathbf{x}}\{\text{ATE}(\mathbf{x})|D = 1\} \tag{1.35}$$

we get, by relying again on the sample equivalent:

$$\widehat{\text{ATET}} = \frac{1}{\sum\limits_{i=1}^{N} D_i} \left[\sum_{i=1}^{N} D_i \cdot \widehat{m}(\mathbf{x}_i) \right] \tag{1.36}$$

Similarly, as:

$$\text{ATENT} = \text{E}_{\mathbf{x}}\{\text{ATE}(\mathbf{x})|D = 0\} \tag{1.37}$$

we also obtain:

$$\widehat{\text{ATENT}} = \frac{1}{\sum\limits_{i=1}^{N}(1 - D_i)} \left[\sum_{i=1}^{N} (1 - D_i) \cdot \widehat{m}(\mathbf{x}_i) \right] \tag{1.38}$$

showing that both the estimations of ATET and ATENT can be recovered once a consistent estimator of $m(\mathbf{x})$ is available.

1.3.2   *Selection on Unobservables (or* Hidden Bias)

When the selection-into-program is governed not only by observable-to-analyst factors but also by unobservable-to-analyst variables (either contingent or genuine) *correlated* with the potential outcomes, then the CI (or CMI) assumption is not sufficient to identify program average effects. Indeed, in this case, what happens is that:

$$\text{E}(Y_1|\mathbf{x}, D) \neq \text{E}(Y_1|\mathbf{x}) \tag{1.39}$$

$$\text{E}(Y_0|\mathbf{x}, D) \neq \text{E}(Y_0|\mathbf{x}) \tag{1.40}$$

and an equivalent bias emerges as in (1.18) although, this time, conditional on $\mathbf{x}$:

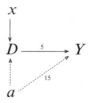

Fig. 1.6 Path diagram of the causal relation between D and Y in case of unobservable selection

$$
\begin{aligned}
E(Y|\mathbf{x}, D = 1) - E(Y|\mathbf{x}, D = 0) &= E(Y_1|\mathbf{x}, D = 1) - E(Y_0|\mathbf{x}, D = 0) \\
&\quad + [E(Y_0|\mathbf{x}, D = 1) - E(Y_0|\mathbf{x}, D = 1)] \\
&= [E(Y_0|\mathbf{x}, D = 1) - E(Y_0|\mathbf{x}, D = 0)] \\
&\quad + \text{ATET}(\mathbf{x})
\end{aligned}
\tag{1.41}
$$

Equation (1.41) illustrates that even in the subset of units identified by $\mathbf{x}$, the DIM produces a *biased* estimation of the causal effect of D on Y that cannot be retrieved observationally as the quantity $E(Y_0 \mid \mathbf{x}, D = 1)$ is unobservable.

Figure 1.6 shows a path diagram offering an intuition of why the causal effect is not identified when the selection depends on unobservables that affect also the target variable.

Suppose that D, the selection (or treatment) variable, is affected by two factors, one observable (x) and one unobservable (a). Suppose that a determines not only D but also the outcome Y in a direct way. In such a situation, we cannot produce autonomous and independent modification of D without moving contemporaneously Y. For instance, suppose that a change in D—originated by a one unit change in a—produces a change in Y of 20. One cannot conclude that the effect of D on Y is 20, as it might be the case that only 5 out of 20 is due to the actual effect of D on Y, while the remaining 15 is due to the effect of a on Y. Since this latter effect is unobservable, we do not have enough information for a correct conclusion about the causal link between D and Y. This effect is thus not identifiable. To correctly identify the direct effect of D on Y, more structural information needs to be added. As we will see later in Chap. 3, this requires either further distributional hypotheses (as in the Heckman Selection model) or the knowledge of at least one instrumental variable for applying Instrumental-variables (IV) estimation.

1.3.3   The Overlap Assumption

Either in the case of selection on observables or selection on unobservables, the identification of ATEs requires a second fundamental assumption besides CMI, i.e., the so-called *overlap assumption*. To show this, we first need to define a key notion of the econometrics of program evaluation, the *propensity-score*, defined as the "probability to get treated, given the knowledge of $\mathbf{x}$," that is:

$$p(D = 1|\mathbf{x}) = \text{propensity-score} \tag{1.42}$$

Given this definition, the overlap assumption states that, for each unit i, it must happen that:

$$0 < p(D_i = 1|\mathbf{x}_i) < 1 \tag{1.43}$$

i.e., units characterized by a set of attributes $\mathbf{x}$ have to belong both to the set of treated and to the set of untreated units. For instance, if for $\mathbf{x} = \mathbf{x}_0$ the propensity-score assumes zero value, it means that there are no units in the treated group having that specific value of $\mathbf{x}$, and this entails that ATEs cannot be calculated (i.e., identified). To better understand how overlap may prevent ATEs identification, consider just eight units and a binary variable x taking value 1 or 0. Table 1.1 shows a simple but instructive example.

Here, we have just two units with $x = 0$ (unit 1 and 2), both in the untreated group ($D = 0$), and no units in the treated group having such a value of x. In a situation like this, $p(D = 1 | x = 0) = 0$ and ATE cannot be identified. Indeed, we have seen above that ATE can be defined as:

$$\begin{aligned} \text{ATE} &= \mathbf{E}_{\mathbf{x}}\{\text{ATE}(\mathbf{x})\} \\ &= p(x = 1) \cdot \text{ATE}(x = 1) + p(x = 0) \cdot \text{ATE}(x = 0) \end{aligned} \tag{1.44}$$

where according to Table 1.1, $p(x = 1) = 6/8$ and $p(x = 0) = 2/8$. Nevertheless, while when $x = 1$ ATE can be identified (both treated and untreated present in fact this kind of attribute) so that:

$$\text{ATE}(x = 1) = [(10 + 20 + 80 + 70)/4] - [(4 + 6)/2] = 45 - 5 = 40 \tag{1.45}$$

the same cannot be done for $\text{ATE}(x = 0)$, as:

$$\text{ATE}(x = 0) = [?] - [(5 + 8)/2] = ? \ => \text{ATE} = ? \tag{1.46}$$

Table 1.1 An example of unfeasible identification of ATE when the overlap assumption fails

	Treatment (D)	Covariate (x)	Outcome (Y)
1	0	0	5
2	0	0	8
3	0	1	6
4	0	1	4
5	1	1	10
6	1	1	20
7	1	1	80
8	1	1	70

so that we are only able to identify ATE in the subpopulation of units having $x = 1$. From a policy assessment perspective, this is a limitation, as relying only on the effect in a subgroup can be insufficient for understanding the effect of a given program. Nevertheless, if we restrict our attention to the set of untreated ($D = 0$), we can properly identify at least ATENT since:

$$\text{ATENT} = (6 + 4)/2 - -(5 + 8)/2 = -1.5 \tag{1.47}$$

while ATET—for the same reason of ATE—is not identifiable. Thus, as a general rule, the identification of ATET just requires that $p(D = 1 \mid \mathbf{x}) < 1$ and that of ATENT that $p(D = 1 \mid \mathbf{x}) > 0$ (or, equivalently, $p(D = 0 \mid \mathbf{x}) < 1$). In other words, we can conclude that in order to identify all ATEs, each cell built by crossing the values taken by the various $\mathbf{x}$—provided that they have finite discrete support—must have both treated and untreated units.

In applications, as a large set of covariates are typically used and many of them take on a continuous support, finding units where $p(D_i = 1 \mid \mathbf{x}_i)$ is exactly equal to one or exactly equal to zero is unlikely, and this helps considerably the identification of ATEs. However, *weak* overlap—as in situations where some specific values of $\mathbf{x}$ appear mostly either in the treated or in the untreated group but not in both, has some (intuitive) consequences in the estimation precision of ATEs. As it will be more clear in Chap. 2, weak overlap entails comparing outcome of individuals belonging to opposite groups having very different relative frequency, thus producing a less reliable estimation of their outcome differences. Statistically, it turns to produce estimates with larger variances independently of the method employed—although some methods might be more sensitive to weak overlap than others (Imbens 2004, pp. 23–24). Some tests for assessing the degree of overlap have been proposed in the literature and will be discussed in Chap. 2 along with sensitivity tests for assessing the reliability of conditional (mean) independence.

1.4   Characterizing Selection Bias

From basic statistics, we know that the DIM estimator of (1.17) is equal to the coefficient α obtained by an OLS regression of this simple univariate linear model:

$$Y = \mu + \alpha \cdot D + u \tag{1.48}$$

Indeed, according to this equation we have, under randomization and for the two regimes separately (treated and untreated):

$$E(Y|D = 1) = \mu + \alpha \tag{1.49}$$

$$E(Y|D = 0) = \mu \tag{1.50}$$

so that:

$$\alpha = E(Y|D = 1) - E(Y|D = 0) = DIM \tag{1.51}$$

Assume now that the selection-into-treatment was driven by a factor x. It entails that the outcome is also a function of x:

$$Y = \mu_a + \alpha_a D + \beta_a x + u_a \tag{1.52}$$

or equivalently:

$$Y^* = \mu_a + \alpha_a D + u_a \tag{1.53}$$

with $Y^* = Y - \beta_a x$. Since the regression is of the same kind of (1.48), it is quite clear that:

$$\alpha_a = E(Y^*|D = 1) - E(Y^*|D = 0) \tag{1.54}$$

which leads to:

$$\alpha_a = \{E(Y|D = 1) - E(Y|D = 0)\} - \beta\{E(x|D = 1) - E(x|D = 0)\} \tag{1.55}$$

or equivalently:

$$\alpha_a = DIM - BIAS \tag{1.56}$$

where $DIM = \alpha = \{E(Y \mid D = 1) - E(Y \mid D = 0)\}$ and $BIAS = \beta\{E(x \mid D = 1) - E(x \mid D = 0)\}$. Equation (1.56) shows that the presence of a selection factor produces a different result for the effect of D on Y compared to the random assignment case, thus modifying the magnitude of the effect. This bias is exactly the difference between the two effects:

$$BIAS = \alpha - \alpha_a \tag{1.57}$$

If the analyst erroneously assumes randomization in cases where this is not present, a bias (different from zero) expressed as in (1.57) may arise. Algebraically, this bias is equal to:

$$BIAS = \beta\{E(x|D = 1) - E(x|D = 0)\} \tag{1.58}$$

It is easy to see that the bias in (1.58) increases either as soon as: (1) β is different from zero, and (2) the average value of x in the treated and untreated group is different. The first cause of bias variation depends on the degree of dependence of the outcome on factor x; the second cause of bias variation depends on how "balanced" are the two groups in terms of the factor x. If the two groups are severely unbalanced in terms of x and the analyst does not control for this, as it may happen if we estimate the effect of the policy by using (1.51) instead of (1.55), then we can obtain a misleading result. An example can help understand this line of reasoning.

Suppose two groups of people, group 1 and group 0, are to be used as treated and control groups, respectively, in the evaluation of a given training program. Suppose that, because of the underlying selection process, group 1 is made of young people (let's say, people with an average age of 20), whereas group 1 is made of older people (with an average age of 60). Furthermore, suppose that we are interested in evaluating the effect of this training program on individuals' comprehension capacity of a complex text, measured by scores associated with a final exam. We might find that group 1 is highly performing with, let's say, an average score of 70, and group 0 is poorly performing with an average of 20. The simple groups' DIM, equal to 50 in this case, would suggest that the training program was effective in fostering people's comprehension capabilities. Nevertheless, this result is misleading as the two groups are far from being balanced in terms of age. In fact, if age has a nonnegligible impact on comprehension, as the common sense would suggest, a selection bias of the kind visible in (1.55) is present. As an acceptable statement, suppose that comprehension is significantly and negatively related to age, so that β is negative and equal to, let's say, -2. In this case we have that:

$$
\alpha_a = \{\underbrace{E(Y \mid D = 1)}_{70} - \underbrace{E(Y|D=0)}_{20}\} - \underbrace{\beta}_{-2} \cdot \{\underbrace{E(x \mid D = 1)}_{60}
$$

$$
- \underbrace{E(x|D=0)}_{20}\} = 50 - (-2) \cdot 40 = -30 \tag{1.59}
$$

showing that the "actual" effect of the policy—once groups are balanced over age—was even negative. In this case, in fact, the BIAS (-80) outweighs the value of DIM (50), thus leading to a final negative value of α_a (-30).

It is now quite clear that randomness is the way in which nature balances samples. On the contrary, when some nonrandomness is at work, sample unbalances can be pervasive and evaluation trickier. It is also more evident at this stage that the knowledge of the unbalance and of the strength of the predicting power of the x-factors on Y are key to restore unbiased results. But what happens when x is not observable? The next chapters will provide a comprehensive exposition of econometric tools to deal with all of these possible cases.

1.4.1   Decomposing Selection Bias

In previous sections, we have been able to show what the selection bias is equal to in a nonrandomized setting. However, a more in-depth analysis of the form assumed by the selection bias can highlight some further interesting aspects. In (1.18) we have seen that:

$$\text{DIM} = \text{ATET} + \text{B}_1 \tag{1.60}$$

where $\text{B}_1 = [E(Y_0 \mid D = 1) - E(Y_0 \mid D = 0)]$ is the selection bias. Nevertheless, it can also be easily proved that:

$$\text{DIM} = \text{ATENT} + \text{B}_2 \tag{1.61}$$

where $\text{B}_2 = [E(Y_1 \mid D = 1) - E(Y_1 \mid D = 0)]$. In other words, this shows that two different selection biases exist, one related to ATET (B_1) and the other related to ATENT (B_0). By summing (1.60) and (1.61), we obtain:

$$\text{DIM} \ = \ \frac{1}{2}(\text{ATET} \ + \ \text{ATENT}) \ + \ \frac{1}{2}(\text{B}_1 + \ \text{B}_0) \tag{1.62}$$

where $\text{B}_1 + \text{B}_0 = \text{B}$ is the overall bias. Equation (1.62) sets out that DIM is just the simple average of ATET and ATET plus the simple average of B_1 and B_0.

A more powerful decomposition of the selection bias has been proposed by Heckman et al. (1998). They show that the selection bias B_1 (similar conclusions can be drawn for B_0) can be decomposed into three sub-biases having interesting interpretation. More specifically they prove that:

$$\text{B}_1 = \text{B}_A + \text{B}_B + \text{B}_C \tag{1.63}$$

In order to see how to get this result, it is first useful to provide some notation: (1) define the bias B_1 conditional on $\mathbf{x}$ as $\text{B}_1(\mathbf{x})$; (2) define $S_{1\mathbf{x}} = \{\mathbf{x} : f(\mathbf{x} \mid D = 1) > 0\}$ and $S_{0\mathbf{x}} = \{\mathbf{x} : f(\mathbf{x} \mid D = 0) > 0\}$ as the support of $\mathbf{x}$ for $D = 1$ and $D = 0$, respectively, with $f(\mathbf{x} \mid D)$ being the conditional density of $\mathbf{x}$ given D; (3) define $S_{\mathbf{x}} = S_{1\mathbf{x}} \cap S_{0\mathbf{x}}$ as the overlap region; and (4) define $\bar{y}_{00} = E(Y_0 \mid \mathbf{x}, D = 0)$ and $\bar{y}_{01} = E(Y_0 \mid \mathbf{x}, D = 1)$. Given these definitions, we have:

$$B_1 = \int_{S_{1x}} \bar{y}_{01} \, dF(\mathbf{x}, D = 1) - \int_{S_{0x}} \bar{y}_{00} \, dF(\mathbf{x}, D = 0)$$

$$= \underbrace{\int_{S_{1x}-S_x} \bar{y}_{01} \, dF(\mathbf{x}, D = 1) - \int_{S_{0x}-S_x} \bar{y}_{00} \, dF(\mathbf{x}, D = 0) + \int_{S_x} \bar{y}_{01} \, dF(\mathbf{x}, D = 1)}_{B_A}$$

$$- \int_{S_x} \bar{y}_{00} \, dF(\mathbf{x}, D = 0) + \left[\underbrace{\int_{S_x} \bar{y}_{00} \, dF(\mathbf{x}, D = 1) - \int_{S_x} \bar{y}_{00} \, dF(\mathbf{x}, D = 1)}_{=0} \right]$$

$$(1.64)$$

where with $\{S_{1x} - S_x\}$ and $\{S_{0x} - S_x\}$ we have indicated the two nonoverlapping sets. By rearranging the terms of the previous equation, it can be shown that:

$$B_1 = \int_{S_{1x}} \bar{y}_{01} \, dF(\mathbf{x}, w = 1) - \int_{S_{0x}} \bar{y}_{00} \, dF(\mathbf{x}, w = 0)$$

$$= \underbrace{\int_{S_{1x}-S_x} \bar{y}_{01} \, dF(\mathbf{x}, w = 1) - \int_{S_{1x}-S_x} \bar{y}_{00} \, dF(\mathbf{x}, w = 0)}_{B_A} +$$

$$\underbrace{\int_{S_x} \bar{y}_{00} \, [dF(\mathbf{x}, w = 1) - dF(\mathbf{x}, w = 0)]}_{B_B} + \underbrace{\int_{S_x} \bar{y}_{01} \, dF(\mathbf{x}, w = 1) - \int_{S_x} \bar{y}_{00} \, dF(\mathbf{x}, w = 1)}_{B_C}$$

$$(1.65)$$

which proves (1.63). How can we interpret the three different biases B_A, B_B, and B_C?

- B_A: bias due to *weak overlap*. Such a bias is present as soon as $\{S_{1x} - S_x\}$ and $\{S_{0x} - S_x\}$ are nonempty. This means that there are subsets of $\mathbf{x}$ in the treated and untreated population with no overlap and thus with no possibility of cross-imputation. In other words, they are individuals that cannot be matched.
- B_B: bias due to *weak balancing*. This bias arises when $dF(\mathbf{x}, D = 1) \neq dF(\mathbf{x}, D = 0)$ although the $\mathbf{x}$ of the two populations overlaps. As soon as covariates $\mathbf{x}$ in the treated and untreated groups do not come from the same distribution—as it occurs in randomization—a bias due to this unbalance emerges and it is measured exactly by B_B.
- B_C: bias due to the presence of *selection on unobservables*. Such a bias appears when some differences in outcomes still remain even after controlling for the

observable confounders included in **x**. This bias is zero when $\bar{y}_{01} = \bar{y}_{00}$, that is, when $E(Y_0 \mid \mathbf{x}, D = 1) = E(Y_0 \mid \mathbf{x}, D = 0)$, which is the condition implied by CMI. In other words, B_C appears when CMI fails so that the selection-into-program was driven by unobservable confounders as well.

Econometric techniques for program evaluation are able to "cure" just some of these biases and generally not all at once. For instance, Matching, as we will see, is rather powerful to reduce the bias terms B_A and B_B, but not B_C. IV methods are generally more suitable to reduce bias B_C than biases B_A and B_B. Regression methods may be particularly problematic in the case of very weak overlap and failure of CMI. Further, in empirical applications, many other aspects than only theoretical biases have to be considered to correctly judge the goodness of a specific estimation procedure. We will discuss this aspect at length in the next chapters. It goes without saying that mixing up different methods may be a good strategy to minimizing biases and thus increasing estimation precision.

1.5   The Rationale for Choosing the Variables to Control for

In previous sections, we saw that controlling for specific observable variables is a "must" if one does not want to run the risk of overlooking important characteristics of individuals that might have been relevant in producing the sample nonrandomness. Fundamental assumptions such as CMI, for instance, strictly require covariates **x** to be controlled for and suitably exploited in the estimation phase.

Which is however the rationale for choosing the variables to control for? Or, in other words, is there some conceivable rule to endorse some variables and discard some others? Answers to these questions are not immediate and need some further elaboration in terms of the "causal chains" the evaluator assumes to lay behind the available data. In choosing confounders, in fact, one should have as clear an understanding as possible of the causal relations linking the variables entering his model. In other words, this suggests that one relies on a clear-cut "theoretical" representation of the relation among treatment, potential confounders, and outcomes. In this sense, context's conditions, theoretical background, past evidence, and even personal beliefs may play a fundamental role in selecting variables to control for.

Lee (2005, pp. 43–49) provided an excellent guideline for establishing how one can wisely choose confounders. In what follows, we will draw heavily on Lee's account, although a bit different organization of his arguments will be presented.

As said, the choice to include or exclude a given covariate x does depend on the specific causal links assumed among x (the potential confounder), D (the binary treatment), and Y (the outcome). Figure 1.7 reports six possible cases that, at least in principle, should account for the majority of real situations. In what follows, we

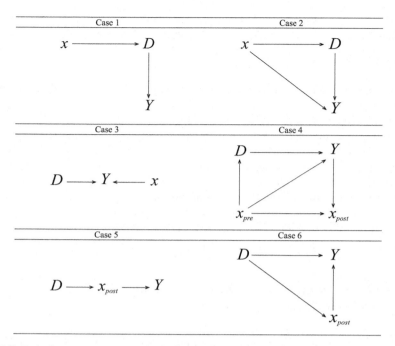

Fig. 1.7 Path diagrams representing causal links among x (the potential confounder), D (the binary treatment), and Y (the outcome)

discuss all these situations, thus suggesting how to deal with x in each of these cases. Observe, for the sake of clarity, that an arrow between A and B means that "A affects (or causes) B."

Case 1 In this pivotal case, x behaves as a pure pretreatment variable. Indeed, x determines D that in turn determines Y. No relation between x and Y is assumed. We show that, in this case, x does not need to be included as a confounder. We first set out a formal explanation and then a more intuitive one.

Translated into equations, Case 1 can be represented by a system of two equations, the *selection equation* (assumed to be linear for simplicity) and the *outcome equation*, taking on this form:

$$D = a_1 + a_x \cdot x + u \tag{1.66}$$
$$Y = b_1 + b_w \cdot D + v \tag{1.67}$$

Throughout this section, we assume that CMI holds, i.e., $u \perp v \mid x$. Since we are working under CMI, we know that:

$$\text{ATE} = E_x\{E(Y|x, D = 1) - E(Y|x, D = 1)\} \tag{1.68}$$

This means that, using the previous Y-equation:

$$E(Y|x, D = 1) = E(Y|D = 1) = b_1 + b_w \qquad (1.69)$$
$$E(Y|x, D = 0) = E(Y|D = 0) = b_1 \qquad (1.70)$$

which results in $\text{ATE} = b_w$. Hence, either if the outcome is balanced or not over x, this has no effect on the estimation of ATE. Therefore, conditioning on x is not necessary in this case. The reason is quite clear: x is relevant in explaining D but with no predictive power on Y; as a consequence, x has no effect on Y. In other words, variables affecting only the selection without having an impact on the outcome should be excluded from the analysis, as their presence does not modify the sign and magnitude of ATE.

Case 2 In this second case, there is a direct effect of x on Y, as well as an effect of x on D as above. The corresponding structural model is the following one (CMI still holds):

$$D = a_1 + a_x \cdot x + u \qquad (1.71)$$
$$Y = b_1 + b_w \cdot D + b_x \cdot x + v \qquad (1.72)$$

In this case x appears in the Y-equation so that:

$$E(Y|D = 1) = E_x\{E(Y|x, D = 1)\} = b_1 + b_w + b_x \cdot E(x|D = 1) \qquad (1.73)$$
$$E(Y|D = 0) = E_x\{E(Y|x, D = 0)\} = b_1 + b_x \cdot E(x|D = 0) \qquad (1.74)$$

resulting in:

$$\text{ATE} = b_w + b_x \cdot [E(x|D = 1) - E(x|D = 0)] \qquad (1.75)$$

Without balancing the treated and untreated group on x we would get that $E(x, D = 1) \neq E(x, D = 0)$, thus conditioning (that is equivalent to "balancing") on x is required. Otherwise, a bias equal to $b_x \cdot [E(x, D = 1) - E(x, D = 0)]$ would appear in the estimation of ATE.

Case 3 In this third case, we assume that D affects Y, x affects Y too, but there is no relation between D and x. For this specific casual chain, we show that there is no difference in controlling or not for x (thus becoming an "optional" choice). In fact, the corresponding structural model becomes (again under CMI):

$$D = a_1 + u \qquad (1.76)$$
$$Y = b_1 + b_w \cdot D + b_x \cdot x + v \qquad (1.77)$$

In this case, x appears in the Y-equation and thus:

$$E(Y|D=1) = E_x\{E(Y|x, D=1)\} = b_1 + b_w + b_x \cdot E(x|D=1)$$
$$= b_1 + b_w + b_x \cdot E(x) \qquad (1.78)$$

$$E(Y|D=0) = E_x\{E(Y|x, D=0)\} = b_1 + b_x \cdot E(x|D=0)$$
$$= b_1 + b_w + b_x \cdot E(x) \qquad (1.79)$$

where we exploited $E(x \mid D) = E(x)$, as x and D are assumed to have no relation in this causal chain. This immediately leads to this result:

$$\text{ATE} = b_w \qquad (1.80)$$

that is the same as what we can get without conditioning on x.

As a conclusion, Cases 1, 2, and 3 lead to the following result: x must be controlled for only if x affects at the same time both D and Y. If x affects either *only* the selection equation or *only* the outcome equation, then controlling for x is not strictly necessary. Nevertheless, adding additional covariates in the Y-equation could result in a more precise estimation of ATEs.

Case 4   This case refers to a situation similar to Case 2, but this time we consider also that: (1) a pretreatment x may have an effect on its posttreatment status (self-effect), and (2) the outcome Y can also affect the posttreatment status of x. In such a situation, while it is clearly needed to control for the pretreatment x (as in Case 2), it is not necessary to control for its posttreatment status. This is because x_{post} is, in this case, just the result of the whole causal chain not explaining any other variable. In this sense, unbalancing on x_{post} is harmless.

Case 5   In this case the treatment D affects x that in turn affects D. As such, x takes the form of a posttreatment variable working as a *mediating* factor (i.e., a factor causally laying between the treatment D and the outcome Y). The corresponding structural system of such a causal chain is:

$$x = c_1 + c_w \cdot D + u_x \qquad (1.81)$$
$$Y = b_1 + b_w \cdot D + v \qquad (1.82)$$

In this case, conditioning on x is not needed as x does not appear in the Y-equation. Thus, one does not need to control for this variable.

Case 6   In this case, the treatment D affects both x and Y that in turn is affected also by x. Again, x takes the form of a posttreatment variable working as a *mediator*. The corresponding structural system is:

$$x = c_1 + c_w \cdot D + u_x \qquad (1.83)$$
$$Y = b_1 + b_w \cdot D + b_x \cdot x + v \qquad (1.84)$$

In this case, by simple substitution, we obtain:

$$Y = b_1 + b_w \cdot D + b_x \cdot (c_1 + c_w \cdot D + u_x) + v$$
$$= (b_1 + b_x \cdot c_1) + (b_w + b_x \cdot c_w) \cdot D + \eta \tag{1.85}$$

with $\eta = (b_x \cdot u_x + v)$ and where the Y-equation is the *reduced-form* of the previous system of two equations. Within this framework, we can define *three* types of effect of D on Y:

- *Direct effect*: $E(Y|D = 1, x) - E(Y|D = 0, x) = b_w$
- *Indirect effect*: $\left[E(x|D = 1) - E(x|D = 0)\right] \cdot \left[E(Y|D, x = 1) - E(Y|D, x = 0)\right]$
  $= c_w \cdot b_x$
- *Total effect*: $E(Y|D = 1) - E(Y|D = 1) = b_w + b_x \cdot c_w$

The total effect $(b_w + b_x \cdot c_w)$ is the sum of the direct (b_w) and indirect effect $(b_x \cdot c_w)$ and can be obtained—under CMI—by an OLS regression of the reduced form of the outcome Y. Instead, the direct effect can be obtained by an OLS of (1.84), where both b_w and b_x are consistently estimated under CMI.

Therefore, it is quite clear that: if the analyst is interested in estimating the total effect of D on Y, then x should not need to be controlled for. Since we are interested in the direct effect of D on Y (i.e., the effect of D on Y "net of the effect of D on x"), then controlling for x is mandatory.

In conclusion, choosing whether to control or not for a given observable variable is not as straightforward as it might appear at first glance. Previous examples, although not exhaustive of all possible situations, might however be a proper point of departure for a wiser decision.

1.6 Partial Identification of ATEs: The Bounding Approach

In Sect. 1.2, we have shown that ATEs cannot be identified because of the missing observation problem of the counterfactual status. In this sense, without introducing additional assumptions—such as the CIA—a point estimation of ATEs would be impossible. Furthermore, imposing assumptions can be sometimes costly, not to say misleading, when such assumptions cannot be tested, as in the case of the CIA.

An assumption-free approach for estimating ATEs, on the contrary, would be more attractive, but it poses further limitations that we will discuss in what follows. Manski et al. (1992) have proposed a simple model for estimating ATEs under partial identification, i.e., without using too much a priori information or assumptions for identifying the causal relation of interest. In what follows, we will reproduce their model.

First, suppose we have a binary target variable Y, a binary treatment D, and a vector of confounders $\mathbf{x}$. In such a case, being Y binomial, we have:

$$\text{ATE}(\mathbf{x}) = \text{E}(Y_1 - Y_0|\mathbf{x}) = p(Y_1 = 1|\mathbf{x}) - p(Y_0 = 1|\mathbf{x}) \qquad (1.86)$$

With no other information or assumptions available, the only conclusion we can reach about the "true" value of ATE(**x**) is that it varies between -1 and $+1$, thus having an interval *width* equal to 2, as given by the difference between the upper and lower bound of such interval.

However, we can exploit some other information and restrict this width. In particular, by applying LIE, we can show that:

$$\text{ATE}(\mathbf{x}) = \text{E}_D\{\text{ATE}(\mathbf{x})\big|D\} = \text{E}_D\{\text{ATE}(\mathbf{x},D)\} \qquad (1.87)$$

This implies that, as for $p(Y_1 = 1|\mathbf{x})$ we have:

$$p(Y_1 = 1|\mathbf{x}) = p(Y_1 = 1|\mathbf{x}, D = 0) \cdot p(D = 0|\mathbf{x}) + p(Y_1 = 1|\mathbf{x}, D = 1) \\ \cdot p(D = 1|\mathbf{x}) \qquad (1.88)$$

where it is clear that the only unidentifiable quantity of the RHS of the previous equation is $p(Y_1 = 1|\mathbf{x}, D = 0)$, while the others are identifiable, as no counterfactual is implicated. Since, by definition:

$$0 \le p(Y_1 = 1|\mathbf{x}, D = 0) \le 1 \qquad (1.89)$$

The substitution of these bounds into (1.88) yields:

$$p(Y_1 = 1|\mathbf{x}, D = 1) \cdot p(D = 1|\mathbf{x}) \le p(Y_1 = 1|\mathbf{x}) \\ \le p(D = 0|\mathbf{x}) + p(Y_1 = 1|\mathbf{x}, D = 1) \\ \cdot p(D = 1|\mathbf{x}) \qquad (1.90)$$

where the width of this interval is $p(D = 0 |\mathbf{x})$. Analogously, for $p(Y_0 = 1|\mathbf{x})$ we follow a similar procedure thus getting:

$$p(Y_0 = 1|\mathbf{x}, D = 0) \cdot p(D = 0|\mathbf{x}) \le p(Y_0 = 1|\mathbf{x}) \\ \le p(D = 1|\mathbf{x}) + p(Y_0 = 1|\mathbf{x}, D = 0) \\ \cdot p(D = 0|\mathbf{x}) \qquad (1.91)$$

whose width is $p(D = 1 | \mathbf{x})$. By considering these bounds for $\text{ATE}(\mathbf{x}) = p(Y_1 = 1 | \mathbf{x}) - p(Y_0 = 1 | \mathbf{x})$ using (1.90) and (1.91), we finally have[6]:

---

[6] Observe that the lower bound of ATE(**x**) is equal to the lower bound of $p(Y_1 = 1 | \mathbf{x})$ minus the upper bound of $p(Y_0 = 1 | \mathbf{x})$, while the upper bound of ATE(**x**) is equal to the upper bound of $p(Y_1 = 1 | \mathbf{x})$ minus the lower bound of $p(Y_0 = 1 | \mathbf{x})$.

$$L_{ATE} \leq p(Y_1 = 1|\mathbf{x}) - p(Y_0 = 1|\mathbf{x}) \leq U_{ATE} \qquad (1.92)$$

where:

$$L_{ATE} = C - p(D = 1|\mathbf{x}) \quad \text{and} \quad U_{ATE} = C + p(D = 0|\mathbf{x}) \qquad (1.93)$$

with:

$$\begin{aligned} C = {} & p(Y_1 = 1|\mathbf{x}, D = 1) \cdot p(D = 1|\mathbf{x}) - p(Y_0 = 1|\mathbf{x}, D = 0) \\ & \cdot p(D = 0|\mathbf{x}) \end{aligned} \qquad (1.94)$$

It is immediate to see that, in such a case, the width of the interval for ATE($\mathbf{x}$) is equal to:

$$p(D = 0|\mathbf{x}) + p(D = 1|\mathbf{x}) = 1 \qquad (1.95)$$

which is half the width of the ATE($\mathbf{x}$) interval obtained above. Thus, as maintained by Manski et al.: "*using sample data alone, we can cut in half the range of uncertainty regarding the treatment effect. Tighter bounds can be obtained only if prior information is available*" (1992, p. 30).

The information contained in the sample, therefore, allows for estimating the quantities entering the lower and upper bounds. In particular, suppose that Y is "obtaining or not obtaining a degree" and that $D = 1$ "if at least one of the parents holds a degree." In such a case, using a sample $\{Y_i, D_i, \mathbf{x}_i\}$, what is needed to estimate the bounds is:

- $p(D = 1|\mathbf{x})$: propensity to have a graduated parent, estimated using all N observations
- $p(Y_1 = 1|\mathbf{x}, D = 1) = p(Y = 1|\mathbf{x}, D = 1)$: probability to get a degree, estimated using only observations for treated units (N_1)[7]
- $p(Y_0 = 1|\mathbf{x}, D = 0) = p(Y = 1|\mathbf{x}, D = 0)$: probability to get a degree, estimated using only observations for untreated units (N_0)

Finally, both parametric and nonparametric estimation of previous probabilities can be performed, and confidence intervals for L_{ATE} and U_{ATE} are possibly obtained, for instance, via bootstrap.

Introducing further assumptions in the data generating process can allow to reduce the range of variation of ATE($\mathbf{x}$) further. A possible way can be that of assuming the so-called *monotonicity* entailing the following condition:

$$0 \leq p(Y_1 = 1|\mathbf{x}, D = 0) \leq p(Y_1 = 1|\mathbf{x}, D = 1) \qquad (1.96)$$

In the previous example, this condition assumes that, *ceteris paribus*, the probability to receive a degree for a given individual is higher when at least one of the

---

[7] Observe that an estimation of $p(D = 0 \mid \mathbf{x})$ is obtained as $[1 - \widehat{p}(D = 1|\mathbf{x})]$.

parents owns a degree. This is a non-testable assumption as $p(Y_1 = 1|\mathbf{x}, D = 0)$ is clearly unobservable. However, in many contexts, monotonicity may be a reasonable assumption. We will come back to this assumption in Chap. 4 when discussing identification in the context of the local average treatment effect (LATE).

It is easy to show that by substituting the monotonicity bounds in place of $0 \leq p$ $(Y_1 = 1|\mathbf{x}, D = 0) \leq 1$ into (1.88), we can find the following new bounds for $p(Y_1 = 1|\mathbf{x})$:

$$p(Y_1 = 1|\mathbf{x}, D = 1) \cdot p(D = 1|\mathbf{x}) \leq p(Y_1 = 1|\mathbf{x}) \leq p(Y_1 = 1|\mathbf{x}, D = 1) \quad (1.97)$$

whose width is:

$$p(D = 0|\mathbf{x}) \cdot p(Y_1 = 1|\mathbf{x}, D = 1) \quad (1.98)$$

proving to be smaller than $p(D = 0 | \mathbf{x})$, i.e., the width of the baseline case. As for $p(Y_1 = 1 | \mathbf{x})$, we can assume an analogous monotonicity assumption:

$$p(Y_0 = 1|\mathbf{x}, D = 0) \leq p(Y_0 = 1|\mathbf{x}, D = 1) \leq 1 \quad (1.99)$$

leading, similarly, to a new bounding relation for $p(Y_0 = 1 | \mathbf{x})$, that is:

$$\begin{aligned} p(Y_0 = 1|\mathbf{x}, D = 0) &\leq p(Y_0 = 1|\mathbf{x}) \\ &\leq p(D = 1|\mathbf{x}) + p(Y_0 = 1|\mathbf{x}, D = 0) \cdot p(D = 0|\mathbf{x}) \end{aligned} \quad (1.100)$$

Given these results, we can get the new bounds for $\text{ATE}(\mathbf{x}) = p(Y_1 = 1|\mathbf{x}) - p(Y_0 = 1|\mathbf{x})$:

$$\begin{aligned} p(Y_1 = 1|\mathbf{x}, D &= 1) \cdot p(D = 1|\mathbf{x}) - p(D = 1|\mathbf{x}) - p(Y_0 = 1|\mathbf{x}, D = 0) \\ &\cdot p(D = 0|\mathbf{x}) \\ &\leq p(Y_1 = 1|\mathbf{x}) - p(Y_0 = 1|\mathbf{x}) \\ &\leq p(Y_1 = 1|\mathbf{x}, D = 1) - p(Y_0 = 1|\mathbf{x}, D = 0) \end{aligned} \quad (1.101)$$

In such a case (we can call the "monotonicity case"), the width of the range of $\text{ATE}(\mathbf{x})$ is smaller than in the baseline case. In particular, while the lower bound is the same, the upper bound is smaller. To show this, call $p(Y_1 = 1|\mathbf{x}, D = 1) = A, p(Y_0 = 1|\mathbf{x}, D = 0) = B, p(Y_0 = 1|\mathbf{x}) = p_0$, and $p(Y_1 = 1|\mathbf{x}) = p_1$. The upper bound in the monotonicity case is $U_{\text{Mon}} = (A - B)$. Consider the upper bound of the baseline model:

$$\begin{aligned} U_{\text{ATE}} &= p_0 + A \cdot p_1 - B \cdot p_0 = p_0 + A - A \cdot p_0 - B \cdot p_0 + (B - B) \\ &= (A - B) + (p_0 - A \cdot p_0) + (B - B \cdot p_0) \geq (A - B) = U_{\text{Mon}} \end{aligned} \quad (1.102)$$

The last inequality follows from the fact that $\{p_0, A, B\}$ are probabilities so that: $(p_0 - A \cdot p_0) \geq 0$ and $(B - B \cdot p_0) \geq 0$.

Another assumption sometimes used to tighten the bounds of ATE($\mathbf{x}$) is based on *exclusion restrictions*, occurring when one assumes that an exogenous variable z affects D, while not affecting Y directly (but only through D). See Lee (2005, pp. 163–167) for a discussion.

In conclusion, we can state that as soon as we increase the number of assumptions to be brought into a treatment model, the level of uncertainty related to the effects' estimation drops. Some assumptions are however generally non-testable and this may cast doubts on the reliability of results thus obtained. This is a risk we can run anytime we wish to achieve *point* identification of a treatment effect to avoid uncertainty in results. On the contrary, the bounding approach responds to the need of sensibly reducing the number of relied upon assumptions. But in doing so, this approach implies *interval* rather than *point* estimates of the effects that might be poorly informative for a policymaker to assess the actual effectiveness of a policy program. Nevertheless, this seems to deal more with the ontology of evaluation exercises than only with technical considerations.

In line with the mainstream literature, however, this book will focus on the more traditional non-bounding approach to treatment effect estimation. This section, however, has shown the limitation of such a choice; as such, it should be taken as a cautionary argument when obtaining and communicating policy evaluation results. More on bounding approach and partial identification can be found in Manski (2003).

1.7   A Guiding Taxonomy of the Econometric Methods for Program Evaluation

In order to reliably measure policy effects, the econometrics of program evaluation has to cope with a very complex system of interrelated phenomena: missing observation, observable and unobservable selection, endogeneity, data availability, and so forth. Two main philosophies have been followed to address this complexity. The first and more extensively adopted approach, developed especially in the last few years, seems to prefer a more empirical-based point of view, where not a great deal of theoretical speculation is brought into the models, except for those specific factors accounting for the selection criteria of supporting programs. Examples of this kind are econometric exercises such as those based on the Control-function regression (CFR), a specific case of the Regression-adjustment (RA), and Matching (MATCH) estimators. Conversely, the second stream of research has tried to make the theoretical background behind the data more explicit by building proper "quasi-structural models," where causal relations are more clearly enlightened (this is the case of, for instance, IV and Selection-models (SM)).

The boundary between these two viewpoints is somewhat less sharp than it might appear at first glance. Nevertheless, for the sake of clarity, Table 1.2—drawing upon a readjustment of that provided by Cerulli (2010)—provides a

Table 1.2 A taxonomy of policy evaluation methods according to the identification assumption, type of specification, and data structure

	Identification assumption		Type of specification		Data structure	
	Selection on observables	Selection on unobservables	Structural	Reduced-form	Cross-section	Longitudinal or repeated cross-section
Regression-adjustment	x			x	x	
Matching	x			x	x	
Reweighting	x				x	
Instrumental-variables	x	x	x		x	
Selection-model	x	x	x		x	
Regression-discontinuity-design	x (sharp)	x (fuzzy)	x (fuzzy)	x (sharp)		
Difference-in-differences	x	x		x		x

tentative *taxonomy* of (binary) treatment models for program evaluation, by distinguishing among the following three analytical dimensions:

Identification assumption: distinguishing between methods suitable to work with selection on observables and/or selection on unobservables, according to the analyst's knowledge of what drives the *self-selection* of individuals and the *selection* of the agency. Only instrumental-variables, Selection-models, and the Difference-in-differences (DID) estimators are able to cope with unobservable selection. Regression-adjustment, Matching, as well as Reweighting (REW) can only deal with selection on observables. The RDD method should deserve a special treatment because this approach—as we will see in Chap. 4—draws upon a different identification assumption, based on locally replicating an experimental setting. However, we have put it into this taxonomy for the sake of comprehensiveness, and because practical estimation follows the observable selection type for sharp RDD (OLS approach), and the unobservable selection type for Fuzzy-RDD (IV approach).

Type of specification: distinguishing between models adopting a *structural/ analytical* approach, where the outcome and the selection-into-program processes are separately modeled in a system of simultaneous equations, and *nonstructural* models where only the outcome equation (the so-called *reduced-form*) is estimated, once controlling for specific covariates.

Data structure: models based on a *cross-section* dataset and models exploiting a *longitudinal* or *repeated cross-section* structure. As evident in the table, only the DID estimator exploits in a substantial way the availability of longitudinal or repeated cross-section data. In applications, the large majority of works uses cross-section datasets, while fewer studies make use of longitudinal data. Longitudinal data are however suitable for before/after policy comparison and for long-run impact assessment.

Although approximate, this taxonomy seems useful for positioning the program evaluation methods we will describe and analyze in detail in the next chapters. The previous taxonomy also offers the opportunity to provide an assessment of the comparative advantages and drawbacks of each econometric method, as illustrated in Table 1.3. We do not discuss the content of this table now, as the reader will find it more useful and understandable after reading the next chapters.

It is however relevant to notice that this table also shows that we cannot identify the "best" method to apply in absolute terms, as each approach presents comparative advantages and drawbacks which are dependent on the specific context of analysis. By and large, at least three elements seem necessary to consider before choosing a specific econometric approach for an ex post program evaluation:

• Program institutional setup and operation
• Subjects' behavior and interaction
• Data availability and data consistency

Paying attention to these aspects is an important precondition for a program evaluation to be econometrically sound. They refer to the qualitative dimension of the analysis, generally based on pilot surveys, interviews to the policy actors involved in the program, and on the collection of program-related documentation.

Table 1.3 An assessment of the comparative advantages and drawbacks of econometric methods for program evaluation

Method	Advantages	Drawbacks
Regression-adjustment (Control-function regression)	*Suitable for observable selection* *Not based on distributional hypotheses*	*Not suitable for unobservable selection* *Based on a parametric estimation*
Matching	*Suitable for observable selection* *Not based on distributional hypotheses* *Based on a nonparametric estimation*	*Not suitable for unobservable selection* *Sensitive to sparseness (weak overlap)* *Sensitive to confounders' unbalancing*
Reweighting	*Suitable for observable selection* *Not based on distributional hypotheses* *Based on a semi-parametric estimation*	*Not suitable for unobservable selection* *Sensitive to propensity-score specification and/or weighting schemes*
Selection-model	*Suitable for both observable and unobservable selection*	*Based on distributional hypotheses* *Based on a parametric estimation*
Instrumental-variables	*Suitable for both observable and unobservable selection* *Not based on distributional hypotheses*	*Availability of instrumental variables* *Based on a parametric estimation*
Regression-discontinuity-design	*Reproducing locally a natural experiment (randomization)* *No distributional hypothesis* *Extendable to nonparametric techniques*	*Availability of a "forcing" variable* *Choice of the cutoff and of an appropriate bandwidth*
Difference-in-differences	*Suitable for both observable and unobservable selection* *Not based on distributional hypotheses*	*Specific form of the error term* *Availability of a longitudinal dataset* *Based on a parametric estimation*

Relying on such information is a necessary step as a proper program evaluation needs qualitative and quantitative analysis to be suitably combined.

1.8 Policy Framework and the Statistical Design for Counterfactual Evaluation

Before describing and applying the various econometric approaches set out in Table 1.2, it is worth stressing that a correct ex post program evaluation analysis first needs to draw upon a rich and qualified set of information. This information generally takes the form of: (1) suitable *indicators*, both qualitative and quantitative, and (2) availability of an accurate *sample of (treated and untreated) units*.

While indicators are primarily aimed at measuring specific aspects of the decisional processes characterizing the subjects involved in the policy, an appropriate sample of units is the basis for implementing a reliable statistical design, since both the set of *beneficiaries* (the supported units) as well as that of the *counterfactual* (approximated by a given set of non-supported units) are to be chosen carefully.

The use of suitable indicators and of an appropriate sample of subjects are the product of the "framework" characterizing the *functioning* of the policy considered. This framework may also suggest what econometric approach might be more suited for the specific context under scrutiny. In a very simplified way, and by restricting the analysis to project-funding programs, Fig. 1.8 tries to set out such a framework showing the actors involved and their role and relation along the policy design. This logical framework, although general, is an essential basis for steering both the choice of indicators and the statistical design for the econometric ex post evaluation exercise (Potì and Cerulli 2011).

In this scheme, we can observe the participation/decision process of two distinct actors: a public agency (managing the program) and a set of units (undergoing the program). Their strategies and interactions, along with those of other subjects that we can roughly identify with the "environment" (whose role, at this stage, is left out for simplicity), represent the basis for identifying the determinants of the policy implementation and effect. Let us briefly describe this framework.

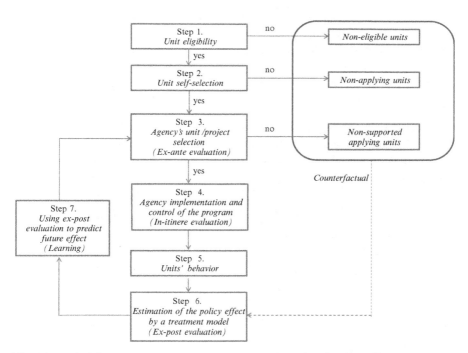

Fig. 1.8 Logical framework for an ex post assessment of a project-funding policy program

It starts from step 1, where each single unit may be distinguished between eligible and non-eligible for the program considered. If the unit is eligible (according to some preconditioning factors, stated in the rules accompanying the program), then it passes to the second step (unit self-selection); otherwise, it becomes part of the potential counterfactual set, being untreated. In the second step, the eligible subjects have to decide whether or not to apply for receiving a given support: it is the process of unit "self-selection" into program. This choice is generally guided by a specific objective function of the unit, comparing benefits and costs of applying. Subjects deciding not to apply are then collected within the group of "non-supported" individuals and potentially used to build the counterfactual set.

Units choosing to apply go to step 3 where the public agency "selects" the beneficiaries of the program on the basis of a specific "welfare function" whose arguments should be consistent with the declared objectives of the policy. Even in this case, the choice might be thought to be driven by a cost-benefit comparison (*ex ante evaluation*). Those subjects that are not selected to benefit from the program become part of the counterfactual set.

Step 4 concerns the factual *implementation* and *control* of the policy as operated by the public agency: after receiving applications and choosing beneficiaries, the public agency has to decide—unit by unit and/or project by project—the magnitude of the support, the number of instalments in the provision of potential monetary assets, etc. and it has to monitor timely the state-of-the-art of supported projects at specific dates (*in itenere evaluation*).

Finally, step 5 concerns the actual behavior of the selected subjects. At this step, given the level and/or quality of treatment, units perform a behavior that might be guided, also in this case, by comparing costs and returns associated to the consequences of their choices.

Step 6 is the downstream part of the program logical framework, where the policy impact is assessed by means of a counterfactual (econometric) method. For estimation purposes, a proper counterfactual set of non-supported units, built along the policy framework (represented in the round frame of Fig. 1.8) is exploited.

Step 7, finally, concludes the framework by producing a *cyclical learning process*. Indeed, by taking stock of past evaluation results, a public agency may upgrade the ex ante choice of beneficiaries in order to increase the likelihood of success in future policy rounds. Of course, an agency's learning process might encompass various program's steps, and not only the one concerning the selection process. Nevertheless, we deem it to be highly related to the exploitation of past impact evaluation results, an essential mechanism for correcting and/or improving future policy performance.

1.9 Available Econometric Software

A final but essential ingredient to perform quantitative program evaluation concerns the availability of specialized software for easily implement evaluation exercises. In this book, we make use of the statistical and econometric software Stata 13 that in recent years has seen a significant increase of both built-in and user-written routines for applying program evaluation methods. Table 1.4 puts forward a list of these Stata routines for treatment effect estimation. Many of them will be presented and extensively used in the applications presented in the following chapters.

It is worth mentioning that Stata 13, the last release of Stata, provides a new far-reaching package, called `teffects`, for estimating treatment effects for observational data.

The `teffects` command can be used to estimate potential-outcome means (POMs) and average treatment effects (ATEs) using observational data. As shown in Table 1.5, this suit covers a large set of methods, such as regression adjustment (RA); inverse-probability weights (IPW); "doubly robust" methods, including inverse-probability-weighted regression adjustment (IPWRA); augmented inverse-probability weights (AIPW); Matching on the propensity-score or nearest-neighbor Matching. Finally, other sub-commands can be used for post-estimation purposes and for testing results' reliability (for instance: `overlap` plots the estimated densities of the probability of getting each treatment level).

In applying `teffects`, the outcome models can be continuous, binary, count, or nonnegative. Binary outcomes can be modeled using logit, probit, or heteroskedastic probit regression; and count and nonnegative outcomes can be modeled using Poisson regression. The treatment model can be binary or multinomial. Binary treatments can be modeled using logit, probit, or heteroskedastic probit regression. For multinomial treatments, one can use pair-wise comparisons and then exploit binary treatment approaches.

Table 1.4 Stata commands for performing econometric program evaluation

`regress`	CFR (or linear RA), linear reweighting, DID (panel data)
`ivreg`	Basic IV, LATE
`treatreg`	Selection-model (HECKIT)
`psmatch2`[a]	Matching (with nearest neighbor on covariates and on propensity-score)
`pscore`[a]	Matching (with propensity-score)
`nnmtach`[a]	Matching (nearest neighbor on covariates)
`rd`[a]	RDD (sharp and fuzzy)
`ivtreatreg`[a]	IV and HECKIT with heterogeneous response to confounders
`treatrew`[a]	Reweighting on propensity-score
`diff`[a]	DID (repeated cross-section)

RA regression-adjustment, *CFR* control-function regression, *HECKIT* Heckman-type selection-model, *IV* instrumental-variables, *DID* difference-in-differences, *RDD* regression-discontinuity-design
[a]User-written routine downloadable from Stata SSC

Table 1.5 Stata 13's sub-commands of the `teffects` for estimating treatment effects for observational data

`aipw`	Augmented inverse-probability weighting
`ipw`	Inverse-probability weighting
`ipwra`	Inverse-probability weighted Regression-adjustment
`nnmatch`	Nearest-neighbor Matching
`overlap`	Overlap plots
`psmatch`	Propensity-score Matching
`ra`	Regression-adjustment

Depending on specific applications, this book will make use of either built-in or user-written commands. Observe that the `teffects` command deals mainly with estimation methods suitable under selection on observables. For methods appropriate for selection on unobservables, we will mainly rely on some user-written commands.

1.10   A Brief Outline of the Book

This book deals with the econometrics of program evaluation in a binary treatment context. It is split into four chapters. Chapter 1 provides a detailed introduction and overview of the main (theoretical and empirical) issues concerning the econometrics of program evaluation. It defines and discusses literature milestone concepts and provides notation for a binary treatment setting. It is greatly recommended to read it before examining the next chapters, where concepts and notation—herein presented—are extensively used. As such, this chapter serves as a basic toolbox for the rest of the book.

Chapter 2 focuses on methods based on selection on observables. Methods such as Regression-adjustment, Matching, and Reweighting are presented, discussed, and applied to real datasets using Stata 13. Besides these methods, specific attention will be devoted also to salient aspects such as results' sensitivity analysis and robustness.

Chapter 3 deals with methods based on selection on unobservables. It presents and examines methods such as: Instrumental-variables (IV), Selection-model (SM), and Difference-in-differences (DID). Moreover, mixture of approaches and methods for time-variant binary treatment are also discussed. Applications to real and simulated datasets are also performed in this chapter using built-in as well as user-written Stata routines (including some developed by the author).

Chapter 4, finally, describes and examines the Regression-discontinuity-design approach, both in its sharp and fuzzy forms. Here, a presentation of the local average treatment effect (LATE) and of its conceptual meaning within a quasi-natural experiment is also illustrated. An application of such methods using simulated data is then provided and discussed at length.

References

Abadie, A., Angrist, J., & Imbens, G. (2002). Instrumental variables estimates of the effect of subsidized training on the quantiles of trainee earnings. *Econometrica, 70*, 91–117.

Althaus, C., Bridgman, P., & Davis, G. (2007). *The Australian policy handbook*. Sydney: Allen & Unwin.

Angrist, J. D. (1991). *Instrumental variables estimation of average treatment effects in econometrics and epidemiology* (NBER Technical Working Papers No. 0115).

Angrist, J. D., & Imbens, G. W. (1995). Two-stage least squares estimation of average causal effects in models with variable treatment intensity. *Journal of the American Statistical Association, 90*, 431–442.

Angrist, J. D., & Pischke, J. S. (2008). *Mostly harmless econometrics: An empiricist's companion*. Princeton, NJ: Princeton University Press.

Blundell, R., & Costa Dias, M. (2002). Alternative approaches to evaluation in empirical microeconomics. *Portuguese Economic Journal, 1*, 91–115.

Cameron, A. C., & Trivedi, P. K. (2005). *Microeconometrics: Methods and applications*. Cambridge: Cambridge University Press.

Cattaneo, M. D. (2010). Efficient semiparametric estimation of multi-valued treatment effects under ignorability. *Journal of Econometrics, 155*, 138–154.

Cerulli, G. (2010). Modelling and measuring the effect of public subsidies on business R&D: Critical review of the economic literature. *Economic Record, 86*, 421–449.

Cerulli, G. (2014a). *Identification and estimation of treatment effects in the presence of neighbourhood interactions* (Working Paper Cnr–Ceris, N° 04/2014).

Cerulli, G. (2014b). *CTREATREG: Stata module for estimating dose–response models under exogenous and endogenous treatment* (Working Paper Cnr–Ceris, N° 05/2014).

Chernozhukov, V., & Hansen, C. (2005). An IV model of quantile treatment effects. *Econometrica, 73*, 245–261.

Cobb-Clark, D. A., & Crossley, T. (2003). Econometrics for evaluations: An introduction to recent developments. *Economic Record, 79*, 491–511.

Cooley, T. F., & LeRoy, S. F. (1985). Atheoretical macroeconometrics: A critique. *Journal of Monetary Economics, 16*, 283–308.

Frölich, M. (2004). Programme evaluation with multiple treatments. *Journal of Economic Surveys, 18*, 181–224.

Frölich, M., & Melly, B. (2010). Estimation of quantile treatment effects with Stata. *Stata Journal, 10*(3), 423–457.

Frölich, M., & Melly, B. (2013). Unconditional quantile treatment effects under endogeneity. *Journal of Business & Economic Statistics, 31*(3), 346–357.

Guo, S., & Fraser, M.-W. (2010). *Propensity score analysis. Statistical methods and applications*. Thousand Oaks, CA: SAGE.

Heckman, J. J. (2000). Causal parameters and policy analysis in economics: A twentieth century retrospective. *Quarterly Journal of Economics, 115*, 45–97.

Heckman, J. J. (2001). Micro data, heterogeneity, and the evaluation of public policy: Nobel lecture. *Journal of Political Economy, 109*, 673–748.

Heckman, J., Ichimura, H., Smith, J., & Todd, P. (1998). Characterizing selection bias using experimental data. *Econometrica, 66*, 1017–1098.

Heckman, J. J., Lalonde, R., & Smith, J. (2000). The economics and econometrics of active labor markets programs. In A. Ashenfelter & D. Card (Eds.), *Handbook of labor economics* (Vol. 3). New York: Elsevier.

Hirano, K., & Imbens, G. (2004). The propensity score with continuous treatments. In A. Gelman & X. L. Meng (Eds.), *Applied Bayesian modeling and causal inference from incomplete-data perspectives* (pp. 73–84). New York: Wiley.

Holland, P. (1986). Statistics and causal inference (with discussion). *Journal of the American Statistical Association, 81*, 945–970.

Hoover, K. D. (2001). *Causality in macroeconomics*. Cambridge: Cambridge University Press.

Hudgens, M. G., & Halloran, M. E. (2008). Toward causal inference with interference. *Journal of the American Statistical Association, 103*(482), 832–842.

Husted, J. A., Cook, R. J., Farewell, V. T., & Gladman, D. D. (2000). Methods for assessing responsiveness: A critical review and recommendations. *Journal of Clinical Epidemiology, 53*, 459–468.

Imai, K., & Van Dyk, D. (2004). Causal inference with general treatment regimes: Generalizing the propensity score. *Journal of the American Statistical Association, 99*, 854–866.

Imbens, G. W. (2000). The role of the propensity score in estimating dose-response functions. *Biometrika, 87*, 706–710.

Imbens, G. W. (2004). Nonparametric estimation of average treatment effects under exogeneity: A review. *The Review of Economics and Statistics, 86*(1), 4–29.

Imbens, G. W., & Wooldridge, J. M. (2009). Recent developments in the econometrics of program evaluation. *Journal of Economic Literature, 47*, 5–86.

Koopmans, T. C. (1947). Measurement without theory. *The Review of Economic Statistics, 29*(3), 161–172.

Koopmans, T. C. (1949). Reply to Rutledge Vining. *The Review of Economic Statistics, 31*, 86–91.

Lee, M. J. (2005). *Micro-econometrics for policy, program and treatment effects.* Oxford: Oxford University Press.

Lucas, R. E. (1976). Econometric policy evaluation: A critique. In K. Brunner & A. H. Meltzer (Eds.), *The Phillips curve and labor markets* (pp. 19–46). Amsterdam: North-Holland.

Lucas, R. E. (1980). Methods and problems in business cycle theory. *Journal of Money, Credit and Banking, 12*, 696–715.

Lucas, R. E., & Sargent, T. J. (1981). After Keynesian macroeconomics. In R. E. Lucas & T. J. Sargent (Eds.), *Rational expectations and econometric practice* (pp. 295–319). Minneapolis, MN: University of Minnesota Press.

Manski, C. F. (1993). Identification of endogenous social effects: The reflection problem. *The Review of Economic Studies, 60*(3), 531–542.

Manski, C. F. (2003). *Partial identification of probability distributions.* New York: Springer.

Manski, C. F. (2013). Identification of treatment response with social interactions. *The Econometrics Journal, 16*(1), S1–S23.

Manski, C. F., Sandefur, G. D., McLanahan, S., & Powers, D. (1992). Alternative estimates of the effect of family structure during adolescence on high school graduation. *Journal of the American Statistical Association, 87*, 417.

Millimet, D., Smith, J., & Vytlacil, E. (Eds.). (2008). *Advances in econometrics, Vol 21. Modelling and evaluating treatment effects in econometrics.* Amsterdam: JAI Press, Elsevier.

Moran, M., Rein, M., & Goodin, R. E. (Eds.). (2008). *The Oxford handbook of public policy.* Oxford: Oxford University Press.

Morgan, S. L., & Winship, C. (2007). *Counterfactuals and causal inference: Methods and principles for social research.* New York: Cambridge University Press.

Neyman, J. (1923). On the application of probability theory to agricultural experiments. Essay on principles. Section 9. Translated in *Statistical Science, 5*(1990), 465–480.

Pearl, J. (2000). *Causality: Models, reasoning and inference.* Cambridge: Cambridge University Press.

Pearl, J. (2009). Causal inference in statistics: An overview. *Statistics Surveys, 3*, 96–146.

Potì, B., & Cerulli, G. (2011). Evaluation of firm R&D and innovation support: New indicators and the ex-ante prediction of ex-post additionality. *Research Evaluation, 20*(1), 19–29.

Rosenbaum, P. R. (2007). Interference between units in randomized experiments. *Journal of the American Statistical Association, 102*(477), 191–200.

Rosenbaum, P., & Rubin, D. (1983). The central role of the propensity score in observational studies for causal effects. *Biometrika, 70*, 41–55.

Rothman, K. J., Greenland, S., & Lash, T. L. (2008). *Modern epidemiology.* Philadelphia: Lippincott Williams & Wilkins.

Rubin, D. (1974). Estimating causal effects of treatments in randomized and non-randomized studies. *Journal of Educational Psychology, 66*, 688–701.

Rubin, D. B. (1977). Assignment to treatment group on the basis of a covariate. *Journal of Educational Statistics, 2*, 1–26.

Rubin, D. B. (1978). Bayesian inference for causal effects: The role of randomization. *Annals of Statistics, 6*(1), 34–58.

Shadish, W., Cook, T., & Campbell, D. (2002). *Experimental and quasi-experimental designs for generalized causal inference*. Boston: Houghton Mifflin.

Sims, C. A. (1980). Macroeconomics and reality. *Econometrica, 48*, 1–48.

Sims, C. A. (1996). Macroeconomics and methodology. *Journal of Economic Perspectives, 10*, 105–120.

Sobel, M. E. (2006). What do randomized studies of housing mobility demonstrate? Causal inference in the face of interference. *Journal of the American Statistical Association, 101* (476), 1398–1407.

Tchetgen-Tchetgen, E. J., & VanderWeele, T. J. (2010). On causal inference in the presence of interference. *Statistical Methods in Medical Research, 21*(1), 55–75.

Trochim, W., & Donnelly, J. P. (2007). *The research methods knowledge base*. Mason, OH: Thomson.

Vining, R. (1949a). Koopmans on the choice of variables to be studied and the methods of measurement. *The Review of Economics and Statistics, 31*, 77–86.

Vining, R. (1949b). Rejoiner. *The Review of Economics and Statistics, 31*, 91–96.

Wooldridge, J. M. (2001). Unobserved heterogeneity and estimation of average partial effects. Michigan State University, Department of Economics, mimeo.

Wooldridge, J. M. (2002). *Econometric analysis of cross section and panel data*. Cambridge: MIT Press.

Wooldridge, J. M. (2010). *Econometric analysis of cross section and panel data*. Cambridge, MA: MIT Press. Chapter 21.

Chapter 2
Methods Based on Selection on Observables

Contents

© Springer-Verlag Berlin Heidelberg 2015
G. Cerulli, *Econometric Evaluation of Socio-Economic Programs*,
Advanced Studies in Theoretical and Applied Econometrics 49,
DOI 10.1007/978-3-662-46405-2_2

2.1 Introduction

This chapter deals with the estimation of average treatment effects (ATEs) under the assumption of selection on observables. In Sect. 1.3.1, we provided a systematic account of the meaning and scope of such an assumption in program evaluation analysis. We argued that working under selection on observables basically means that all the relevant information about the true nonrandom selection-into-treatment process, producing the observed sets of treated and untreated observations, is known to the analyst. Hence, by assumption, we are ruling out any possible presence of loosely defined *unobservables* as hidden drivers of the selection process.

A plethora of econometric methods have been developed so far in the literature to provide correct inference for causal parameters in such a setting. Here, we discuss the four most popular approaches: Regression-adjustment (RA), Matching (MATCH), Reweighting (REW), and the Doubly-robust (DR) estimator. Along this chapter, the presentation of these methods will follow this order.

Section 2.2 develops the main notation and formulas for estimating ATEs by Regression-adjustment. We interpret such a method as a generalized approach to ATEs' estimation under observable selection and discuss inference for the parametric (linear and nonlinear), the semi-parametric, and nonparametric case.

Section 2.3 examines at length the popular Matching estimators. Here, we start by introducing the main conceptual framework in order to understand the philosophy underlying the implementation of Matching approach. We then distinguish between covariates and propensity-score Matching, discussing also the implications of ATEs' identification assumptions in these cases. We go on to examine the large sample properties of Matching, focusing on the propensity-score Matching (PS Matching), probably the most frequently implemented Matching estimator. Finally, we present some empirical tests for assessing Matching's quality and reliability.

Section 2.4 is dedicated to the Reweighting estimators. This class of ATEs' estimators is a valuable alternative to Regression-adjustment and Matching; although, in many ways, it is strictly linked to both approaches. Particular attention is given to inverse-probability weighting estimators and to ATEs' analytical standard errors formulas in such a case.

Section 2.5, which concludes the theoretical part of this chapter, presents the Doubly-robust estimator, a robustness approach combining Reweighting on inverse probabilities with Regression-adjustment.

Finally, Sects. 2.6–2.8 and subsections offer a number of applications in a comparative perspective.

2.2 Regression-Adjustment

This section presents and develops the main conceptual building blocks, notation, and formulas for estimating ATEs using the Regression-adjustment (RA) approach. In the course of the discussion, we illustrate how one can interpret such an estimator as a generalized approach to ATEs' estimation under observable selection, and discuss parametric (both linear and nonlinear), semi-parametric, and nonparametric RA.

2.2.1 Regression-Adjustment as Unifying Approach Under Observable Selection

In this section, we present the Regression-adjustment (RA) approach for estimating consistently ATEs and illustrate how it can be seen as a general estimation procedure under selection on observables. Indeed, RA is suitable only when the conditional independence assumption (CIA) holds. In order to obtain the form of this estimator, we start by rewriting explicitly what CIA implies, that is:

$$(Y_1; Y_0) \perp D | \mathbf{x}$$

where $(Y_1; Y_0)$ are the two potential outcomes, $\mathbf{x}$ is a vector of pretreatment exogenous covariates, D the treatment binary indicator, and the symbol $\perp$ refers to probabilistic independence. As stated in Chap. 1, however, in order to identify ATEs, a less restrictive assumption which only limits independence to the mean is required. It is known as conditional mean independence (or CMI) and implies that:

$$E(Y_1 | \mathbf{x}, D) = E(Y_1 | \mathbf{x})$$
$$E(Y_0 | \mathbf{x}, D) = E(Y_0 | \mathbf{x})$$

As showed, CMI leads to the following two identification conditions of the unobservable counterfactual mean potential outcomes:

$$E(Y_0 | \mathbf{x}, D = 1) = E(Y_0 | \mathbf{x}, D = 0) \tag{2.1}$$
$$E(Y_1 | \mathbf{x}, D = 0) = E(Y_1 | \mathbf{x}, D = 1) \tag{2.2}$$

where the right-hand side (RHS) of both previous equations are observable quantities used to "impute" the unobservable quantities in the left-hand side (LHS). We have also seen that under CMI:

$$\text{ATE}(\mathbf{x}) = \text{E}(Y|\mathbf{x}, D = 1) - \text{E}(Y|\mathbf{x}, D = 0)$$

that can be interpreted as a conditional DIM estimator. By simply denoting:

$$m_1(\mathbf{x}) = \text{E}(Y|\mathbf{x}, D = 1) \tag{2.3}$$

and

$$m_0(\mathbf{x}) = \text{E}(Y|\mathbf{x}, D = 0) \tag{2.4}$$

we have that:

$$\text{ATE}(\mathbf{x}) = m_1(\mathbf{x}) - m_0(\mathbf{x})$$

This implies that as soon as *consistent* estimators of $m_1(\mathbf{x})$ and $m_0(\mathbf{x})$ are available, we can estimate causal parameters ATEs through the sample equivalents of previous formulas:

$$\widehat{\text{ATE}} = \frac{1}{N}\sum_{i=1}^{N}[\widehat{m}_1(\mathbf{x}_i) - \widehat{m}_0(\mathbf{x}_i)] \tag{2.5}$$

$$\widehat{\text{ATET}} = \frac{1}{N_1}\sum_{i=1}^{N}D_i \cdot [\widehat{m}_1(\mathbf{x}_i) - \widehat{m}_0(\mathbf{x}_i)] \tag{2.6}$$

$$\widehat{\text{ATENT}} = \frac{1}{N_0}\sum_{i=1}^{N}(1 - D_i) \cdot [\widehat{m}_1(\mathbf{x}_i) - \widehat{m}_0(\mathbf{x}_i)] \tag{2.7}$$

where the "hat" refers to an estimator of $m_1(\mathbf{x})$ and $m_0(\mathbf{x})$.

This estimation method is known as Regression-adjustment (RA) and can be seen as a general estimation approach for ATEs; indeed, other approaches assuming CMI can be seen as particular types of Regression-adjustment. Both $m_1(\mathbf{x})$ and $m_0(\mathbf{x})$ can be estimated either *parametrically, semi-parametrically,* or *nonparametrically*: the choice depends on the assumption made on the form of the potential outcome, which can be modeled in a parametric as well as nonparametric or semi-parametric way. Note that the Regression-adjustment approach only uses the potential outcome means to recover ATEs and does not use the propensity-score.[1]

Table 2.1 presents a simple example explaining the estimation logic behind RA. As will become evident, it is mostly based on an *imputation* logic, where imputation can be performed in various ways. This example represents a case in

[1] We have two different approaches for estimating ATEs under CMI (Imbens 2004): (1) the first uses some specification and estimation of $\text{E}(Y_g \mid \mathbf{x})$ for $g = 0,1$; (2) the second uses some specification and estimation of $\text{E}(D \mid \mathbf{x}) = \text{prob}(D = 1 \mid \mathbf{x})$, denoted as the *propensity-score*. We start by considering case (1).

Table 2.1 An example explaining the estimation logic of the Regression-adjustment

Unit	D	x	$m_1 = E(Y|D=1;x)$	$m_0 = E(Y|D=0;x)$	$m_1 - m_0$	ATET	ATENT	ATE
1	1	A	25	68	−43			
2	1	B	65	25	40			
3	1	C	36	74	−38	−1.5		
4	1	D	47	12	35			
5	0	B	65	25	40			6.3
6	0	D	47	12	35			
7	0	D	47	12	35			
8	0	A	25	68	−43		11.5	
9	0	C	36	74	−38			
10	0	B	65	25	40			

which imputation is based on conditioning over the values of one single variable x, which is supposed to take on four values: {A, B, C, D}. In the table, the numbers reported in bold are those imputed according to the value assumed by x in the sample. For instance, consider m_1 for unit 5. In the sample, this unit is untreated: for such a unit, we observe m_0 but we do not observe the counterfactual m_1.

Given $E(Y_1 \mid D=0, \mathbf{x}) = E(Y_1 \mid D=1, \mathbf{x}) = E(Y \mid D=1, \mathbf{x})$, using CMI, we can impute the missing observation $m_{1,i=5} = E(Y_{1,i=5} \mid D_{i=5}=0, x_{i=5}=B)$ with the observable quantity $E(Y_{1,i=2} \mid D_{i=2}=1, x_{i=2}=B)$ being equal to the value of m_1 for another unit in the treated set having the same $x=B$ as unit 5, i.e., unit 2. Similarly, the value of m_0 for unit 3 can be imputed using the value of m_1 of unit 9, since both have $x=C$, and so forth.

In this example, once all missing observations are imputed (see the numbers in bold in Table 2.1), we can calculate the differences $(m_{1i} - m_{0i})$. The average of these differences over the treated units returns the ATET, the one over the untreated units the ATENT; finally, the average over the whole sample provides the value of ATE. Notice that, by definition, ATE = ATET · (4/10) + ATENT · (6/10).

This example clearly proves that RA imputation works well only if we are able to "impute" $m_1(x_i)$ to each individual i belonging to the control group with $x=x_i$ and $m_0(x_i)$ to each individual i belonging to the treatment group with $x=x_i$. Therefore, some minimal units' *overlap* over x is necessary for imputation to be achieved (and, thus, for identifying treatment effects).

Generally, however, perfect overlap between treated and untreated units (as in the previous example) may not occur in real contexts. For instance, in the case of a variable x assuming continuous values, it is unlikely that two units in the opposite treatment status have exactly the same x. In such a case, imputation through RA can be performed using "prediction" of Y conditional on x, using observations in the opposite treatment status.

These predictions can be obtained by assuming either a parametric relation between Y and x or a nonparametric one. Nevertheless, as it will be clearer later on, a certain degree of overlap is still necessary for imputation to be reliable, both in parametric and nonparametric approaches. In general, however, a lack of overlap seems more problematic for semi- and nonparametric methods (Kernel and Matching methods, for instance) than for parametric approaches, although even in this case, poor overlap may have adverse effects on the estimation precision of ATEs.

In order to illustrate clearly this important issue, Figs. 2.1 and 2.2 report the imputation procedure, respectively, used by a parametric (linear, for simplicity) and a nonparametric (Kernel) approach.

In this example, we have to impute the missing observation $E(Y_1 \mid D = 0, x = 5)$ using the prediction from a regression of Y on x on the set of treated units, i.e., we have to first estimate:

$$E\big(Y_1 \big| D = 1, x = 5\big) = E\big(Y \big| D = 1, x = 5\big)$$

and then use it for imputing $E(Y_1 \mid D = 0, x = 5)$.

Figure 2.1 imputes this value by adopting a linear regression of the type:

$$E\big(Y \big| D = 1, x\big) = \alpha + \beta x$$

so that $E(Y_1 \mid D = 0, x = 5) = \alpha + \beta \cdot 5$. This imputation method—also known as the Control-function regression (CFR)—is able to overcome identifying problems, without excluding—however—possible overlap problems. To see this, suppose we wish to impute the counterfactual mean potential outcome at, say, $x = 40$, a

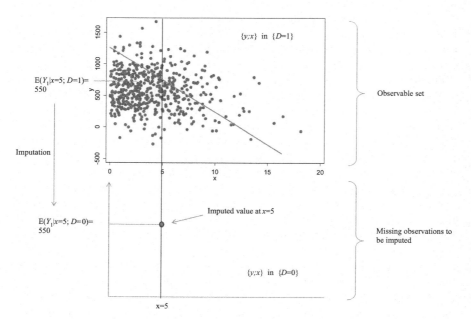

Fig. 2.1 Missing observation imputation in the linear (parametric) case

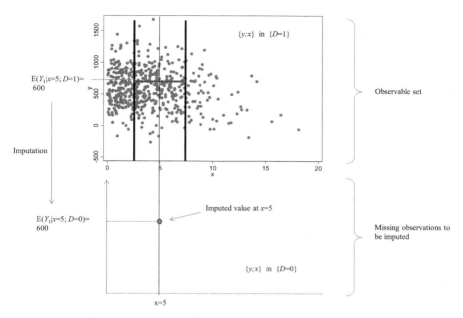

Fig. 2.2 Missing observation imputation using local (nonparametric) average

larger value than $x = 5$. This implies that we need to find an imputation for $E(Y_1 \mid D = 0, x = 40)$. As evident from Fig. 2.1, there are no units in the set of treated with $x = 40$. Nevertheless, we could trust the reliability of the estimated regression function and impute $E(Y_1 \mid D = 0, x = 40)$ with $(\alpha + \beta \cdot 40)$. This prediction can be computed even if no treated units appear with $x = 40$ in our dataset. Of course, such an *extrapolation* might be worrying when the x of the untreated unit is very far from the support of x in the treated set. Moreover, even if some of the treated units have such a value, imputation remains problematic when such units are few, as predictions for that part of the cloud are clearly less reliable (due to a lack of data). Therefore, parametric imputation overcomes identification problems due to weak overlapping, but with the caveat that prediction might be not reliable in the nonoverlapping region.

Figure 2.2 imputes the same value by adopting a local smoothness approach. Basically, it estimates $E(Y \mid D = 1, x = 5)$ by fixing a bandwidth $h = 2.5$ around $x = 5$ and by taking the average of Y within $I = \{x + h \le x \le x - h\}$:

$$E\left(Y_1 \mid D = 0; x = 5\right) = \frac{1}{N_I}\sum_{i \in I} Y_i = 550$$

This imputation method—also known as the local average—can have more complicated identification problems due to weak overlap than a parametric approach. Why? Suppose—as above—that we wish to impute the counterfactual mean potential outcome at, say, $x = 40$. This means that we need to find an imputation for $E(Y_1 \mid D = 0, x = 40)$. As evident, there are no units in the set of treated within the interval $[x - h; x + h] \equiv [37.5; 42.5]$. This means that we cannot compute the value to be imputed; thus, ATE is not identified. In order to obtain identification, one possible solution might be to enlarge the bandwidth so as to obtain a new interval containing at least some observations. The reliability of imputation under such an enlargement is, however, highly questionable since, in order to calculate the prediction, we are now considering values of Y whose x are very far from the point of interest, that is, $x = 40$. Moreover, even if some treated units were present in the interval around $x = 40$, smoothing techniques are very sensitive to observation *sparseness*: in points like, for example, $x = 15$ imputation is based on an average of few observations, thus questioning the quality of this imputation.

In conclusion, nonparametric imputation might be more reliable as it does not assume a parametric form of the potential outcomes, but it barely overcomes the identification problems due to weak overlap. In this sense, the use of parametric and nonparametric methods depends on the degree of overlap and sparseness of the available data.

In what follows, we first present identification and estimation of ATEs in both parametric and nonparametric case. We begin with the parametric approach, by presenting and discussing the linear parametric RA, i.e., the so-called Control-function regression (CFR), and nonlinear parametric RA. Subsequently, we give an account of the semi- and nonparametric approaches proposed in the literature discussing their statistical properties. Among the nonparametric methods, special attention will be devoted to the Matching approach.

2.2.2   Linear Parametric Regression-Adjustment: The Control-Function Regression

The linear parametric RA assumes that $m_0(\mathbf{x}) = \mu_0 + \mathbf{x}\boldsymbol{\beta}_0$ and $m_1(\mathbf{x}) = \mu_1 + \mathbf{x}\boldsymbol{\beta}_1$, where μ_0 and μ_1 are scalars and $\boldsymbol{\beta}_0$ and $\boldsymbol{\beta}_1$ are two vectors of parameters. In such a case, applying RA implies estimating two distinct OLS regressions: $Y_i = \mu_0 + \mathbf{x}_i\boldsymbol{\beta}_0$ only on untreated and $Y_i = \mu_1 + \mathbf{x}_i\boldsymbol{\beta}_1$ only on treated units, thus getting the predicted values $\widehat{m}_1(\mathbf{x}_i)$ and $\widehat{m}_0(\mathbf{x}_i)$. These quantities can be used to recover all the causal parameters of interest by inserting them into the RA formulas (2.5)–(2.7).

It seems worth to link this approach with the more familiar regression setting so to get all the elements necessary for ordinary inference, including obtaining standard errors. We therefore develop a standard regression model that can be shown to lead to exactly the same results as the linear parametric RA. In other words, we show that CFR is just a particular case of RA, the one in which a parametric/linear form of the conditional expectation of Y given $\mathbf{x}$ and D is assumed.

As a specific RA, the Control-function regression is a method identifying ATEs under CMI. As such, it is still useful to stress that CFR is suited only when the selection-into-program is due to observable determinants (i.e., *overt bias*). We know that CMI states that:

$$E(Y_1|\mathbf{x}, D) = E(Y_1|\mathbf{x}) \tag{2.8}$$

$$E(Y_0|\mathbf{x}, D) = E(Y_0|\mathbf{x}) \tag{2.9}$$

where (2.8) and (2.9) restrict the independence only over the mean. To proceed further, we first need to model the potential outcomes in a simple additive form as follows:

$$Y_0 = \mu_0 + v_0 \tag{2.10}$$

$$Y_1 = \mu_1 + v_1 \tag{2.11}$$

$$Y = Y_0 + D(Y_1 - Y_0) \tag{2.12}$$

where v_0 and v_1 are random variables and μ_1 and μ_0 are scalars. In other words, we are assuming that outcomes consist of a constant term *plus* a random component. Additionally, we also assume that the random components take on the following form:

$$v_0 = g_0(\mathbf{x}) + e_0 \tag{2.13}$$

$$v_1 = g_1(\mathbf{x}) + e_1 \tag{2.14}$$

with $E(e_0) = E(e_1) = 0$. This implies that:

$$Y_0 = \mu_0 + g_0(\mathbf{x}) + e_0 \tag{2.15}$$

$$Y_1 = \mu_1 + g_1(\mathbf{x}) + e_1 \tag{2.16}$$

making it explicit the dependence of the potential outcomes on the observable vector of covariates $\mathbf{x}$. As seen in Chap. 1, we also assume $\mathbf{x}$ to be an *exogenous* set of factors, a condition implying that:

$$E(e_0|\mathbf{x}) = E(e_1|\mathbf{x}) = 0 \tag{2.17}$$

By substituting (2.10) and (2.11) into (2.12), we thus obtain:

$$Y = \mu_0 + D(\mu_1 - \mu_0) + v_0 + D(v_1 - v_0) \tag{2.18}$$

and by plugging (2.15) and (2.16) into (2.18), we get:

$$Y = \mu_0 + D(\mu_1 - \mu_0) + g_0(\mathbf{x}) + D[g_1(\mathbf{x}) - g_0(\mathbf{x})] + e \tag{2.19}$$

where $e = e_0 + D (e_1 - e_0)$. Consider now a *parametric* form of the expected value of the potential outcomes over $\mathbf{x}$, i.e., $g_0(\mathbf{x}) = \mathbf{x}\boldsymbol{\beta}_0$ and $g_1(\mathbf{x}) = \mathbf{x}\boldsymbol{\beta}_1$, where $\boldsymbol{\beta}_0$ and $\boldsymbol{\beta}_1$

are two unknown vector parameters. By taking the expectation of (2.19) over the support of $(D, \mathbf{x})$ and assuming (2.17) we have, under CMI, that:

$$E(Y|D,\mathbf{x}) = \mu_0 + D(\mu_1 - \mu_0) + g_0(\mathbf{x}) + D[g_1(\mathbf{x}) - g_0(\mathbf{x})] \qquad (2.20)$$

since: $E(e \mid D, \mathbf{x}) = E(e_0 \mid D, \mathbf{x}) + D \ [E(e_1 \mid D, \mathbf{x}) - E(e_0 \mid D, \mathbf{x})] = E(e_0 \mid \mathbf{x}) + D \ [E(e_1 \mid \mathbf{x}) - E(e_0 \mid \mathbf{x})] = 0$, where the second equality comes from CMI, and the third and final ones from assumption (2.17), i.e., the exogeneity of $\mathbf{x}$.

According to (2.20), two different models can be drawn. The first under the hypothesis of a homogenous reaction function of Y_0 and Y_1 to $\mathbf{x}$ and the second under a heterogeneous reaction.

Case 1 Homogenous reaction function of Y_0 and Y_1 to $\mathbf{x}$: $g_1(\mathbf{x}) = g_0(\mathbf{x})$.

In this case, we can show that:

$$\begin{aligned} ATE = ATE(\mathbf{x}) = ATET = ATET(\mathbf{x}) = ATENT = ATENT(\mathbf{x}) \\ = \mu_1 - \mu_0 \end{aligned} \qquad (2.21)$$

$$E(Y|D,\mathbf{x}) = \mu_0 + D \cdot ATE + \mathbf{x}\beta \qquad (2.22)$$

Thus no heterogeneous average treatment effect (over $\mathbf{x}$) exists. Indeed, by definition:

$$\begin{aligned} ATE = E(Y_1 - Y_0) = E[(\mu_1 + g_1(\mathbf{x}) + e_1) - (\mu_0 + g_0(\mathbf{x}) + e_0)] \\ = \mu_1 - \mu_0 \end{aligned} \qquad (2.23)$$

is a scalar. Moreover, (2.22) follows immediately from (2.20); thus, the coefficient of D in an ordinary least squares (OLS) estimation of (2.22) consistently estimates $ATE = ATET = ATENT$, as the error term has by construction a zero mean conditional on $(D, \mathbf{x})$. This procedure can therefore be applied on a sample of units with size N:

$$OLS: \quad Y_i = \mu_0 + D_i\alpha + \mathbf{x}_i\boldsymbol{\beta}_0 + error_i, \quad i = 1, \ldots, N \qquad (2.24)$$

where $\alpha = ATE$.

Case 2 Heterogeneous reaction function of Y_0 and Y_1 to $\mathbf{x}$: $g_1(\mathbf{x}) \neq g_0(\mathbf{x})$.

In this second case, we can show that:

$$ATE \neq ATE(\mathbf{x}) \neq ATET \neq ATET(\mathbf{x}) \neq ATENT \neq ATENT(\mathbf{x}) \qquad (2.25)$$

$$E(Y|D,\mathbf{x}) = \mu_0 + D \cdot ATE + \mathbf{x}\beta_0 + D(\mathbf{x} - \mu_\mathbf{x})\beta \qquad (2.26)$$

where $\boldsymbol{\mu}_\mathbf{x} = E(\mathbf{x})$ and $\boldsymbol{\beta} = (\boldsymbol{\beta}_1 - \boldsymbol{\beta}_0)$. In this case, heterogeneous average treatment effects (over $\mathbf{x}$) exist and the population causal parameters take on the following form:

$$\text{ATE} = (\mu_1 - \mu_0) + \boldsymbol{\mu_x}\boldsymbol{\beta} \qquad (2.27)$$

$$\text{ATE}(\mathbf{x}) = \text{ATE} + (\mathbf{x} - \boldsymbol{\mu_x}) \qquad (2.28)$$

$$\text{ATET} = \text{ATE} + \text{E}_{\mathbf{x}}\{\mathbf{x} - \boldsymbol{\mu_x}|D = 1\}\boldsymbol{\beta} \qquad (2.29)$$

$$\text{ATET}(\mathbf{x}) = \left[\text{ATE} + (\mathbf{x} - \boldsymbol{\mu_x})\boldsymbol{\beta}|D = 1\right] \qquad (2.30)$$

$$\text{ATENT} = \text{ATE} + \text{E}_{\mathbf{x}}\{\mathbf{x} - \boldsymbol{\mu_x}|D = 0\}\boldsymbol{\beta} \qquad (2.31)$$

$$\text{ATENT}(\mathbf{x}) = \left[\text{ATE} + (\mathbf{x} - \boldsymbol{\mu_x})\boldsymbol{\beta}|D = 0\right] \qquad (2.32)$$

Given these formulas for the population causal parameters, the sample estimates can be obtained by relying on the sample equivalents, that is:

$$\widehat{\text{ATE}} = \widehat{\alpha} \qquad (2.33)$$

$$\widehat{\text{ATE}}(\mathbf{x}) = \widehat{\alpha} + (\mathbf{x} - \overline{\mathbf{x}})\widehat{\boldsymbol{\beta}} \qquad (2.34)$$

$$\widehat{\text{ATET}} = \widehat{\alpha} + (N_1)^{-1}\sum_{i=1}^{N} D_i(\mathbf{x}_i - \overline{\mathbf{x}})\widehat{\boldsymbol{\beta}} \qquad (2.35)$$

$$\widehat{\text{ATET}}(\mathbf{x}) = \left[\widehat{\alpha} + (\mathbf{x} - \overline{\mathbf{x}})\widehat{\boldsymbol{\beta}}\right]_{(D=1)} \qquad (2.36)$$

$$\widehat{\text{ATENT}} = \widehat{\alpha} + (1/N_0)^{-1}\sum_{i=1}^{N} (1 - D_i)(\mathbf{x}_i - \overline{\mathbf{x}})\widehat{\boldsymbol{\beta}} \qquad (2.37)$$

$$\widehat{\text{ATENT}}(\mathbf{x}_i) = \left[\widehat{\alpha} + (\mathbf{x}_i - \overline{\mathbf{x}})\widehat{\boldsymbol{\beta}}\right]_{(D=0)} \qquad (2.38)$$

In (2.33)–(2.38), the estimated causal parameters of interest depend in turn on the unknown parameters: μ_1, μ_0, $\boldsymbol{\beta}_1$, $\boldsymbol{\beta}_0$, and $\boldsymbol{\mu_x}$. If a consistent estimation of these parameters is available, then we can recover (consistently) all the causal effects, thus using regression (2.26) and applying the following procedure:

- Estimate $Y_i = \mu_0 + D_i\,\alpha + \mathbf{x}_i\boldsymbol{\beta}_0 + D_i\,(\mathbf{x}_i - \boldsymbol{\mu_x})\boldsymbol{\beta} + error_i$ by OLS, thus getting consistent estimates of μ_0, α, $\boldsymbol{\beta}_0$, and $\boldsymbol{\beta}$
- Plug these estimated parameters into the sample formulas (2.33)–(2.38) and recover all the causal effects
- Obtain standard errors for ATET and ATENT via bootstrap.

Indeed, while the standard error of ATE is estimated directly within the regression, as $\text{ATE} = \alpha$, no direct estimation is available for ATET and ATENT. Fortunately, a bootstrap procedure can be reliably used in this case.

Before proceeding further, it might be useful to shed more light on the implications of assuming heterogeneity in the potential outcome response to $\mathbf{x}$. Figure 2.3 draws the expected values implied by (2.13) and (2.14) on $\mathbf{x} = x$ (i.e., by assuming just one confounding variable) when $g_1(\mathbf{x}) = g_0(\mathbf{x})$ (Fig. 2.3a) and when $g_1(\mathbf{x}) \neq g_0(\mathbf{x})$ (Fig. 2.3b). In the first case, the ATE(x) does not vary over the support

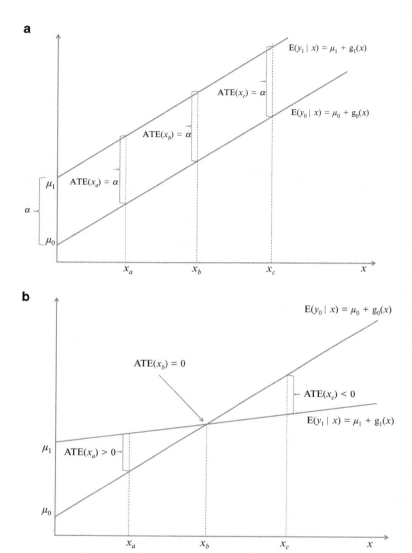

Fig. 2.3 A graphical representation of the potential outcomes function and of the corresponding ATE(x) under homogeneous (**a**) and heterogeneous (**b**) response to x

of x. It is steadily constant and equal to $\alpha = (\mu_1 - \mu_0)$. In the second case, in contrast, the ATE(x) varies along the support of x, taking a positive value for $x = x_a$, a zero value for $x = x_b$, and a negative one for $x = x_c$.

In some contexts, however, assuming homogeneous response to confounders might be questionable. For example, allowing that individuals or companies react in the same manner to, let's say, their gender, location, or size when they are treated and when they are untreated may be a somewhat strong assumption. In many sociological environments, for instance, people's perception of the context may change according to a different state of the world (treated vs. untreated situations). In the economic context, a company characterized by a weak propensity to bearing risks may become more prone to invest in a riskier business when public funding is available: for instance, such a company might change its reaction to, let's say, its stock of fixed capital when financed, by increasing its productive response to this asset. Similar conclusions can be reached from many psychological or sociological programs, as passing from the untreated to the treated status may produce different mental, relational, and environmental situations.

Interestingly, this econometric framework allows one to test for the presence of such heterogeneity. In (2.26), a simple F-test of joint significance for the coefficients in vector $\boldsymbol{\beta}$ can be exploited to check the presence of heterogeneity; if the null hypothesis H_0: $\boldsymbol{\beta} = (\boldsymbol{\beta}_1 - \boldsymbol{\beta}_0) = \mathbf{0}$ is rejected, then it means that heterogeneity is at work, and vice versa.

2.2.3 Nonlinear Parametric Regression-Adjustment

The Control-function regression method presented in the previous section assumes a linear form of the potential outcome conditional means. When the outcome is binary or count, however, the linearity assumption can be relaxed, and a proper parametric form of $m_0(\mathbf{x})$ and $m_1(\mathbf{x})$ can be assumed. Table 2.2 presents common possible nonlinear models with the corresponding outcome conditional mean.

By substituting previous formulas into the Regression-adjustment formulas (2.5)–(2.7), we can obtain the corresponding non linear Regression-adjustment estimators for ATEs. For instance, when the outcome variable is a count, a consistent estimation of ATET is:

$$\widehat{\text{ATET}} = \frac{1}{N_1}\sum_{i=1}^{N} D_i \cdot \left[\exp\left(\mathbf{x}_i\widehat{\boldsymbol{\beta}}_1\right) - \exp\left(\mathbf{x}_i\widehat{\boldsymbol{\beta}}_0\right)\right]$$

and similarly for ATE and ATENT.

Table 2.2 Type of outcome and distribution for parametric Regression-adjustment

Type of outcome	Distribution	$m_g(\mathbf{x})$, $g = 1,0$
Linear		$\mathbf{x}\boldsymbol{\beta}_g$
Binary	Logit	$\exp(\mathbf{x}\boldsymbol{\beta}_g)/\{1 + \exp(\mathbf{x}\boldsymbol{\beta}_g)\}$
	Probit	$\Phi(\mathbf{x}\boldsymbol{\beta}_g)$
	Heteroskedastic probit	$\Phi[\mathbf{x}\boldsymbol{\beta}_g/\exp(\mathbf{z}\boldsymbol{\gamma}_g)]$
Count	Poisson	$\exp(\mathbf{x}\boldsymbol{\beta}_g)$

Note: in the heteroskedastic probit, $\mathbf{z}$ and $\boldsymbol{\gamma}_g$ are the variables and the parameters (excluding the constant) explaining the idiosyncratic variance of the error term of the latent single-index model

The problem with nonlinear models of this kind is with the estimation of the standard errors for ATEs estimators. More specifically, the previous equation contains estimators from a first-step estimation (generally, of a maximum likelihood (ML) type); thus, the implied nested estimation error has to be taken into account. As illustrated in the following example, a solution can be obtained however.

Consider the case of ATE (for ATET and ATENT, it is similar), and consider a generic parametric nonlinear form of the Regression-adjustment estimator:

$$\widehat{\text{ATE}} = \frac{1}{N}\sum_{i=1}^{N}\left[m_1\left(\mathbf{x}_i; \widehat{\boldsymbol{\beta}}_1\right) - m_1\left(\mathbf{x}_i; \widehat{\boldsymbol{\beta}}_0\right)\right]$$

Suppose that both $\widehat{\boldsymbol{\beta}}_0$ and $\widehat{\boldsymbol{\beta}}_1$ are $\sqrt{N}$ consistent and asymptotically normal M-estimator with objective function $q_i(\mathbf{x}_i; \boldsymbol{\beta})$, score $s_i(\mathbf{x}_i; \boldsymbol{\beta})$, and expected Hessian $\mathbf{A}$, derived from a first-step estimation (a probit, for instance). For compactness purposes, we assume that:

$$m(\mathbf{x}_i; \boldsymbol{\beta}) = m_1\left(\mathbf{x}_i; \widehat{\boldsymbol{\beta}}_1\right) - m_1\left(\mathbf{x}_i; \widehat{\boldsymbol{\beta}}_0\right)$$

with $\widehat{\boldsymbol{\beta}} = \left[\widehat{\boldsymbol{\beta}}_0; \widehat{\boldsymbol{\beta}}_1\right]$. As $\widehat{\text{ATE}}$ is in turn an M-estimator, it eventually takes the form of a two-step M-estimator (see Wooldridge 2010, pp. 409–420), thus implying that $\widehat{\text{ATE}}$ is also $\sqrt{N}$ consistent and asymptotically normal for ATE. In such cases, it can be showed that the estimated asymptotic variance is:

$$\widehat{\text{Asyvar}}\left[\widehat{\text{ATE}}\right] = \frac{1}{N}\left[\widehat{\text{Var}}[m(\mathbf{x}_i; \boldsymbol{\beta})] + \widehat{\mathbf{G}}\left[\widehat{\text{Asyvar}}\sqrt{N}\left(\widehat{\boldsymbol{\beta}} - \boldsymbol{\beta}\right)\right]\widehat{\mathbf{G}}'\right]$$

where:

$$\widehat{\text{Var}}[m(\mathbf{x}_i; \boldsymbol{\beta})] = \frac{1}{N}\sum_{i=1}^{N}\left[m_1\left(\mathbf{x}_i; \widehat{\boldsymbol{\beta}}_1\right) - m_1\left(\mathbf{x}_i; \widehat{\boldsymbol{\beta}}_0\right) - \widehat{\text{ATE}}\right]^2$$

$$\widehat{\mathbf{G}} = \left\{\frac{1}{N}\sum_{i=1}^{N}\frac{\partial m_i\left(\mathbf{x}_i; \widehat{\boldsymbol{\beta}}\right)}{\partial\widehat{\boldsymbol{\beta}}}\right\}$$

and

$$\widehat{\text{Asyvar}}\sqrt{N}\left(\widehat{\boldsymbol{\beta}} - \boldsymbol{\beta}\right) = \widehat{\mathbf{A}}^{-1}\widehat{\mathbf{B}}\,\widehat{\mathbf{A}}^{-1}$$

At this point, we only need to see to which matrix $\mathbf{A}$ and $\mathbf{B}$ in the last formula are equal. By defining the score of the first-step M-estimator as:

$$s_i\left(\mathbf{x}_i; \widehat{\boldsymbol{\beta}}\right) = \left\{\frac{\partial q_i\left(\mathbf{x}_i; \widehat{\boldsymbol{\beta}}\right)}{\partial \widehat{\boldsymbol{\beta}}}\right\}$$

one can prove that:

$$\widehat{\mathbf{B}} = \left\{\frac{1}{N}\sum_{i=1}^{N} s_i\left(\mathbf{x}_i; \widehat{\boldsymbol{\beta}}\right) \cdot s_i\left(\mathbf{x}_i; \widehat{\boldsymbol{\beta}}\right)'\right\}$$

and

$$\widehat{\mathbf{A}} = \left\{\frac{1}{N}\sum_{i=1}^{N} \frac{\partial q_i\left(\mathbf{x}_i; \widehat{\boldsymbol{\beta}}\right)}{\partial \widehat{\boldsymbol{\beta}} \, \partial \widehat{\boldsymbol{\beta}}'}\right\}$$

In conclusion, once the asymptotic variance of $\widehat{\text{ATE}}$ is computed using the above-mentioned formula, the usual significance test can be correctly employed. Note also that bootstrapping can in this case be a suitable option, provided that all sources of uncertainty due to first-step estimation are taken into account when resampling from the observed distribution.

2.2.4 Nonparametric and Semi-parametric Regression-Adjustment

We have argued that the general estimator implied by the Regression-adjustment in (2.5)–(2.7) takes the form of a sample average from the data that can be estimated by parametric, nonparametric, or semi-parametric imputation methods for $m_1(\mathbf{x})$ and $m_0(\mathbf{x})$ based on conditioning on $\mathbf{x}$. Control-function regression represents the parametric case. Local smoothing techniques such as kernel or local linear regression can be used to obtain nonparametric estimation of $m_1(\mathbf{x})$ and $m_0(\mathbf{x})$. As illustrated in Fig. 2.2, these approaches are, however, unfeasible when no minimal overlap between treated and control group is present over $\mathbf{x}$. This may occur in datasets where the support of the covariates $\mathbf{x}$ in the treated and untreated group is very different, and thus, the overlap is poor. Figure 2.4 shows two cases in which the distribution of a covariate x in the treated and untreated group results, respectively, in a good and a poor overlap. We will return to this issue in Sect. 2.3.11 and illustrate how to test the degree of overlap in a given dataset.

Anyway, when an acceptable level of overlap is present, it is possible to use (local) kernel methods for estimating $m_g(\mathbf{x})$, with $g = 1,0$. Heckman et al. (1997, 1998) consider kernel methods for estimating $m_g(\mathbf{x})$, focusing in particular on the

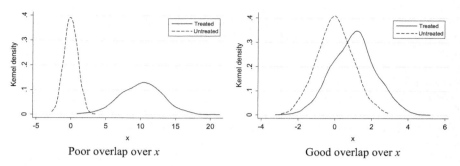

Fig. 2.4 Overlap over the covariate x

local linear regression approach. The logic of this approach is very close to the example provided in Fig. 2.2. Their simple kernel estimator has the following form:

$$\widehat{m}_g(\mathbf{x}) = \sum_{i:D_i=g} Y_i \cdot K\left(\frac{\mathbf{x}_i - \mathbf{x}}{h}\right) \bigg/ \sum_{i:D_i=g} K\left(\frac{\mathbf{x}_i - \mathbf{x}}{h}\right)$$

where $\mathbf{x}$ is the point in which the previous function is evaluated, $K(\cdot)$ a specific kernel function, and h the bandwidth parameter. In the local linear kernel regression, the function $m_g(\mathbf{x})$ is instead estimated as the intercept b_0 in the following minimization problem:

$$\min_{b_0, \mathbf{b}_1} \left\{ \sum_{i:D_i=g} [Y_i - b_0 - \mathbf{b}_1(\mathbf{x}_i - \mathbf{x})]^2 \cdot K\left(\frac{\mathbf{x}_i - \mathbf{x}}{h}\right) \right\}$$

The authors require specific kernel functions to control for the *bias* of their estimators. Indeed, as known, kernel regressions are biased in finite samples, although the bias disappears asymptotically if the bandwidth h goes to zero as N goes to infinity: it is only in this case that the kernel is a consistent estimator. From the central limit theorem, however, we can prove that the *bias-corrected* kernel estimators of $m_0(\mathbf{x})$ and $m_1(\mathbf{x})$ are $(hN_g)^{-1/2}$ consistent and asymptotically normal with zero mean and finite variance. The problem here, however, is how to deal with the estimation of the bias when it is thought to be non-negligible even if N is sufficiently large; a further problem is then how to estimate the variance which generally depends on unknown functions. We will come back to this issue in the next section and again when analyzing Matching estimators, where it will become clearer that kernel approaches are also inefficient in estimating ATEs.

Semi-parametric approaches can be also suitably exploited (Cattaneo 2010). In such cases, however, the question is: which types of semi-parametric imputation methods should be used and which are the related asymptotic properties of these estimators? In a parametric case like CFR, we can invoke the classical asymptotic theory suggesting that OLS are consistent, asymptotically normal, and efficient since they reach the Cramér–Rao lower bound of the variance when the normality assumption of the population probability density is satisfied.

In the case of semi-parametric methods, things are a bit more complicated. Nevertheless, in the specific case of semi-parametric Regression-adjustment, Hahn (1998) has shown that, under CMI, it is possible to identify the *semi-parametric efficiency bound* for ATE and ATET by exploiting a previous result on the semi-parametric analog of the (parametric) Cramér–Rao variance lower bound. Hahn's theorem states that if a $N^{-1/2}$ consistent and asymptotically normal estimator of $m_1(\mathbf{x})$ and $m_0(\mathbf{x})$ are available, then the asymptotic variance of $\widehat{\text{ATE}}$ is equal to:

$$\sigma\widehat{\text{ATE}}^2 = \frac{1}{N_0 + N_1} \cdot \text{E}\left[\frac{\sigma_1^2(\mathbf{x})}{p(\mathbf{x})} + \frac{\sigma_0^2(\mathbf{x})}{1 - p(\mathbf{x})} + (m_1(\mathbf{x}) - m_0(\mathbf{x}) - \text{ATE})^2\right] \quad (2.39)$$

where $\sigma_g^2(\mathbf{x}) = \text{Var}\left(y_g | \mathbf{x}\right) = \text{Var}\left(y_g | \mathbf{x}, D = g\right)$ with $g = 1,0$—i.e., the variances of Y_0 and Y_1 conditional on $\mathbf{x}$.

In the case of $\widehat{\text{ATET}}$, two different lower bounds, therefore, emerge: one when the propensity-score is assumed to be unknown:

$$\sigma^2_{\widehat{\text{ATET}}}\big|_{\{p(\mathbf{x}) \text{ is unknown}\}} = \frac{1}{N_0 + N_1 p^2} \cdot \text{E}\left[\sigma_1^2(\mathbf{x}) \cdot p(\mathbf{x}) + \frac{\sigma_0^2(\mathbf{x}) \cdot p(\mathbf{x})^2}{1 - p(\mathbf{x})} + p(\mathbf{x}) \cdot (m_1(\mathbf{x}) - m_0(\mathbf{x}) - \text{ATET})^2\right]$$
$$(2.40)$$

and one when the propensity-score is assumed to be known:

$$\sigma^2_{\widehat{\text{ATET}}}\big|_{\{p(\mathbf{x}) \text{ is known}\}} = \frac{1}{N_0 + N_1 p^2} \cdot \text{E}\left[\sigma_1^2(\mathbf{x}) \cdot p(\mathbf{x}) + \frac{\sigma_0^2(\mathbf{x}) \cdot p(\mathbf{x})^2}{1 - p(\mathbf{x})} + p(\mathbf{x})^2 \cdot (m_1(\mathbf{x}) - m_0(\mathbf{x}) - \text{ATET})^2\right]$$
$$(2.41)$$

It is worth emphasizing that the variance in (2.41) is lower than that in (2.40), so that knowledge of the propensity-score in this case increases efficiency.

Hahn (1998) also proposes a specific semi-parametric and efficient estimator of ATE and ATET. Indeed, under CMI, he shows that:

$$\text{E}\left(D \cdot Y | \mathbf{x}\right) = \text{E}\left(D \cdot Y_1 | \mathbf{x}\right) = \text{E}\left(D | \mathbf{x}\right) \cdot \text{E}\left(Y_1 | \mathbf{x}\right) = \text{E}\left(D | \mathbf{x}\right) \cdot m_1(\mathbf{x}) \quad (2.42)$$

implying that:

$$m_1(\mathbf{x}) = \frac{\text{E}\left(DY | \mathbf{x}\right)}{\text{E}\left(D | \mathbf{x}\right)} \quad (2.43)$$

and similarly:

$$m_0(\mathbf{x}) = \frac{\mathrm{E}\left[(1-D)Y|\mathbf{x}\right]}{1 - \mathrm{E}(D|\mathbf{x})} \tag{2.44}$$

By using these results and (2.5), we obtain:

$$\widehat{\mathrm{ATE}} = \frac{1}{N}\sum_{i=1}^{N}\left[\frac{\widehat{\mathrm{E}}\left(D_iY_i|\mathbf{x}_i\right)}{\widehat{\mathrm{E}}\left(D_i|\mathbf{x}_i\right)} - \frac{\widehat{\mathrm{E}}\left[(1-D_i)Y_i|\mathbf{x}_i\right]}{1 - \widehat{\mathrm{E}}\left(D_i|\mathbf{x}_i\right)}\right] \tag{2.45}$$

When **x** has a finite support, the previous formula can be directly estimated by substituting the following three estimations of the elements included into (2.45):

$$\widehat{\mathrm{E}}\left(D_iY_i|\mathbf{x}_i = x\right) = \sum_i D_iY_i \cdot 1(\mathbf{x}_i = x)\bigg/\sum_i 1(\mathbf{x}_i = x) \tag{2.46}$$

$$\widehat{\mathrm{E}}\left((1 - D_i)Y_i|\mathbf{x}_i = x\right) = \sum_i (1 - D_i)Y_i \cdot 1(\mathbf{x}_i = x)\bigg/\sum_i 1(\mathbf{x}_i = x) \tag{2.47}$$

$$\widehat{\mathrm{E}}\left(D_i|\mathbf{x}_i = x\right) = \sum_i D_i \cdot 1(\mathbf{x}_i = x)\bigg/\sum_i 1(\mathbf{x}_i = x) \tag{2.48}$$

On the contrary, when **x** has a continuous support, Hahn recommends estimating the previous three conditional expectations using *series estimators* that are asymptotically normal. The efficient estimator proposed by Hahn for ATET takes therefore the following form:

$$\widehat{\mathrm{ATET}} = \frac{1}{N}\sum_{i=1}^{N}\widehat{p}(\mathbf{x}_i)\left[\frac{\widehat{\mathrm{E}}\left(D_iY_i|\mathbf{x}_i\right)}{\widehat{p}(\mathbf{x}_i)} - \frac{\widehat{\mathrm{E}}\left[(1 - D_i)Y_i|\mathbf{x}_i\right]}{1 - \widehat{p}(\mathbf{x}_i)}\right]\bigg/\frac{1}{N}\sum_{i=1}^{N}\widehat{p}(\mathbf{x}_i) \tag{2.49}$$

where $\widehat{p}(\mathbf{x}_i) = \widehat{\mathrm{E}}\left(w_i|\mathbf{x}_i\right)$ is a *series estimator* of the propensity-score. Series estimators are global smoothing techniques approximating—uniformly on **x**—an unknown function $m_g(\mathbf{x})$ as linear combination of $K+1$ basis-functions, that is:

$$m(\mathbf{x}) = \sum_{j=0}^{K}\theta_j\varphi_j(\mathbf{x})$$

with $K+1$ representing the number of basis-functions to be used in estimation. The set of basis-functions can be chosen among various typologies, for example, polynomials (power series) such as $\varphi_j(\mathbf{x}) = \mathbf{x}^j$. The set of parameters $\{\theta_0, \ldots, \theta_K\}$ are simply estimated by a linear regression of Y_i on $\varphi(\mathbf{x})' = \{\varphi_0(\mathbf{x}_i), \ldots, \varphi_K(\mathbf{x}_i)\}$. Under regularity conditions and, in particular, under the assumption that K is chosen as a function of N growing slower than N, series estimators are uniformly consistent and asymptotically normal with an estimable asymptotic variance $\varphi(\mathbf{x})'\widehat{\mathbf{V}}_K\varphi(\mathbf{x})$. See Newey (1997) for more technical details.

Observe, finally, the difference between the nonparametric and the semi-parametric approach; in the first case, just two unknown functions need to be recovered in order to estimate ATEs, i.e., $m_1(\mathbf{x})$ and $m_0(\mathbf{x})$; in the semi-parametric estimator proposed by Hahn (1998), however, we also need to estimate $p(\mathbf{x})$.

As far as the estimation of the asymptotic variance for ATEs is concerned, we have illustrated above that it is theoretically possible to calculate nonparametric and semi-parametric estimators of ATEs that are consistent, asymptotically normal, and (semi-parametrically) efficient. The estimation of the asymptotic variance of such an estimator may nonetheless be cumbersome to calculate since (2.39), for instance, entails the estimation of three unknown functions: two regressions—$m_1(\mathbf{x})$ and $m_0(\mathbf{x})$—two conditional variances—$\sigma_1(\mathbf{x})$ and $\sigma_0(\mathbf{x})$—and the propensity-score—$p(\mathbf{x})$. As suggested by Imbens (2004, p. 21), there are three possible estimation approaches for these variances:

1. *Brute force*: consistent estimation of the five functions of the asymptotic variance can be estimated by *kernel* methods or by *series*.
2. *Series polynomials*: in the case where either the regression functions or the propensity-score are estimated by series methods, they become parametric. Thus, given the number of terms in the series, the analyst can directly calculate the asymptotic variance of the ATEs from their formula. Under general conditions, this will produce valid standard errors and confidence intervals.
3. *Bootstrapping*: given that previous nonparametric estimators of ATEs are rather smooth, it is likely that bootstrapping will lead to valid standard errors and confidence intervals.

2.3 Matching

Matching is a popular statistical procedure for estimating treatment effect parameters in nonexperimental settings (Stuart 2010). Developed in the statistic and epidemiological literature, Matching has become a relevant approach also in the current theoretical and applied econometrics, as illustrated by the increasing number of applications using this approach in many economic and social studies (Caliendo and Kopeinig 2008). This section starts by introducing the main conceptual framework to understand the philosophy lying behind the development of Matching. We start by distinguishing between covariates and propensity-score Matching, discussing also the implications of ATEs' identification assumptions in the Matching case. We then both examine the large sample properties of Matching and how to perform a correct inference when such an approach is used. Given its popularity, special attention is devoted to propensity-score Matching (PS Matching). Finally, some useful tests for assessing the reliability and quality of the estimated Matching are presented in the last two subsections of this section.

2.3.1 Covariates and Propensity-Score Matching

From a technical point of view, Matching is equivalent to the nonparametric RA estimator seen above where, instead of using a nonparametric estimation of the observable conditional mean, one uses directly the observed outcome. The Matching formulas for ATEs are:

$$\widehat{\text{ATET}}_M = \frac{1}{N_1}\sum_{i=1}^{N} D_i \cdot [Y_i - \widehat{m}_0(\mathbf{x}_i)] \tag{2.50}$$

$$\widehat{\text{ATENT}}_M = \frac{1}{N_0}\sum_{i=1}^{N} (1 - D_i) \cdot [\widehat{m}_1(\mathbf{x}_i) - Y_i] \tag{2.51}$$

$$\widehat{\text{ATE}}_M = \frac{1}{N}\sum_{i=1}^{N} \{D_i[Y_i - \widehat{m}_0(\mathbf{x}_i)] + (1 - D_i)[\widehat{m}_1(\mathbf{x}_i) - Y_i]\} \tag{2.52}$$

As CFR and smoothing techniques, Matching also identifies ATEs under the CMI assumption. In applications, Matching is sometimes preferred to parametric regression models as it entails a nonparametric estimation of ATE, ATET, and ATENT and does not require to specify a specific parametric relation between potential outcomes and confounding variables. Moreover, in contrast to the CFR approach, a wide set of different Matching procedures can be employed, thus enabling one to compare various estimators and provide robustness to results. Another characteristic of the Matching approach is that it reduces the number of untreated to a subsample (the so-called *selected controls*) having structural characteristics more homogeneous to the those of treated units; furthermore, Matching usually considers treated and untreated units to be compared only in the so-called *common support*, dropping out all those controls whose confounders values are either higher or smaller than that of the treated units. Many scholars interpret these characteristics of Matching as more robust compared to usual parametric regression, although the statistical justification for this conclusion is questionable (Zhao 2004).

The idea behind Matching is simple, intuitive, and attractive, and this can partly explain its popularity. It can be summarized in the following statement: "*recovering the unobservable potential outcome of one unit using the observable outcome of similar units in the opposite status.*" To better understand this statement, take the case of the estimation of ATET. We know from Chap. 1 that, for a single treated unit *i*, the *treatment effect* and the ATET are, respectively, equal to:

$$\text{TE}_i = Y_{1i} - Y_{0i}$$
$$\text{ATET} = \text{E}(Y_{1i}|D_i = 1) - \text{E}(Y_{0i}|D_i = 1) \tag{2.53}$$

where we only observe Y_{1i}, while Y_{0i} is unknown and TE_i not computable. Suppose, however, that Y_{0i} is perfectly estimated by using some average of the outcome of (matched) untreated individuals and call this quantity $\hat{Y}_{0i}$. Then, we will simply have that:

$$Y_{0i} \xrightarrow{\text{imputed through a distance function } f} \widehat{Y}_{0i}$$

The choice of the function f corresponds to a specific *distance metric* between treated and untreated units. Measuring such a distance can be done in two ways: either (1) based on the vector of covariates $\mathbf{x}$, so that one can calculate, in a meaningful manner, how far $\mathbf{x}_i$ is from $\mathbf{x}_j$, where unit j is assumed to be in the opposite treatment group, i.e., $D_j = 1 - D_i$ (covariates Matching or C Matching) (2) or on the basis of only one single index-variable, the propensity-score $p(\mathbf{x}_i)$, synthesizing all covariates in a one-dimension variable (propensity-score Matching or PS Matching).

In either of the cases, we can use, however, different approaches: for example, the one-to-one nearest-neighbor method selects only one unit j from the set of untreated units whose $\mathbf{x}_j$ or $p(\mathbf{x}_j)$ is the "closest" value to $\mathbf{x}_i$ or $p(\mathbf{x}_i)$ according to a prespecified metric. The kernel methods, in contrast, use all units in the untreated set and downweights untreated observations that are more distant.

Irrespective of the specific method chosen, the estimation of the $\text{ATE}_i(\mathbf{x}_i)$ would be simply given by:

$$\widehat{\text{ATE}}_i(\mathbf{x}_i) = Y_{1i} - \widehat{Y}_{0i} \tag{2.54}$$

and an estimation of ATE, ATET, and ATENT obtained by averaging properly previous quantities over i:

$$\widehat{\text{ATE}} = \frac{1}{N}\sum_{i=1}^{N}\left(\widehat{Y}_{1i} - \widehat{Y}_{0i}\right) \tag{2.55}$$

$$\widehat{\text{ATET}} = \frac{1}{N_1}\sum_{i\in\{D=1\}}\left(Y_{1i} - \widehat{Y}_{0i}\right) = \frac{1}{N_1}\sum_{i=1}^{N} D_i\left(Y_{1i} - \widehat{Y}_{0i}\right) \tag{2.56}$$

$$\widehat{\text{ATENT}} = \frac{1}{N_0}\sum_{i\in\{D=0\}}\left(\widehat{Y}_{1i} - Y_{0i}\right) = \frac{1}{N_0}\sum_{i=1}^{N}(1 - D_i)\left(\widehat{Y}_{1i} - Y_{0i}\right) \tag{2.57}$$

where $\{D=1\}$ identifies the set of treated units and $\{D=0\}$ that of untreated units.

By looking at previous formulas, it is easy to observe that Matching can be seen as a special case of the nonparametric Regression-adjustment: ATET, for instance, can be obtained from (2.6) by setting $\widehat{m}_1(\mathbf{x}_i) = Y_{1i}$ and $\widehat{m}_0(\mathbf{x}_i) = \widehat{Y}_{0i}$; equivalently, ATENT can be obtained by substituting $\widehat{m}_1(\mathbf{x}_i) = \widehat{Y}_{1i}$ and $\widehat{m}_0(\mathbf{x}_i) = Y_{0i}$. Thus, Matching directly uses the observed outcome for treated (ATET) and untreated (ATENT) instead of an estimation of the conditional predictions as in the Regression-adjustment. However, before presenting how Matching is implemented in practice, it is important to highlight the statistical properties of this estimator. The next section will focus on this important aspect.

2.3.2 Identification of ATEs Under Matching

In Sect. 1.4.1, we saw that the *selection bias* may be decomposed into three terms as follows:

$$B_1 = B_A + B_B + B_C$$

Where, B_A is the bias due to *weak overlap*; B_B is bias due to *weak balancing*; and B_C is bias due to the presence of *unobservable selection*.

Under specific assumptions, Matching is suited for eliminating biases B_A and B_B but not B_C. In principle, Matching identifies ATEs only under two hypotheses, i.e.,

A.1 Conditional mean independence (CMI), i.e., $E(Y_1 \mid \mathbf{x}, D) = E(Y_1 \mid \mathbf{x})$ and $E(Y_0 \mid \mathbf{x}, D) = E(Y_0 \mid \mathbf{x})$
A.2 Overlap: $0 < p(\mathbf{x}) < 1$, where:

$$p(\mathbf{x}) = \Pr(D = 1 \mid \mathbf{x}) \qquad (2.58)$$

is the *propensity-score*, defined as the probability to be treated given the conditioning variables $\mathbf{x}$ (see, Sect. 1.3.3).

More precisely, however, ATEs are only identified under assumptions A.1 and A.2 if the Matching is *exact*, i.e., only if it is possible to build a finite number of cells based on crossing the values taken by the various $\mathbf{x}$ (see Sect. 2.3.7). When this is not possible, as usually happens, when $\mathbf{x}$ contains at least one continuous variable, then we need a third hypothesis in order to identify ATEs:

A.3 Balancing: $\{(D \perp \mathbf{x}) \mid Matching\}$, i.e., after matching, the covariates' distribution in the treated and control group has to be equal.

It would appear worthwhile to shed further light on the implications of these three assumptions for the Matching estimator.

2.3.2.1 Implications of Assuming "CMI"

We know that the conditional independence assumption implies, for ATET($\mathbf{x}$), that:

$$\text{ATET}(\mathbf{x}) = E(Y_1 \mid D = 1, \mathbf{x}) - E(Y_0 \mid D = 1, \mathbf{x})$$
$$= E(Y_1 \mid D = 1, \mathbf{x}) - E(Y_0 \mid D = 1, \mathbf{x})$$
$$+ \left[E(Y_0 \mid D = 0, \mathbf{x}) - E(Y_0 \mid D = 0, \mathbf{x})\right] \qquad (2.59)$$

However, since according to CMI the mean of Y_0 given $\mathbf{x}$ *does not* depend on variation of D, this mean is the same for any value of D, so that:

$$E(Y_0|D = 1, \mathbf{x}) = E(Y_0|D = 0, \mathbf{x}) \qquad (2.60)$$

This relation suggests one should estimate (or impute) the unobservable (or missing) value on the left side of (2.60) using the observable quantity on the right side. Thus, following (2.59), ATET($\mathbf{x}$) becomes:

$$\begin{aligned} \text{ATET}(\mathbf{x}) &= E(Y_1|D = 1, \mathbf{x}) - E(Y_0|D = 0, \mathbf{x}) \\ &= E(Y|D = 1, \mathbf{x}) - E(Y|D = 0, \mathbf{x}) \end{aligned} \qquad (2.61)$$

that is a function of all observable quantities. An estimate of the "unconditional" ATET is then obtained by averaging (2.61) over the support of $\mathbf{x}$.

Similarly, the condition identifying ATENT is:

$$E(Y_1|D = 0, \mathbf{x}) = E(Y_1|D = 1, \mathbf{x}) \qquad (2.62)$$

so that the unobservable quantity in the left side of (2.62) becomes equivalent to the observable quantity on the right side. ATE can be finally obtained as the usual weighted average of ATET and ATENT.

2.3.2.2 Implications of Assuming "Overlap"

As seen, the overlap assumption states that $0 < p(\mathbf{x}) < 1$. If this assumption does not hold, there might exist units with specific characteristic $\mathbf{x}$ that either always receive treatment (i.e., $p(\mathbf{x}) = 1$) or never receive treatment (i.e., $p(\mathbf{x}) = 0$), thus not permitting us to identify ATEs. To better understand why, assume that there is an $\mathbf{x}^*$ with $p(\mathbf{x}^*) = 1$. All units in the sample having exactly $\mathbf{x} = \mathbf{x}^*$ are included in the treated group. No units with $\mathbf{x} = \mathbf{x}^*$ are in the untreated group, thus preventing to find a similar untreated set for units characterized by $\mathbf{x} = \mathbf{x}^*$. In this case then, the ATET ($\mathbf{x}^*$) cannot be recovered and ATET is not identified.

In empirical practice, fortunately, finding cases in which $p(\mathbf{x}) = 1$ or $p(\mathbf{x}) = 0$ is unlikely. Thus, in the case of Matching, some imprecision in the capacity of $\mathbf{x}$ to explain all the variability of $p(\mathbf{x})$ solves the identification problem. As a result, the model used to predict program participation should not be "too" good!

2.3.2.3 Implications of Assuming "Balancing"

As already mentioned, this assumption matters when Matching is not exact, a case typically occurring when $\mathbf{x}$ presents at least one continuous variable. Indeed, in such a case, finding two observations in the opposite status having the same covariates' value might be infeasible, and frequencies are expected to be unevenly distributed over $\mathbf{x}$ in a comparison between the treated and untreated set of observations. In such cases, however, Matching should help to restore some balancing over $\mathbf{x}$,

Fig. 2.5 Distribution of the
covariate x by treatment
status. Case in which a good
overlap combines with
some imbalance. By
assumption, x varies within
$[0; 1]$

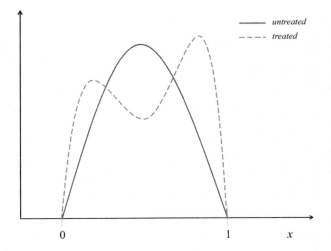

although a perfect balancing is in general impossible to achieve empirically. In
order for Matching to be a reliable procedure for estimating the actual ATEs, we
have to rely on a "plausible degree" of balancing over the observables; this should
be possible to test using some suitable test statistics after Matching is completed.
Therefore, at least in principle, only when Matching passes the "balancing test," can
we conclude that the unbalancing bias (B_B) has been eliminated. In all other cases,
conclusions to be drawn with respect to the actual value of the treatment effect
estimated by Matching remain questionable.

Observe that the overlap and the balancing one are two distinct, although
partially linked, assumptions. Indeed, in usual datasets, we might find a good degree
of covariates' overlap, sometimes accompanied with some strong imbalance.
Typically, overlap should help balancing, but the two concepts remain distinct.
Figure 2.5 shows an example of a good overlap over the covariate x in the presence
of relevant imbalance.

2.3.3   Large Sample Properties of Matching Estimator(s)

As said, Matching can be seen as a particular nonparametric RA estimator.
Nevertheless, the procedure used by Matching to recover the unobserved outcomes—based on some type of comparison between treated and untreated matched
units—generally involves algorithms characterized by high non-smoothness. This
renders the identification of Matching's asymptotic properties rather problematic.
In the literature so far, large sample properties have been clearly singled out only
for some types of Matching methods, while for other types, no clear understanding
of the behavior of this method when N becomes sufficiently large has been achieved
(this is the case, for instance, of stratification Matching).

Generally speaking, Matching might be neither $N^{-1/2}$ consistent nor efficient, thus questioning sometimes the extensive use of this approach in empirical studies. There are two types of Matching, however, for which asymptotic results are known: *kernel* Matching (Heckman et al. 1998) and *nearest-neighbor* Matching (Abadie and Imbens 2006, 2011).

Heckman et al. (1998), hereinafter HIT (1998), provided the following important results for ATET. Assume that CMI and the overlap assumptions hold, that observations are i.i.d., and that we know the actual value of $m_0(\mathbf{x}_i) = \widehat{Y}_{0i} = Y_{0i}$. Under these assumptions, the Matching estimator of ATET:

$$\widehat{\mathrm{ATET}} = \frac{1}{N_1}\sum_{i\in\{D=1\}}(Y_{1i} - Y_{0i}) = \frac{1}{N_1}\sum_{i\in\{D=1\}}\left[Y_{1i} - \mathrm{E}\left(Y_0|D=0,\mathbf{x}=\mathbf{x}_i\right)\right] \quad (2.63)$$

is consistent for ATET, and $\sqrt{N_1}\left(\widehat{\mathrm{ATET}} - \mathrm{ATET}\right)$ is asymptotically normally distributed with zero mean and variance equal to:

$$\mathrm{V}_{\mathbf{x}} = \mathrm{E}\left[\mathrm{Var}\left(Y_1|D=1,\mathbf{x}\right)|D=1\right] + \mathrm{Var}\left[\mathrm{E}\left(Y_1 - Y_0|D=1,\mathbf{x}\right)|D=1\right] \quad (2.64)$$

Likewise, if Matching is done using only the known propensity-score (instead of the entire bundle of $\mathbf{x}$), then:

$$\begin{aligned}\mathrm{V}_{p(\mathbf{x})} = {} & \mathrm{E}\left[\mathrm{Var}\left(Y_1|D=1,p(\mathbf{x})\right)|D=1\right] \\ & + \mathrm{Var}\left[\mathrm{E}\left(Y_1 - Y_0|D=1,p(\mathbf{x})\right)|D=1\right]\end{aligned} \quad (2.65)$$

In this case, the two variances do not dominate each other (Theorem 1, p. 270).

In real applications, however, these variances are unknown, as both the conditional expected outcomes and the propensity-score are unknown functions and have thus to be estimated. HIT (1998) established large sample properties for a specific class of Matching estimators of ATET, the kernel types, estimating the missing observation as:

$$\widehat{Y}_{0i} = \sum_{j\in\{D=0\}}Y_jK\left(\frac{\mathbf{x}_i - \mathbf{x}_j}{a}\right)\Bigg/ \sum_{j\in\{D=0\}}K\left(\frac{\mathbf{x}_i - \mathbf{x}_j}{a}\right) \quad (2.66)$$

where $K(\cdot)$ is a convenient kernel function, and a is a prespecified bandwidth parameter. The authors show that $\sqrt{N_1}\left(\widehat{\mathrm{ATET}} - \mathrm{ATET}\right)$, using (2.66), is in this case asymptotically biased but normally distributed with the mean as function of the bias b and asymptotic variance equal to:

$$V = \frac{1}{\Pr(\mathbf{x}|D=1)}$$
$$\cdot \left\{ \text{var}_{\mathbf{x}} \left[E_{\mathbf{x}} \left(Y_1 - Y_1 | \mathbf{x}, D = 1 \right) | D = 1 \right] + E_{\mathbf{x}} \left[\text{var}_{\mathbf{x}} \left(Y_1 | \mathbf{x}, D = 1 \right) \right] \right\}$$
$$+ \frac{1}{\Pr(\mathbf{x}|D=1)^2} [V_1 + 2 \cdot \text{cov}_1 + \theta V_0] \qquad (2.67)$$

Therefore, HIT (1998) show that kernel Matching is in general not $N^{-1/2}$ consistent and only under particular sequence of the smoothing parameter $N^{-1/2}$ consistency can be guaranteed. To better understand previous formulas and how asymptotic properties are drawn, HIT (1998) prove that the kernel Matching is a special case of an *asymptotically linear estimator* that for a generic parameter β takes the following form:

$$\widehat{\beta}_N - \beta = N^{-1} \sum_{i=1}^{N} \psi(\mathbf{z}_i) + \widehat{b}(\mathbf{z}_i) + \widehat{r}(\mathbf{z}_i) \qquad (2.68)$$

where $\mathbf{z}_i$ is the random sample of observations, $\psi(\cdot)$ a function of $\mathbf{z}_i$ depending on the type of estimator used (parametric or nonparametric type), $\widehat{b}(\mathbf{z}_i)$ a stochastic bias that is not $N^{-1/2}$ consistent, and $\widehat{r}(\mathbf{z}_i)$ is a $N^{-1/2}$ consistent residual term.[2]

This explains why the kernel approach leads to a biased estimation of ATET when N is large, but finite. Observe that in the last term of the previous variance, V_1 and V_0 represent respectively the asymptotic conditional variance of $\psi_1(\cdot)$ and $\psi_0(\cdot)$ as two distinct functions estimated from observations with $D = 1$ and $D = 0$ have to be set; cov_1 is a limit probability of the product of the conditional expectation of $\psi_1(\cdot)$ and the expectation of $\left(Y_1 - \widehat{\beta}_N \right)$, and θ is the finite limit of N_1/N_0. This last definition means that as soon as N_0 increases in comparison with N_1, then the variance reduces accordingly. In particular, HIT (1998) illustrate that if only untreated observations are used (i.e., $\psi_1(\cdot) = 0$) for estimating the kernel function, then $V_1 + 2 \cdot \text{cov}_1 = 0$. As a consequence, the last variance term becomes θV_0 implying that if one assumes θ goes to zero with N going to infinity, the kernel becomes $N^{-1/2}$ consistent as the variance becomes approximately equal to the case of HIT (1998) Theorem 1 (see Theorem 2).

As for the comparison between the asymptotic variances, when Matching is done over all $\mathbf{x}$ or over $p(\mathbf{x})$, the authors suggest that if one restricts the comparison to kernel estimators that are $N^{-1/2}$ consistent, no variance dominates each other even in this case. Thus, Matching on covariates or Matching on propensity-score does not provide ground for efficiency gain, even when the propensity-score is estimated nonparametrically (pp. 269–271). Nevertheless, the use of the propensity-score—by reducing dimensionality—can sensibly shrink the amount of calculation needed

---

[2] An estimator b_N of the population parameter β is said to be $N^{-1/2}$ consistent if $\sqrt{N}(b_N - \beta) \xrightarrow{P} 0$.

when conditioning on all covariates, so that the use of propensity-score is justified on the basis of computational burden but not in terms of efficiency.

Another fundamental contribution to the large sample properties of Matching estimators is that provided by Abadie and Imbens (2006), focusing on the nearest-neighbor Matching. The authors consider nearest-neighbor with replacement and a fixed number of matched units M and show that although this Matching estimation of ATE and ATET is consistent, it is generally not $N^{-1/2}$ consistent being the order of convergence of magnitude $N^{-1/k}$, where k is the number of covariates used to match units. More in details, and taking for simplicity the case of ATE, they show that:

$$\widehat{\text{ATE}} - \text{ATE} = A_M + E_M + B_M \tag{2.69}$$

where $A_M = \left\{ E_x \left[E(Y_1 | x) - E(Y_0 | x) \right] - \text{ATE} \right\}$, E_M is a residual term and B_M, a bias term. Indeed, while the first two terms on the right side of previous equation are $N^{-1/2}$ consistent and asymptotically normal with zero mean and finite variance, the bias term B_M is only $N^{-1/k}$ consistent. It means that, as soon as N increases and $k \geq 3$, B_M goes to zero in probability slower than A_M and E_M, thus dominating asymptotically these two last terms. Of course, when Matching is exact, the bias disappears and the nearest-neighbor procedure will be fully $N^{-1/2}$ consistent and asymptotically normal. In real applications, however, exact matching is rare as covariates usually take the form of continuous variables. However, when $k = 1$, then the bias has an order of convergence equal to N^{-1} that is faster than $N^{-1/2}$; in this case, as N becomes larger, the bias vanishes and the nearest-neighbor estimator is $N^{-1/2}$ consistent and asymptotically normal. In the more general case of k higher than one, Abadie and Imbens (2006) show, however, that:

$$(V_A + V_E)^{-1/2} \sqrt{N} \left(\widehat{\text{ATE}} - \text{ATE} - B_M \right) \xrightarrow{\text{d}} N(0,1) \tag{2.70}$$

where V_A and V_E are the variance of A_M and E_M, respectively, so that if a consistent estimation of the bias term is available, then one can use the previous result for doing usual inference.

Another important aspect related to the nearest-neighbor Matching is regarding its asymptotic efficiency properties. The authors show that when $k \geq 2$, the nearest-neighbor estimator is not efficient as it does not reach the Hahn (1998) lower bound. In particular, they show that:

$$\lim_{N \to \infty} \frac{N \cdot V_{\widehat{\text{ATE}}} - V^{\text{eff}}}{V^{\text{eff}}} < \frac{1}{2M} \tag{2.71}$$

where the first term is the *asymptotic efficiency loss* of the nearest-neighbor Matching (with V^{eff} the asymptotic variance lower bound) and M the fixed number of matches. It is clear that, as soon as M becomes sufficiently large when N goes to infinity, the efficiency loss becomes negligible.

As for the estimation of ATET, similar conclusions can be reached; in this case, however, it can be proved that the bias can be approximately neglected if the number of potential controls increases faster than the number of treated units as N goes to infinity.

Finally, Abadie and Imbens (2011) propose a bias-corrected estimation making Matching estimators $N^{-1/2}$ consistent and asymptotically normal and provide an estimation of the correct asymptotic variance. This approach is presented through a Stata implementation in Sect. 2.7.1.

2.3.4 Common Support

We saw that the fundamental identification condition for Matching is (2.60):

$$E(Y_0|D = 1, \mathbf{x}) = E(Y_0|D = 0, \mathbf{x})$$

thus—to make it meaningful—we require that $0 < p(\mathbf{x}) < 1$. HIT (1998), nevertheless, illustrate that a weaker assumption is needed in order to identify Matching. They call it *common support* and it states that Matching can be equally consistently estimated not only over the all support of $\mathbf{x}$ but also on the support of $\mathbf{x}$ common to both participant and comparison groups. We may define it as S:

$$S = \text{Supp}(\mathbf{x}|w = 1) \cap \text{Supp}(\mathbf{x}|w = 0) \tag{2.72}$$

When the set in (2.72) is not empty, we may estimate Matching using a reduced sample by applying a *trimming rule*, which is a rule to reduce the number of units employed in estimation to the common support S. In general, the quality of the matches may be improved by imposing the *common support* restriction. Note, however, that in this way, high-quality matches may be lost at the boundaries of the common support and the sample may be considerably reduced. Imposing the common support restriction is not necessarily better, therefore, than not considering it at all (Lechner 2008).

2.3.5 Exact Matching and the "Dimensionality Problem"

Equations (2.1) and (2.2) suggest a simple strategy for the estimation of ATEs by Matching when $\mathbf{x}$ has a finite support. This procedure exploits the idea that—within cells identified by $\mathbf{x}$—the condition for random assignment is restored so that intracell DIM is a consistent estimator. More specifically, the procedure suggests that:

- The data are stratified into *cells* defined by each particular value of $\mathbf{x}$.
- Within each cell (i.e., conditioning on $\mathbf{x}$), one should compute the *difference* between the average outcomes of the treated and that of the controls.
- These differences should be averaged with respect to the distribution of $\mathbf{x}$ in the population of treated (for ATET) or untreated (for ATENT) units.

This procedure leads to the following estimators of ATEs:

$$\widehat{\text{ATET}} = \text{E}_{\mathbf{x}}\{\text{E}(Y_{1i} - \widehat{Y}_{0i}|D = 1, \mathbf{x}\} = \sum_{\mathbf{x}} \widehat{\text{TE}}_{\mathbf{x}} \cdot p(\mathbf{x}_i = \mathbf{x}|D_i = 1)$$

$$\widehat{\text{ATENT}} = \text{E}_{\mathbf{x}}\{\text{E}(\widehat{Y}_{1i} - Y_{0i}|D = 0, \mathbf{x}\} = \sum_{\mathbf{x}} \widehat{\text{TE}}_{\mathbf{x}} \cdot p(\mathbf{x}_i = \mathbf{x}|D_i = 0)$$

$$\widehat{\text{ATE}} = \text{E}_D\{\text{E}_{\mathbf{x}}\{\text{E}(\widehat{Y}_{1i} - \widehat{Y}_{0i}|D, \mathbf{x}\}\}$$

$$= p(D = 1) \cdot \widehat{\text{ATET}} + p(D = 0) \cdot \widehat{\text{ATENT}} \tag{2.73}$$

In other words, they are a weighted average of the treatment effects with weights equal to the probability of $\mathbf{x}$ within the set of treated or untreated units.

The ATEs estimators in (2.73) is called exact Matching, and it is feasible only when $\mathbf{x}$ has a very small dimensionality (taking, for instance, just three values). But if the sample is small, the set of covariates $\mathbf{x}$ is large and many of them take discrete multivalues or, even worse, they are continuous variables, then exact Matching is unfeasible. For example, if $\mathbf{x}$ is made of K binary variables, then the number of cells becomes 2^K, and this number increases further if some variables take more than two values.

If the number of cells (or "blocks") is very large with respect to the size of the sample, it is possible that some cells contain only treated or only control subjects. Thus, the calculus of ATEs might become unfeasible and ATEs not identified. If variables are all continuous, as happens in many socioeconomic applications, it would be even impossible to build cells.

To avoid this drawback, known as the *dimensionality problem*, Rosenbaum and Rubin (1983) have suggested that units are matched according to the propensity-score (defined, as said above, as the "probability of being treated conditional on $\mathbf{x}$"). Using the propensity-score permits to reduce the multidimensionality to a *single scalar dimension*, $p(\mathbf{x})$.

In a parametric context, the estimation of the propensity-score is usually obtained through a probit (or logit) regression of D on the variables contained in $\mathbf{x}$. Once the scores are obtained, one may match treated and control units with the *same* propensity-score and then averaging on the differences so obtained. The problem is that although the propensity-score is a singleton index, it is still a "continuous" variable, and this prevents us from being able to perform an exact Matching.

Despite this, Dehejia and Wahba (1999) have provided a procedure estimating ATEs using the propensity-score, which is capable of dealing with its continuous nature. As we will see in Sect. 2.3.7, this procedure is based on the idea of building intervals of the propensity-score so to transform it into a variable with finite support. Before presenting the Dehejia and Wahba (1999) procedure, it is worth to briefly discuss some fundamental properties of the propensity-score, which justify its popularity and extensive use in many program evaluation applications.

2.3.6 The Properties of the Propensity-Score

According to the definition of Rosenbaum and Rubin (1983, 1984), the propensity-score is the *conditional probability of receiving the treatment, given the confounding variables* **x**. Interestingly, since D is binary, the following equalities apply:

$$p(\mathbf{x}) = \Pr(D = 1|\mathbf{x}) = E(D|\mathbf{x}) \tag{2.74}$$

that is, the propensity-score is the expectation of the treatment variable, conditional on **x**. The propensity-score has *two* important properties which account for its appeal: the *balancing* and *unconfoundedness* properties.

P1. *Balancing of confounding variables, given the propensity-score*:
  If $p(\mathbf{x})$ is the propensity-score, then:

$$D \perp \mathbf{x}|p(\mathbf{x}) \tag{2.75}$$

which implies that, conditionally on $p(\mathbf{x})$, the treatment and the observables are independent. To prove relation (2.75), we can first observe that:

$$\Pr[D = 1|\mathbf{x}, p(\mathbf{x})] = E[D|\mathbf{x}, p(\mathbf{x})] = E[D|\mathbf{x}] = \Pr[D = 1|\mathbf{x}] = p(\mathbf{x}) \tag{2.76}$$

Similarly, using the law of iterated expectations (LIE):

$$\Pr[D = 1|p(\mathbf{x})] = E[D|p(\mathbf{x})] = E_{p(\mathbf{x})}\big[E[D|\mathbf{x}, p(\mathbf{x})]\big|p(\mathbf{x})\big]$$
$$= E_{p(\mathbf{x})}[p(\mathbf{x})|p(\mathbf{x})] = p(\mathbf{x}) \tag{2.77}$$

where the third equality uses the fact that $p(\mathbf{x})$ is a function of **x**, thus setting **x** implies setting $p(\mathbf{x})$. By comparing (2.76) and (2.77), we obtain that:

$$\Pr[D = 1|\mathbf{x}, p(\mathbf{x})] = \Pr[D = 1|p(\mathbf{x})] = p(\mathbf{x}) \tag{2.78}$$

which entails that conditionally on $p(\mathbf{x})$, the treatment D and the observables $\mathbf{x}$ are independent.

P2. *Unconfoundedness, given the propensity-score*

Suppose that the conditional independence assumption (CIA) holds, in other words:

$$(Y_1, Y_0) \perp D|\mathbf{x} \tag{2.79}$$

then assignment to treatment is random, also given the propensity-score, that is:

$$(Y_1, Y_0) \perp D|p(\mathbf{x}) \tag{2.80}$$

Property (2.80) is not tricky to prove. In fact, using LIE again, we initially have that:

$$\Pr[D = 1|Y_1, Y_0, p(\mathbf{x})] = \mathrm{E}[D|Y_1, Y_0, p(\mathbf{x})]$$
$$= \mathrm{E}\left[\mathrm{E}[D|\mathbf{x}, p(\mathbf{x}), Y_1, Y_0]|Y_1, Y_0, p(\mathbf{x})\right] = \mathrm{E}\left[\mathrm{E}D|\mathbf{x}, Y_1, Y_0]|Y_1, Y_0, p(\mathbf{x})\right]$$
$$= \mathrm{E}\left[\mathrm{E}[D|\mathbf{x}]|Y_1, Y_0, p(\mathbf{x})\right] = \mathrm{E}\left[p(\mathbf{x})|Y_1, Y_0, p(\mathbf{x})\right] = p(\mathbf{x}) \tag{2.81}$$

where the last equality comes from (2.79). From (2.78) we saw that:

$$\Pr[D = 1|\mathbf{x}, p(\mathbf{x})] = \Pr[D = 1|p(\mathbf{x})] = p(\mathbf{x})$$

and looking at (2.81) this implies that:

$$\Pr[D = 1|Y_1, Y_0, p(\mathbf{x})] = \Pr[D = 1|p(\mathbf{x})] \tag{2.82}$$

which shows that conditionally on $p(\mathbf{x})$ the treatment D and the potential outcomes (Y_1, Y_0) are stochastically independent.

Property P2 states that stratifying units according to $p(\mathbf{x})$ produces the same orthogonal condition between the potential outcomes and the treatment that is stratifying on $\mathbf{x}$, but with the advantage to rely just on one dimension variable. Property P1, additionally, states that if the propensity-score is correctly specified, then we should see that units stratified according to the propensity-score should be indistinguishable in terms of their $\mathbf{x}$ (i.e., they are *balanced*). Thus, testing empirically whether the balancing property holds is a way for assuring that the correct propensity-score is being used to stratify units. As said, balancing observations is an essential ingredient to draw reliable Matching results.

2.3.7   Quasi-Exact Matching Using the Propensity-Score

Assumption P2 suggests to match treated units and controls directly on the basis of the (estimated) propensity-score instead of using the larger set of variables in **x**. As previously mentioned, even if the "dimensionality curse" is solved as a k-dimension problem that reduces to just one dimension, the problem related to the continuous form of the propensity-score still remains. In that, exact Matching with a continuous variable is impossible, as none of the units have exactly the same value of such a variable. Nevertheless, a *discretization* procedure of the propensity-score may still be implemented to approximate the Exact-Matching approach.

Dehejia and Wahba (1999), hereinafter DW (1999), proposed a quasi-exact-Matching procedure for estimating ATEs using propensity-score's discretization. The authors' procedure exploits properties P1 and P2 to obtain reliable Matching estimation of ATEs. A Stata implementation of this procedure has been provided by Becker and Ichino (2002).

The idea underlying this approach is rather straightforward; in the first instance, a stratification of the units is generated according to discrete intervals of the propensity-score; secondly, DIMs within each interval are calculated; and thirdly, ATEs by averaging over these DIMs are computed. This procedure is very close to the exact matching, except that here strata have to be found empirically, whereas in the exact matching, they are prior knowledge.

The problem with this approach, however, is how to choose the appropriate number of strata to be considered in the averaging of the DIMs over strata. Fortunately, the balancing property (P1) of the propensity-score suggests a criterion to set the right number of strata, based on the idea that, when propensity-score is used to stratifying units, in each stratum a quasi-randomization should be produced. In this case, the values assumed by the covariates **x** for treated and untreated in each stratum should be approximately equal. Thus, the optimal number of strata (also called "blocks") are those satisfying the balancing property as defined above. Following DW (1999) and Becker and Ichino (2002), the algorithm to produce the appropriate number of strata entails the following steps:

1. *Estimating the propensity-score*:

   - First, start with a parsimonious specification in order to estimate the propensity-score for each individual, using the following function:

   $$p(\mathbf{x}) = \Pr\{D = 1 | \mathbf{x}\} = G[f(\mathbf{x})] \qquad (2.83)$$

   where $G[\cdot]$ can be probit, logit, or linear, and $f(\mathbf{x})$ is a function of covariates with linear and higher order terms.
   - Second, order the units according to the estimated propensity-score (from the lowest to the highest value).

2. *Identify the number of strata by satisfying the balancing property*:

- Third, stratify all observations into blocks such that in each block, the estimated propensity-scores for the treated and the controls are *not* statistically different:

  - Start with five blocks of equal score range {0–0.2, ..., 0.8–1}
  - Test whether the means of the scores for the treated and the controls are statistically different in each block (balancing of the propensity-score)
  - If they are, increase the number of blocks and test again
  - If not, proceed to the next step

- Fourth, test whether the balancing property holds in all strata for all covariates:

  - For each covariate, test whether the means for the treated and for the controls are statistically different in all strata (balancing for covariates)
  - If one covariate is not balanced in one block, split the block and test again within each finer block
  - If one covariate is not balanced in all blocks, modify the logit/probit/linear estimation of the propensity-score adding more interaction and higher order terms and then test the balancing property again.

3. *Estimating ATEs*:

- Fifth, once the balancing property is satisfied and, thus, the optimal number of strata is found, then an (weighted) average of the DIM estimators calculated in the final blocks provides an estimation of ATEs.

It is clear that the previous procedure approximates the exact matching by a discretization of the propensity-score. Nonetheless, the large sample properties of such an estimator, called *stratification Matching*, have yet to be proved. Stratification Matching is, however, only one of many types of Matching estimators that can be implemented. Later on in this chapter, we will discuss other types of Matching that do not require a stratification procedure to be reliably used (although they need to satisfy some balancing test too). In fact, in standard applications, the quasi-exact-Matching procedure proposed by DW (1999) may be rather demanding, as it may be difficult to assure balancing for all covariates within all strata.

Other Matching methods provide a less restrictive and, thus, easier way to obtain reliable estimates of ATEs, without requiring to build blocks. A typical procedure for estimating ATEs by these approaches takes the following form (see also Fig. 2.6):

- First, choose a specification of the logit/probit and calculate the propensity-score for each unit (both treated and untreated).
- Second, identify a specific *type of Matching* using some distance metric between treated and untreated units and then match all units with the other units of opposite treatment.

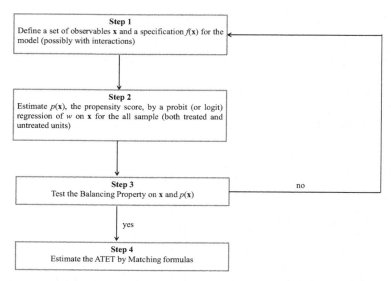

Fig. 2.6 Flow diagram of a Matching protocol

- Third, test the balancing property by comparing, for each x in $\mathbf{x}$, the mean of the treated with the mean of the controls selected by the specific Matching type used.
- Fourth, if the balancing is satisfied, then calculate ATEs with the Matching formula specified in step 2, otherwise modify the probit/logit specification until the balancing is satisfied.

In this case, one should apply Matching estimation just when for each x and for $p(\mathbf{x})$, no difference emerges in terms of the mean of treated and matched untreated units. The advantage of this approach is that it does not require balancing for each x in $\mathbf{x}$ and for $p(\mathbf{x})$ in each stratum since, comparatively, it is "as if" only one single block was built. The limits reside in the use of a less sophisticated test of the balancing property.

Of course, in practical situations, one generally modifies the propensity-score specification by adding other variables and/or interactions, or—in the worst case— by dropping a given x if unbalancing persists after several modifications, only if x is not relevant to explain the outcome Y. Of course, evaluators must ponder and clarify any choice made in order to attain balancing, as reaching balancing—at least at an acceptable level of statistical significance—is neither easy nor sure. That is, however, probably a limit of Matching compared, for instance, to regression approaches that do not need to comply with this property (although they assume a parametric form of the imbalance).

It is clear that perfect balancing is impossible due to the random nature of the data and even more importantly because the analyst rarely has access to the entire set of confounders explaining the selection-into-program. Nevertheless, some diagnostic test to evaluate the quality of the Matching provided is useful.

As a good place to start, one could assume that a good Matching on propensity-score occurs when treated and selected untreated units are similar in terms of **x** and *a fortiori* in term of $p(\mathbf{x})$. Thus, if treated and control units are largely different in terms of observables, the reached Matching is not sufficiently *robust* and it might be questionable. Comparison of the estimated propensity-scores across treated and controls therefore provides a useful diagnostic tool to evaluate how similar treated subjects and controls are and how reliable the estimation strategy is. More precisely, it would be useful to:

- Calculate the frequency of matched untreated cases having a propensity-score lower than the minimum or higher than the maximum of the propensity-scores of the treated units. Preferably, one would hope that the range of variation of propensity-scores is the same in both groups.
- Draw histograms and kernel densities of the estimated propensity-scores for the treated and the controls, before and after Matching when possible. In case of stratification Matching, one should use histogram bins corresponding to the strata constructed for the estimation of propensity-scores. One hopes to get an equal frequency of treated and untreated units in each bin.

2.3.8 Methods for Propensity-Score Matching

Previous considerations have led to prefer propensity-score Matching over covariates Matching for at least three reasons: (1) conditioning on $p(\mathbf{x})$ rather than **x** does not undermine consistency and does not increase the variance (precision) of estimation; (2) working with $p(\mathbf{x})$ is easier than working with **x**, as $p(\mathbf{x})$ is a single variable indexing the overall **x**. It is computationally preferable to work on only one dimension rather than on k dimensions; (3) knowing $p(\mathbf{x})$ may be interesting per se, having a meaningful theoretical interpretation as it derives from the behavioral *selection rule* adopted by the individuals within the program/experiment. Thus, in the remainder of this chapter, we will focus mainly on the propensity-score Matching approach.

According to the previous procedures, once the balancing property is statistically satisfied to a certain appreciable extent, results from Matching can be reliably accepted. In the literature, different types of Matching methods have been proposed: one-to-one nearest-neighbor, multiple-nearest-neighbors, radius (with various calipers), kernel, local linear, ridge, and stratification are among the most used (Busso et al. 2009; Caliendo and Kopeinig 2008; Dehejia and Wahba 2002; Heckman et al. 1998).

What is interesting is that all these methods can be retrieved as specific case of a general Matching formula, as showed by Smith and Todd (2005). Indeed, in the case of Matching, the imputation of the missing counterfactual follows this rule:

$$\widehat{Y}_{0i} = \begin{cases} Y_i & \text{if } D_i = 0 \\ \displaystyle\sum_{j \in C(i)} h(i,j)Y_j & \text{if } D_i = 1 \end{cases}$$

and

$$\widehat{Y}_{1i} = \begin{cases} \displaystyle\sum_{j \in C(i)} h(i,j)Y_j & \text{if } D_i = 0 \\ Y_i & \text{if } D_i = 1 \end{cases}$$

where the unobserved outcome is estimated as an average of the observed outcomes for the observations j chosen as matches for i in the opposite treatment group of i. Given this, we have:

$$\widehat{\text{ATET}} = \frac{1}{N_1} \sum_{i \in \{D=1\}} \left(Y_i - \widehat{Y}_{0i}\right) = \frac{1}{N_1} \sum_{i \in \{D=1\}} \left(Y_i - \sum_{j \in C(i)} h(i,j)Y_j\right) \qquad (2.84)$$

$$\widehat{\text{ATENT}} = \frac{1}{N_0} \sum_{i \in \{D=0\}} \left(\widehat{Y}_{1i} - Y_i\right) = \frac{1}{N_0} \sum_{i \in \{D=0\}} \left(\sum_{j \in C(i)} h(i,j)Y_j - Y_i\right) \qquad (2.85)$$

$$\widehat{\text{ATE}} = \left(\frac{1}{N}\sum_i D_i\right) \cdot \widehat{\text{ATET}} + \left(\frac{1}{N}\sum_i (1 - D_i)\right) \cdot \widehat{\text{ATENT}} \qquad (2.86)$$

where $C(i)$, called the "neighborhood" of i, is the set of indices j for the units matched with unit i, that is: $C(i) = \{j: \text{matched with } i\}$; $0 < h(i,j) \leq 1$ are weights to apply to the single j matched with i, and they generally increase as soon as j is closer to i. Observe that i may be treated or untreated.

Different propensity-score Matching methods can be obtained by specifying different forms of the weights $h(i,j)$ and of the set $C(i)$ as showed in Table 2.3 (Busso et al. 2009).[3] We briefly review these methods.

Nearest-neighbor Matching The classical nearest-neighbor Matching suggests to match each treated unit with the closest untreated unit in the dataset, where "closeness" is defined according to some distance metric over $p(\mathbf{x})$ (or $\mathbf{x}$ in the

---

[3] Notation in Table 2.3 means as follows: $\widehat{\Delta}_{ij} = p(\mathbf{x}_i) - p(\mathbf{x}_j)$; $K_{ij} = K\left(\widehat{\Delta}_{ij}/h\right)$ where $K(\cdot)$ is a kernel function and h a bandwidth; $L_i^d = \sum_{j \in C} K_{ij}\widehat{\Delta}_{ij}^d$ for $d = 1,2$; $\widetilde{\Delta}_{ij} = p(\mathbf{x}_i) - \overline{p}(\mathbf{x}_j)$, where $\overline{p}(\mathbf{x}_j) = \sum_{j \in C} p(\mathbf{x}_j)K_{ij} / \sum_{j \in C} K_{ij}$; r_L is an adjustment factor suggested by Fan (1992), r_R is an adjustment factor suggested by Seifert and Gasser (2000), B is an interval that gives the bth stratum for the stratification estimator, and B is the number of blocks used. For a Gaussian kernel, $r_L = 0$ and for an Epanechnikov kernel, $r_L = 1/N^2$. For a Gaussian kernel, $r_R = 0.35$ and for an Epanechnikov kernel, $r_R = 0.31$.

Table 2.3 Different Matching methods for estimating ATEs according to the specification of $C(i)$ and $h(i, j)$

Matching method	$C(i)$	$h(i,j)$
One-nearest-neighbor	$\left\{ \text{Singleton } j : \min_j \lVert p_i - p_j \rVert \right\}$	1
M-nearest-neighbors	$\left\{ \text{First } M \, j : \min_j \lVert p_i - p_j \rVert \right\}$	$\frac{1}{M}$
Radius	$\left\{ j : \lVert p_i - p_j \rVert < r \right\}$	$\frac{1}{N_{C(i)}}$
Kernel	All control units (C)	$\dfrac{K_{ij}}{\sum_{j \in C} K_{ij}}$
Local-linear	All control units (C)	$\dfrac{K_{ij} L_i^2 - K_{ij} \widehat{\Delta}_{ij} L_i^1}{\sum_{j \in C} \left(K_{ij} L_i^2 - K_{ij} \widehat{\Delta}_{ij} L_i^1 + r_L \right)}$
Ridge	All control units (C)	$\dfrac{K_{ij}}{\sum_{j \in C} K_{ij}} + \dfrac{\widehat{\Delta}_{ij}}{\sum_{j \in C} \left(K_{ij} \widehat{\Delta}^2_{ij} + r_R h \lvert \widehat{\Delta}_{ij} \rvert \right)}$
Stratification	All control units (C)	$\dfrac{\sum_{b=1}^{B} \mathbf{1}[p(\mathbf{x}_i) \in I(b)] \cdot \mathbf{1}[p(\mathbf{x}_j) \in I(b)]}{\sum_{b=1}^{B} \mathbf{1}[p(\mathbf{x}_j) \in I(b)]}$

case of Matching on covariates). When pair-wise matching is allowed, we have the so-called one-to-one nearest-neighbor Matching. Generally, however, each unit in a given treatment status is matched with the closest M neighbors in the opposite status, and an average of them is thus produced as counterfactual. Observe that matching may be done with and without replacement. When replacement is allowed, then the same unit can be used for more than one unit in the opposite status; on the contrary, when matching is done without replacement, the same unit can be used only once per each unit in the opposite status. As we will see, adopting replacement can have an impact on the variance of the Matching estimator.

The procedure for implementing the one-to-one Matching with replacement is rather simple. Taking the case of ATET as example, we have:

- First, for each treated unit i find the *nearest* control unit j using the Mahalanobis/ Euclidean distance:

$$
d_{ij} = \begin{cases} \sqrt{(\mathbf{x}_j - \mathbf{x}_i)' \mathbf{\Omega}^{-1} (\mathbf{x}_j - \mathbf{x}_i)} & \text{for Covariates Matching} \\ d_{ij} = \lVert p(\mathbf{x}_j) - p(\mathbf{x}_i) \rVert & \text{for Propensity score Matching} \end{cases}
$$

where $\mathbf{\Omega}$ is the covariance Matrix of the covariates $\mathbf{x}$.
- Second, if the nearest control unit has already been used, use it again (replacement).
- Third, drop the unmatched controlled units.
- Fourth, calculate ATEs applying formulas (2.84)–(2.86).

In the case of ATET estimation, this algorithm delivers a set of N_1 pairs of treated and control units in which control units may appear more than once. Of course, if for each treated i we consider M nearest-neighbors, then the mean of their outcomes is considered as the counterfactual outcome of i.

Radius(or caliper) Matching A limit of the nearest-neighbor Matching is that it does not consider the "level" of the distance between matches. This means that it could match pairs even when they are very different (as p_i and p_j are far). To avoid this shortcoming, radius Matching is sometimes preferred (Cochran and Rubin 1973). It can be seen as a variant of the nearest-neighbor, trying to avoid the occurrence of "bad" matches by imposing a threshold on the maximum distance permitted between p_i and p_j. It means that two units are matched only when their distance in absolute terms is lower than a tolerance limit, identified by a prespecified *caliper* "r" as illustrated in Table 2.3. Those treated units with no matches within the caliper are eliminated. Thus, radius Matching naturally imposes a common support restriction. Of course, defining a priori which is the correct caliper to use can be sometimes difficult. There exists a tension between a larger caliper and a higher precision: using a larger caliper increases the sample size but reduces the extent of similarity among units; using a smaller caliper increases the similarity but reduces the sample size. Thus, the choice of the correct caliper should take into account this trade-off. The steps for implementing radius Matching with replacement to calculate ATEs are as follows:

- First, for each treated unit i identify all the control units whose **x** differs by less than a given tolerance r (the *caliper*) chosen by the researcher.
- Second, allow for replacement of control units.
- Third, when a treated unit has no control closer than r, take the nearest control or delete it.
- Fourth, estimate ATEs applying formulas (2.84)–(2.86).

Observe that if in the third step, the unmatched unit is deleted, then the algorithm delivers a set of $N_1(r) \leq N_1$ treated units and $N_{C(i)}$ untreated units, some of which are used more than once. On the contrary, when this unit is matched with its nearest control instead of being eliminated, then the algorithm delivers a set of $N_1(r) = N_1$ treated units.

According to (2.84)–(2.86), the ATEs formulas for both nearest-neighbor and radius Matching estimators are easy to be calculated:

$$\widehat{\text{ATET}} = \frac{1}{N_1} \sum_{i \in \{D=1\}} \left(Y_i - \sum_{j \in C(i)} h(i,j) Y_j \right)$$

$$= \frac{1}{N_1} \sum_{i \in \{D=1\}} Y_i - \frac{1}{N_1} \sum_{i \in \{D=1\}} \sum_{j \in C(i)} h(i,j) Y_{0j}$$

$$= \frac{1}{N_1} \sum_{i \in \{D=1\}} Y_{1i} - \frac{1}{N_1} \sum_{j \in \{D=0\}} \left(\sum_{i \in \{D=1\}} h(i,j) \right) Y_j$$

$$= \frac{1}{N_1} \sum_{i \in \{D=1\}} Y_i - \frac{1}{N_1} \sum_{j \in \{D=0\}} h_{1j} Y_j \tag{2.87}$$

$$\widehat{\text{ATENT}} = \frac{1}{N_0} \sum_{j \in \{D=1\}} h_{0j} Y_j - \frac{1}{N_0} \sum_{i \in \{D=0\}} Y_i$$

$$\widehat{\text{ATE}} = \left(\frac{1}{N} \sum_i D_i \right) \cdot \widehat{\text{ATET}} + \left(\frac{1}{N} \sum_i (1 - D_i) \right) \cdot \widehat{\text{ATENT}}$$

where $h_{gj} = \sum_{i \in \{D=g\}} h_{ij}$, $g = 1, 0$ and $h(i,j) = 1/N_{C(i)}$ if $j \in C(i)$ and $h_{ij} = 0$ otherwise.

Kernel and local linear Matching The kernel Matching estimator can be interpreted as a particular version of the radius Matching in which every treated unit is matched with a weighted average of *all* control units with weights that are inversely proportional to the distance between the treated and the control units. Formally, the kernel Matching estimator for ATET (for ATE and ATENT formulas can be similarly derived) is given by:

$$\widehat{\text{ATET}} = \frac{1}{N_1} \sum_{i \in \{D=1\}} \left(Y_{1i} - \sum_{j \in \{D=0\}} \left(\frac{K(p_j - p_i/h)}{\sum_{k \in \{D=0\}} K(p_j - p_i/h)} \right) Y_{0j} \right) \tag{2.88}$$

In (2.88), $K(\cdot)$ is a kernel function (Gaussian or Epanechnikov, for instance) and h the bandwidth parameter, which has the same role of the caliper in radius Matching.

Local linear Matching is a variant of the kernel Matching, where a linear component in the weights is introduced. As showed by Fan (1992), Local linear Matching can have some advantages compared with standard kernel estimation methods including, for instance, a faster rate of convergence close to boundary points and greater robustness to different data design densities.

Stratification Matching As seen above, this method exploits directly the propensity-score property P2 as stated in (2.45), i.e., independence conditional to the propensity-score. If this assumption holds, then it suggests that within cells (or blocks), identified by splitting the sample according to the values assumed by $\mathbf{x}$, the random assignment is restored. Thus, by construction, stratification Matching exploits the fact that in each block, defined by a given splitting procedure, the covariates are balanced and the assignment to treatment can be assumed as random within each block. Using the propensity-score, hence, and letting b index the B blocks defined over intervals of the propensity-score, the stratification Matching assumes for ATEs the following formulas:

$$\widehat{\text{ATE}} = \sum_{b=1}^{B} \widehat{\text{ATE}}_b \cdot \left[\frac{N^b}{N} \right]$$

$$\widehat{\text{ATET}} = \sum_{b=1}^{B} \widehat{\text{ATE}}_b \cdot \left[\frac{\sum_{i \in I(b)} D_i}{\sum_i D_i} \right] \qquad (2.89)$$

$$\widehat{\text{ATENT}} = \sum_{b=1}^{B} \widehat{\text{ATE}}_b \cdot \left[\frac{\sum_{i \in I(b)} (1 - D_i)}{\sum_i (1 - D_i)} \right]$$

where $\widehat{\text{ATE}}_b = \left(1/N_1^b \right) \sum_{i \in I(b)} y_i - \left(1/N_0^b \right) \sum_{j \in I(b)} y_j$, $I(b)$ is the set of units present in block b, N_1^b is the number of treated units in block b, N_0^b is the number of control units in block b, and $N^b = N_0^b + N_1^b$. The number of blocks B are those obtained when the balancing property is satisfied according to the procedure described in Sect. 2.3.7.

2.3.9 Inference for Matching Methods

As suggested in previous sections, large sample properties for previous matching methods show—generally speaking—that Matching(s) generally have no really appealing asymptotic properties. We saw, for example, that the nearest-neighbor Matching on k covariates is not in general $N^{-1/2}$ consistent and its asymptotic Normal distribution contains a nonzero bias when $k \geq 3$.

However, when $k = 1$, namely when matching is done over just one variable, the bias has an order of convergence equal to N^{-1} that is faster than $N^{-1/2}$; in this case, as N becomes larger, the bias vanishes and the nearest-neighbor Matching estimator is $N^{-1/2}$ consistent and asymptotically normal (although it is not fully efficient). Thus, if the nearest neighbor is used by calculating only the propensity-score, clearly equivalent to the case in which $k = 1$, we could rely on its "well-known" asymptotic properties. The problem is that the propensity-score is a "generated variable," and this introduces an additional complication into the model, especially when the parametric hypothesis behind the probit or logit specification can be questionable.

However, a recent paper by Abadie and Imbens (2012) derives the asymptotic distribution of the nearest-neighbor Matching when the propensity-score is estimated. Abadie and Imbens (2006, 2012) show that for Matching with replacement, using the "true" propensity-score as the only matching variable, we have that:

$$\sqrt{N}\left(\widehat{\text{ATE}} - \text{ATE}\right) \overset{d}{\to} N\left(0, \sigma^2\right) \tag{2.90}$$

where σ^2 takes on the following form:

$$\sigma^2 = \text{E}\left[\left(m\left(1, p(x)\right) - m\left(0, p(x)\right) - \text{ATE}\right)^2\right]$$

$$+ \text{E}\left[\sigma^2\left(1, p(x)\right)\left(\frac{1}{p(x)} + \frac{1}{2M}\left(\frac{1}{p(x)} - \left(p(x)\right)\right)\right)\right]$$

$$+ \text{E}\left[\sigma^2\left(0, p(x)\right)\left(\frac{1}{1 - p(x)} + \frac{1}{2M}\left(\frac{1}{1 - p(x)} - \left(1 - p(x)\right)\right)\right)\right] \tag{2.91}$$

with $\sigma^2(D, p(x)) = \text{Var}(Y \mid D = g, p(x) = p)$, $g = 1,0$. Suppose we are now interested in estimating $p(x)$ using a parametric model (logit or probit) $F(x\theta)$, and let θ_{ML} be the maximum likelihood estimation of this model. Then, it can be proved that:

$$\sqrt{N}\left(\widehat{\text{ATE}} - \text{ATE}\right) \overset{d}{\to} N\left(0, \sigma^2 - c' I_{\theta_{\text{ML}}}^{-1} c\right) \tag{2.92}$$

where $I_{\theta_{\text{ML}}}$ is the Fisher information matrix, c a vector depending on the joint distribution of the outcome, the treatment, and the covariates. Since $I_{\theta_{\text{ML}}}$ is positive semi-definite, nearest-neighbor Matching on the estimated propensity-score has, in large samples, a smaller asymptotic variance than matching on the true propensity-score. As for ATET, a similar formula appears; although in this case, it can be shown that the variance adjustment can be either positive or negative, so that no dominance emerges between knowing and estimating the propensity-score.

In practical applications, however, one could use the procedure implemented by Abadie et al. (2004) (from here on ADHI (2004)). This approach is a Stata implementation of the nearest-neighbor Matching as developed by Abadie and Imbens (2006) reviewed above, thus it is suitable for nearest-neighbor on covariates, although one could also use it for nearest-neighbor on the propensity-score, even if it *does not* consider adjustment for estimating the propensity-score. This approach might be useful as it provides the corrected standard errors compared to other implementations of the nearest-neighbor Matching (see later on).

The ADHI (2004) approach, starts by considering the set $C_M(i)$ defined as the "set of indices" for the units matched with unit i that are at least as close as the M-th match:

$$C_M(i) \equiv \{j = 1, \ldots, N : D_j = 1 - D_i, \|\mathbf{x}_j - \mathbf{x}_i\| \le d_M(i)\}$$

where $d_M(i)$ is the distance between the covariates of the unit i, i.e. $\mathbf{x}_i$, and the covariates of the M-th nearest match of i in the opposite treatment status. Then, they define the following quantity[4]:

$$K_M(i) = \sum_{j=1}^{N} 1\{i \in C_M(j)\} \cdot \frac{1}{\#C_M(j)}$$

$$K'_M(i) = \sum_{j=1}^{N} 1\{i \in C_M(j)\} \cdot \left\{\frac{1}{\#C_M(j)}\right\}^2$$

with $\#C_M(i)$ indicating the number of elements in $C_M(i)$, as the number of times i is used as a match for all observations j of the opposite treatment group, weighted by the total number of matches for observation j. It is quite clear that potential outcomes are estimated as follows:

$$\widehat{Y}_{0i} = \begin{cases} Y_i & \text{if } D_i = 0 \\ \dfrac{1}{\#C_M(i)} \displaystyle\sum_{j \in C_M(i)} Y_j & \text{if } D_i = 1 \end{cases}$$

and

$$\widehat{Y}_{1i} = \begin{cases} \dfrac{1}{\#C_M(i)} \displaystyle\sum_{j \in C_M(i)} Y_j & \text{if } D_i = 0 \\ Y_i & \text{if } D_i = 1 \end{cases}$$

where the unobserved outcome is estimated as an average of the observed outcomes for the observations j chosen as matches for i in the opposite treatment group. The authors prove that estimators for ATEs are in this case equal to:

$$\widehat{\text{ATE}} = \frac{1}{N}\sum_{i=1}^{N} \left(\widehat{Y}_{1i} - \widehat{Y}_{0i}\right) = \frac{1}{N}\sum_{i=1}^{N} (2D_i - 1)\{1 + K_M(i)\}Y_i \qquad (2.93)$$

$$\widehat{\text{ATET}} = \frac{1}{N_1}\sum_{i \in \{D=1\}} \left(Y_{1i} - \widehat{Y}_{0i}\right) = \frac{1}{N_1}\sum_{i=1}^{N} \{D_i - (1 - D_i)K_M(i)\}Y_i \qquad (2.94)$$

$$\widehat{\text{ATENT}} = \frac{1}{N_0}\sum_{i \in \{D=0\}} \left(\widehat{Y}_{1i} - Y_{0i}\right) = \frac{1}{N_0}\sum_{i=1}^{N} \{D_i K_M(i) - (1 - D_i)\}Y_i \qquad (2.95)$$

As discussed in Sect. 2.3.3, previous estimators are asymptotically biased as exact

---

[4] Observe that: $\sum_i K_M(i) = N$, $\sum_{i \in \{D=1\}} K_M(i) = N_1$ and $\sum_{i \in \{D=0\}} K_M(i) = N_0$.

matching is not possible. When k continuous covariates are considered, they will have a bias term depending on the matching discrepancies (i.e., difference in covariates between matched units and their matches) that will be of the order $N^{-1/k}$. The bias-corrected matching estimator eliminates the bias by adjusting the difference within the matches for the differences in their values of $\mathbf{x}$. In practice, the adjustment is carried out by estimating the following two OLS regressions weighted by $K_M(i)$ using only the data on the matched sample:

$$\widehat{\mu}_1(\mathbf{x}) = \widehat{\beta}_{0,1} + \mathbf{x}\widehat{\beta}_{1,1}$$
$$\widehat{\mu}_0(\mathbf{x}) = \widehat{\beta}_{0,0} + \mathbf{x}\widehat{\beta}_{1,0}$$

and then taking the difference of these predictions for estimating the bias, so that:

$$\widehat{Y}_{0i} = \begin{cases} Y_i & \text{if } D_i = 0 \\ \dfrac{1}{\#C_M(i)} \displaystyle\sum_{j \in C_M(i)} \left\{ Y_j + \widehat{\mu}_0(\mathbf{x}_i) - \widehat{\mu}_0(\mathbf{x}_j) \right\} & \text{if } D_i = 1 \end{cases}$$

and

$$\widehat{Y}_{1i} = \begin{cases} \dfrac{1}{\#C_M(i)} \displaystyle\sum_{j \in C_M(i)} \left\{ Y_j + \widehat{\mu}_1(\mathbf{x}_i) - \widehat{\mu}_1(\mathbf{x}_j) \right\} & \text{if } D_i = 0 \\ Y_i & \text{if } D_i = 1 \end{cases}$$

Observe that one only estimates a regression function over the controls to get $\widehat{Y}_{0i}$ and only a regression function over the treated to get $\widehat{Y}_{1i}$.

As for the estimation of the variance for the population parameters of (2.93)–(2.95), ADHI (2004) provide these formulas:

$$\mathrm{Var}\left(\widehat{\mathrm{ATE}}\right) = \frac{1}{N^2}\sum_{i=1}^{N}\left[\left(\widehat{Y}_{1i} - \widehat{Y}_{0i} - \widehat{\mathrm{ATE}}\right)^2 + \left\{K_M^2(i) + 2K_M(i) - K_M'(i)\right\}\widehat{\sigma}_{w_i}(\mathbf{x}_i)\right] \tag{2.96}$$

$$\mathrm{Var}\left(\widehat{\mathrm{ATET}}\right) = \frac{1}{N_1^2}\sum_{i=1}^{N}\left[D_i\left(\widehat{Y}_{1i} - \widehat{Y}_{0i} - \widehat{\mathrm{ATET}}\right)^2 + (1-D_i)\left\{K_M^2(i) - K_M'(i)\right\}\widehat{\sigma}_{D_i}(\mathbf{x}_i)\right] \tag{2.97}$$

$$\mathrm{Var}\left(\widehat{\mathrm{ATENT}}\right) = \frac{1}{N_0^2}\sum_{i=1}^{N}\left[(1-D_i)\left(\widehat{Y}_{1i} - \widehat{Y}_{0i} - \widehat{\mathrm{ATENT}}\right)^2\right.$$
$$\left. + D_i\left\{K_M^2(i) - K_M'(i)\right\}\widehat{\sigma}_{D_i}(\mathbf{x}_i)\right] \tag{2.98}$$

In order to estimate these variances, it is necessary to estimate consistently the conditional variance of the outcomes, $\sigma_{D_i}(\mathbf{x}_i) = \mathrm{Var}\left(Y_{ig}|D_i = g, X_i = \mathbf{x}_i\right)$ with

$g = 1,0$, using the available sample. ADHI (2004) distinguish between two cases: (1) the case in which this variance is constant for both the treatment and control group and for all values of $\mathbf{x}$ (*homoskedasticity*) and (2) the case in which it is not constant but may depend either on D or $\mathbf{x}$ (*heteroskedasticity*). The authors provide the formulas for both cases under the assumption of a *constant* treatment effect (i.e., $Y_{1i} - Y_{1i} = \alpha = $ constant).

It should be noted that it may be possible to use the previous formulas by considering the propensity-score as unique covariate. In this case, $k = 1$ and the previous formulas would return unbiased estimations. Nevertheless, those formulas do not take into account the fact that the propensity-score is estimated in the first step, so that they are not in principle "fully correct." As discussed, however, Abadie and Imbens (2012) have provided the correct formulas and estimation of the variances for the nearest-neighbor Matching when $k = 1$ and matching is done on a parametric estimation of the propensity-score. A Stata implementation for the latter case is available using the command `teffects psmatch`.

Although these important results, in many applications variances are still calculated using software which do not consider previous formulas. Normally, an approximation is assumed treating weights *as if* they are fixed scalars, so that standard results from Difference-in-means (DIM) estimation under randomization is exploited (although it might be incorrect). Starting from (2.84) to (2.86), this approximation assumes that if (1) CMI holds, (2) overlapping holds, and (3) $\{Y_{1i}; \mathbf{x}_i\}$ are i.i.d., then previous Matching estimators are consistent statistics for ATEs with a normal asymptotic distribution having mean zero and variance equal to:

$$\mathrm{Var}\left(\widehat{\mathrm{ATE}}\right) = \left(\frac{N_1}{N}\right)^2 \cdot \mathrm{Var}\left(\widehat{\mathrm{ATET}}\right) + \left(\frac{N_0}{N}\right)^2 \cdot \mathrm{Var}\left(\widehat{\mathrm{ATENT}}\right)$$

$$\mathrm{Var}\left(\widehat{\mathrm{ATET}}\right) = \frac{1}{N_1^2} \sum_{i \in \{D=1\}} \mathrm{Var}(Y_{1i}) + \frac{1}{N_1^2} \sum_{j \in \{D=0\}} h_{1j}^2 \mathrm{Var}(Y_{0j})$$

$$= \frac{1}{N_1^2}\left[N_1 \sigma_1 + \sigma_0 \sum_{j \in \{D=0\}} h_{1j}^2\right] = \frac{1}{N_1}\sigma_1 + \frac{1}{N_1^2}\sigma_0 \sum_{j \in \{D=0\}} h_{1j}^2$$

$$= \frac{1}{N_1}\sigma^2\left(1 + \frac{1}{N_1}\sum_{j \in \{D=0\}} h_{1j}^2\right) \tag{2.99}$$

$$\mathrm{Var}\left(\widehat{\mathrm{ATENT}}\right) = \frac{1}{N_0^2} \sum_{j \in \{D=1\}} h_{0j} \mathrm{Var}(Y_j) + \frac{1}{N_0^2} \sum_{i \in \{D=0\}} \mathrm{Var}(Y_i)$$

$$= \frac{1}{N_0^2}\sigma_1 \sum_{j \in \{D=1\}} h_{0j}^2 + \frac{1}{N_0}\sigma_0 = \frac{1}{N_0}\sigma\left(\frac{1}{N_0}\sum_{j \in \{D=1\}} h_{0j}^2 + 1\right)$$

where we have assumed that $\sigma_1 = \sigma_0 = \sigma$, since observations are i.i.d. (otherwise, treatment group heteroskedasticity can also be assumed and in this case $\sigma_1 \neq \sigma_0$).

Previous variances are thus used to perform usual inference tests on ATEs, once a common sample estimation of σ (or σ_1 and σ_0 in the heteroskedastic case) is computed and plugged-into (2.99).

As for kernel Matching, under specific conditions showed by HIT (1998) on the bandwidth and on the kernel function used, the estimator in (2.88) is a consistent estimation of ATET (and ATE and ATENT) and thus of the counterfactual outcomes. In particular, one needs to assume that $K(\cdot)$ has a zero mean and integrates to one and that h converges to zero as N and $N \cdot h$ go to infinity. Available software uses bootstrap techniques to obtain standard errors, although it has however been shown that bootstrapping may not be the correct technique to implement in the case of Matching (Abadie and Imbens 2008).

In the case of the stratification Matching, by assuming once again independence of outcomes across units (i.i.d.), the variance of the stratification Matching of ATEs is easily shown to be equal to:

$$\text{Var}\left(\widehat{\text{ATET}}\right) = \frac{1}{N_1}\left[\sigma_1 + \sum_{b=1}^{B} \frac{N_1^b N_1^b}{N_1 N_0^b}\sigma_0\right] \tag{2.100}$$

$$\text{Var}\left(\widehat{\text{ATENT}}\right) = \frac{1}{N_0}\left[\sum_{b=1}^{B} \frac{N_0^b N_0^b}{N_0 N_1^b}\sigma_1 + \sigma_0\right] \tag{2.101}$$

Once again, this is only an approximation of the true variance, as weights should not be considered as fixed. Unfortunately, to date, large sample properties for this matching estimator have to be provided yet. It is, however, useful to consider the previous formulas, as they emphasize that a penalty arises when an unequal number of treated and control units appears in a given stratum; if there is a stratum in which the number of controls is smaller than the number of treated, the variance increases, and the loss of efficiency is larger, the larger is the fraction of treated in that stratum. Observe that, if $N_1^b = N_0^b$, then:

$$\text{Var}\left(\widehat{\text{ATET}}\right) = \frac{1}{N_1}[\sigma_1 + \sigma_0] = \frac{2}{N_1}\sigma$$

$$\text{Var}\left(\widehat{\text{ATET}}\right) = \frac{1}{N_0}[\sigma_1 + \sigma_0] = \frac{2}{N_0}\sigma$$

$$\text{Var}\left(\widehat{\text{ATE}}\right) = \frac{2}{N}\sigma$$

Observe, finally, that one could obtain the outcomes within each stratum as predicted values from the estimation of linear (or more articulated) functions of the propensity-score. DW (1999) illustrated, however, that the gain from using this approach does not appear to be significant.

2.3.10   Assessing the Reliability of CMI by Sensitivity Analysis

Generally speaking, the aim of sensitivity analysis is that of assessing whether results obtained by applying a given estimation method are sufficiently reliable when the main assumptions under which the results are drawn may not be fully satisfied (Saltelli et al. 2008).

For observational studies invoking Conditional (Mean) Independence as in the case of Matching, sensitivity analysis is an important post-estimation practice for checking the robustness of treatment effects estimation when such an assumption can be questionable.

Rosenbaum (2002, 2005) provides a powerful sensitivity analysis test when Matching is used in observational studies. The aim of this test is that of assessing the reliability of ATEs estimations when unobservable selection (and thus "hidden bias") might be present.[5]

Suppose we have a set of S matched pairs derived from one-to-one nearest-neighbor Matching satisfying the balancing property. As such, two units (one treated and one untreated) forming a single matched pair are indistinguishable in terms of observables $\mathbf{x}$, and if no hidden bias is at work, they must have the same probability to be treated: in fact, the intent of propensity-score Matching is exactly that of matching units with the same probability to be treated, given $\mathbf{x}$. Nevertheless, if selection-into-program was due also to, let's say, one additional non-observable variable v, then two matched units should not have the same probability to be treated although balanced on observable variables.

By assuming a logistic distribution, two matching units i and j, having $\mathbf{x}_i = \mathbf{x}_j$, have the following odds ratio:

$$\frac{\frac{p_i}{1-p_i}}{\frac{p_j}{1-p_j}} = \frac{p_i(1-p_j)}{p_j(1-p_i)} = \frac{\exp(\mathbf{x}_i\boldsymbol{\beta} + \gamma v_i)}{\exp(\mathbf{x}_j\boldsymbol{\beta} + \gamma v_j)} = \exp\{\gamma(v_i - v_j)\} \qquad (2.102)$$

showing that, as soon as $v_i \neq v_j$, the two probabilities to be treated are different, actual balancing does not hold and a hidden bias arises. Suppose that v_i and v_j take values in the interval [0; 1] and that $\gamma \geq 0$. This implies that $-1 \leq v_i - v_j \leq 1$, so that the odds ratio is in turn bounded this way:

$$\frac{1}{e^\gamma} \leq \frac{p_i(1-p_j)}{p_j(1-p_i)} \leq e^\gamma \qquad (2.103)$$

---

[5] Stata implementations to deal with sensitivity analysis in observational studies under observable selection can be found in: Nannicini (2007), Becker and Caliendo (2007), DiPrete and Gangl (2004), and Gangl (2004).

where odds are equal only when $\gamma = 0$, that is when no hidden bias is present because unobservables have no effect on selection. Thus, given a positive value of γ, we can depict a situation in which the odds ratio is maximum (the best case) and one in which it is minimum (the worst case). This reflects the uncertainty due to the presence of an unobservable confounder. By putting $\Gamma = e^\gamma$, we can also say that in the presence of a potential hidden bias, one unit has an odds of treatment that is up to $\Gamma \geq 1$ times greater than the odds of another unit. When randomization is allowed, however, the odds ratio is equal to one by definition and $\Gamma = 1$.

Rosenbaum proposes a sensitivity analysis test based on the *Wilcoxon's signed rank* statistic. The procedure to calculate this statistic is quite straightforward. Consider S matched pairs, with $s = 1, \ldots, S$, where each pair is formed by one treated and one untreated unit. For each pair, calculate the treated-minus-control difference (DIM) in outcomes and call it D_s, thus getting the absolute differences $|D_s|$. Then, eliminate from the sample any absolute difference score taking value zero, thereby yielding a set of S' nonzero absolute differences, where $S' \leq S$ becomes the new sample size. Assign ranks R_s ranging from 1 to S' to each $|D_s|$, so that the smallest absolute difference gets rank 1 and the largest one rank S'. If ties occur, assign the average rank. The Wilcoxon test statistic W is obtained as the sum of the positive ranks:

$$W = \sum_{s=1}^{S'} R_s^+ \tag{2.104}$$

The Wilcoxon test statistic W varies from a minimum of 0—where all the observed differences are negative—to a maximum of $S'(S' - 1)/2$—where all the observed difference scores are positive. For a quite large randomized experiment and under the null hypothesis of equality in the two (treated and untreated) populations' medians (i.e., no-effect assumption), the W statistic is approximately normal distributed with mean equal to $S'(S' - 1)/4$ and variance $S'(S' + 1)(2S' + 1)/24$. If the null hypothesis is true, the test statistic W should take on a value approximately close to its mean. Rosenbaum, however, shows that for a quite large observational study, again under the null hypothesis of equality in the populations' medians, the distribution of W is approximately bounded between two normal distributions with the following expectations:

$$\mu_{\max} = \lambda S' \left(S' + 1 \right) \Big/ 2$$

$$\mu_{\min} = (1 - \lambda) S' \left(S' + 1 \right) \Big/ 2$$

and same variance:

$$\sigma_W^2 = \lambda (1 - \lambda) S' \left(S' + 1 \right) \left(2S' + 1 \right) \Big/ 6$$

where $\lambda = \Gamma/(1 + \Gamma)$. It is immediate to see that in the randomization case $\Gamma = 1$, the two formulas become the same and are equal to the case of randomized experiment.

Different levels of Γ (and thus of λ) modify the p-value of the W-test, thus producing uncertainty in the results. For $\Gamma \geq 2$, the p-value is bounded between a minimum and a maximum and one can use the upper bound to see up to which value of Γ the usual 5 % significance is maintained in the experiment.

Suppose we have implemented a one-to-one Matching and the calculated treatment effect is significant. Suppose we then test the robustness of this finding via the W-test and discover that the 5 % significance of the test is attained up to a value of $\Gamma = 5$. In this case, we can then trust our initial finding of a significant effect, as such a value of Γ is very high and thus unlikely: it should mean that the probability to be treated is five times higher for one unit than for another one, a situation that should be really rare in reality. If, on the contrary, for a value of Γ equal, let's say, to 1.2, the p-value upper bound of W is higher than 0.05, thus very slight departures from perfect randomization produce no significant results. In this case, we should be really careful in coming to a positive effect of the treatment.

2.3.11 Assessing Overlap

As suggested several times in previous sections, a good overlap of treated and control units over the covariates' support is required in order to obtain reliable estimates for ATEs. A question arises, however, how can we assess the goodness of overlap in a given dataset? Imbens and Rubin (forthcoming) suggest three types of overlap measures: (1) standardized difference in averages; (2) logarithm of the ratio of standard deviations; and (3) Frequency coverage.

(i) *Standardized difference in averages*

Consider a covariate x. The formula for computing standardized difference in averages is:

$$\frac{\bar{x}_1 - \bar{x}_0}{\sqrt{(s_1^2 + s_0^2)/2}}$$

where the numerator contains the difference of the means of x in the treated and control group and the denominator the squared root of the unweighted mean of the two variances. This measure is scale-free (it does not depend on the unit of measure of x), but it has the limit to refer to a specific moment of the distribution, the average.

(ii) *Logarithm of the ratio of standard deviations*

In addition to the previous approach, one may use a measure of the differences in the dispersion of the treated and control distribution over x, by computing the logarithm of the ratio of standard deviations:

$$\ln(s_1) - \ln(s_0)$$

This approach is straightforward, but it fails to take into account the overall shape of the two distributions.

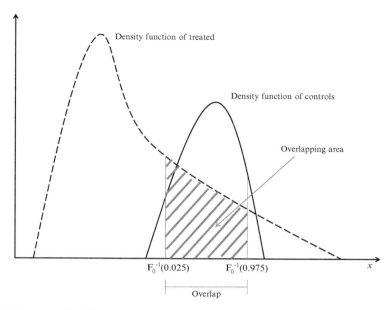

Fig. 2.7 An example of *frequency coverage* measure

(iii) *Frequency coverage*

   Local measures described above are useful but somewhat limited in their scope. A more reliable way to assess overlap is that of computing the share of the treated (control) units taking covariate values that are near the center of the distribution of the covariate values of the controls (treated). This can be achieved for either the treated or control units by employing the following formulas:

$$\pi_1^{0.95} = F_1\left\{F_0^{-1}(0.975)\right\} - F_1\left\{F_0^{-1}(0.025)\right\}$$
$$\pi_0^{0.95} = F_0\left\{F_1^{-1}(0.975)\right\} - F_0\left\{F_1^{-1}(0.025)\right\}$$

where $F_1(x)$ and $F_1(x)$ are the cumulative distribution functions for treated and untreated units, respectively; $F_1^{-1}(\alpha)$ and $F_0^{-1}(\alpha)$ are the α-th quintile of the treated and control units distribution, and $\pi_1^{0.95}$ and $\pi_0^{0.95}$ are the treated and untreated units' overlapping areas corresponding to a 95 % probability mass.

   Figure 2.7 (referring just to $\pi_1^{0.95}$) shows why previous measures can assess the degree of data overlap. The overlapping area drawn in the middle contains just a small share of the treated units' frequency. Most of the treated individuals have a value of x laying on the left of $F_0^{-1}(0.025)$, thus implying that a very large number of treated cannot find good control matches in that interval. As such, this figure entails that $\pi_1^{0.95}$ will be low and overlap for treated units weak. However, the opposite may happen for the control units, as in the same dataset, $\pi_0^{0.95}$ can be sufficiently large. In general, we have that:

$$0 \le \pi_g^{0.95} \le 0.95, \quad g = 1, 0$$

In the case of random assignment, one should have that $\pi_g^{0.95} \cong 0.95$, so that the higher this probability, the higher the overlap and the more reliable the ATEs estimation. An advantage of the frequency coverage measures is that of offering two distinct overlapping measures, one for treated and one for untreated units. A further useful tool for assessing overlap is the inspection and comparison of the various quintiles, plotting jointly the two distributions and doing a Kolmogorov–Smirnov test for the equality of distributions.

In a multivariate context, when many covariates are considered, we need, however, a synthetic measure of overlap. An overall summary measure of the difference in location of the two distributions may be:

$$\sqrt{(\bar{\mathbf{x}}_1 - \bar{\mathbf{x}}_0)'[(\Sigma_1 + \Sigma_0)/2]^{-1}(\bar{\mathbf{x}}_1 - \bar{\mathbf{x}}_0)}$$

where $\bar{\mathbf{x}}_1$ and $\bar{\mathbf{x}}_0$ are $M \times 1$ vectors of averages for the M covariates, and Σ_1 and Σ_0 are corresponding covariance matrices.

In a multivariate case, assessing overlap using the propensity-score, taken as a synthesis of the entire set of covariates, can also be a suitable and proper strategy. Instead of considering M dimensions, one can consider just one dimension, with significant advantages. Indeed, it is easy to see that: (1) any differences in the covariate distributions by treatment status involve variation in the propensity-score, and (2) a change in the propensity-score is equivalent to nonzero differences in average propensity-score values by treatment status. This is sufficient to allow for assessing overlap with one of the previous univariate method using the propensity-score as reference covariate.

2.3.12   Coarsened-Exact Matching

In this section, we discuss an alternative approach to standard Matching models, known as coarsened exact Matching (CEM), proposed by Blackwell et al. (2009). The basic idea behind CEM is that of allowing the analyst to choose ex ante the degree of the balancing of covariates, thus avoiding the necessity for its ex post assessment and repeatedly reestimating the propensity-score until balancing is satisfied. CEM aims to overcome such a laborious procedure.

We saw that, when covariates are continuous or discrete with high dimensionality, exact Matching is infeasible. One could, however, *discretize* continuous variables, as well as reduce the number of values that a discrete covariate can take. Such a procedure, which the authors call "coarsening mechanism," enables one to build a tractable number of cells by: crossing all covariates' values, deleting cells that do not contain at least one treated and one control unit, and estimating ATEs on the remaining cells (over a reduced number of either treated or untreated units). More specifically, the CEM algorithm is as follows:

1. *First*, start with the covariates $\mathbf{x}$ and generate a copy, which we indicate by $\mathbf{x}^c$.
2. *Second*, "coarsen" $\mathbf{x}^c$ according to user-defined cut points (the CEM's automatic binning algorithm can also be exploited).
3. *Third*, produce cells by crossing all values of $\mathbf{x}^c$ and place each observation in its corresponding cell.
4. *Fourth*, drop any observation whose cell does not contain at least one treated and one control unit.
5. *Fifth*, estimate ATEs by stratification Matching on the remaining cells (or, equivalently, run a WLS regression of Y on D using the remaining cells' weights).

It is clear that the CEM approach does not overcome the typical trade-off arising in Matching methods "with pruning": indeed, if one increases the level of coarsening (i.e., he chooses larger intervals), this will result in a lower number of cells. With fewer cells, however, it is highly more likely to observe observations with very diverse covariates. In other words, an increasing degree of coarsening is generally accompanied by higher imbalance in the covariates. In the opposite case, we have that reducing coarsening increases balancing, but it increases also the likelihood of finding cells which do not contain at least one treated and one control unit, thereby reducing sample size and estimation precision.

To assess CEM quality, Iacus et al. (2012) suggest to examine a specific measure of (global) imbalance:

$$L_1(f,g) = \frac{1}{2}\sum_{b=1}^{B} |f_b - g_b| \qquad (2.105)$$

where b indexes the generic cell; B is the number of cells produced by coarsening; f_b and g_b are the relative frequencies for the treated and control units within cell b, respectively. It is easy to see that a value of L_1 equal to zero signals perfect global balance; vice versa, the larger the L_1 is, the larger the extent of imbalance, until reaching a maximum of one which occurs when there is complete separation of treated and control units in each cell.

The authors suggest to take the value of L_1 obtained after coarsening (but without trimming) as a benchmark to be compared with the value of L_1 obtained when observations with cells not containing at least one treated and one control unit are dropped (trimming). By calling the first $L_{1,\text{unmtach}}$ and the second $L_{1,\text{match}}$, we expect that CEM has worked well if:

$$L_{1,\text{match}} \leq L_{1,\text{unmtach}}$$

i.e., if some improvement in balancing occurs. Of course, both values of L_1 in the previous inequality will depend on the cut points chosen. Such a choice—similar to fixing the caliper in the radius Marching—can be either theoretically or heuristically driven.

In conclusion, in order to obtain reliable estimates from CEM, one needs to find a good compromise between the reduction of the imbalance achieved using CEM on the one hand and the size of the sample obtained by deleting nonmatched cells, on the other hand.

It is worthwhile noting that the ATEs' standard errors obtained in the last-step WLS regression take weights as fixed numbers, while they are subject to sampling randomness. This implies—as in previous Matching methods—that the CEM standard errors are not fully correct and should be taken just as approximations of the actual ones.

2.4 Reweighting

Reweighting represents a large class of estimators of ATEs and is a powerful approach to estimate (binary) treatment effects in a nonexperimental setting when units' nonrandom assignment to treatment is due to observable selection. As such, Reweighting can be seen as an alternative option to previously discussed estimation approaches, although we will illustrate that, in many regards, previous methods and Reweighting are strictly linked.

Early developments and applications of Reweighting date back to the 1950s with the works of Daniel G. Horvitz and Donovan J. Thompson who derived an inverse-probability weighting estimator of totals and means for accounting for different proportions of observations within strata in finite populations. As will be shown, such an estimator can be also employed in program evaluation econometrics without substantial changes.

This section provides an introduction to this subject. We set out by showing the link between Reweighting and Weighted least squares (WLS) in estimating ATEs; subsequently, we discuss a specific Reweighting estimator, the one based on the propensity-score inverse-probability; Finally, we show how to obtain correct analytical standard errors for such an estimator when it is assumed that the propensity-score is correctly specified.

2.4.1 Reweighting and Weighted Least Squares

The idea behind the reweighting estimation procedure is quite straightforward; when the treatment is not randomly assigned, we expect that the treated and untreated units present very different distributions of their observable characteristics. As seen in Chap. 1, this may happen either because of the units' self-selection into the experiment or because the selection process is operated by an external entity (such as, for instance, a public agency). Many examples of such a situation can be drawn both from socioeconomic and epidemiological contexts.

If this is the case, the distribution of the variables feeding into **x** could be strongly unbalanced. To reestablish some balance in the covariates' distributions, a suitable way could be that of weighting the observations by suitable weights and then using a Weighted least squares (WLS) framework to estimate the ATEs. As such, the WLS framework can also be seen as a generalized approach to ATEs estimation under selection on observables. Indeed, it can be proved that both Matching and Reweighting estimators can be retrieved as the coefficient of the treatment indicator D in a weighted regression, where different weighting functions are considered.

A general formula for the Reweighting estimator of ATEs takes the following form:

$$\widehat{\text{ATE}} = \frac{1}{N_1}\sum_{i=1}^{N} \omega_1(i) \cdot D_i \cdot Y_i - \frac{1}{N_0}\sum_{j=1}^{N} (1 - D_j) \cdot \omega_0(j) \cdot Y_j \qquad (2.106)$$

$$\widehat{\text{ATET}} = \frac{1}{N_1}\sum_{i=1}^{N} D_i \cdot Y_i - \frac{1}{N_0}\sum_{j=1}^{N} (1 - D_j) \cdot \omega(j) \cdot Y_j \qquad (2.107)$$

$$\widehat{\text{ATENT}} = \frac{1}{N_0}\left(N \cdot \widehat{\text{ATE}} - N_1 \cdot \widehat{\text{ATET}}\right) \qquad (2.108)$$

where the weights $\omega_0(\cdot)$ and $\omega_1(\cdot)$ in previous equations add to one in specific cases only. As for ATET, when the weights add to one, we have that:

$$\frac{1}{N_0}\sum_{j=1}^{N} (1 - D_j) \cdot \omega(j) = 1$$

The Reweighting estimator of ATET can be obtained as the coefficient of the binary treatment D in a regression of the outcome Y on a constant and D using:

$$W = D + (1 - D) \cdot \omega(\cdot)$$

as weights. Likewise, if the weights $\omega_0(\cdot)$ and $\omega_1(\cdot)$ add to one, that is:

$$\frac{1}{N_0}\sum_{j=1}^{N} (1 - D_j) \cdot \omega_0(j) = 1 \quad \text{and} \quad \frac{1}{N_1}\sum_{j=1}^{N} D_j \cdot \omega_1(j) = 1$$

then it can be showed that the Reweighting estimation of ATE can be obtained by the same previous regression with weights equal to:

$$W = D \cdot \omega_1(\cdot) + (1 - D) \cdot \omega_0(\cdot)$$

If weights do not add to one, then one can retrieve the estimations of ATEs by directly implementing the previous formulas. The advantage of relying on a WLS framework is that standard errors for the Reweighting estimates of ATEs are directly obtained by the regression analysis. Interestingly, one can notice that the usual DIM estimator of standard statistics can be interpreted as a Reweighting estimator where $\omega(j) = 1$, that is:

$$\widehat{\text{DIM}} = \frac{1}{N_1}\sum_{i=1}^{N}D_i \cdot Y_i - \frac{1}{N_0}\sum_{j=1}^{N}\left(1 - D_j\right) \cdot Y_j$$

where, of course, $(1/N_1)\sum_{i=1}^{N}D_i = (1/N_0)\sum_{j=1}^{N}\left(1 - D_j\right) = 1$, and the DIM is simply obtained by an OLS regression of Y on D.

It appears worthwhile briefly commenting on the contents of Table 2.4 illustrating a number of weighting functions generally used in applications. The IPW_1 is a popular weighting function provided by Rosenbaum and Rubin (1983) and considered in Dehejia and Wahba (1999), Wooldridge (2010), and Hirano et al. (2003). When referring to Reweighting estimators, many scholars refer to IPW_1. This estimator has a number of interesting properties which will be discussed in more depth in the following section. The drawback of IPW_1 is that its weights do not add to one, thus WLS regression is not feasible. Johnston and DiNardo (1996) and Imbens (2004) have therefore proposed the IPW_2 function which, by rescaling weights in IPW_1 so as to add to one, allows one to estimate ATEs by WLS and thus obtain standard errors. Finally, weights for IPW_3 have been derived by Lunceford and Davidian (2004), but they are rarely used in the evaluation literature.

Interestingly, Matching estimators of ATEs can be seen as peculiar Reweighting estimators, and thus performed by WLS (Busso et al. 2009). By taking the case of ATET, in fact, we can show that:

$$\widehat{\text{ATET}}_{\text{Matching}} = \frac{1}{N_1}\sum_{i\in\{D=1\}}\left(Y_i - \sum_{j\in C(i)}h(i,j)Y_j\right)$$

$$= \frac{1}{N_1}\sum_{i=1}^{N}D_iY_i - \sum_{j=1}^{N}\left(1 - D_j\right)Y_j\frac{1}{N_1}\sum_{i=1}^{N}D_ih(i,j)$$

$$= \frac{1}{N_1}\sum_{i=1}^{N}D_iy_i - \frac{1}{N_0}\sum_{j=1}^{N}\left(1 - D_j\right)Y_j\omega(j) = \widehat{\text{ATET}}_{\text{Reweighting}}$$

where $\omega(j) = (N_0/N_1)\sum_{i=1}^{N}D_ih(i,j)$ are reweighting factors, $C(i)$ is the untreated units' neighborhood for the treated unit i, and $h(i,j)$ are matching weights that— once appropriately specified—produce different types of Matching methods. A valuable aspect of this version of the Matching estimator is that it can be directly estimated by WLS, as we can show that:

Table 2.4 A number of weighting functions generally used in applications

	ATET	ATE	
	ω	ω_0	ω_0
IPW$_1$	$\dfrac{p(\mathbf{x}_j)}{1-p(\mathbf{x}_j)}\Big/\dfrac{p}{1-p}$	$\dfrac{1-p}{1-p(\mathbf{x}_j)}$	$\dfrac{p}{1-p(\mathbf{x}_j)}$
IPW$_2$	$\dfrac{\frac{p(\mathbf{x}_j)}{1-p(\mathbf{x}_j)}}{\frac{1}{N_0}\sum_{j=1}^{N}\frac{(1-D_j)\,p(\mathbf{x}_j)}{1-p(\mathbf{x}_j)}}$	$\dfrac{\frac{1}{1-p(\mathbf{x}_j)}}{\frac{1}{N_0}\sum_{j=1}^{N}\frac{1-D_j}{1-p(\mathbf{x}_j)}}$	$\dfrac{\frac{1}{p(\mathbf{x}_j)}}{\frac{1}{N_1}\sum_{j=1}^{N}\frac{D_j}{p(\mathbf{x}_j)}}$
IPW$_3$	$\dfrac{\frac{p(\mathbf{x}_j)}{1-p(\mathbf{x}_j)}\left(1-C_j\right)}{\frac{1}{N_0}\sum_{j=1}^{N}\frac{(1-D_j)\,p(\mathbf{x}_j)}{1-p(\mathbf{x}_j)}\left(1-C_j\right)}$	$\dfrac{\frac{1}{1-p(\mathbf{x}_j)}\left(1-C_j^0\right)}{\frac{1}{N_0}\sum_{j=1}^{N}\frac{1-D_j}{1-p(\mathbf{x}_j)}\left(1-C_j^0\right)}$	$\dfrac{\frac{1}{p(\mathbf{x}_j)}\left(1-C^1\right)}{\frac{1}{N_1}\sum_{j=1}^{N}\frac{D_j}{p(\mathbf{x}_j)}\left(1-C_j^1\right)}$

$$p=\frac{N_1}{N},\quad A_i=\frac{1-D_i}{1-p(\mathbf{x}_i)},\quad B_i=\frac{D_i}{p(\mathbf{x}_i)},\quad C_i=\frac{\left(1-\frac{p(\mathbf{x}_j)}{p}A_i\right)\frac{1}{N}\sum_{j=1}^{N}\left(1-\frac{p(\mathbf{x}_j)}{p}A_j\right)}{\frac{1}{N}\sum_{j=1}^{N}\left(1-\frac{p(\mathbf{x}_j)}{p}A_j\right)^2}$$

$$C_i^0=\frac{\left(\frac{1}{1-p(\mathbf{x}_j)}\right)\frac{1}{N}\sum_{j=1}^{N}\left(A_j p(\mathbf{x}_j)-D_i\right)}{\frac{1}{N}\sum_{j=1}^{N}\left(A_j p(\mathbf{x}_j)-D_i\right)^2},\quad C_i^1=\frac{\left(\frac{1}{p(\mathbf{x}_j)}\right)\frac{1}{N}\sum_{j=1}^{N}\left(B_j(1-p(\mathbf{x}_j))-(1-D_i)\right)}{\frac{1}{N}\sum_{j=1}^{N}\left(B_j(1-p(\mathbf{x}_j))-(1-D_i)\right)^2}$$

Source: Busso et al. (2009)

$$\frac{1}{N_0}\sum_{j=1}^{N}(1-D_j)\omega(j) = \frac{1}{N_0}\sum_{j=1}^{N}\left\{(1-D_j)\left[\frac{N_0}{N_1}\sum_{i=1}^{N}D_ih(i,j)\right]\right\}$$

$$= \frac{1}{N_1}\sum_{i=1}^{N}\left\{D_i\left[\sum_{j\in C(i)}h(i,j)\right]\right\} = \frac{1}{N_1}\sum_{i=1}^{N}D_i = 1$$

since $\sum_{j\in C(i)}h(i,j) = 1$ being $h(i,j)=1/N_{C(i)}$ so that $\sum_{j\in C(i)}h(i,j) = (1/N_{C(i)})\sum_{j\in C(i)}1 = (N_{C(i)}/N_{C(i)}) = 1$.

In the case of kernel Matching, a similar result can be achieved, since in that case:

$$\omega(j) = \frac{N_0}{N_1}\sum_{i=1}^{N}D_ih(i,j) = \frac{\sum_{i=1}^{N}D_iK_{ij}\Big/\sum_{i=1}^{N}D_iK_{ij}}{\sum_{i=1}^{N}(1-D_i)K_{ij}\Big/\sum_{i=1}^{N}D_iK_{ij}}\Big/\frac{p}{1-p}.$$

Thus, a possible Reweighting estimation protocol for ATET is as follows:

1. Estimate the propensity-score (based on **x**) by a logit or a probit to obtain the predicated probability p_i.
2. Given a chosen specification of $\omega(\cdot)$, build regression weights as:

$$W_i = D_i + (1-D_i)\cdot\omega(i)$$

3. If weights satisfy (at least approximately) the property of summing to one, run a WLS regression of the outcome Y_i on a constant and D_i using W_i as regression weights.
4. The coefficient of the binary treatment D in the previous regression is a consistent estimation of ATET, provided that the propensity-score is correctly specified.

This Reweighting procedure is a generalization of the popular *inverse-probability regression* (Robins et al. 2000; Brunell and Dinardo 2004), and the intuitive idea is that of penalizing (advantaging) treated units with higher (lower) probability to be treated and advantaging (penalizing) untreated units with higher (lower) probability to be treated, thus rendering the two groups as similar as possible. In this simplistic case, the previous procedure becomes:

1. Estimate the propensity-score (based on **x**) by a logit or a probit getting the predicated probability p_i;
2. Build weights as $1/p_i$ for the treated observations, and $1/(1-p_i)$ for the untreated observations.
3. Calculate the ATE simply by a comparison of the weighted means of the two groups (this is what indeed the *weighted regression* does).

For each observation, the weight eliminates a component induced by the extent of the nonrandom assignment to the program (a confounding element).

Compared with previous approaches, Reweighting estimators have the very attractive advantage that they do not require one to estimate the regression functions $m_0(\mathbf{x})$ and $m_1(\mathbf{x})$, but they provide estimations of ATEs only by relying on an estimation of $p(\mathbf{x})$, the propensity-score. This advantage may also be somewhat a limitation, as Reweighting estimators are very sensitive to the specification of the propensity-score, so that measurement errors in this specification could produce severe bias.

As such, this approach relies on the assumption that the propensity-score specification is correctly estimated. This means that the Reweighting approach can be inconsistent either if the specification of the explanatory variables is incorrect or the parametric probit/logit approach does not properly explain the conditional probability of becoming treated.

Due to its popularity, the next section provides a more detailed treatment of Reweighting under IPW_1, showing how to obtain correct standard errors. This seems relevant as weights for IPW_1 do not add to one.

2.4.2 Reweighting on the Propensity-Score Inverse-Probability

In what follows, we focus on type 1 Reweighting on propensity-score inverse-probability (IPW_1) as proposed in the seminal paper by Rosenbaum and Rubin (1983). In this case, we start with the following assumptions about the data generating process (DGP)[6]:

$$
\begin{cases}
Y_1 = g_0(\mathbf{x}) + e_0, & E(e_0) = 0 \\
Y_0 = g_1(\mathbf{x}) + e_1, & E(e_1) = 0 \\
Y = DY_1 + Y_0(1 - D) \\
\text{CMI} \\
0 < p(\mathbf{x}) < 1 \\
\mathbf{x}\,\text{exogenous}
\end{cases}
\tag{2.109}
$$

where Y_1 and Y_0 are the unit's outcomes when it is treated and untreated, respectively; $g_1(\mathbf{x})$ and $g_0(\mathbf{x})$ are the unit's reaction functions to the confounder $\mathbf{x}$ when the unit is, respectively, treated and untreated; e_0 and e_1 are two errors with unconditional zero mean; $\mathbf{x}$ is a set of observable exogenous confounding variables assumed to drive the nonrandom assignment into treatment. It can be proved that, when assumptions in (2.109) hold, then:

---

[6] As reminder, we consider the following version of the Law of Iterated Expectations: LIE1: $E_y(Y) = \mu_Y = E_\mathbf{x}[E_y(Y/\mathbf{x})]$; LIE2: $E_y(Y \mid \mathbf{x}) = \mu_2(\mathbf{x}) = E_\mathbf{z}[E_y(Y \mid \mathbf{x}, \mathbf{z}) \mid \mathbf{x}] = E_\mathbf{z}[\mu_1(\mathbf{x}, \mathbf{z}) \mid \mathbf{x}]$; LIE3: $E(h) = p_1 \cdot E(h \mid \mathbf{x}_1) + p_2 \cdot E(h \mid \mathbf{x}_2) + \cdots + p_M \cdot E(h \mid \mathbf{x}_M)$.

$$\text{ATE} = \text{E}\left\{\frac{[D - p(\mathbf{x})]Y}{p(\mathbf{x})[1 - p(\mathbf{x})]}\right\} \tag{2.110}$$

$$\text{ATET} = \text{E}\left\{\frac{[D - p(\mathbf{x})]Y}{p(D = 1)[1 - p(\mathbf{x})]}\right\} \tag{2.111}$$

$$\text{ATENT} = \text{E}\left\{\frac{[D - p(\mathbf{x})]Y}{p(D = 0)p(\mathbf{x})}\right\} \tag{2.112}$$

To this purpose, observe first that: $DY = D[DY_1 + Y_0 \ (1 - D)] = D^2 Y_1 + DY_0 - D^2 Y_0 = DY_1$, since $D^2 = D$. Thus:

$$\text{E}\left[\frac{DY}{p(\mathbf{x})}|\mathbf{x}\right] = \text{E}\left[\frac{DY_1}{p(\mathbf{x})}|\mathbf{x}\right] \overset{\text{LIE2}}{=} \text{E}\left\{\text{E}\left[\frac{DY_1}{p(\mathbf{x})}|\mathbf{x}, D\right]|\mathbf{x}\right\}$$

$$= \text{E}\left\{\frac{DE(Y_1|\mathbf{x}, D)}{p(\mathbf{x})}|\mathbf{x}\right\} \overset{\text{CMI}}{=} \text{E}\left\{\frac{DE(Y_1|\mathbf{x})}{p(\mathbf{x})}|\mathbf{x}\right\}$$

$$= \text{E}\left\{\frac{Dg_1(\mathbf{x})}{p(\mathbf{x})}|\mathbf{x}\right\} = g_1(\mathbf{x}) \cdot \text{E}\left\{\frac{D}{p(\mathbf{x})}|\mathbf{x}\right\} = \frac{g_1(\mathbf{x})}{p(\mathbf{x})} \cdot \text{E}\{D|\mathbf{x}\}$$

$$= \frac{g_1(\mathbf{x})}{p(\mathbf{x})} \cdot p(\mathbf{x}) = g_1(\mathbf{x}) \tag{2.113}$$

since: $\text{E}(D \mid \mathbf{x}) = p(\mathbf{x})$. Similarly, we can show that:

$$\text{E}\left[\frac{(1 - D)Y}{[1 - p(\mathbf{x})]}|\mathbf{x}\right] = g_0(\mathbf{x}) \tag{2.114}$$

Combining (2.113) and (2.114), we have that:

$$\text{ATE}(\mathbf{x}) = g_1(\mathbf{x}) - g_0(\mathbf{x}) = \text{E}\left[\frac{DY}{p(\mathbf{x})}|\mathbf{x}\right] - \text{E}\left[\frac{(1 - D)Y}{[1 - p(\mathbf{x})]}|\mathbf{x}\right]$$

$$= \text{E}\left[\frac{[D - p(\mathbf{x})]Y}{p(\mathbf{x})[1 - p(\mathbf{x})]}|\mathbf{x}\right] \tag{2.115}$$

provided that $0 < p(\mathbf{x}) < 1$. In order to obtain the ATE, it is sufficient to take the expectation over $\mathbf{x}$:

$$\text{ATE} = \text{E}_{\mathbf{x}}\{\text{ATE}(\mathbf{x})\} = \text{E}_{\mathbf{x}}\text{E}\left[\frac{[D - p(\mathbf{x})]Y}{p(\mathbf{x})[1 - p(\mathbf{x})]}|\mathbf{x}\right] = \text{E}\left[\frac{[D - p(\mathbf{x})]Y}{p(\mathbf{x})[1 - p(\mathbf{x})]}\right] \tag{2.116}$$

It is interesting to show that the previous formula for ATE is equal to the famous Horvitz and Thompson (1952) estimator of the population mean. Indeed:

Table 2.5 Dataset coming from a nonexperimental statistical setting

id	Y	D	Inclusion probability
1	y_1	1	$\pi_1 = p_1(\mathbf{x})$
2	y_2	0	$\pi_2 = 1 - p_2(\mathbf{x})$
3	y_3	1	$\pi_3 = p_3(\mathbf{x})$
4	y_4	1	$\pi_4 = p_4(\mathbf{x})$
5	y_5	0	$\pi_5 = 1 - p_5(\mathbf{x})$

$$
\begin{aligned}
\text{ATE} &= \mathrm{E}\left[\frac{[D - p(\mathbf{x})]Y}{p(\mathbf{x})[1 - p(\mathbf{x})]}\right] = \mathrm{E}\left[\frac{DY - p(\mathbf{x})Y + [p(\mathbf{x})DY - p(\mathbf{x})DY]}{p(\mathbf{x})[1 - p(\mathbf{x})]}\right] \\
&= \mathrm{E}\left[\frac{p(\mathbf{x})DY}{p(\mathbf{x})[1 - p(\mathbf{x})]} + \frac{DY[1 - p(\mathbf{x})]}{p(\mathbf{x})[1 - p(\mathbf{x})]} - \frac{p(\mathbf{x})Y}{p(\mathbf{x})[1 - p(\mathbf{x})]}\right] \\
&= \mathrm{E}\left[\frac{DY}{1 - p(\mathbf{x})} + \frac{DY}{p(\mathbf{x})} - \frac{Y}{1 - p(\mathbf{x})}\right] = \mathrm{E}\left[\frac{DY - Y}{1 - p(\mathbf{x})} + \frac{DY}{p(\mathbf{x})}\right] \\
&= \mathrm{E}\left[\frac{DY}{p(\mathbf{x})} - \frac{Y - DY}{1 - p(\mathbf{x})}\right] = \mathrm{E}\left[\frac{DY}{p(\mathbf{x})} - \frac{(1 - D)Y}{1 - p(\mathbf{x})}\right] = \mathrm{E}\left[\frac{DY}{p(\mathbf{x})}\right] - \mathrm{E}\left[\frac{(1 - D)Y}{1 - p(\mathbf{x})}\right]
\end{aligned}
$$

Thus, by summing, we obtain:

$$
\text{ATE} = \mathrm{E}\left[\frac{DY}{p(\mathbf{x})}\right] - \mathrm{E}\left[\frac{(1 - D)Y}{1 - p(\mathbf{x})}\right] \tag{2.117}
$$

whose sample equivalent is:

$$
\widehat{\text{ATE}} = \frac{1}{N}\sum_{i=1}^{N}\frac{D_i Y_i}{p(\mathbf{x}_i)} - \sum_{i=1}^{N}\frac{(1 - D_i)Y_i}{1 - p_i(\mathbf{x})} \tag{2.118}
$$

This can be easily seen through the following example. Suppose we have a dataset with variables $\{Y, D, \mathbf{x}\}$ as described in Table 2.5.

If we define the *inclusion probability* of unit i into the sample S as:

$$
\pi_i = \Pr\{i \in S\}
$$

it is immediate to see that:

- For *treated* units, the inclusion probability is equal to the propensity-score: $p(D = 1 \mid \mathbf{x})$;
- For *untreated* units, the inclusion probability is equal to: $p(D = 0 \mid \mathbf{x}) = 1 - p(D = 1 \mid \mathbf{x})$.

Thus, applying formula (2.118), we have:

$$
\begin{aligned}
\widehat{ATE} &= \frac{1}{5}\left[\frac{y_1}{p(\mathbf{x}_1)} + \frac{y_3}{p(\mathbf{x}_3)} + \frac{y_4}{p(\mathbf{x}_4)}\right] - \frac{1}{5}\left[\frac{y_2}{1-p(\mathbf{x}_2)} + \frac{y_5}{1-p(\mathbf{x}_5)}\right]\\
&= \frac{1}{5}\left[\frac{y_1}{p(\mathbf{x}_1)} + \frac{y_3}{p(\mathbf{x}_3)} + \frac{y_4}{p(\mathbf{x}_4)} + \frac{y_2}{1-p(\mathbf{x}_2)} + \frac{y_5}{1-p(\mathbf{x}_5)}\right]\\
&= \frac{1}{5}\left[\frac{y_1}{p(\mathbf{x}_1)} + \frac{y_2}{1-p(\mathbf{x}_2)} + \frac{y_3}{p(\mathbf{x}_3)} + \frac{y_4}{p(\mathbf{x}_4)} + \frac{y_5}{1-p(\mathbf{x}_5)}\right]\\
&= \frac{1}{5}\left[\frac{y_1}{\pi_1} + \frac{y_2}{\pi_2} + \frac{y_3}{\pi_3} + \frac{y_4}{\pi_4} + \frac{y_5}{\pi_5}\right] = \frac{1}{5}\sum_{i=1}^{5}\frac{y_i}{\pi_i}
\end{aligned}
\tag{2.119}
$$

Thus, we have proved that:

$$
\widehat{ATE} = \hat{\mu}_{HT} = \frac{1}{N}\sum_{i=1}^{N}\frac{y_i}{\pi_i}
\tag{2.120}
$$

The inverse-probability Reweighting estimation of ATE is thus equivalent to the Horvitz–Thompson estimator. As said previously, in sampling theory, it is a general method for estimating the total and mean of finite populations when samples are drawn without replacement and units have unequal selection probabilities.

Similarly, we can also calculate the ATET by considering that:

$$
\begin{aligned}
[D - p(\mathbf{x})]Y &= [D - p(\mathbf{x})]\\
&\quad\cdot[Y_0 + D\cdot(Y_1 - Y_0) = D - p(\mathbf{x})\cdot Y_0 + D\cdot D - p(\mathbf{x})]\\
&\quad\cdot(Y_1 - Y_0)\\
&= [D - p(\mathbf{x})]\cdot Y_0 + D\cdot[1 - p(\mathbf{x})]\cdot(Y_1 - Y_0)
\end{aligned}
$$

since $D^2 = D$. Thus, dividing the previous expression by $[1 - p(\mathbf{x})]$:

$$
\frac{[D - p(\mathbf{x})]Y}{[1 - p(\mathbf{x})]} = \frac{[D - p(\mathbf{x})]Y_0}{[1 - p(\mathbf{x})]} + D(Y_1 - Y_0)
\tag{2.121}
$$

Consider now the quantity $[D - p(\mathbf{x})]Y_0$ in the RHS of (2.121). We have that:

$$
\begin{aligned}
[D - p(\mathbf{x})]Y_0 &= E\{[D - p(\mathbf{x})]Y_0|\mathbf{x}\} = E\big(E\{[D - p(\mathbf{x})]Y_0|\mathbf{x},D\}|\mathbf{x}\big)\\
&= E\big([D - p(\mathbf{x})]\cdot E\{Y_0|\mathbf{x},D\}|\mathbf{x}\big) = E\big([D - p(\mathbf{x})]\cdot E\{Y_0|\mathbf{x}\}|\mathbf{x}\big)\\
&= E\big([D - p(\mathbf{x})]\cdot g_0(\mathbf{x})|\mathbf{x}\big) = g_0(\mathbf{x})\cdot E\big([D - p(\mathbf{x})]|\mathbf{x}\big)\\
&= g_0(\mathbf{x})\cdot\big[E(D|\mathbf{x}) - E(p(\mathbf{x})|\mathbf{x})\big] = g_0(\mathbf{x})\cdot[p(\mathbf{x}) - p(\mathbf{x})] = 0.
\end{aligned}
$$

Taking relation (2.121) and applying the expectation conditional on $\mathbf{x}$, we get:

$$\mathrm{E}\left\{\frac{[D-p(\mathbf{x})]Y}{[1-p(\mathbf{x})]}\Big|\mathbf{x}\right\} = \mathrm{E}\left\{\frac{[D-p(\mathbf{x})]Y_0}{[1-p(\mathbf{x})]}\Big|\mathbf{x}\right\} + \mathrm{E}\{D(Y_1-Y_0)|\mathbf{x}\}$$
$$= \mathrm{E}\{D(Y_1-Y_0)|\mathbf{x}\}$$

since we have shown that $[D-p(\mathbf{x})]Y_0$ is zero. By LIE, we obtain that:

$$\begin{cases} \mathrm{E}_{\mathbf{x}}\mathrm{E}\left\{\dfrac{[D-p(\mathbf{x})]Y}{[1-p(\mathbf{x})]}\Big|\mathbf{x}\right\} & = \mathrm{E}\left\{\dfrac{[D-p(\mathbf{x})]Y}{[1-p(\mathbf{x})]}\right\} \\ \mathrm{E}_{\mathbf{x}}\mathrm{E}\{D(Y_1-Y_0)|\mathbf{x}\} & = \mathrm{E}\{D(Y_1-Y_0)\} \end{cases}$$

In other words:

$$\mathrm{E}\left\{\frac{[D-p(\mathbf{x})]Y}{[1-p(\mathbf{x})]}\right\} = \mathrm{E}\{D(Y_1-Y_0)\}$$

From LIE we know that if x is a generic discrete variable assuming values $x=(x_1, x_2, \ldots, x_M)$ with probabilities $p=(p_1, p_2, \ldots, p_M)$, then $\mathrm{E}(h)=p_1 \cdot \mathrm{E}(h \mid x_1)+p_2 \cdot \mathrm{E}(h \mid x_2)+\cdots+p_M \cdot \mathrm{E}(h \mid x_M)$. Thus, by assuming $h=D(Y_1-Y_0)$, we obtain that: $\mathrm{E}(h)=\mathrm{E}[D(Y_1-Y_0)]=p(D=1) \cdot \mathrm{E}[D(Y_1-Y_0) \mid D=1]+p(D=0) \cdot \mathrm{E}[D(Y_1-Y_0) \mid D=0]=p(D=1) \cdot \mathrm{E}[(Y_1-Y_0) \mid D=1]=p(D=1) \cdot \text{ATET}$. Thus:

$$\mathrm{E}\left\{\frac{[D-p(\mathbf{x})]Y}{[1-p(\mathbf{x})]}\right\} = \mathrm{E}\{D(Y_1-Y_0)\} = p(D=1) \cdot \text{ATET}$$

proving that:

$$\text{ATET} = \mathrm{E}\left\{\frac{[D-p(\mathbf{x})]Y}{p(D=1)[1-p(\mathbf{x})]}\right\} \tag{2.122}$$

Recall that: $\text{ATE}=p(D=1)\cdot\text{ATET}+p(D=0)\cdot\text{ATENT}$, thus:

$$\text{ATENT} = \frac{\text{ATE}}{p(D=0)} - \frac{p(D=1)}{p(D=0)}\text{ATET} =$$
$$= \frac{1}{p(D=0)}\mathrm{E}\left\{\frac{[D-p(\mathbf{x})]Y}{p(\mathbf{x})[1-p(\mathbf{x})]} - p(D=1)\frac{[D-p(\mathbf{x})]Y}{p(D=1)[1-p(\mathbf{x})]}\right\} =$$
$$= \frac{1}{p(D=0)}\mathrm{E}\left\{\frac{[D-p(\mathbf{x})]Y}{p(\mathbf{x})[1-p(\mathbf{x})]} - \frac{[D-p(\mathbf{x})]Y}{[1-p(\mathbf{x})]}\right\}$$
$$= \frac{1}{p(D=0)}\mathrm{E}\left\{\frac{[D-p(\mathbf{x})]Y-p(\mathbf{x})[D-p(\mathbf{x})]Y}{p(\mathbf{x})[1-p(\mathbf{x})]}\right\} =$$
$$= \frac{1}{p(D=0)}\mathrm{E}\left\{\frac{[D-p(\mathbf{x})]Y[1-p(\mathbf{x})]}{p(\mathbf{x})[1-p(\mathbf{x})]}\right\} = \frac{1}{p(D=0)}\mathrm{E}\left\{\frac{[D-p(\mathbf{x})]Y}{p(\mathbf{x})}\right\} =$$
$$= \mathrm{E}\left\{\frac{[D-p(\mathbf{x})]Y}{p(D=0)p(\mathbf{x})}\right\}$$

This implies, finally, that:

$$\text{ATENT} \ = \ \mathrm{E}\left\{\frac{[D - p(\mathbf{x})]Y}{p(D = 0)\,p(\mathbf{x})]}\right\} \tag{2.123}$$

2.4.3   Sample Estimation and Standard Errors for ATEs

Assuming that the propensity-score is *correctly specified*, we can estimate previous parameters simply by using the "sample equivalent" of the population parameters, that is:

$$\widehat{\text{ATE}} \ = \ \frac{1}{N}\sum_{i=1}^{N}\frac{[D_i - \widehat{p}\,(\mathbf{x}_i)]Y_i}{\widehat{p}\,(\mathbf{x}_i)\left[1 - \widehat{p}\,(\mathbf{x}_i)\right]}] \tag{2.124}$$

$$\widehat{\text{ATET}} = \ \frac{1}{N}\sum_{i=1}^{N}\frac{[D_i - \widehat{p}\,(\mathbf{x}_i)]Y_i}{\widehat{p}\,(D = 1)[1 - \widehat{p}_i(\mathbf{x})]} \tag{2.125}$$

$$\widehat{\text{ATENT}} \ = \ \frac{1}{N}\sum_{i=1}^{N}\frac{[D_i - \widehat{p}_i(\mathbf{x}_i)]Y_i}{\widehat{p}\,(D = 0)\,\widehat{p}\,(\mathbf{x}_i)} \tag{2.126}$$

The estimation is a two-step procedure: (1) first, estimate the propensity-score $p(\mathbf{x}_i)$ getting $\widehat{p}\,(\mathbf{x}_i)$; (2) second, substitute $\widehat{p}\,(\mathbf{x}_i)$ into the formulas to get the parameter estimation. Observe that consistency is guaranteed by the fact that these estimators are M-estimators. In order to obtain the standard errors for these estimations, we exploit the fact that the first step is an ML-estimation and the second step an M-estimation. In our case, the first step is an ML based on logit or probit, and the second step is a standard M-estimator. In such a case, Wooldridge (2007, 2010, pp. 922–924) has proposed a straightforward procedure to estimate standard errors, provided that the propensity-score is correctly specified. We briefly illustrate the Wooldridge's procedure and formulas for obtaining these (analytical) standard errors.

(i) *Standard errors estimation for* ATE
   First: define the estimated ML score of the first step (probit or logit), which is by definition equal to:

$$\widehat{\mathbf{d}}_i = \widehat{\mathbf{d}}\,(D_i, \mathbf{x}_i, \widehat{\boldsymbol{\gamma}}) = \frac{[\nabla_{\boldsymbol{\gamma}}\widehat{p}\,(\mathbf{x}_i, \widehat{\boldsymbol{\gamma}})]' \cdot [D_i - \widehat{p}\,(\mathbf{x}_i, \widehat{\boldsymbol{\gamma}})]}{\widehat{p}\,(\mathbf{x}_i, \widehat{\boldsymbol{\gamma}})[1 - \widehat{p}\,(\mathbf{x}_i, \widehat{\boldsymbol{\gamma}})]} \tag{2.127}$$

Observe that $\mathbf{d}$ is a row vector of the $R - 1$ parameters $\boldsymbol{\gamma}$ and $\nabla_{\boldsymbol{\gamma}}\widehat{p}\,(\mathbf{x}_i, \widehat{\boldsymbol{\gamma}})$ is the gradient of the function $p(\mathbf{x}, \boldsymbol{\gamma})$.
   Second: define the generic estimated summand of ATE as:

$$\widehat{k}_i = \frac{[D_i - \widehat{p}(\mathbf{x}_i)]Y_i}{\widehat{p}(\mathbf{x}_i)[1 - \widehat{p}(\mathbf{x}_i)]} \tag{2.128}$$

Third: calculate the OLS *residuals* from this regression:

$$\widehat{k}_i \text{ on } \left(1, \widehat{\mathbf{d}}'_i\right) \quad \text{with } i = 1, \ldots, N \tag{2.129}$$

and call them $\hat{e}_i$ $(i = 1, \ldots, N)$. The *asymptotic standard error* for ATE is equal to:

$$\frac{\left[\frac{1}{N}\sum_{i=1}^{N}\widehat{e}^2_i\right]^{1/2}}{\sqrt{N}} \tag{2.130}$$

which can be used to test the significance of ATE. Notice that $\mathbf{d}$ will have a different expression according to the probability model considered. Here, we consider the *logit* and *probit* case.

Case 1   Logit

Suppose that the correct probability follows a logistic distribution. This means that:

$$p(\mathbf{x}_i, \boldsymbol{\gamma}) = \frac{\exp(\mathbf{x}_i\boldsymbol{\gamma})}{1 + \exp(\mathbf{x}_i\boldsymbol{\gamma})} = \Lambda(\mathbf{x}_i\boldsymbol{\gamma}) \tag{2.131}$$

Thus, by simple algebra, we obtain that:

$$\underbrace{\widehat{\mathbf{d}}'_i}_{1\times R} = \mathbf{x}_i(D_i - \widehat{p}_i) \tag{2.132}$$

Case 2   Probit

Suppose that the right probability follows a Normal distribution. In other words:

$$p(\mathbf{x}_i, \boldsymbol{\gamma}) = \Phi(\mathbf{x}_i\boldsymbol{\gamma}) \tag{2.133}$$

Thus, by simple algebra, we have that:

$$\widehat{\mathbf{d}}'_i == \frac{\phi(\mathbf{x}_i, \widehat{\boldsymbol{\gamma}})\mathbf{x}_i \cdot [D_i - \Phi(\mathbf{x}_i\boldsymbol{\gamma})]}{\Phi(\mathbf{x}_i\boldsymbol{\gamma})[1 - \Phi(\mathbf{x}_i\boldsymbol{\gamma})]} \tag{2.134}$$

Observe that one can add also functions of $\mathbf{x}$ to estimate previous formulas. This reduces the standard errors if these functions are partially correlated with k.

Observe that the previous procedure produces standard errors that are lower than those produced by ignoring the first step (i.e., the propensity-score estimation via ML). Indeed, the naïve standard error:

$$
\frac{\left[\frac{1}{N} \sum_{i=1}^{N} \left(\widehat{k}_i - \widehat{ATE} \right)^2 \right]^{1/2}}{\sqrt{N}}
\tag{2.135}
$$

is higher than the one produced by the previous procedure.

(ii) *Standard error for* ATET

Following a similar procedure to that implemented for ATE, define:

$$
\widehat{q}_i = \frac{[D_i - \widehat{p}(\mathbf{x}_i)] Y_i}{\widehat{p}(D=1)[1 - \widehat{p}_i(\mathbf{x})]}
\tag{2.136}
$$

and calculate:

$$
\widehat{r}_i = \text{residuals from the regression of } \widehat{q}_i \text{ on } \left(1, \, \widehat{\mathbf{d}}' \right)
\tag{2.137}
$$

Then, the asymptotic standard error for ATET is given by:

$$
\frac{[\widehat{p}(D=1)]^{-1} \cdot \left[\frac{1}{N} \sum_{i=1}^{N} \left(\widehat{r}_i - D_i \cdot \widehat{ATET} \right)^2 \right]^{1/2}}{\sqrt{N}}
\tag{2.138}
$$

(iii) *Standard error for* ATENT

In this case, define:

$$
\widehat{b}_i = \frac{[D_i - \widehat{p}_i(\mathbf{x}_i)] Y_i}{\widehat{p}(D=0) \widehat{p}(\mathbf{x}_i)}
\tag{2.139}
$$

and then calculate:

$$
\widehat{s}_i = \text{residuals from the regression of } \widehat{b}_i \text{ on } \left(1, \, \widehat{\mathbf{d}}' \right)
\tag{2.140}
$$

The *asymptotic standard error* for ATENT is therefore:

$$\frac{[\widehat{p}\,(D=0)]^{-1} \cdot \left[\frac{1}{N}\sum_{i=1}^{N}\left(\widehat{s}_i - (1-D_i)\cdot\widehat{\text{ATENT}}\,\right)^2\right]^{1/2}}{\sqrt{N}} \tag{2.141}$$

Previous standard errors are correct as long as the probit or the logit are the correct probability rules in the DGP. If this is not the case, then measurement error is present and previous estimations might be inconsistent. The literature has provided more flexible nonparametric estimation of previous standard errors; see, for example, Hirano et al. (2003) or in Li et al. (2009). Under a correct specification, a straightforward alternative is to use bootstrap, where the binary response estimation and the averaging are included in each bootstrap iteration.

2.5   Doubly-Robust Estimation

Combining different methods may sometimes lead to an estimation of the treatment effects having better properties in terms of robustness. This is the case of the so-called *Doubly-robust* estimator, which combines Reweighting (through an inverse-probability regression) and Regression-adjustment (Robins and Rotnitzky 1995; Robins et al. 1994; Wooldridge 2007).

The robustness of this approach lies in the fact that either the conditional mean or the propensity-score needs to be correctly specified but not both. This in itself is a non-negligible advantage of this method.

In practice, the application of the Doubly-robust estimator is as follows:

- Define a parametric function for the conditional mean of the two potential outcomes as $m_0(\mathbf{x}, \boldsymbol{\delta}_0)$ and $m_1(\mathbf{x}, \boldsymbol{\delta}_1)$, respectively, and let $p(\mathbf{x}, \boldsymbol{\gamma})$ be a parametric model for the propensity-score.
- Estimate $\widehat{p}_i(\mathbf{x}_i)$ by the maximum likelihood (logit or probit).
- Apply a WLS regression using as weights the inverse probabilities to obtain, by assuming a linear form of the conditional mean, the parameters' estimation as:

$$\min_{a_1,\mathbf{b}_1}\sum_{i=1}^{N} D_i(y_i - a_1 - \mathbf{b}_1\mathbf{x}_i)^2/\widehat{p}\,(\mathbf{x}_i) \tag{2.142}$$

$$\min_{a_0,\mathbf{b}_0}\sum_{i=1}^{N} (1-D_i)(y_i - a_0 - \mathbf{b}_0\mathbf{x}_i)^2/(1-\widehat{p}\,(\mathbf{x}_i)) \tag{2.143}$$

- Finally, estimate ATEs by Regression-adjustment as:

$$\widehat{\text{ATE}} = 1/N \sum_{i=1}^{N} \left[\left(\widehat{a}_1 - \widehat{\mathbf{b}}_1 \mathbf{x}_i \right) - \left(\widehat{a}_0 - \widehat{\mathbf{b}}_0 \mathbf{x}_i \right) \right] \qquad (2.144)$$

$$\widehat{\text{ATET}} = 1/N_1 \sum_{i=1}^{N} D_i \left[\left(\widehat{a}_1 - \widehat{\mathbf{b}}_1 \mathbf{x}_i \right) - \left(\widehat{a}_0 - \widehat{\mathbf{b}}_0 \mathbf{x}_i \right) \right] \qquad (2.145)$$

$$\widehat{\text{ATENT}} = 1/N_0 \sum_{i=1}^{N} (1 - D_i) \left[\left(\widehat{a}_1 - \widehat{\mathbf{b}}_1 \mathbf{x}_i \right) - \left(\widehat{a}_0 - \widehat{\mathbf{b}}_0 \mathbf{x}_i \right) \right] \qquad (2.146)$$

Two different arguments are invoked to illustrate why the Doubly-robust estimator is consistent (see Wooldridge 2010, pp. 931–932):

1. In the first case, the conditional mean is correctly specified but the propensity-score function is freely misspecified. In this case, robustness is assured by the fact that WLS consistently estimate the parameters independently of the specific function of $\mathbf{x}$ used to build weights. Thus, even an incorrect propensity-score does not affect ATEs consistency.
2. In the second case, the conditional mean is misspecified but the propensity-score function is correctly specified. In this case, the argument is somewhat tricky. Under CMI, it can be showed that the parameters $(\boldsymbol{\delta}_0^*, \boldsymbol{\delta}_1^*)$ estimated by the inverse-probability regression (with the true weights) are also the (minimum) solution of an unweighted "population" regression, such as $E[(Y_g - a_g - \mathbf{b}_g \mathbf{x})^2]$ that identifies the parameters of the linear projection of Y_g in the vector space generated by $(1, \mathbf{x})$. Since a constant is included in the regression, then $E(Y_g) = E\left(a_g^* - \mathbf{b}_g^* \mathbf{x} \right)$, so that $\text{ATE} = E(Y_1) - E(Y_0) = E\left[(a_1^* - \mathbf{b}_1^* \mathbf{x}) - (a_0^* - \mathbf{b}_0^* \mathbf{x}) \right]$ independently of the linearity of the conditional means. This also continues to hold when we consider functions of $\mathbf{x}$.

The previous results can be seen to hold, with slight modifications, even in the case of binary, fractional and count response variables, provided that the corresponding conditional mean function is considered (Wooldridge 2010, pp. 932–934).

2.6 Implementation and Application of Regression-Adjustment

In this section, we illustrate how to estimate ATEs in Stata using the parametric linear and nonlinear Regression-adjustment approaches. We use the dataset JTRAIN2.DTA, freely available in Stata by typing:

```
. net from http://www.stata.com/data/jwooldridge/
. net describe eacsap
. net get eacsap
```

The dataset comes from the National Supported Work (NSW) demonstration, a labor market experiment in which 185 participants were randomized into treatment and 260 units were used as controls. In this experiment, treatment took the form of a "on-the-job training" lasting between 9 months and a year in between 1976 and 1977. This dataset contains 445 observations.

The dataset, originally used by Lalonde (1986), was also used by Dehejia and Wahba (1999, 2002) in their seminal papers on propensity-score Matching. In their applications, the authors start by using the 260 experimental control observations to obtain a *benchmark* estimate for the treatment impact. Subsequently, for the 185 treated units, they alternatively consider different sets of control groups coming from the "Population Survey of Income Dynamics (PSID)" and the "Current Population Survey (CPS)." In the empirical work of this section, we use the original dataset of 445 observations.

Data refer to the real earnings and demographics of a sample of the men who participated in this job training experiment. We are mainly interested in assessing the effect of training on earnings. The objective is to calculate: (1) the simple Difference-in-means (DIM) estimator; (2) the parameters ATE, ATE(x); ATET, ATET(x); and ATENT, ATENT(x); (3) the combined density plot of ATE(x), ATET(x), and ATENT(x); (4) the standard error and confidence interval for ATET and ATENT by bootstrap. We begin with a description of the dataset:

```
. describe

-----------------------------------------------------------------------------
  obs:            445
  vars:            19                              5 Oct 2012 12:44
  size:        16,910
-----------------------------------------------------------------------------
                storage   display    value
variable name   type      format     label     variable label
-----------------------------------------------------------------------------
train           byte      %9.0g                =1 if assigned to job training
age             byte      %9.0g                age in 1977
educ            byte      %9.0g                years of education
black           byte      %9.0g                =1 if black
hisp            byte      %9.0g                =1 if Hispanic
married         byte      %9.0g                =1 if married
nodegree        byte      %9.0g                =1 if no high school degree
mosinex         byte      %9.0g                # mnths prior to 1/78 in expmnt
re74            float     %9.0g                real earns., 1974, $1000s
re75            float     %9.0g                real earns., 1975, $1000s
re78            float     %9.0g                real earns., 1978, $1000s
unem74          byte      %9.0g                =1 if unem. all of 1974
unem75          byte      %9.0g                =1 if unem. all of 1975
unem78          byte      %9.0g                =1 if unem. all of 1978
lre74           float     %9.0g                log(re74); zero if re74 == 0
```

lre75	float	%9.0g	log(re75); zero if re75 == 0
lre78	float	%9.0g	log(re78); zero if re78 == 0
agesq	int	%9.0g	age^2
mostrn	byte	%9.0g	months in training

We wish to assess whether individual's real earnings in 1978, measured in thousands of dollars, were affected by participating in a training program up to 2 years before 1978. We consider a series of covariates as observable confounders, such as real earnings in 1974 ("re74") and 1975 ("re75"), individual age ("age"), individual age squared ("agesq"), a binary high school degree indicator ("nodegree"), marital status ("married"), and a binary variable for being black ("black") and hispanic ("hisp").

In order to carry out this analysis we use two Stata commands: the user-written ivtreatreg (Cerulli 2014b) and the built-in Stata13 teffects ra. The syntax for both is reported below.

Syntax for ivtreatreg

The basic syntax of ivtreatreg takes the following form:

```
ivtreatreg outcome treatment [varlist] [if] [in] [weight], model(cf-ols)
[hetero(varlist_h) graphic]
```

where varlist represents the set of confounders **x**. This command allows one to compute the parametric Regression-adjustment under the linear assumption (i.e., the Control-function regression). It assumes a heterogeneous response to the confounders declared in varlist_h and estimates ATE, ATET, and ATENT as well as these parameters conditional on varlist_h. Since ivtreatreg also estimates other treatment models (more of which is discussed in the next chapter), the Control-function regression is estimated by adding the option model(cf-ols).[7]

Syntax for teffects ra

The basic syntax of teffects ra takes this form:

```
teffects ra (ovar omvarlist [, omodel noconstant)] (tvar) [if] [in]
[weight] [, stat options]
```

where ovar is the output variable, omvarlist the confounders **x**, tvar the binary treatment variable, and omodel specifies the model for the outcome variable that can be one of these depending on the nature of the outcome:

---

[7] Note that the ivtreatreg option cf-ols is only available in a previous version of this command. The present version of the command, as published in *The Stata Journal*, does not provide such option. The old version can be obtained on request.

```
--------------------------------------------------------------------------
     omodel                       Description
--------------------------------------------------------------------------
     linear                       linear outcome model; the default
     logit                        logistic outcome model
     probit                       probit outcome model
     hetprobit(varlist)           heteroskedastic probit outcome model
     poisson                      exponential outcome model
--------------------------------------------------------------------------
```

Including the `linear` option in `teffects ra` produces the same results as `ivtreatreg`. The latter, however, permits one to also select a subset of heterogeneous confounders (depending on analyst's choice), while the former does not. Moreover, `ivtreatreg` also provides, by default, an estimation of ATET, ATENT, and of ATE(**x**), ATET(**x**), and ATENT(**x**). In contrast, `teffects ra` does not provide an estimation of ATENT. `teffects ra` is, however, more suited in the case of binary and count outcomes. Of course, one can elaborate further on the results from `teffects ra` in order to eventually recover that which is not directly provided by the command.

We start by renaming the target variable ("re78") and the treatment variable ("train"):

```
. gen y = re78
. gen w = train
```

In order to simplify the notation, we put all the confounders into a global macro `xvars`:

```
. global xvars re74 re75 age agesq nodegree married black hisp
```

and generate a global macro called `xvarsh` affecting the heterogeneous response to treatment, as follows:

```
. global xvarsh re74 re75age agesq nodegree married black hisp
```

Before going into ATEs estimation, it seems useful to look at some descriptive statistics with regard to the variables employed in the model. To this aim, we use the `tabstat` command:

```
. tabstat y w $xvars, columns(statistics) s(n mean sd min max)
       variable |        N        mean          sd        min         max
   -------------+------------------------------------------------------------
              y |      445    5.300765    6.631493          0      60.3079
              w |      445    .4157303    .4934022          0            1
           re74 |      445    2.102266    5.363584          0      39.5707
```

```
         re75 |        445    1.377139    3.150961            0     25.1422
          age |        445    25.37079    7.100282           17          55
        agesq |        445    693.9775    429.7818          289        3025
     nodegree |        445    .7820225    .4133367            0           1
      married |        445    .1685393    .3747658            0           1
        black |        445    .8337079    .3727617            0           1
         hisp |        445    .0876404    .2830895            0           1
-----------------------------------------------------------------------------
```

It is also useful to report the descriptive statistics by treatment status:

```
. bysort w: tabstat y $xvars , columns(statistics)

-> w = 0                          -> w = 1
    variable |        mean            variable |        mean
-------------+----------          -------------+----------
           y |    4.554802                   y |    6.349145
        re74 |    2.107027                re74 |    2.095574
        re75 |    1.266909                re75 |    1.532056
         age |    25.05385                 age |    25.81622
       agesq |    677.3154               agesq |    717.3946
    nodegree |    .8346154            nodegree |    .7081081
     married |    .1538462             married |    .1891892
       black |    .8269231               black |    .8432432
        hisp |    .1076923                hisp |    .0594595
-------------------------         -------------------------
```

As we can see, the difference between the outcome means is quite high, but at this stage, we cannot conclude that this observed difference was caused by attending the training course.

Given this preliminary analysis of the data, we can estimate a series of regression using first `ivtreatreg`:

```
*** MODEL 1: SIMPLE DIFFERENCE-IN-MEAN (DIM) ***
. qui xi: reg y w
estimates store DIM
*** MODEL 2: "cf-ols" WITH HOMOGENEOUS RESPONSE TO TREATMENT STATUS
. qui xi: ivtreatreg y w $xvars , model(cf-ols)
estimates store CFOLS1
*** MODEL 3: "cf-ols" WITH HETEROGENEOUS RESPONSE TO TREATMENT STATUS
. qui xi: ivtreatreg y w $xvars , hetero($xvarsh) model(cf-ols)
estimates store CFOLS2
*** COMPARE ESTIMATES OF ATE:
. estimates table DIM CFOLS1 CFOLS2 ,         ///
```

```
b(%9.5f) star keep(w) stats(r2) ///
title("ATE comparison between DIM, CFOLS1, CFOLS2")
ATE comparison between DIM, CFOLS1, CFOLS2

-------------------------------------------------------------
   Variable |     DIM          CFOLS1         CFOLS2
------------+------------------------------------------------
          w |  1.79434**      1.62517*       1.54472*
------------+------------------------------------------------
         r2 |  0.01782        0.04896        0.06408
-------------------------------------------------------------
              legend: * p<0.05; ** p<0.01; *** p<0.001
```

Results from previous estimators are very similar indeed. This reflects the random assignment entailed by the NSW demonstration: in such a case, controlling for covariates was expected not to provide significant change in the ATE estimation, and this is properly confirmed.

We can, in such a setting, also calculate ATET and ATENT and then test their statistical significance by applying bootstrap procedures as follows:

```
*** BOOTSTRAP STD. ERR. FOR "ATET" AND "ATENT"
. xi: bootstrap atet=e(atet) atent=e(atent), rep(200): ///
ivtreatreg y w $xvars , hetero($xvarsh) model(cf-ols)

Bootstrap replications (200)
----+--- 1 ---+--- 2 ---+--- 3 ---+--- 4 ---+--- 5
..................................................    50
..................................................   100
..................................................   150
..................................................   200
Bootstrap results                        Number of obs   =      445
                                         Replications    =      200
     command: ivtreatreg y w re74 re75 age agesq nodegree married black hisp,
hetero(re74 re75 age agesq nodegree married black hisp) model(cf-ols)
        atet:  e(atet)
       atent:  e(atent)
------------------------------------------------------------------------------
             |  Observed   Bootstrap                      Normal-based
             |    Coef.    Std. Err.      z    P>|z|    [95% Conf. Interval]
-------------+----------------------------------------------------------------
        atet |  1.764007   .6654867    2.65   0.008    .4596768    3.068337
       atent |  1.38869    .682661     2.03   0.042    .0506991    2.726681
------------------------------------------------------------------------------
```

The results obtained in regression CFOLS2 can be obtained using `teffects` `ra`:

```
. teffects ra (y $xvars , linear) (w)
Iteration 0:    EE criterion =  1.808e-27
Iteration 1:    EE criterion =  1.929e-30
Treatment-effects estimation                    Number of obs    =       445
Estimator       : regression adjustment
Outcome model   : linear
Treatment model: none
------------------------------------------------------------------------------
                 |               Robust
             y   |     Coef.   Std. Err.      z    P>|z|     [95% Conf. Interval]
-----------------+------------------------------------------------------------
ATE              |
             w   |
       (1 vs 0)  |   1.544721   .6619304    2.33   0.020     .2473607    2.84208
-----------------+------------------------------------------------------------
POmean           |
             w   |
             0   |   4.567414   .3374549   13.53   0.000     3.906015   5.228814
------------------------------------------------------------------------------
```

To obtain ATET, one simply types:

```
. teffects ra (y $xvars , linear) (w) , atet
Iteration 0:    EE criterion =  1.808e-27
Iteration 1:    EE criterion =  9.663e-31
Treatment-effects estimation                    Number of obs    =       445
Estimator       : regression adjustment
Outcome model   : linear
Treatment model: none
------------------------------------------------------------------------------
                 |               Robust
             y   |     Coef.   Std. Err.      z    P>|z|     [95% Conf.   Interval]
-----------------+------------------------------------------------------------
ATET             |
             w   |
       (1 vs 0)  |   1.764007   .6719526    2.63   0.009     .4470038    3.08101
-----------------+------------------------------------------------------------
POmean           |
             w   |
             0   |   4.585139   .3576414   12.82   0.000     3.884174   5.286103
------------------------------------------------------------------------------
```

while, to get the potential outcome means with confidence interval:

```
. teffects ra (y $xvars , linear) (w) , pomeans
Iteration 0:   EE criterion =  1.808e-27
Iteration 1:   EE criterion =  2.272e-30
Treatment-effects estimation              Number of obs     =     445
Estimator      : regression adjustment
Outcome model  : linear
Treatment model: none
------------------------------------------------------------------------------
             |               Robust
          y  |    Coef.   Std. Err.     z    P>|z|    [95% Conf. Interval]
------------------------------------------------------------------------------
POmeans      |
          w  |
          0  |  4.567414   .3374549   13.53  0.000    3.906015    5.228814
          1  |  6.112135   .5725393   10.68  0.000    4.989978    7.234291
------------------------------------------------------------------------------
```

Optionally, it is also possible to predict the ATE(**x**) by typing:

```
. predict ATE_x , te
```

thus showing that ATE, ATET, and ATENT are given by the following means:

```
. qui sum ATE_x
. display r(mean)
1.5447205  // ATE
. sum ATE_x if w==1
. display r(mean)
1.7640067  // ATET
. sum ATE_x if w==0
. display r(mean)
1.38869    // ATENT
```

Observe that the standard errors for ATENT can be obtained by bootstrap (not reported).

Sometimes, it may be useful to report the estimated treatment effect as a percentage of the untreated potential outcome mean. To this aim, we can include the coeflegend option so that teffects ra reports the names of the parameters. One can then exploit the command nlcom to obtain the percentage change with standard errors calculated with the delta method:

```
. teffects ra (y $xvars , linear) (w) , coeflegend
Iteration 0:   EE criterion =  1.808e-27
Iteration 1:   EE criterion =  1.929e-30
Treatment-effects estimation                    Number of obs    =      445
Estimator      : regression adjustment
Outcome model  : linear
Treatment model: none
------------------------------------------------------------------------------
            y |    Coef.  Legend
--------------+---------------------------------------------------------------
ATE           |
            w |
     (1 vs 0) |   1.544721   _b[ATE:r1vs0.w]
--------------+---------------------------------------------------------------
POmean        |
            w |
            0 |   4.567414   _b[POmean:r0.w]
------------------------------------------------------------------------------

. nlcom _b[ATE:r1vs0.w]/ _b[POmean:r0.w]
     _nl_1:  _b[ATE:r1vs0.w]/_b[POmean:r0.w]
------------------------------------------------------------------------------
            y |    Coef.   Std. Err.     z    P>|z|    [95% Conf. Interval]
--------------+---------------------------------------------------------------
        _nl_1 |  .3382046   .1589424    2.13   0.033    .0266832    .649726
------------------------------------------------------------------------------
```

The results indicate a significant 33 % increase in real earnings due to training. One advantage of ivtreatreg over teffects ra is that it allows for the possibility of plotting jointly the distributions of ATE(**x**), ATET(**x**), and ATENT(**x**), by typing:

```
. ivtreatreg y w $xvars , hetero($xvarsh) model(cf-ols) graphic
      Source |      SS      df      MS           Number of obs =     445
-------------+------------------------------     F( 17,   427) =    1.72
       Model |  1251.29175   17  73.6053972     Prob > F      =   0.0367
    Residual |  18274.3649  427  42.7971074     R-squared     =   0.0641
-------------+------------------------------     Adj R-squared =   0.0268
       Total |  19525.6566  444  43.9767041     Root MSE      =  6.5419
------------------------------------------------------------------------------
           y |    Coef.   Std. Err.     t    P>|t|     [95% Conf. Interval]
-------------+----------------------------------------------------------------
           w |  1.544721   .6426025    2.40   0.017     .2816628    2.807778
        re74 |  .0772563   .0976092    0.79   0.429    -.1145981    .2691106
        re75 |  .0580198   .1841072    0.32   0.753    -.3038494    .4198891
         age | -.0710885   .3397475   -0.21   0.834    -.7388741    .5966972
```

agesq	.0016875	.0055277	0.31	0.760	-.0091773	.0125523
nodegree	-.3707108	1.141044	-0.32	0.745	-2.613473	1.872051
married	-.7515524	1.222282	-0.61	0.539	-3.153992	1.650887
black	-2.913191	1.684909	-1.73	0.085	-6.224939	.3985567
hisp	-.6138299	2.055351	-0.30	0.765	-4.653694	3.426035
_ws_re74	-.0579181	.1651987	-0.35	0.726	-.3826219	.2667858
_ws_re75	.0232402	.2744957	0.08	0.933	-.5162907	.5627711
_ws_age	.9239745	.5771688	1.60	0.110	-.210471	2.05842
_ws_agesq	-.0147917	.0094685	-1.56	0.119	-.0334024	.003819
_ws_nodegree	-1.588303	1.606886	-0.99	0.323	-4.746694	1.570088
_ws_married	1.748556	1.80549	0.97	0.333	-1.800198	5.29731
_ws_black	1.827491	2.360635	0.77	0.439	-2.812421	6.467403
_ws_hisp	.7387987	3.273411	0.23	0.822	-5.695206	7.172803
_cons	7.856682	5.309304	1.48	0.140	-2.578942	18.29231

to obtain:

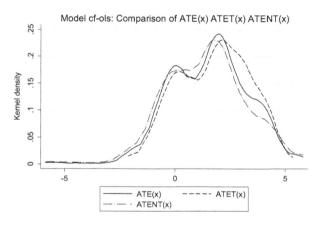

Model cf-ols: Comparison of ATE(x) ATET(x) ATENT(x)

The graphical representation can be useful to analyze the dispersion of the effect around the mean. As such, it may offer interesting information about the effect's heterogeneity over observations and about the potential presence of influential data. Moreover, it can emphasize the presence of a different effect's distribution pattern between treated and untreated units.

A final remark relates to the standard errors of ATEs when using the ivtreatreg versus using teffects ra command. As is evident from the results, the standard errors are in fact slightly different due to the fact that teffects ra does not make the small-sample adjustment that regression-based methods do.

In addition, an interesting option available for teffects ra is that of reporting the two potential outcomes estimations separately. In some contexts,

this can be interesting in itself. To obtain this, we simply add the option
`aequations` as follows:

```
. teffects ra (y $xvars , linear) (w) , aequations
Some output omitted
--------------------------------------------------------------------------------
                |                 Robust
            y  |    Coef.   Std. Err.      z     P>|z|    [95% Conf. Interval]
----------------+---------------------------------------------------------------
ATE             |
            w  |
      (1 vs 0) |  1.544721   .6619304    2.33   0.020    .2473607    2.84208
----------------+---------------------------------------------------------------
POmean          |
            w  |
            0  |  4.567414   .3374549   13.53   0.000    3.906015   5.228814
----------------+---------------------------------------------------------------
OME0            |
         re74  |  .0772563   .0930324    0.83   0.406   -.1050838   .2595963
         re75  |  .0580198   .1697555    0.34   0.733   -.2746948   .3907345
          age  | -.0710885   .2469855   -0.29   0.773   -.5551712   .4129942
        agesq  |  .0016875   .0038335    0.44   0.660    -.005826    .009201
     nodegree  | -.3707108   .9035178   -0.41   0.682   -2.141573   1.400152
      married  | -.7515524    .994725   -0.76   0.450   -2.701178   1.198073
        black  | -2.913191    1.31429   -2.22   0.027   -5.489152  -.3372307
         hisp  | -.6138299   1.590098   -0.39   0.699   -3.730364   2.502704
        _cons  |  7.856682   4.031418    1.95   0.051   -.0447516   15.75812
----------------+---------------------------------------------------------------
OME1            |
         re74  |  .0193382   .2576129    0.08   0.940   -.4855738   .5242502
         re75  |  .0812601   .1941968    0.42   0.676   -.2993587   .4618788
          age  |  .8528861   .5519752    1.55   0.122   -.2289655   1.934738
        agesq  | -.0131042   .0088728   -1.48   0.140   -.0304946   .0042862
     nodegree  | -1.959013   1.303733   -1.50   0.133   -4.514283    .596256
      married  |  .9970032    1.50374    0.66   0.507   -1.950273   3.944279
        black  |  -1.0857    1.602923   -0.68   0.498   -4.227372   2.055971
         hisp  |  .1249687   2.646375    0.05   0.962   -5.061831   5.311769
        _cons  | -4.326628   8.146136   -0.53   0.595   -20.29276   11.63951
--------------------------------------------------------------------------------
```

In conclusion, `ivtreatreg` and `teffects ra` provide similar and complementary reports of results. The combined use of both commands can be a beneficial
strategy for linear potential outcomes models.

When linearity is not appropriate, as in the case of a binary or count outcome, using `teffects ra` is preferable, although `ivtreatreg` also provides in this case a consistent estimation of ATEs.

To illustrate how one can exploit the `teffects ra` command in a nonlinear case, take a binary outcome within the same dataset. Suppose, we wish to study the effect of training on the probability of becoming unemployed using as outcome the variable "unem78." In this case, we can define

```
. teffects ra (unem78 $xvars , probit) (w)
Some output omitted
Treatment-effects estimation                 Number of obs    =      445
Estimator        : regression adjustment
Outcome model    : probit
Treatment model: none
-----------------------------------------------------------------------------
             |               Robust
      unem78 |      Coef.   Std. Err.      z    P>|z|     [95% Conf. Interval]
-------------+---------------------------------------------------------------
ATE          |
          w  |
     (1 vs 0)|   -.105289   .0432818    -2.43   0.015    -.1901198   -.0204583
-------------+---------------------------------------------------------------
POmean       |
          w  |
          0  |   .3555628   .0298023    11.93   0.000     .2971513    .4139742
-----------------------------------------------------------------------------
```

The coefficient is negative and significant, so that the probability to remain unemployed decreases due to attending the training course. In order to estimate the potential outcome means, we can type:

```
. teffects ra (unem78 $xvars , probit) (w) , pomeans
Treatment-effects estimation                 Number of obs    =      445
Estimator        : regression adjustment
Outcome model    : probit
Treatment model: none
-----------------------------------------------------------------------------
             |               Robust
      unem78 |      Coef.   Std. Err.      z    P>|z|     [95% Conf. Interval]
-------------+---------------------------------------------------------------
POmeans      |
          w  |
          0  |   .3555628   .0298023    11.93   0.000     .2971513    .4139742
          1  |   .2502737   .0318015     7.87   0.000      .187944    .3126035
-----------------------------------------------------------------------------
```

These results indicate that on average over observations, the probability of being unemployed when one is treated is around 25 %, while this probability increases to around 35 % when one is untreated. Thus, the training has a positive effect on employment.

2.7 Implementation and Application of Matching

In this section, we focus on ATEs estimation using nonparametric methods, in particular, focusing on Matching. We consider the same dataset as we have used for Regression-adjustment, and we proceed first by presenting an application using covariates matching (C Matching) and then one using propensity-score matching (PS Matching).

2.7.1 Covariates Matching

In order to apply C Matching, we use the Stata built-in command nnmatch, part of the teffects package. The syntax of this command is very similar to that of Regression-adjustment and takes the form:

Basic syntax of teffects nnmatch

```
teffects nnmatch (ovar omvarlist) (tvar) [if] [in] [weight] [, stat options]
stat                    Description
--------------------------------------------------------------------------------
  ate                   estimate average treatment effect in population
  atet                  estimate average treatment effect on the treat
--------------------------------------------------------------------------------
Main options            Description
--------------------------------------------------------------------------------
  nneighbor(#)          specify number of matches per observation
  biasadj(varlist)      correct for large-sample bias using varlist
  ematch(varlist)       match exactly on specified variables
--------------------------------------------------------------------------------
```

Note that the above table contains only some of the options available for the teffects nnmatch command (see the Stata 13 manual for the other options). As for those considered here, according to the Stata help file of this command, we have that nneighbor(#) specifies the number of matches per observation. The default is nneighbor(1); biasadj(*varlist*), which specifies that a linear function of the specified covariates can be used to correct for a large sample bias that exists when matching on more than one continuous covariate. By default, no correction is performed. As we have seen, Abadie and Imbens (2006, 2012) have

shown that nearest-neighbor matching estimators are not consistent when matching
is done on two or more continuous covariates and have proposed a bias-corrected
estimator that is consistent. The correction term uses a linear function of variables
specified in `biasadj()`; `ematch(varlist)` specifies that the variables in
`varlist` match exactly. All variables in `varlist` must be numeric and may
be specified as factors. `teffects nnmatch` exits with an error if any observation
does not have the requested exact match.

Given this premise, we can apply `teffects nnmatch` to the previous job
training example in the following manner:

```
. teffects nnmatch (y $xvars) (w)
Treatment-effects estimation                   Number of obs      =        445
Estimator       : nearest-neighbor matching    Matches: requested =          1
Outcome model   : matching                                   min =          1
Distance metric: Mahalanobis                                 max =         16
------------------------------------------------------------------------------
             |               AI Robust
           y |      Coef.   Std. Err.      z    P>|z|     [95% Conf. Interval]
-------------+----------------------------------------------------------------
ATE          |
           w |
      (1 vs 0) |   1.625655   .6652704     2.44   0.015     .3217487    2.929561
------------------------------------------------------------------------------
```

The results obtained are in line with those found using Regression-adjustment; in
other words, a significant positive effect of training on earnings.

We can now consider the possibility of performing an exact matching on some
specific covariates and of increasing, up to three, the number of neighbors. In this
case, we have:

```
. teffects nnmatch (y $xvars) (w) , nneighbor(3) ematch(hisp black)
Treatment-effects estimation                   Number of obs      =        445
Estimator       : nearest-neighbor matching    Matches: requested =          3
Outcome model   : matching                                   min =          3
Distance metric: Mahalanobis                                 max =         18
------------------------------------------------------------------------------
             |               AI Robust
           y |      Coef.   Std. Err.      z    P>|z|     [95% Conf. Interval]
-------------+----------------------------------------------------------------
ATE          |
           w |
      (1 vs 0) |   1.263357   .6265118     2.02   0.044     .0354166    2.491298
------------------------------------------------------------------------------
```

Finally, we consider an estimation incorporating bias adjustment in large samples. We assume that such bias depends on aging ("age") and real earnings in 1974 ("re74"), so that:

```
. teffects nnmatch (y $xvars) (w) , biasadj(age re74)
Treatment-effects estimation                Number of obs      =        445
Estimator       : nearest-neighbor matching  Matches: requested =          1
Outcome model  : matching                                min =          1
Distance metric: Mahalanobis                             max =         16
------------------------------------------------------------------------------
             |              AI Robust
          y |    Coef.   Std. Err.      z    P>|z|     [95% Conf. Interval]
-------------+----------------------------------------------------------------
ATE          |
         w  |
   (1 vs 0)  |  1.501995   .6651594    2.26   0.024    .1983066    2.805684
------------------------------------------------------------------------------
```

The adjustment provided slightly modifies the bias result, decreasing from around 1.6 to 1.5.

2.7.2 Propensity-Score Matching

Matching on the propensity-score is probably the most diffused approach for applying Matching within the program evaluation empirical literature. This popularity can be understood given the previously discussed properties of the propensity-score, but it is also due to its ability to provide direct information on the factors driving the selection-into-treatment.

In what follows, we present three Stata commands available for PS Matching: the first is the Stata built-in psmatch, part of the package teffects; the second is pscore a user-written command provided by Becker and Ichino (2002); the third is psmatch2, a user-written command carried out by Leuven and Sianesi (2003).

2.7.2.1 PS Matching Using teffects psmatch

We start by providing the estimation of ATEs on the JTRAIN2 dataset, using teffects psmatch. The syntax of the command is as follows:

Basic syntax of teffects psmatch

```
            teffects psmatch (ovar) (tvar tmvarlist [, tmodel]) [if] [in] [weight] [,
stat options]

    tmodel                   Description
--------------------------------------------------------------------------------

    Model
      logit                  logistic treatment model; the default
      probit                 probit treatment model
      hetprobit(varlist)     heteroskedastic probit treatment model
--------------------------------------------------------------------------------

    tmodel specifies the model for the treatment variable.
    For multivariate treatments, only logit is available and multinomial
    Logit used.

    stat                     Description
--------------------------------------------------------------------------------

      ate                    estimate average treatment effect in population; the
      atet                   estimate average treatment effect on the treated
--------------------------------------------------------------------------------

    options                  Description
--------------------------------------------------------------------------------

      nneighbor(#)           specify number of matches per observation;
      caliper(#)             specify the maximum distance for which two
                             observations are potential neighbours
      generate(stub)         generate variables containing the observation
                             numbers of the nearest neighbors
--------------------------------------------------------------------------------
```

Note that the syntax of `teffects psmatch` is slightly different from that of `teffects ra` and `teffects nnmatch`, although easily manageable too. Moreover, in contrast to C Matching, PS Matching does not require a bias correction, since it matches units on a single continuous covariate. Of course, the underlying assumption is that the probability rule according to which the propensity-score is estimated is correctly specified. Finally, `teffects psmatch` also estimates standard errors adjusted for the first-step estimation of the propensity-score, as suggested by Abadie and Imbens (2012).

We start with the baseline application, which by default is `nneighbor(1)` and the estimation model for the propensity-score is a logit.

```
. teffects psmatch (y) (w $xvars)
Treatment-effects estimation              Number of obs    =        445
Estimator      : propensity-score matching  Matches: requested =        1
Outcome model  : matching                                    min =        1
Treatment model: logit                                       max =       16
--------------------------------------------------------------------------------
               |             AI Robust
             y |    Coef.   Std. Err.     z    P>|z|    [95% Conf. Interval]
```

```
-------------+-----------------------------------------------------------
ATE          |
          w  |
   (1 vs 0)  |   1.936551    .7433629    2.61    0.009    .4795867    3.393516
-------------+-----------------------------------------------------------
```

As is evident from the table above, the result on ATE is a little higher than that obtained in the previous estimations, although statistical significance and sign are consistent.

An important post-estimation command that can be employed after running `teffects psmatch` is the command `teffects overlap`, which enables one to assess graphically the degree of overlap. In order to obtain the graphical representation of the degree of overlap, we run the previous PS Matching command using the option `generate(stub)`:

```
. qui teffects psmatch (y) (w $xvars) , generate(near_obs)
. teffects overlap
```

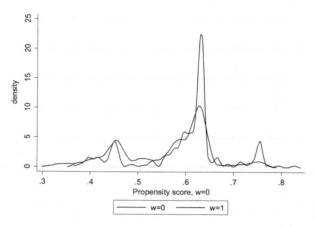

As it is clearly evident, problems of overlap do not appear in this dataset, neither plot indicating the presence of a probability mass close to 0 or 1. Moreover, the probability mass of the two estimated densities is concentrated in regions where overlap occurs, thus indicating that the results obtained from the matching procedure are reliable.

2.7.2.2 PS Matching Using `pscore`

In this section, we present an application of PS Matching performed using the user-written command `pscore` provided by Becker and Ichino (2002). The basic syntax of `pscore` is:

```
pscore treatment varlist [weight] [if exp] [in range] , pscore(newvar)
[blockid(newvar) detail logit comsup level(#) numblo(#)]
```

The `pscore` routine estimates the propensity-score of the treatment on the control variables using a probit (or logit) model and stratifies individuals in blocks according to the propensity-score. It displays summary statistics of the propensity-score and of the stratification. Moreover, it checks whether the balancing property is satisfied or not; if it is not, it asks for a less parsimonious specification of the propensity-score; it also saves the estimated propensity-score and optionally the blocks' number. The estimated propensity-scores can then be used together with the sub-commands `attr`, `attk`, `attnw`, `attnd`, and `atts` to obtain estimates of the average treatment effect on the treated using, respectively, radius Matching, kernel Matching, nearest-neighbor Matching (in one of the two versions: equal weights and random draw), and stratification Matching, the latter using the blocks number as an input.

In this application, which is similar in sprit to the exercise presented in Cameron and Trivedi (2005, Chapter 25), we use again data from the National Supported Work (NSW) demonstration to evaluate the effect of training on earnings. In this application, however, instead of considering the dataset with 260 control units (i.e., the dataset JTRAIN2.DTA), we consider a comparison group of individuals taken from the Population Survey of Income Dynamics (PSID), and in particular the subset PSID-1 including 2,490 controls.[8] We call this dataset JTRAIN_CPS1.DTA; the dataset includes 2,675 units.

The benchmark estimate obtained from the NSW experiment is $1,794, which is equal to the average of RE78 for NSW treated units *minus* the average of RE78 for NSW controls. This value is obtained using the DIM estimator (see Sect. 2.4.1).

We perform PS Matching by `pscore` using the same specification of the propensity-score proposed in Dehejia and Wahba (2002). Firstly, we fix the number of bootstrap replications:

```
. global breps 100
```

We then create a global macro, `xvars_ps`, containing the variables entering the propensity-score specification:

```
. global xvars_ps age agesq educ educsq marr nodegree black   ///
hisp re74 re74sq re75 u74 u75 u74hisp
```

The command `pscore` tabulates the treatment variable; estimates the propensity-score by visualizing the logit/probit regression results; and tests whether the balancing property is satisfied by identifying the optimal numbers of blocks. In

---

[8] The subset PSID-1 is made of "all male household heads under age 55 who did not classify themselves as retired in 1975" (see Dehejia and Wahba 1999, p. 1055).

other words, it implements the algorithm presented in Sect. 2.3.7. If the balancing property is not satisfied, then we are asked to change the propensity-score specification by introducing other variables, powers, and/or interactions. According to Dehejia and Wahba (2002)'s specification, we can estimate:

```
. pscore w $xvars_ps, pscore(myscore) comsup ///
blockid(myblock) numblo(5) level(0.005) logit
******************************************************
Algorithm to estimate the propensity-score
******************************************************
The treatment is w
        w |      Freq.      Percent        Cum.
------------+-----------------------------------
        0 |      2,490       93.08       93.08
        1 |        185        6.92      100.00
------------+-----------------------------------
    Total |      2,675      100.00

Estimation of the propensity-score
Logistic regression                       Number of obs   =      2675
                                          LR chi2(14)     =    951.10
                                          Prob > chi2     =    0.0000
Log likelihood = -197.10175               Pseudo R2       =    0.7070
-------------------------------------------------------------------------------
        w |     Coef.   Std. Err.      z    P>|z|     [95% Conf. Interval]
------------+------------------------------------------------------------------
      age |  .2628422   .120206     2.19   0.029     .0272428    .4984416
    agesq | -.0053794   .0018341   -2.93   0.003    -.0089742   -.0017846
     educ |  .7149774   .3418173    2.09   0.036     .0450278    1.384927
   educsq | -.0426178   .0179039   -2.38   0.017    -.0777088   -.0075269
     marr | -1.780857   .301802    -5.90   0.000    -2.372378   -1.189336
 nodegree |  .1891046   .4257533    0.44   0.657    -.6453564    1.023566
    black |  2.519383   .370358     6.80   0.000     1.793495    3.245272
     re75 | -.0002678   .0000485   -5.52   0.000    -.0003628   -.0001727
     hisp |  3.087327   .7340486    4.21   0.000     1.648618    4.526036
     re74 | -.0000448   .0000425   -1.05   0.292    -.000128     .0000385
    re74sq |  1.99e-09   7.75e-10    2.57   0.010     4.72e-10    3.51e-09
      u74 |  3.100056   .5187391    5.98   0.000     2.083346    4.116766
      u75 | -1.273525   .4644557   -2.74   0.006    -2.183842   -.3632088
  u74hisp | -1.925803   1.07186    -1.80   0.072    -4.02661     .1750032
    _cons | -7.407524   2.445692   -3.03   0.002    -12.20099   -2.614056
-------------------------------------------------------------------------------
Note: 65 failures and 0 successes completely determined.
Note: the common support option has been selected
The region of common support is [.00036433, .98576756]
Description of the estimated propensity-score
```

in region of common support

Estimated propensity-score

```
-----------------------------------------------------------------
     Percentiles      Smallest
 1%    .0003871       .0003643
 5%    .0004805       .0003669
10%    .0006343       .0003702     Obs              1271
25%    .0016393       .0003714     Sum of Wgt.      1271
50%    .0090427                    Mean          .1447205
                      Largest      Std. Dev.     .2809511
75%    .0897599       .9803043
90%     .656286       .9830988     Variance      .0789335
95%    .9392306       .9855413     Skewness      2.049999
99%    .9640553       .9857676     Kurtosis      5.748631
*******************************************************
Step 1: Identification of the optimal number of blocks
Use option detail if you want more detailed output
*******************************************************

The final number of blocks is 6
This number of blocks ensures that the mean propensity-score
is not different for treated and controls in each blocks
***********************************************************
Step 2: Test of balancing property of the propensity-score
Use option detail if you want more detailed output
***********************************************************

The balancing property is satisfied
This table shows the inferior bound, the number of treated
and the number of controls for each block

  Inferior |
  of block |            w
 of pscore |         0          1 |    Total
-----------+----------------------+----------
  .0003643 |       960          9 |      969
        .1 |        56         10 |       66
        .2 |        33         14 |       47
        .4 |        22         24 |       46
        .6 |         7         33 |       40
        .8 |         8         95 |      103
-----------+----------------------+----------
     Total |     1,086        185 |    1,271
```

Note: the common support option has been selected

```
*******************************************
End of the algorithm to estimate the pscore
*******************************************
```

The results indicate that the balancing property is satisfied with a final optimal number of propensity-score blocks equal to 6. This is a good news, as it ensures that we can reliably apply matching, since observable covariates are balanced within blocks (i.e., PS strata); this implies that differences in the output between treated and control units should only be attributed to the effect of the treatment variable. Observe that the command, as it is written above, generates three important variables: the estimated propensity-score ("myscore"), the block identification number ("myblock"), and the binary common support variable ("comsup"); each observation will have a given estimated propensity-score, will belong to a specific block, and will be (or will be not) in the common support. We can perform the same estimation without the common support option. In what follows, however, we will use this option in calculating all causal effects.

After running `pscore`, once the balancing property is properly satisfied, one can estimate ATEs with various Matching methods by typing the proper sub-command:

(a) Nearest-neighbor Matching

```
. set seed 10101
. attnd re78 w $xvars_ps , comsup logit
-----------------------------------------------------------
n. treat.  n. contr.      ATT     Std. Err.        t
-----------------------------------------------------------
     185         60    1285.782    3895.044     0.330
-----------------------------------------------------------
Note: the numbers of treated and controls refer to actual
nearest neighbour matches
```

(b) Radius Matching for radius = 0.001

```
. set seed 10101
. attr re78 w $xvars_ps , comsup  logit radius(0.001)
ATT estimation with the Radius Matching method
Analytical standard errors
-----------------------------------------------------------
n. treat.  n. contr.      ATT    Std. Err.        t
-----------------------------------------------------------
      51        541   -7808.241   1146.418    -6.811
-----------------------------------------------------------
Note: the numbers of treated and controls refer to actual
matches within radius
```

(c)   Radius Matching for radius = 0.0001

```
. set seed 10101
. attr re78 w $xvars_ps , comsup logit radius(0.0001)
ATT estimation with the Radius Matching method
Analytical standard errors
---------------------------------------------------------------
n. treat.   n. contr.        ATT   Std. Err.            t
---------------------------------------------------------------
      27          91   -6401.345   2054.218       -3.116
---------------------------------------------------------------
Note: the numbers of treated and controls refer to actual
matches within radius
```

(d)   Radius Matching for radius = 0.00001

```
. set seed 10101
. attr re78 w $xvars_ps , comsup logit radius(0.00001)
ATT estimation with the Radius Matching method
Analytical standard errors
---------------------------------------------------------------
n. treat.   n. contr.        ATT   Std. Err.            t
---------------------------------------------------------------
      16          17   -1135.184   3189.367       -0.356
---------------------------------------------------------------
Note: the numbers of treated and controls refer to actual
matches within radius
```

(e)   Stratification Matching

```
. set seed 10101
. atts re78 w , pscore(myscore) blockid(myblock) comsup
ATT estimation with the Stratification method
Analytical standard errors
---------------------------------------------------------------
n. treat.   n. contr.        ATT   Std. Err.            t
---------------------------------------------------------------
     185        1086    1452.370    920.769        1.577
---------------------------------------------------------------
```

(f)   Kernel Matching

```
. set seed 10101
. attk re78 w $xvars_ps , comsup boot reps($breps) dots logit
ATT estimation with the Kernel Matching method
```

```
Bootstrapped standard errors

------------------------------------------------------------
 n. treat.   n. contr.        ATT   Std. Err.          t
------------------------------------------------------------
       185        1086   1342.016     864.064      1.553
------------------------------------------------------------
```

Observe that for kernel Matching, the `attk` routine does not provide analytical standard errors, only bootstrapped standard errors. The results are reported in Table 2.6, together with the results obtained by Dehejia and Wahba (2002).

The obtained results show a strong variability of the treatment effect across the type of Matching procedure. In particular, radius Matching estimators set out a dramatic bias, showing even a negative estimate of ATET. Dehejia and Wahba (2002, p. 155, Table 3), on the contrary, reported positive effects using caliper Matching. This difference is due to the fact that the approach adopted does not discard those treated units which do not find matches within the caliper's area, but they are matched with the nearest-neighbor found outside the area identified by the caliper. This is a simple but significant example of how slight changes in the algorithm used to match units can lead to very different and, possibly, contrasting results.

2.7.2.3   PS Matching Using `psmatch2`

Another Stata routine available for implementing Matching is `psmatch2` (Leuven and Sianesi 2003). The basic syntax of `psmatch2` is as follows:

```
psmatch2 depvar [indepvars] [if exp] [in range] [, outcome(varlist)  ///
pscore(varname) neighbor(integer) radius caliper(real) mahalanobis(varlist)
common
```

although many further options are included. The routine `psmatch2` implements full Mahalanobis Matching and a variety of propensity-score Matching methods to

Table 2.6 Comparison of ATET estimates over different matching methods

	ATET (this application)	ATET as % of 1,794	Dehejia and Wahba (2002)	ATET as % of 1,794	Benchmark: NSW experiment
Nearest-neighbor	1,286	72	1,890	105	1,794
Radius = 0.001	−7,808	−435	1,824	102	
Radius = 0.0001	−6,401	−357	1,973	110	
Radius = 0.00001	−1,135	−63	1,893	106	
Stratification	1,452	81			
Kernel	1,342	75			

Note: In the two ATET columns, nearest-neighbor estimates differ because of replacement

adjust for pretreatment observable differences between a group of treated and a group of untreated units. Treatment status is identified by depvar = 1 for the treated and depvar = 0 for the untreated observations. In this application, we use psmatch2 with the propensity-score calculated by pscore, but we may directly calculate the propensity-score within psmatch2.

By considering again the JTRAIN_PSID1.DTA, we can estimate a 3-NN Matching:

```
. psmatch2 w , out(re78) pscore(myscore) neighbor(3) common
----------------------------------------------------------------------------------
         Variable    Sample |   Treated    Controls   Difference        S.E.   T-stat
----------------------------------------------------------------------------------
            RE78   Unmatched | 6349.14537  21553.9213  -15204.7759  1154.61435   -13.17
                        ATT | 6349.14537   5022.4331   1326.71227  2923.22823     0.45
----------------------------------------------------------------------------------
Note: S.E. does not take into account that the propensity-score is estimated.
            | psmatch2:
 psmatch2: |    Common
 Treatment |   support
assignment | On support|    Total
-----------+-----------+----------
 Untreated |     2,490 |    2,490
   Treated |       185 |      185
-----------+-----------+----------
     Total |     2,675 |    2,675
```

The ATET is equal to around 1,326 and, although not significant, it is of the same magnitude of previous nearest-neighbor Matching estimates.

In order to test the balancing property, psmatch2 takes a different route compared to that of pscore. More specifically, it does not provide a test before matching but after matching is realized. This is done by a useful accompanying routine called pstest, which performs a difference-in-mean test for the covariates before and after Matching. The syntax of pstest is:

```
    pstest varlist [,summary quietly mweight(varname) treated(varname)
support(varname)]
```

pstest calculates several measures of the balancing of the variables included in varlist before and after matching. In particular, for each variable in varlist, it calculates:

(a) *t*-tests for equality of means in the treated and untreated groups, both before and after matching. *t*-tests are based on a regression of the variable on a treatment indicator. Before matching, this is an unweighted regression on the whole sample; after matching the regression is weighted using the matching weight variable "_weight" and based on the on-support sample;

(b) The standardized bias before and after matching, together with the achieved percentage reduction in abs(bias). The standardized bias is the difference of the sample means in the treated and untreated (full or matched) subsamples as a percentage of the square root of the average of the sample variances in the treated and untreated groups.

We first calculate a before/after difference-in-mean test for the estimated propensity-score:

```
. pstest myscore
```

Variable	Sample	Mean Treated	Control	%bias	%reduct |bias|	t	p>|t|
myscore	Unmatched	.69994	.02229	310.5		76.66	0.000
	Matched	.69994	.70236	-1.1	99.6	-0.08	0.937

and for all the covariates:

```
. pstest $xvars_ps
```

Variable	Sample	Mean Treated	Control	%bias	%reduct |bias|	t	p>|t|
age	Unmatched	25.816	34.851	-100.9		-11.57	0.000
	Matched	25.816	24.773	11.7	88.5	1.61	0.108
agesq	Unmatched	717.39	1323.5	-97.1		-10.59	0.000
	Matched	717.39	639.96	12.4	87.2	1.96	0.051
educ	Unmatched	10.346	12.117	-68.1		-7.69	0.000
	Matched	10.346	10.741	-15.2	77.7	-2.01	0.045
educsq	Unmatched	111.06	156.32	-78.5		-8.52	0.000
	Matched	111.06	118.43	-12.8	83.7	-1.89	0.060
marr	Unmatched	.18919	.86627	-184.2		-25.81	0.000
	Matched	.18919	.13874	13.7	92.5	1.31	0.191
nodegree	Unmatched	.70811	.30522	87.9		11.49	0.000
	Matched	.70811	.68288	5.5	93.7	0.53	0.599

black	Unmatched	.84324	.2506	148.0		18.13	0.000
	Matched	.84324	.87027	-6.7	95.4	-0.74	0.459
hisp	Unmatched	.05946	.03253	12.9		1.94	0.053
	Matched	.05946	.05045	4.3	66.5	0.38	0.705
re74	Unmatched	2095.6	19429	-171.8		-17.50	0.000
	Matched	2095.6	2448.2	-3.5	98.0	-0.67	0.504
re75	Unmatched	1532.1	19063	-177.4		-17.50	0.000
	Matched	1532.1	1700.4	-1.7	99.0	-0.49	0.621
re74sq	Unmatched	2.8e+07	5.6e+08	-85.7		-8.30	0.000
	Matched	2.8e+07	3.3e+07	-0.8	99.0	-0.45	0.655
u74	Unmatched	.70811	.08635	164.2		27.54	0.000
	Matched	.70811	.64324	17.1	89.6	1.33	0.184
u75	Unmatched	.6	.1	122.8		20.70	0.000
	Matched	.6	.56757	8.0	93.5	0.63	0.528
u74hisp	Unmatched	.03243	.00361	21.7		5.09	0.000
	Matched	.03243	.03063	1.4	93.7	0.10	0.921

It may be useful to show how to get `pstest`'s results by hand. As example, we consider only the propensity-score:

```
. *1. For Treated
. sum myscore [aweight=_weight] if w==0
. *2. For Untreated
. sum myscore [aweight=_weight] if w==0
```

In order to assess the quality of the Matching, we can plot the distribution of the propensity-score for treated and untreated before and after Matching in the same graph. One should remember that weights can also be used when calculating the density. We first define a label for the treatment status:

```
. label define tstatus 0 Comparison_sample 1 Treated_sample
. label values w tstatus
. label variable w "Treatment Status"
```

The propensity-score density graph "before" Matching can be obtained by the following command:

```
. qui graph twoway (kdensity myscore if TREAT==1, msize(small) ) ///
(kdensity myscore if TREAT==0, msize(small) lpattern(shortdash_dot)), ///
subtitle(, bfcolor(none)) ///
xtitle("propensity-score (Before)", size(medlarge)) ///
xscale(titlegap(*7) ytitle("Density", size(medlarge)) yscale(titlegap(*5)) ///
legend(pos(12) ring(0) col(1)) ///
legend( label(1 "Treated") label(2 "Untreated")) saving(BEFORE, replace)
```

Similarly, the propensity-score density graph "after" Matching can be obtained using:

```
. qui graph twoway (kdensity myscore [aweight=_weight] if TREAT==1,
msize(small)) ///
(kdensity myscore [aweight=_weight] if TREAT==0, msize(small)
lpattern(shortdash_dot)), ///
subtitle(, bfcolor(none)) ///
xtitle(" propensity-score (After) ", size(medlarge))
xscale(titlegap(*7)) ///
ytitle("Density", size(medlarge)) yscale(titlegap(*5)) ///
legend(pos(12) ring(0) col(1)) ///
legend( label(1 "Treated") label(2 "Untreated")) saving(AFTER , replace)
```

Finally, we can combine the two previous graphs in a single graph by typing:

```
. graph combine BEFORE.gph AFTER.gph
```

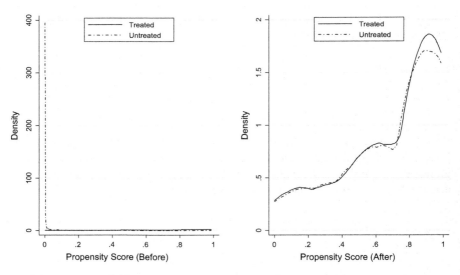

This above graph illustrates the improvement of post-matching propensity-score and visually indicates that the matching operated was successful. When this does

not occur, so that balancing is not fully achieved, one should find another specification of the propensity-score or, in the worst case, try to carefully justify why
accepting results, despite the fact that full covariates' balancing has not been
achieved. This is a limitation of Matching as an evaluation technique, since in
real datasets, it is not always possible to reach balancing (at least to some acceptable
extent), even in the presence of a rich set of covariates. This leads the researcher
sometimes to prefer methods for which such a problem is less relevant (e.g.,
Reweighting on the propensity-score).

Before concluding this section, we present an application of the Rosenbaum
sensitivity test, using the Stata user-written routine rbounds (Gangl 2004).

Syntax of rbounds

```
rbounds varname [if exp], gamma(numlist) [alpha(#) acc(#) sigonly dots]
```

Description
----

rbounds calculates Rosenbaum bounds for average treatment effects on the treated
    in the presence of unobserved heterogeneity (hidden bias) between treatment
    and control cases. rbounds takes the difference in the response variable
    between treatment and control cases as input variable varname. The procedure
    then calculates Wilcoxon sign-rank tests that give upper and lower bound
    estimates of significance levels at given levels of hidden bias. Under the
    assumption of additive treatment effects, rbounds also provides Hodges-
    Lehmann point estimates and confidence intervals for the average treatment
    effect on the treated. If installed, the input variable varname may be
    generated from psmatch or psmatch2. Currently, rbounds implements the
    sensitivity tests for matched (1x1) pairs only.

Main options
----

gamma(numlist) specifies the values of gamma for which to carry out
    the sensitivity analysis. Estimates at cap gamma = 1 (no heterogeneity)
    are included in the calculations by default. gamma() is required by
    rbounds.
alpha(#) specifies the values of alpha in the calculation of confidence
    intervals for the Hodges-Lehmann point estimate of the average treatment
    effect.
acc(#) specifies the convergence criterion of the line search algorithm
    used to find the Hodges-Lehmann point estimates. Convergence level is set
    to 1e-acc, the preset value is acc=6.
sigonly restricts rbounds to calculate Wilcoxon signrank tests for
    significance levels only.
dots may be specified for status information. The option is useful for
    checking total execution time with large samples.

Although `psmatch2` has been already run, we rerun it just for the sake of completeness.

```
. global xvars re74 re75 age agesq nodegree married black hisp
. pscore w $xvars_ps, pscore(myscore) comsup
. psmatch2 w , out(re78) pscore(myscore) common
```

Before running `rbounds`, we first calculate, for each unit, the difference between the actual and the imputed outcome by typing:

```
. gen delta = RE78 - _RE78 if _treat==1 & _support==1
```

Now, we run the `rbounds` command by writing:

```
. rbounds delta, gamma(1 (1) 3)
Rosenbaum bounds for delta (N = 185 matched pairs)
```

Gamma	sig+	sig-	t-hat+	t-hat-	CI+	CI-
1	0	0	5251.77	5251.77	4318.09	6209.05
2	1.4e-15	0	3404.07	7255.29	2505.17	8674.72
3	5.7e-11	0	2443.75	8767.93	1598.29	10253
4	1.2e-08	0	1940.64	9678.02	976.635	11562.7
5	2.9e-07	0	1505.64	10548.3	647.205	12783.4

```
* gamma   - log odds of differential assignment due to unobserved factors
  sig+    - upper bound significance level
  sig-    - lower bound significance level
  t-hat+  - upper bound Hodges-Lehmann point estimate
  t-hat-  - lower bound Hodges-Lehmann point estimate
  CI+     - upper bound confidence interval (a=  .95)
  CI-     - lower bound confidence interval (a=  .95)
```

The W-test's p-value upper bound (sig+) maintains the 5 % significance up to a value of Γ equal to 5. In this case, we can therefore sufficiently trust our Matching, since the results remain significant even with a very high and unlikely value of Γ; indeed, $\Gamma = 5$ means that the probability to be treated is five times higher for one unit than for another one, a situation that should be really rare in reality. Therefore, our matching can be taken as soundly reliable.

2.7.3 An Example of Coarsened-Exact Matching Using cem

This section provides an illustrative example of Coarsened-exact Matching (CEM) using the user-written Stata command `cem` provided by Blackwell et al. (2009).

We consider again the dataset JTRAIN_PSID1.dta. The basic cem syntax is reported below.

Syntax of cem

```
cem varname1 [(cutpoints1)] [varname2 [(cutpoints2)]] ... [, options]
```

Main options	Description
treatment(varname)	name of the treatment variable
showbreaks	display the cutpoints used for each variable
autocuts(string)	method used to automatically generate cutpoints
k2k	force cem to return a k2k solution

Description

cem implements the Coarsened Exact Matching method described in Iacus, King, and
  Porro (2012). The main input for cem are the variables to use and the
  cutpoints that define the coarsening. Users can either specify cutpoints for
  a variable or allow cem to automatically coarsen the data based on a binning
  algorithm, chosen by the user. To specify a set of cutpoints for a variable,
  place a numlist in parentheses after the variable's name. To specify an
  automatic coarsening, place a string indicating the binning algorithm to use
  in parentheses after the variable's name. To create a certain number of
  equally spaced cutpoints, say 10, place "#10" in the parentheses (this will
  include the extreme values of the variable). Omitting the parenthetical
  statement after the variable name tells cem to use the default binning
  algorithm, itself set by autocuts.

In this example, we start first by evaluating the degree of imbalance when cells are not deleted. Of course, we first need to coarsen variables. To this aim, we leave cem to apply its automated coarsening algorithm (although it is possible to choose a user-defined level of coarsening). To calculate the state of "starting" imbalance within our dataset, we make use of the imb command (provided by Stata when cem is installed). The imb syntax is in what follows:

Syntax of imb

```
imb varlist [if] [in] [, options]
```

Main options	Description
treatment(varname)	name of the treatment variable
breaks(string)	method used to generate cutpoints

Description

Imb returns a number of measures of imbalance in covariates between treatment

and control groups. A multivariate L1 distance, univariate L1 distrances,
difference in means and empirical quatiles difference are reported. The L1
measures are computed by coarsening the data according to breaks and
comparing across the multivariate histogram.

Considering a simple model with a parsimonious specification of the covariates,
we run the imb command:

```
. imb age educ black nodegree re74, treatment(treat)
Multivariate L1 distance: .94819277
-----------------------------------------------------------------------------

Univariate imbalance:
              L1       mean      min      25%      50%      75%      max
     age   .37598   -9.0344      -1       -6       -8      -15       -7
    educ   .44049   -1.7709       4       -2       -1       -2       -1
   black   .59264    .59264       0        1        1        0        0
nodegree   .40289    .40289       0        0        1        0        0
    re74   .72282    -17333       0   -10776   -18417   -25159  -1.0e+05
-----------------------------------------------------------------------------
```

The overall multivariate imbalance, as calculated by the statistic L_1, provides
evidence of a strong imbalance in this dataset, since the statistic is very close to one.
This is also reflected in univariate imbalances that are especially strong for real
earnings in 1974 ("re74", with a value of 0.72) and the variable "black" (with a
value of 0.59).

Given this initial state of imbalance, we run the cem command to see whether
there is some balancing improvement when cells that do not contain at least one
treated unit and one control unit are dropped out:

```
. cem age educ black nodegree re74, treatment(treat)
Matching Summary:
-----------------
Number of strata: 553
Number of matched strata: 61
              0       1
    All    2490     185
Matched     348     163
Unmatched  2142      22
Multivariate L1 distance: .69399345
-----------------------------------------------------------------------------

Univariate imbalance:
             L1      mean      min      25%      50%      75%      max
    age   .01132   -.29306      -1        0        1        0        1
   educ   .05817    .05608       1        0        0        0        0
```

black	2.8e-16	3.3e-16	0	0	0	0	0
nodegree	4.2e-16	-7.8e-16	0	0	0	0	0
re74	.62824	-4832.4	0	-3526.7	-6857.4	-8249.6	-226.7

We immediately see from previous results that a quite significant improvement of multivariate balancing is achieved; the statistic L_1 passes from 0.948 to 0.693 (with a decrease of around 27 %). The imbalance for "re74" (0.628), however, remains fairly strong.

What is striking is the large number of cells deleted by the cem algorithm: we started with 553 cells but only 61 out of them have matched. This is a rate of cells' survivorship of just 11 %, which is quite low and is well reflected in the significant decrease of untreated units, from 2,490 to 348 (just 13 %).

Although questionable, we accept this result at this stage and calculate the ATET through a WLS approach, using as weights those automatically generated by cem, i.e., cem_weights:

```
. regress re78 treat [iweight=cem_weights]

      Source |       SS       df       MS              Number of obs =      511
-------------+------------------------------           F(  1,   509) =    16.47
       Model |  1.6537e+09     1  1.6537e+09           Prob > F      =   0.0001
    Residual |  5.1108e+10   509   100408432           R-squared     =   0.0313
-------------+------------------------------           Adj R-squared =   0.0294
       Total |  5.2762e+10   510   103454192           Root MSE      =    10020

------------------------------------------------------------------------------
        re78 |      Coef.   Std. Err.      t    P>|t|     [95% Conf. Interval]
-------------+----------------------------------------------------------------
       treat |  -3859.77   951.0692    -4.06   0.000    -5728.275   -1991.266
       _cons |  10221.63   537.1499    19.03   0.000     9166.326    11276.93
------------------------------------------------------------------------------
```

The results indicate a negative, significant, and remarkable effect of training on real earnings in 1978. The estimated value ($-3,859$) is, however, too far from the true one (1,794), thus illustrating the bias induced by this Matching approach. As in the case of radius Matching, this bias is probably due to a too strong trimming process operated by the cem balancing algorithm. Thus, the trade-off between estimation precision and balancing tended to be mainly against the first, implying that one has to be very careful in drawing conclusions when a relatively high reduction of observations is carried out by the Matching process. This is indeed true for any Matching relying on some trimming procedure.

2.8   Implementation and Application of Reweighting

In this section, we present a Stata implementation of the Reweighting method to consistently estimate ATE, ATET, and ATENT. We first present the user-written Stata command `treatrew` (Cerulli 2014a), to be going on, by comparing it with the built-in Stata routine `teffects ipw`.

2.8.1   The Stata Routine *treatrew*

The user-written Stata module `treatrew` estimates ATEs by Reweighting on the propensity-score as proposed by Rosenbaum and Rubin (1983). Either analytical or bootstrapped standard errors are provided. The syntax follows the typical Stata command syntax.

Syntax of `treatrew`

```
    treatrew outcome treatment [varlist] [if] [in] [weight], model(modeltype)
[graphic range(a b) conf(number) vce(robust)]
-------------------------------------------------------------------------------
Description

treatrew estimates Average Treatment Effects by reweighting on propensity-score.
    Depending on the model specified, treatrew provides consistent estimation of
    Average Treatment Effects under the hypothesis of "selection on observables".
    Conditional on a pre-specified set of observable exogenous variables x -
    thought of as those driving the non-random assignment to treatment - treatrew
    estimates the Average Treatment Effect (ATE), the Average Treatment Effect on
    Treated (ATET) and the Average Treatment Effect on Non-Treated (ATENT), as
    well as the estimates of these parameters conditional on the observable
    factors x (i.e., ATE(x), ATET(x) and ATENT(x)). Parameters standard errors
    are provided either analytically (following Wooldridge, 2010, p. 920-930) and
    via bootstrapping. treatrew assumes that the propensity-score specification
    is correct.
-------------------------------------------------------------------------------
Main Options
-------------------------------------------------------------------------------
model(modeltype): specifies the model for estimating the propensity-score, where
    modeltype must be one out of these two: "probit" or "logit". It is always
    required to specify one model.
graphic: allows for a graphical representation of the density distributions of
    ATE(x), ATET(x) and ATENT(x)within their whole support.
range(a b): allows for a graphical representation of the density distributions
    of ATE(x), ATET(x) and ATENT(x) within the support [a;b] specified by the
    user. It has to be specified along with the graphic option.
```

```
modeltype_options        description
-------------------------------------------------------------------------------
    probit               The propensity-score is estimated by a probit regression
    logit                The propensity-score is estimated by a logit regression
-------------------------------------------------------------------------------
```

The user has to set: (a) the outcome variable, i.e., the variable over which the treatment is expected to have an impact (outcome); (b) the binary treatment variable (treatment); (c) a set of confounding variables (varlist); and finally (d) a series of options. Two options are of particular importance: the option model (modeltype) sets the type of model, probit or logit, that has to be used in estimating the propensity-score; the option graphic and the related option range(a b) produce a chart where the distribution of ATE(**x**), ATET(**x**), and ATENT(**x**) are jointly plotted within the interval $[a; b]$.

As treatrew is an e-class command, it provides an ereturn list of objects (such as scalars and matrices) to be used in subsequent elaborations. In particular, the values of ATE, ATET, and ATENT are returned in the scalars e(ate), e(atet), and e(atent), and they can be used to obtain bootstrapped standard errors. Observe that, by default, treatrew provides analytical standard errors.

To illustrate a practical application of treatrew, we use an illustrative dataset called FERTIL2.DTA accompanying the manual "Introductory Econometrics: A Modern Approach" by Wooldridge (2013), which collects cross-sectional data on 4,361 women of childbearing age in Botswana. This dataset is freely downloadable at http://fmwww.bc.edu/ec-p/data/wooldridge/FERTIL2.dta. It contains 28 variables on various woman and family characteristics.

Using FERTIL2.DTA, we are interested in evaluating the impact of the variable "educ7" (taking value 1, if a woman has more than or exactly 7 years of education, and 0 otherwise) on the number of children in the family ("children"). Several conditioning (or confounding) observable factors are included in the dataset, such as the age of the woman ("age"), whether or not the family owns a TV ("tv"), whether or not the woman lives in a city ("urban"), and so forth. In order to investigate the relationship between education and fertility and according to the model's specification of Wooldridge (2010, example 21.3, p. 940), we estimate ATE, ATET and ATENT (as well as ATE(**x**), ATET(**x**), and ATENT(**x**)) by "reweighting" using the treatrew command. We also compare Reweighting results with other popular program evaluation methods, such as (1) the Difference-in-means (DIM), which is taken as the benchmark case, (2) the OLS regression-based random-coefficient model with "heterogeneous reaction to confounders," estimated through the user-written Stata routine ivtreatreg (Cerulli 2014b), and (3) a one-to-one nearest-neighbor Matching, computed by the psmatch2 Stata module (Leuven and Sianesi 2003). Results from all these estimators are reported in Table 2.7.

The results in column (1) refer to the Difference-in-means (DIM) and are obtained by typing:

```
. reg children educ7
```

Table 2.7 Comparison of ATE, ATET, and ATENT estimation among DIM, CFR, REW, and MATCH

	(1) DIM	(2) CFR	(3) REW (probit) Analytical std. err.	(4) REW (logit) Analytical std. err.	(5) REW (probit) Bootstrapped std. err.	(6) REW (logit) Bootstrapped std. err.	(7) MATCH[a]
ATE	-1.77***	-0.374***	-0.43***	-0.415***	-0.434***	-0.415***	-0.316***
	0.062	0.051	0.068	0.068	0.070	0.071	0.080
	-28.46	-7.35	-6.34	-6.09	-6.15	-5.87	-3.93
ATET		-0.255***	-0.355**	-0.345***	-0.355***	-0.345***	-0.131
		0.048	0.15	0.104	0.065	0.054	0.249
		-5.37	-2.37	-3.33	-5.50	-6.45	-0.52
ATENT		-0.523***	-0.532***	-0.503**	-0.532***	-0.503***	-0.549***
		0.075	0.19	0.257	0.115	0.119	0.135
		-7.00	-2.81	-1.96	-4.61	-4.21	-4.07

Note: b/se/t, DIM difference-in-means, CFR control-function regression, REW reweighting on propensity- score, MATCH one-to-one nearest-neighbor Matching on propensity-score

[a]Standard errors for ATE and ATENT are computed by bootstrapping

**5 %, ***1 % of significance

Results on column (2) refer to CF-OLS and are obtained by typing:

```
. ivtreatreg children educ7 age agesq evermarr urban electric tv , ///
hetero(age agesq evermarr urban electric tv) model(cf-ols)
```

In the case of CF–OLS, standard errors for ATET and ATENT are obtained via bootstrap procedures and can be obtained in Stata by typing:

```
. bootstrap atet=r(atet) atent=r(atent), rep(200):   ///
ivtreatreg children educ7 age agesq evermarr urban electric tv ,  ///
hetero(age agesq evermarr urban electric tv) model(cf-ols)
```

Results set out in columns (3)–(6) refer to the Reweighting estimator (REW). In column (3) and (4), standard errors are computed analytically, whereas in column (5) and (6), they are calculated via bootstrap for the logit and probit model, respectively. These results can be retrieved by typing sequentially:

```
. treatrew children educ7 age agesq evermarr urban electric tv , ///
model(probit)
. treatrew children educ7 age agesq evermarr urban electric tv , ///
model(logit)
. bootstrap e(ate) e(atet) e(atent) , reps(200): ///
treatrew children educ7 age agesq evermarr urban electric tv , model(probit)
. bootstrap e(ate) e(atet) e(atent) , reps(200): ///
treatrew children educ7 age agesq evermarr urban electric tv , model(logit)
```

Finally, column (7) presents an estimation of ATEs obtained by implementing a one-to-one nearest-neighbor Matching on propensity-score (MATCH). Here, the standard error for ATET is obtained analytically, whereas those for ATE and ATENT are computed by bootstrapping. Matching results can be obtained by typing:

```
. psmatch2 educ7 age agesq evermarr urban electric tv, ate out(children) com
. bootstrap r(ate) r(atu): psmatch2 educ7 $xvars , ate out(children) com
```

where the option com restricts the sample to units with common support. In order to test the balancing property for such a Matching estimation, we provide a DIM on the propensity-score *before* and *after* matching treated and untreated units, using the psmatch2's post-estimation command pstest:

```
. pstest _pscore

-----------------------------------------------------------------------
                        |       Mean              %reduct  |     t-test
    Variable    Sample  | Treated  Control    %bias  |bias| |    t    p>|t|
------------------------+---------------------------------+---------------
     _pscore  Unmatched |  .65692   .42546    111.7          |  37.05  0.000
              Matched   |  .65692   .65688      0.0   100.0  |   0.01  0.994
                        |                                    |
-----------------------------------------------------------------------
```

This test suggests that with regard to the propensity-score, the Matching procedure implemented by psmatch2 is balanced; thus we can sufficiently trust the Matching results (indeed, the propensity-score was unbalanced before Matching and balanced after Matching).

A number of results warrant commenting. Unlike DIM, results from CF-OLS and REW are fairly comparable, both in terms of coefficients' size and significance; the values of ATE, ATET, and ATENT obtained using Reweighting on propensity-score are only slightly higher than those obtained by CF-OLS. This means that the linearity of the potential outcome equations assumed by the CF-OLS is an acceptable approximation. Looking at the value of ATET, obtained by REW (reported in column 3, Table 2.7), an educated woman in Botswana would have been—*ceteris paribus*—significantly more fertile if she had been less educated. We can conclude that "education" has a negative impact on fertility, resulting a woman having around 0.5 fewer children. Observe that, if confounding variables were not considered, as in using DIM, this negative effect would appear dramatically higher, of approximately 1.77 children. The difference between 1.77 and 0.5 (around 1.3) is an estimation of the bias induced by the presence of selection on observables.

Columns (3) and (4) contain REW results using Wooldridge's analytical standard errors in the case of probit and logit respectively. As one might expect, these results are very similar. Of more interest are the REW results when standard errors are obtained via bootstrap (columns (5) and (6)). Here statistical significance is confirmed when comparing these to the results derived from analytical formulas. What is immediate to see is that bootstrap procedures seem to increase significance both for ATET and ATENT, while ATE's standard error is in line with the analytical one.

Some differences in results emerge when applying the one-to-one nearest-neighbor Matching (column (7)) to this dataset. In this case, ATET becomes insignificant with a magnitude that is around one-third lower than that obtained by Reweighting. As previously discussed, ATE and ATENT's standard errors are obtained here via bootstrap, given that psmatch2 does not provide analytical solutions for these two parameters. As illustrated by Abadie and Imbens (2008), bootstrap performance is nevertheless generally poor in the case of Matching; thus, these results have to be taken with some caution.

Fig. 2.8 Estimation of the distribution of ATE(**x**), ATET(**x**), and ATENT(**x**) by Reweighting on propensity-score with range equal to (–30; 30)

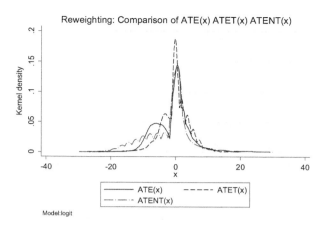

Finally, Fig. 2.8 sets out the estimated kernel density for the distribution of ATE(**x**), ATET(**x**), and ATENT(**x**) when `treatrew` is used with the options "`graphic`" and "`range(-30 30)`". It is evident that the distribution of ATET(**x**) is slightly more concentrated around its mean (equal to ATET) than ATENT(**x**), thus indicating that more educated women respond more homogenously to a higher level of education. On the contrary, less educated women react much more heterogeneously to a potential higher level of education.

2.8.2 The Relation Between `treatrew` and Stata 13's `teffects ipw`

As said, stata 13 provides a new far-reaching package, `teffects`, for estimating treatment effects for observational data. Among the many estimation methods provided by this suit, the sub-command `teffects ipw` (hereafter IPW) implements a Reweighting estimator based on inverse-probability weighting.

This routine estimates the parameters ATE, ATET, and the mean potential outcomes using a WLS regression, where weights are function of the propensity-score estimated in the first step. To see the equivalence between IPW and WLS, we apply the new command to our previous dataset by computing ATE:

```
. teffects ipw (children) (educ7 $xvars, probit) , ate
Iteration 0:   EE criterion =   6.624e-21
Iteration 1:   EE criterion =   4.111e-32
Treatment-effects estimation                Number of obs     =        4358
Estimator       : inverse-probability weights
Outcome model   : weighted mean
Treatment model: probit
```

```
---------------------------------------------------------------------
             |              Robust
    children |    Coef.   Std. Err.      z    P>|z|    [95% Conf. Interval]
-------------+-------------------------------------------------------
ATE          |
       educ7 |
     (1 vs 0)|  -.1531253  .0755592   -2.03   0.043   -.3012187  -.0050319
-------------+-------------------------------------------------------
POmean       |
       educ7 |
           0 |   2.208163  .0689856   32.01   0.000    2.072954   2.343372
---------------------------------------------------------------------
```

In this results table, we see that the value of ATE is -0.153 with a standard error of 0.075 resulting in a moderately significant effect of "educ7" on "children."

We can show that this value of ATE can also be obtained using a simple WLS regression of y on w and a constant, with weights h_i designed in this way:

$$h_i = h_{i1} = 1/p(\mathbf{x}_i) \qquad \text{if } D_i = 1$$
$$h_i = h_{i0} = 1/[1 - p(\mathbf{x}_i)] \quad \text{if } D_i = 0$$

The Stata code for computing such a WLS regression is as follows:

```
. global xvars age agesq evermarr urban electric tv
. probit educ7 $xvars , robust // estimate the probit regression
. predict _ps , p  // call the estimated propensity-score as _ps
. gen H=(1/_ps)*educ7+1/(1-_ps)*(1-educ7) // weighing function H for D=1 and D=0
. reg children educ7 [pw=H] , vce(robust) // estimate ATE by a WLS regression
---------------------------------------------------------------------
Linear regression                        Number of obs =     4358
                                         F( 1,  4356) =     2.00
                                         Prob > F      =   0.1576
                                         R-squared     =   0.0013
                                         Root MSE      =   2.1324

             |              Robust
    children |    Coef.   Std. Err.      t    P>|t|    [95% Conf. Interval]
-------------+-------------------------------------------------------
       educ7 |  -.1531253  .1083464   -1.41   0.158   -.3655393   .0592887
       _cons |   2.208163  .0867265   25.46   0.000    2.038135   2.378191
---------------------------------------------------------------------
```

This table shows that the IPW and WLS values for ATE are identical. One difference, however, is in the estimated standard errors, which are quite divergent: 0.075 in IPW compared to 0.108 in WLS. Moreover, observe that ATE calculated by WLS becomes nonsignificant.

Why do these standard errors differ? The answer resides in the difference in the approach used for estimating the variance of ATE (and, possibly, ATET): WLS regression employs the usual OLS variance–covariance matrix adjusted for the presence of a matrix of weights, let's say Ω; WLS does not, however, consider the presence of a "generated regressor"—namely—the weights computed through the propensity-scores estimated in the first step. Stata 13's IPW, in contrast, takes into account also the variability introduced by the generated weights, by exploiting a GMM approach for estimating the correct variance–covariance matrix in this case (see StataCorp 2013, pp. 68–88). In this sense, Stata 13's IPW is a more robust approach than a standard WLS regression.

Both WLS and IPW in Stata make use by default of "normalized" weights, that is, weights that add up to one. `treatrew`, instead, uses "non-normalized" weights and this is the reason why the ATEs values obtained from `treatrew` (see the previous section) are numerically different from those obtained from WLS and IPW. Moreover, as illustrated by Busso et al. (2009, p. 7), it is easy to show that a general formula for estimating ATE by Reweighting is:

$$\widehat{\text{ATE}} = \frac{1}{N}\sum_{i=1}^{N} D_i Y_i h_{i1} - \frac{1}{N}\sum_{i=1}^{N} (1 - D_i) Y_i h_{i0} \qquad (2.147)$$

`treatrew` employs non-normalized inverse-probability weights defined as above, that is:

$$h_{i1} = 1/p(\mathbf{x}_i)$$
$$h_{i0} = 1/[1 - p(\mathbf{x}_i)]$$

The weights do not sum up to one; thus, analytical standard errors cannot be retrieved by a weighted regression. The method suggested by Wooldridge (implemented by `treatrew`) for obtaining correct analytical standard errors of ATE, ATET, and ATENT is thus required, since a generated regressor from the first-step estimation is employed in the second step.

The normalized weights used in WLS and IPW are instead:

$$h_{i1} = \frac{1/p(\mathbf{x}_i)}{\dfrac{1}{N_1}\sum_{i=1}^{N} D_i/p(\mathbf{x}_i)}$$

$$h_{i0} = \frac{1/[1 - p(\mathbf{x}_i)]}{\dfrac{1}{N_0}\sum_{i=1}^{N} (1 - D_i)/[1 - p(\mathbf{x}_i)]}$$

Cerulli (2014a, appendix B) shows that if the formula for ATE uses "normalized" (rather than "non-normalized") weights, then the `treatrew`'s ATE estimation would become numerically equivalent to the value of ATE obtained by WLS and IPW.

To conclude, we can assert that both IPW and `treatrew` lead to correct analytical standard errors, as both take into account the fact that the propensity-score is a generated regressor from a first-step (probit or logit) regression. The different values of ATE and ATET obtained in the two approaches lie in the different weighting scheme (normalized vs. non-normalized) adopted.

In short, `treatrew` is useful when considering non-normalized weights, i.e. when a "pure" inverse-probability weighting scheme is employed. Moreover, compared to Stata 13's IPW, `treatrew` also provides an estimation of ATENT, although it does not provide by default an estimation of the mean potential outcome (s).

2.8.3 An Application of the Doubly-Robust Estimator

This last subsection illustrates how one can estimate ATEs using the Doubly-robust estimator discussed in Sect. 2.4. In Stata 13, this can be performed using the command `teffects aipw` where `aipw` stands for "augmented inverse-probability weighting" estimator. As discussed, the Doubly-robust estimator uses jointly Regression-adjustment and Reweighting methods for estimating ATEs and also for estimating the potential outcome means. The Doubly-robust estimator performs the following three-step procedure: (1) estimate the parameters of the selection equation and compute inverse-probability weights; (2) estimate two regressions of the outcome, one for treated and one for untreated units, to obtain the unit-specific predicted outcomes; (3) calculate the weighted means of the unit-specific predicted outcomes, where the weights are the inverse-probability weights estimated in the first step; (4) take the difference between these two averages to obtain ATEs.

It is important to note that this command allows also for various choices of the functional forms of the outcome, including the possibility to model count and binary outcomes. The basic syntax of this command is as follows:

Basic syntax of `teffects aipw`

```
teffects aipw (ovar omvarlist [, omodel noconstant]) (tvar tmvarlist [,
tmodel noconstant)] [if] [in] [weight] [, stat options]
--------------------------------------------------------------------------------
    omodel                   Description
--------------------------------------------------------------------------------
    Model
      linear                 linear outcome model; the default
      logit                  logistic outcome model
      probit                 probit outcome model
      hetprobit(varlist)     heteroskedastic probit outcome model
      poisson                exponential outcome model
--------------------------------------------------------------------------------
```

```
 tmodel                            Description
------------------------------------------------------------------------------
  Model
    logit                    logistic treatment model; the default
    probit                   probit treatment model
    hetprobit(varlist)       heteroskedastic probit treatment model
------------------------------------------------------------------------------
  stat                              Description
------------------------------------------------------------------------------
  Stat
    ate                      estimate average treatment effect; the default
    pomeans                  estimate potential-outcome means
------------------------------------------------------------------------------
```

The syntax follows the other teffects package's sub-commands, except that in this case, we can specify two distinct set of confounders, one for the outcome (omvarlist) and one for the selection (or treatment) equation (tmvarlist). The treatment binary variable is indicated by tvar and the outcome variable by ovar.

We apply an estimation of ATE and POMs to the FERTIL2.DTA dataset:

```
. global xvars age agesq evermarr urban electric tv
. teffects aipw (children $xvars) (educ7 $xvars) atet
------------------------------------------------------------------------------
Treatment-effects estimation                   Number of obs      =      4358
Estimator       : augmented IPW
Outcome model   : linear by ML
Treatment model: logit
------------------------------------------------------------------------------
             |              Robust
    children |     Coef.   Std. Err.      z    P>|z|     [95% Conf. Interval]
-------------+----------------------------------------------------------------
ATE          |
       educ7 |
    (1 vs 0) |  -.4012974   .0587055   -6.84   0.000    -.5163581   -.2862367
-------------+----------------------------------------------------------------
POmean       |
       educ7 |
           0 |   2.494768   .0481193   51.85   0.000     2.400456    2.58908
------------------------------------------------------------------------------
```

The ATE value (−0.401) is significant and very close to the one obtained using the treatrew command (−0.415), which simply implements a Reweighting estimator. Moreover, the standard errors are very close (0.059 vs. 0.068). To conclude then, the use of a three, rather than two-step approach would not appear to result in appreciable improvements in the ATE estimation within this dataset.

By including the options `pomeans` and `aequations`, we can obtain estimates of both POMs and also visualize the results of the three regressions performed to obtain previous estimation of ATE:

```
. teffects aipw (children $xvars) (educ7 $xvars) , pomeans aequations
```
```
----------------------------------------------------------------------------
Treatment-effects estimation                    Number of obs    =      4358
Estimator       : augmented IPW
Outcome model   : linear by ML
Treatment model: logit
----------------------------------------------------------------------------
```

children	Coef.	Robust Std. Err.	z	P>|z|	[95% Conf. Interval]	
POmeans						
educ7						
0	2.494768	.0481193	51.85	0.000	2.400456	2.58908
1	2.093471	.0481605	43.47	0.000	1.999078	2.187864
OME0						
age	.3606572	.0311193	11.59	0.000	.2996646	.4216498
agesq	-.0031604	.0005198	-6.08	0.000	-.0041793	-.0021416
evermarr	.8375024	.0903669	9.27	0.000	.6603864	1.014618
urban	-.3860406	.0835026	-4.62	0.000	-.5497027	-.2223786
electric	-.3695401	.1851556	-2.00	0.046	-.7324384	-.0066419
tv	-.2011699	.2748112	-0.73	0.464	-.7397899	.3374501
_cons	-4.991605	.4118896	-12.12	0.000	-5.798894	-4.184316
OME1						
age	.2356515	.0261468	9.01	0.000	.1844048	.2868983
agesq	-.0014569	.0005144	-2.83	0.005	-.0024652	-.0004487
evermarr	.5700708	.0562416	10.14	0.000	.4598392	.6803024
urban	-.1214004	.0449316	-2.70	0.007	-.2094648	-.033336
electric	-.2762289	.0702917	-3.93	0.000	-.4139981	-.1384596
tv	-.3248643	.0820202	-3.96	0.000	-.4856209	-.1641077
_cons	-3.358809	.3099163	-10.84	0.000	-3.966233	-2.751384
TME1						
age	-.0182638	.0312554	-0.58	0.559	-.0795233	.0429957
agesq	-.0013532	.0005193	-2.61	0.009	-.0023711	-.0003353
evermarr	-.5350235	.0799502	-6.69	0.000	-.691723	-.378324
urban	.5037746	.0709056	7.10	0.000	.3648023	.642747
electric	.7766193	.1373618	5.65	0.000	.5073952	1.045843

tv	1.741456	.2073006	8.40	0.000	1.335154	2.147758
_cons	1.61559	.434969	3.71	0.000	.7630665	2.468114

With the exception of the variable "tv" in the estimation of the untreated potential outcome regression (OME0 in the previous table), all covariates are highly significant in all three estimated regressions. Of course, one can be selective in deciding which covariates have to explain the selection equation and which the outcomes equations. One should, however, have convincing arguments to justify which variables to include/exclude in the potential outcomes and the selection equations, since this choice may remarkably change the causal links lying behind the model (and, as a consequence, the magnitude and significance of estimates). We will come back to this important question in the next chapter, where Instrumental-variables (IV) and Selection-model (SM) approaches will be presented and extensively discussed.

References

Abadie, A., Drukker, D., Herr, H., & Imbens, G. (2004). Implementing matching estimators for average treatment effects in Stata. *The Stata Journal, 4*, 290–311.

Abadie, A., & Imbens, G. W. (2006). Large sample properties of matching estimators for average treatment effects. *Econometrica, 74*(1), 235–267.

Abadie, A., & Imbens, G. W. (2008). On the failure of the bootstrap for matching estimators. *Econometrica, 76*(6), 1537–1557.

Abadie, A., & Imbens, G. (2011). Bias-corrected matching estimators for average treatment effects. *Journal of Business & Economic Statistics, 29*, 1–11.

Abadie, A., & Imbens, G. W. (2012). Matching on the estimated propensity score. Harvard University and National Bureau of Economic Research.

Becker, S. O., & Caliendo, M. (2007). Sensitivity analysis for average treatment effects. *The Stata Journal, 7*(1), 71–83.

Becker, S., & Ichino, A. (2002). Estimation of average treatment effects based on propensity scores. *The Stata Journal, 2*, 358–377.

Blackwell, M., Iacus, S. M., King, G., & Porro, G. (2009). CEM: Coarsened exact matching. *The Stata Journal, 9*, 524–546.

Brunell, T. L., & DiNardo, J. E. (2004). A propensity score reweighting approach to estimating the partisan effects of full turnout in American presidential elections. *Political Analysis, 12*, 28–45.

Busso, M., DiNardo, J., & McCrary, J. (2009). *New evidence on the finite sample properties of propensity score matching and reweighting estimators.* Unpublished manuscript, Dept. Of Economics, UC Berkeley.

Caliendo, M., & Kopeinig, S. (2008). Some practical guidance for the implementation of propensity score matching. *Journal of Economic Surveys, 22*, 31–72.

Cameron, A. C., & Trivedi, P. K. (2005). *Microeconometrics: Methods and applications.* New York: Cambridge University Press.

Cattaneo, M. D. (2010). Efficient semiparametric estimation of multi–valued treatment effects under ignorability. *Journal of Econometrics, 155*, 138–154.

Cerulli, G. (2014a). TREATREW: A user–written Stata routine for estimating average treatment effects by reweighting on propensity score. *The Stata Journal, 14*(3), 541–561.

Cerulli, G. (2014b). IVTREATREG: A new Stata routine for estimating binary treatment models with heterogeneous response to treatment and unobservable selection. *The Stata Journal, 14* (3), 453–480.

Cochran, W. G., & Rubin, D. B. (1973). Controlling bias in observational studies: A review. *Sankhya, Series A, 35*, 417–446.

Dehejia, R., & Wahba, S. (1999). Causal effects in nonexperimental studies: Reevaluating the evaluation of training programs. *Journal of the American Statistical Association, 94*, 1053–1062.

Dehejia, R., & Wahba, S. (2002). Propensity score–matching methods for nonexperimental causal studies. *The Review of Economics and Statistics, 84*, 151–161.

DiPrete, T., & Gangl, M. (2004). Assessing bias in the estimation of causal effects: Rosenbaum bounds on matching estimators and instrumental variables estimation with imperfect instruments. *Sociological Methodology, 34*, 271–310.

Fan, J. (1992). Local linear regression smoothers and their minimax efficiencies. *Annals of Statistics, 21*, 196–216.

Gangl, M. (2004). RBOUNDS: Stata module to perform Rosenbaum sensitivity analysis for average treatment effects on the treated. Statistical Software Components S438301, Boston College Department of Economics.

Hahn, J. (1998). On the role of the propensity score in efficient semiparametric estimation of average treatment effects. *Econometrica, 66*(2), 315–332.

Heckman, J. J., Ichimura, H., & Todd, P. E. (1997). Matching as an econometric evaluation estimator: Evidence from evaluating a job training programme. *Review of Economic Studies, 64*(4), 605–54.

Heckman, J. J., Ichimura, H., & Todd, P. (1998). Matching as an econometric evaluation estimator. *Review of Economic Studies, 65*(2), 261–94.

Hirano, K., Imbens, G. W., & Ridder, G. (2003). Efficient estimation of average treatment effects using the estimated propensity score. *Econometrica, 71*(4), 1161–1189.

Horvitz, D. G., & Thompson, D. J. (1952). A generalization of sampling without replacement from a finite universe source. *Journal of the American Statistical Association, 47*, 663–685.

Iacus, S. M., King, G., & Porro, G. (2012). Causal inference without balance checking: Coarsened exact matching. *Political Analysis, 20*, 1–24.

Imbens, G. W. (2004). Nonparametric estimation of average treatment effects under exogeneity: A review. *Review of Economics and Statistics, 86*(1), 4–29.

Imbens, G. W., & Rubin, D. (forthcoming). *Causal inference in statistics*. Cambridge: Cambridge University Press.

Johnston, J., & DiNardo, J. E. (1996). *Econometric methods*. New York: McGraw-Hill.

LaLonde, R. (1986). Evaluating the econometric evaluations of training programs with experimental data. *American Economic Review, 76*, 604–620.

Lechner, M. (2008). A note on the common support problem in applied evaluation studies. *Annals of Economics and Statistics/Annales d'Économie et de Statistique, 91/92*, 217–235.

Leuven, E., & Sianesi, B. (2003). PSMATCH2: Stata module to perform full Mahalanobis and propensity score matching, common support graphing, and covariate imbalance testing. Statistical Software Components S432001, Boston College Department of Economics, revised 12 Feb 2014.

Li, Q., Racine, J. S., & Wooldridge, J. M. (2009). Efficient estimation of average treatment effects with mixed categorical and continuous data. *Journal of Business and Economic Statistics, 27*, 206–223.

Lunceford, J. K., & Davidian, M. (2004). Stratification and weighting via the propensity score in estimation of causal treatment effects: A comparative study. *Statistics in Medicine, 15*, 2937–2960.

Nannicini, T. (2007). Simulation–based sensitivity analysis for matching estimators. *The Stata Journal, 7*, 3.

Newey, W. K. (1997). Convergence rates and asymptotic normality for series estimators. *Journal of Applied Econometrics, 5*, 99–135.

Robins, J. M., Hernan, M. A., & Brumback, B. A. (2000). Marginal structural models and causal inference in epidemiology. *Epidemiology, 11*, 550–560.

Robins, J., & Rotnitzky, A. (1995). Semiparametric efficiency in multivariate regression models with missing data. *Journal of the American Statistical Association, 90*, 122–129.

Robins, J., Rotnitzky, A., & Zhao, L. P. (1994). Estimation of regression coefficients when some regressors are not always observed. *Journal of the American Statistical Association, 89*, 846–866.

Rosenbaum, P. R. (2002). *Observational studies* (2nd ed.). New York: Springer.

Rosenbaum, P. R. (2005). Sensitivity analysis in observational studies. In B. S. Everitt & D. C. Howell (Eds.), *Encyclopedia of statistics in behavioral science* (Vol. 4, pp. 1809–1814). Chichester, UK: Wiley.

Rosenbaum, P., & Rubin, D. (1983). The central role of the propensity score in observational studies for causal effects. *Biometrika, 70*, 41–55.

Rosenbaum, P. R., & Rubin, D. B. (1984). Reducing bias in observational studies using subclassification on the propensity score. *Journal of the American Statistical Association, 79*(387), 147–156.

Saltelli, A., Ratto, M., Andres, T., Campolongo, F., Cariboni, J., Gatelli, D., Saisana, M., & Tarantola, S. (2008). *Global sensitivity analysis. The primer*. Chichester, UK: Wiley.

Seifert, B., & Gasser, T. (2000). Data adaptive ridging in local polynomial regression. *Journal of Computational and Graphical Statistics, 9*, 338–360.

Smith, J. A., & Todd, P. E. (2005). Does matching overcome LaLonde's critique of nonexperimental estimators? *Journal of Econometrics, 125*, 305–353.

StataCorp. (2013). *Stata 13 Treatment-effects reference manual*. College Station, TX: Stata Press.

Stuart, E. A. (2010). Matching methods for causal inference: A review and a look forward. *Statistical Science, 25*(1), 1–21.

Wooldridge, J. M. (2007). Inverse probability weighted estimation for general missing data problems. *Journal of Econometrics, 141*, 1281–1301.

Wooldridge, J. M. (2010). *Econometric analysis of cross section and panel data* (Vol. 2). Cambridge, MA: MIT Press. Chapter 21.

Wooldridge, J. M. (2013). *Introductory econometrics: A modern approach* (5th ed.). Mason, OH: South-Western.

Zhao, Z. (2004). Using matching to estimate treatment effects: data requirements, matching metrics, and Monte Carlo evidence. *Review of Economics and Statistics, 86*, 91–107.

Chapter 3
Methods Based on Selection on Unobservables

Contents

3.1 Introduction

This chapter covers econometric methods for estimating ATEs under "selection on unobservables," also known in the literature as "hidden bias." When nonobservable factors significantly drive the nonrandom assignment to treatment, recovering

© Springer-Verlag Berlin Heidelberg 2015

G. Cerulli, *Econometric Evaluation of Socio-Economic Programs*,
Advanced Studies in Theoretical and Applied Econometrics 49,
DOI 10.1007/978-3-662-46405-2_3

161

consistent estimations of ATEs relying only on observables (basically, the vector of covariates **x**) is no longer possible. As a consequence, econometric methods based on the conditional independence assumption (CIA) reviewed in Chap. 2 are no longer appropriate for estimating the actual program effect on target variables.

As already suggested in Chap. 1, the nature of the unobservables can be twofold. On one hand, there are unobservable elements due to some lack of information in the available datasets. This is more of a problem of data availability than genuine incapacity of gauging specific phenomena; for convenience, we will call these *contingent* unobservables. On the other hand, there are *genuine* unobservables that would be fairly impossible to measure also in case of abundant information (for instance, individual entrepreneurial innate ability, propensity to bear risks, ethical attitudes, and so on).

Regardless of what kind of "unobservableness" the analyst has to deal with, the problem becomes one of finding suitable econometric procedures in order to produce consistent estimation of ATEs under this more complicated setting. Fortunately, the literature has provided three methods to cope with selection on unobservables: Instrumental-variables (IV), Selection-models (SM), and Difference-in-differences (DID). All the three approaches offer a solution to the hidden bias problem. Their implementation requires, however, either additional information or further assumptions, which are not always available or viable.

More specifically, the application of IV requires the availability of at least one instrumental-variable, i.e., a variable in the dataset which is directly correlated with the selection process, but (directly) uncorrelated with the outcome. Similarly, Selection-models restore consistency under the assumption of joint normality of the error terms of the potential outcomes and of the selection equation. Finally, the DID estimator requires to have observations before and after the policy event, either for different or for the same set of individuals.

It is quite clear that in many program evaluation contexts, such additional assumptions and information are not always available. For this reason, working under the potential presence of a hidden bias is generally recognized as much more tricky than working under overt bias. Nevertheless, it is possible to find a solution for some situations, and knowing how to technically and computationally implement a correct estimation in these cases is of the utmost importance. For this reason, this chapter presents and discusses program evaluation econometric approaches which deal with hidden bias along with related applications either with real and artificial data.

The chapter is organized as follows: Sect. 3.2 and subsections present various IV approaches and discuss some of their limitations; Sect. 3.3 discusses the Heckman Selection-model; Sect. 3.4 sets out the DID estimator in a repeated cross section and in a longitudinal (or panel) data structure; Sect. 3.5 focuses on an application of IV and Selection-model on simulated and real data; Sect. 3.6 offers an implementation of DID both in repeated cross sections and panel data.

3.2 Instrumental-Variables

When selection into a program is driven not only by observables but also by unobservable-to-the-analyst factors, then the conditional mean independence (CMI) hypothesis no longer holds and Regression-adjustment (including Control-function regression), Matching, and Reweighting generally bring biased estimates of ATE, ATET, and ATENT (see Chap. 1).

In the regression approach, the treatment binary variable D becomes *endogenous*, that is, correlated with the error term, thus preventing ordinary least squares (OLS) from producing consistent estimates of regression parameters, including ATE, ATET, and ATENT. In the case of Matching (and propensity-score based Reweighting, for instance), the bias depends on excluding relevant covariates from the variables generating the actual propensity-score and/or from the matching procedure applied on units (as, for instance, in the nearest-neighbor approach).

In a regression setting, the typical econometric solution to deal with endogeneity problems is represented by Instrumental-variables estimation (Sargan 1958; Angrist and Krueger 1991; Abadie et al. 2002; Angrist and Imbens 1995; Angrist and Pischke 2008; Angrist 1991; Angrist et al. 1996; Imbens and Angrist 1994; Lee 2005). The virtue of this approach lays in its capacity to restore causal parameters' consistency, even under selection on unobservables (Angrist and Krueger 2001).

In practical cases, however, the application of IV has important limitations, mainly due to the need for at least one exogenous variable z, the "instrumental-variable," which is assumed to have the following two fundamental properties:

- z is (directly) correlated with treatment D
- z is (directly) uncorrelated with outcome Y

These two requirements imply that the selection into program should possibly depend on the same factors affecting the outcome *plus z*, the instrument, assumed to not directly affect the outcome. The relation between the endogenous variable D and the outcome Y can exist (so that empirical correlation might not be zero), but it can be only an "indirect link" produced by the "direct effect" of z on D. Algebraically, this represents the classical *exclusion restriction* assumption under which IV methods identify the casual parameters of interest (Heckman and Vytlacil 2001).

The causal rationale lying behind the IV approach has been widely discussed in Chap. 1, where we acknowledged that finding good instruments is neither easy nor so common in applications. Indeed, according to Angrist and Pischke (2008, p. 117), sources of instruments come "*from a combination of institutional knowledge and ideas about the processes determining the variable of interest.*" In this sense, institutional constraints may play a key role in generating suitable instruments, thus providing grounds for creating quasi-randomized settings approximating "natural experiments." For instance, in the celebrated paper of Angrist and Krueger (1991) looking for the causal relation between years of schooling and personal earning, the authors use "quarter-of-birth" in order to instrument years of education, assumed to be endogenous. Why should this be a good instrument? The authors argue that as it is compulsory to attend school until the age of 16 in many US states (and only after this threshold can a student freely drop out of school), and as individuals born in the first quarters of the year start school before the age of 6, while ones later born are more than 6 years old at that time, this induces a situation in which earlier born children have a longer education time than those born later. Empirically, the authors find a positive relation between years of education and quarter-of-birth, thus showing that this variable can serve as a good instrument for years of education. In fact, the date of birth seems unrelated to the (unobservable) variables which may influence earnings such as family background, personal motivation, and genetic attitude; as such, quarter-of-birth can be reliably assumed as randomly determined and, as such, purely exogenous. Further analytical developments on the connection between IV and causality will be presented in the next chapter where the notion of local average treatment effect (LATE) will be set out and discussed. In this chapter, we will focus mainly on how to restore consistency using IV when program's selection on unobservables is assumed. Unless stated otherwise, we assume that a reliable instrumental-variable is available.

3.2.1 IV Solution to Hidden Bias

In Chap. 1 we saw that the Difference-in-means (DIM) estimator is equal to the coefficient α obtained by an OLS regression of this simple univariate linear model:

$$Y = \mu + \alpha D + u \tag{3.1}$$

so that:

$$\alpha = E(Y|D = 1) - E(Y|D = 0) = \text{DIM} \tag{3.2}$$

It is also known that in a univariate regression such as (3.1):

$$\alpha = \text{Cov}(Y; D)/\text{Var}(D) \tag{3.3}$$

Suppose now that the selection-into-treatment was driven by a factor x, that is unobservable-to-the-analyst. We want to characterize this situation and show that IV provides an unbiased estimate of α. Such a situation entails that the outcome is also function of x. In other words, the true process generating Y is:

$$Y = \mu + \alpha D + \beta x + u \tag{3.4}$$

Since in (3.4) x is unobservable, it is part of the error term; thus the model becomes:

$$Y = \mu + \alpha D + u^* \tag{3.5}$$

with $u^* = \beta x + u$ showing that the treatment D and the new error term u^* are related, for the selection-into-treatment is supposed to depend on x. A simple OLS of regression (3.5), therefore, leads to a biased estimation of α; in fact:

$$\alpha_{OLS} = \text{Cov}(Y; D)/\text{Var}(D) = \text{Cov}(\mu + \alpha D + \beta x + u; D)/\text{Var}(D)$$
$$= \alpha \text{Var}(D)/\text{Var}(D) + \beta \text{Cov}(x; D)/\text{Var}(D) \tag{3.6}$$

that is:

$$\alpha_{OLS} = \alpha + \beta \text{Cov}(x; D)/\text{Var}(D) \tag{3.7}$$

where, similarly to what is stated in (3.3), we get that:

$$\alpha_{OLS} = \alpha + \beta \{ E(x|D = 1) - E(x|D = 0) \} \tag{3.8}$$

which is also equivalent to (1.58). Equation (3.8) proves that in the case of unobservable selection, a standard OLS is a biased estimator. This depends on the fact that the basic assumption for OLS to be consistent in (3.5), i.e., $\text{Cov}(D; u^*) = 0$, fails when the error contains factors driving the selection-into-treatment, which results in $\text{Cov}(D; u^*) \neq 0$.

In such a situation, an IV approach can restore consistency, provided that an instrumental-variable z, correlated with D but uncorrelated with u^*, is available. If we assume that u is a pure random component, thus uncorrelated by definition with z, we can show that:

$$\text{Cov}(z; u^*) = \text{Cov}(z; \beta x + u) = \beta \text{Cov}(z; x) + \text{Cov}(z; u) = \beta \text{Cov}(z; x) = 0 \tag{3.9}$$

implying that $\text{Cov}(z; x) = 0$. By starting from (3.5), and assuming that $\text{Cov}(z; u^*)$ is zero, with z as an instrument, we have that:

$$\text{Cov}(z; u^*) = \text{Cov}(z; Y - \mu - \alpha D) = \text{Cov}(Y; z) - \alpha \text{Cov}(D; z) = 0 \tag{3.10}$$

implying immediately that:

$$\alpha_{IV} = \text{Cov}(Y; z)/\text{Cov}(D; z) \tag{3.11}$$

We can now show that this estimator is consistent. In fact:

$$\alpha_{IV} = \text{Cov}(Y; z)/\text{Cov}(D; z) = \frac{\text{Cov}(\mu + \alpha D + \beta x + u; z)}{\text{Cov}(D; z)}$$

$$= \frac{\alpha \cdot \text{Cov}(D; z) - \beta \cdot \text{Cov}(x; z)}{\text{Cov}(D; z)} = \alpha \tag{3.12}$$

as $\text{Cov}(x; z) = 0$ as assumed in (3.9). Equation (3.12) proves that the IV estimator of the effect of D on Y is consistent for the true causal parameter α.

3.2.2 IV Estimation of ATEs

This section, which presents IV methods for consistently estimating ATEs, relies on a vast literature on IV methods in the econometrics of program evaluation. In what follows, however, we will refer to the excellent review by Wooldridge (2010, pp. 937–954) and Angrist and Pischke (2008, Chap. 4), as well as to papers by Angrist et al. (1996), Heckman (1997), and Heckman and Vytlacil (1998).

To see how IV can consistently estimate ATE, ATET, and ATENT consider, as done in Chap. 2, the switching random coefficient regression derived from the potential outcome model (POM):

$$Y = \mu_0 + D(\mu_1 - \mu_0) + v_0 + D(v_1 - v_0) \tag{3.13}$$

This equation, assuming that CMI does not hold, yields:

$$E(v_1|D, \mathbf{x}) \neq E(v_1|\mathbf{x}) \tag{3.14}$$

and

$$E(v_0|D, \mathbf{x}) \neq E(v_0|\mathbf{x}) \tag{3.15}$$

As in the case of Control-function regression, we can distinguish two cases: (1) the *homogenous* and (2) the *heterogeneous* cases.

Case 1 $v_1 = v_0$ *(homogenous case)*

As seen for Control-function regression, in this case one assumes that $v_1 = v_0$, thus:

$$Y = \mu_0 + D(\mu_1 - \mu_0) + v_0 \tag{3.16}$$

This equation implies that:

$$\text{ATE} = \text{ATET} = \text{ATENT} = \mu_1 - \mu_0 \tag{3.17}$$

Suppose, however, one has an instrumental-variable z. Formally, the two properties that such a variable should have can be written as:

$$\text{E}(v_0|\mathbf{x}, z) = \text{E}(v_0|\mathbf{x}) \quad \Leftrightarrow \quad z \text{ is uncorrelated with } v_0 \tag{3.18}$$

$$\text{E}(D|\mathbf{x}, z) \neq \text{E}(D|\mathbf{x}) \quad \Leftrightarrow \quad z \text{ is correlated with } D \tag{3.19}$$

By considering firstly (3.18), we can assume that $\text{E}(v_0 \mid \mathbf{x}, z) = \text{E}(v_0 \mid \mathbf{x}) = g(\mathbf{x}) = \mathbf{x}\boldsymbol{\beta}$, which means that $\text{E}(v_0 \mid \mathbf{x}, z) \neq 0$. Simple algebra yields a regression model containing an error term with zero unconditional mean of this type (see Wooldridge 2010, pp. 937–938):

$$Y = \mu_0 + D \cdot \text{ATE} + \mathbf{x}\beta + u \tag{3.20}$$

that is a model in which $(\mathbf{x}, z)$ are uncorrelated with the error term u, i.e., $(\mathbf{x}, z)$ are exogenous, but the error term u is still correlated with D, the treatment.

The previous assumptions and relationships can be more compactly summarized in the following two-equation structural system:

$$\begin{cases} \text{(a)} & Y_i = \mu_0 + D_i \text{ATE} + \mathbf{x}_i \boldsymbol{\beta} + u_i \\ \text{(b)} & D_i^* = \eta + \mathbf{q}_i \boldsymbol{\delta} + \varepsilon_i \\ \text{(c)} & D_i = \begin{cases} 1 & \text{if } D_i^* \geq 0 \\ 0 & \text{if } D_i^* < 0 \end{cases} \\ \text{(d)} & \mathbf{q}_i = (\mathbf{x}_i, z_i) \end{cases} \tag{3.21}$$

where ATE cannot be consistently estimated by an OLS of (3.21a), since without invoking CMI, we have that $\text{Cov}(u_i; \varepsilon_i) \neq 0$, thus D is endogenous in this equation. In the previous system, (3.21a) is known as the *outcome equation*, whereas (3.21b)—or, equivalently, (3.21c)—is known as the *selection equation* and (3.21d) as the identifying *exclusion restriction*.

In program evaluation, (3.21b) represents the latent selection function derived from: (1) an objective function of a supporting external agency choosing whether a unit is, or is not, suitable for treatment; (2) self-selection into the program operated by units themselves, according to some cost/benefit contrast within a proper unit pay-offs function. Generally, it is assumed that D_i^*, a rescaled scalar score associated with each eligible unit, is unknown to the evaluator as he only knows the (final) binary decision indicator D_i (selected vs. not selected for the program), along with some other observable unit characteristics (covariates) affecting this choice.

In a system like (3.21), endogeneity arises when one assumes that the unobservable factors affecting the selection into program (i.e., ε_i) are correlated with the unobservable factors affecting the realization of units' outcome (i.e., u_i). In the case of zero correlation between these two terms, OLS of (3.21a) produces consistent estimation of ATE.

Table 3.1 Common binary outcome probability rules for the selection-into-treatment

Model	$p(D = 1 \mid \mathbf{x}) = E(D = 1 \mid \mathbf{x}) = F(\mathbf{x}\boldsymbol{\beta})$
Lineal	$\mathbf{x}\boldsymbol{\beta}$
Probit	$\Phi(\mathbf{x}\boldsymbol{\beta})$
Logit	$\Lambda(\mathbf{x}\boldsymbol{\beta}) = \exp(\mathbf{x}\boldsymbol{\beta})/[1 + \exp(\mathbf{x}\boldsymbol{\beta})]$

An important question is: how can we estimate consistently ATE in system (3.21) when $\mathrm{Cov}(u_i; \varepsilon_i) \neq 0$? In general, we may rely on three IV methods:

- Direct-2SLS
- Probit-OLS
- Probit-2SLS

They have different properties, and in what follows, we provide a brief exposition of these three approaches. As will be seen, an important role to qualify the properties of such estimators is played by the assumption about the process generating the selection-into-treatment indicator D: Table 3.1 reports three classical cases usually adopted in applications.

3.2.2.1   Direct Two-Stage Least Squares

This approach is the traditional IV procedure used in textbook econometrics (Cameron and Trivedi 2005; Wooldridge 2010). It is based on two sequential OLS regressions in order to calculate the predictions of the endogenous variable D in the first step, and on using these predictions as a regressor in the outcome equation in place of the actual D in the second step. This approach assumes that the probability to be treated given $\mathbf{x}$ takes a linear form. As such, the selection equation can be consistently estimated by OLS, regardless of the fact that the treatment endogenous variable is binary. The implementation of direct two-stage least squares (Direct-2SLS), therefore, follows this procedure:

1. Estimate the selection equation by running an OLS regression of D on $\mathbf{x}$ and z of the type: $D_i = \eta + \mathbf{x}_i \boldsymbol{\delta}_\mathbf{x} + z_i \delta_z + error_i$, to obtain the "predicted values" of D_i, denoted by $D_{\mathrm{fv},i}$;
2. Estimate the outcome equation by running a second OLS of Y on $\mathbf{x}$ and $D_{\mathrm{fv},i}$. The coefficient of $D_{\mathrm{fv},i}$ is a consistent estimation of ATE.

It is evident that in step 1, what is fitted is a linear probability model, while in step 2, a standard OLS regression is estimated. The second step also provides the analytical estimation of ATE and of its standard error to perform usual significance tests. As we will clarify later on, the robustness of this approach hinges mainly on the quality of the chosen variable z, as a *weak* instrument (a z poorly correlated with the treatment D) can inflate parameters' standard errors, thus making estimates highly imprecise.

3.2.2.2 Probit-OLS (Logit-OLS)

Generally, assuming that the treatment probability varies linearly with **x,** and z is too demanding, and nonlinear probability functions such as probit or logit are generally preferred. The probit, for instance, assumes that the error term of the latent selection equation in (3.21b) is standard normally distributed, while the logit supposes a logistic distribution.

Take the case of the probit (the logit follows a similar argument), since it implies the normality assumption of the selection error, using Direct-2SLS leads to efficiency loss of estimations, as this latter method does not exploit suitably the normality of the error term ε. This is an important limitation of Direct-2SLS. Nevertheless, a more efficient estimation procedure (we call here Probit-OLS) can be found in the normality case. To see how, we have to first observe that:

$$E(D|\mathbf{x}, z) = p(D = 1|\mathbf{x}, z) \qquad (3.22)$$

showing that, when D is binary, the propensity-score is equivalent to the orthogonal projection of the vector D in the vector space generated by the exogenous variable $(\mathbf{x}, z)$. Among all the projections of D on the $(\mathbf{x}, z)$ subspace, the orthogonal one produces the "smallest" projection error: Fig. 3.1 provides a visual representation of this important property of the orthogonal projection.

Figure 3.1 illustrates that the projection error of D is minimized when the projection is E($D \mid \mathbf{x}$, z); in fact, the vector norm of the error e_{op} is always the smallest one compared with the vector norm of any other generic projection vector h. This derives from the following property of the conditional expectation:

$$E(D|\mathbf{x}, z) = \mathrm{argmin}_{f(\mathbf{x}, z)}\left\{\sum_{i=1}^{n} [D_i - f(\mathbf{x}, z)]^2\right\}$$

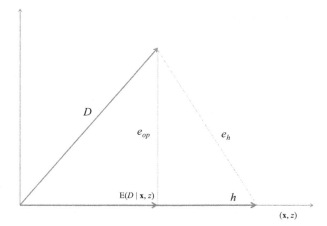

Fig. 3.1 Visualization of the orthogonal projection of D on the vector space generated by $(\mathbf{x}, z)$

Thus, if one (erroneously) uses Direct-2SLS when $E(D = 1 \mid \mathbf{x}) = \Phi(\mathbf{x}\boldsymbol{\beta})$, then one is not using the best representation of D as function of $(\mathbf{x}; z)$. This reduces the precision of the estimation of the selection equation and thus that of ATE. Note, however, that in this setup, Direct-2SLS is still consistent.

If the selection equation is estimated by a probit, a higher level of efficiency is obtained, since the correct orthogonal projection is used. This suggests, therefore, that a slightly different procedure—the Probit-OLS (or Logit-OLS)—should be implemented:

1. Estimate the selection equation by running a probit (or logit) regression of D on $\mathbf{x}$ and z thus obtaining the "predicted probabilities" of D_i, denoted by $p_{1D,i}$;
2. Estimate the outcome equation by running a second OLS of Y on $\mathbf{x}$ and $p_{1D,i}$. The estimated coefficient of $p_{1D,i}$ provides a consistent estimation of ATE.

Once again, the choice between a logit and a probit depends on whether a standard normal or a logistic distribution of ε is assumed. Focus on the probit case although the same augments apply for the logit model. The Probit-OLS can be directly derived from the outcome equation. By taking the expectation of Y conditional on $(\mathbf{x}, z)$ in (3.21a), we obtain:

$$E\big(Y\big|\mathbf{x}, z\big) = \mu_0 + \text{ATE} \cdot E\big(D\big|\mathbf{x}, z\big) + \mathbf{x}\boldsymbol{\beta} \qquad (3.23)$$

since $E(u \mid \mathbf{x}, z) = 0$ being $\mathbf{x}$ and z exogenous by definition. Substituting (3.22) into the previous equation we obtain:

$$E\big(Y\big|\mathbf{x}, z\big) = \mu_0 + \text{ATE} \cdot p\big(D = 1\big|\mathbf{x}, z\big) + \mathbf{x}\boldsymbol{\beta} \qquad (3.24)$$

This relation suggests that one is able to consistently estimate ATE with a simple OLS regression of Y on $(1, p_{1D,i}, \mathbf{x})$, which is exactly what Probit-OLS does. Observe, however, that standard errors for ATE need to be corrected for both the presence of a generated regressor in (3.24) and for heteroscedasticity.

This approach does, however, have an important limitation. In order to preserve estimation efficiency, Probit-OLS requires that the probit is the "actual probability rule" governing the conditional probability of being treated. This is somewhat of a drawback, given that specification errors may occur frequently in applied work. It is immediate to see that in such a case, inconsistency depends on the presence of a "measurement error" from the first-step estimation of the propensity-score, which directly enters the outcome equation in (3.24).

3.2.2.3 Probit-2SLS (Logit-2SLS)

As previously mentioned, consistency for Probit-OLS depends on relying on a correctly specified propensity-score model. When this assumption does not hold, previous procedure can lead to inconsistent results. A way to overcome this limitation is that of using instead of OLS a 2SLS after running the probit. This alternative procedure, called here Probit-2SLS (or Logit-2SLS), works as follows: first, apply a probit (logit) of D on $\mathbf{x}$ and z, thus obtaining the "predicted probability of D"; then, use these probabilities to apply a (direct) 2SLS with the predicted probabilities obtained from the probit (logit) estimation being used as an instrument for D. In other words, the Probit-2SLS uses the estimated propensity-score as instrument for D.

This procedure leads to higher efficiency than that of Direct-2SLS. Why? In the case of Direct-2SLS, the instrument used for D is z; however, functions of $(\mathbf{x}; z)$ might be more correlated with D than the z alone. In particular, as argued above, there is a function of $(\mathbf{x}; z)$ which has the highest correlation with D, namely $\mathrm{E}(D \mid \mathbf{x}, z) = $ propensity-score , i.e., the orthogonal projection of D on all exogenous variables (including the instrument).

To conclude, when the probit (or logit, depending on the case) model is correctly specified, Probit-2SLS uses the best instrument available in the class of all instruments that are functions of $(\mathbf{x}, z)$. Probit-2SLS, therefore, is more efficient than Direct-2SLS but generally no more than Probit-OLS (although with slight differences in this latter case).

The very advantage of using Probit-2SLS is that, unlike Probit-OLS, it returns consistent estimations even when the first-step probit is incorrectly specified (although, it is no more efficient in this case). This occurs since, unlike Probit-OLS, the (incorrect) estimation of the probit does not enter directly in the outcome equation. Furthermore, the propensity-score estimated by the probit, although incorrect, still remains a function of $\mathbf{x}$ and z, and thus, it is a valid instrument. Of course, in an incorrectly specified setting, Probit-2SLS loses efficiency. In practice, Probit-2SLS follows these three steps:

1. Estimate a probit of D on $\mathbf{x}$ and z, getting $p_{1D,i}$, i.e., the "predicted probability of D."
2. Run an OLS of D on $(1, \mathbf{x}, p_{1D,i})$, thus getting the fitted values $D_{2\mathrm{fv},i}$.
3. Finally, estimate a second OLS of Y on $(1, \mathbf{x}, D_{2\mathrm{fv},i})$.

The estimated coefficient of $D_{2\mathrm{fv},i}$ is a consistent estimate of ATE, which does not require that the process generating D is correctly specified in order to obtain consistency.

Finally, in contrast to Probit-OLS, a further robust characteristic of Probit-2SLS is that the standard errors in this case do not need to be adjusted for the presence of a generated instrument, given that this estimator meets the condition for consistency required in cases like this (see Wooldridge 2010, pp. 124–125).

3.2.2.4 The Identification Issue

From a technical point of view, when using Probit-OLS or Probit-2SLS, identifying $(\mu_0, \mathrm{ATE}, \boldsymbol{\beta})$ in the outcome equation (3.21a) does not require one to introduce z as additional regressor in the selection equation (3.21b). Indeed, for identification purposes, it is sufficient that the selection equation contains just the vector of covariates $\mathbf{x}$. Since $F(\mathbf{x}\boldsymbol{\beta})$ is a nonlinear function of $\mathbf{x}$, then it is not perfectly collinear with $\mathbf{x}$. $F(\mathbf{x}\boldsymbol{\beta})$ can, therefore, be used as an instrument along with $\mathbf{x}$, since it does not produce problems of collinearity. Problems due to collinearity can, however, emerge when $F(\cdot)$ is assumed to be linear (as in the case of the linear probability model).

Nevertheless, since $\mathbf{x}$ and $F(\mathbf{x}\boldsymbol{\beta})$ are strongly correlated and are used jointly as instruments, it can be proven that the previous IV estimators have larger variances, thereby providing a more imprecise estimation of the actual policy effect. When using IV methods such as Probit-OLS and Probit-2SLS, it is, therefore, recommended to have access to at least one instrument z, which can be exploited in the estimation of the selection equation.

3.2.3 IV with Observable and Unobservable Heterogeneities

The previous IV estimators did not take into account either observable or unobservable heterogeneity. When we eliminate this assumption, minor changes need to be incorporated into these IV procedures. It seems worth emphasizing how one, however, proceeds in the case of both observable and unobservable heterogeneities, which we label as IV Case 2.

Case 2 $v_1 \neq v_0$ (heterogeneous case)

Consider now the case in which $v_1 \neq v_0$, so that $Y = \mu_0 + D\,(\mu_1 - \mu_0) + v_0 + D\,(v_1 - v_0)$. As in the Control-function regression, this assumption implies that ATE $\neq$ ATET $\neq$ ATENT. This is the case of observable heterogeneity, where ATE $(\mathbf{x})$, ATET$(\mathbf{x})$, and ATENT$(\mathbf{x})$ can be separately defined and estimated. As suggested in Chap. 1, this assumption states that the same unit has a different reaction to variations in the vector of observables $\mathbf{x}$ when it is treated and untreated. For many empirical applications, this seems a more general and reasonable assumption.

Suppose that v_1 and v_0 are independent of z: thus, z is assumed to be exogenous in this model, that is:

$$E\left(v_0 \big| \mathbf{x}, z\right) = E\left(v_0 \big| \mathbf{x}\right) = g_0(\mathbf{x}) \tag{3.25}$$

$$E\left(v_1 \big| \mathbf{x}, z\right) = E\left(v_1 \big| \mathbf{x}\right) = g_1(\mathbf{x}) \tag{3.26}$$

This is equivalent to writing:

$$v_0 = g_0(\mathbf{x}) + e_0 \quad \text{with} \quad E\left(e_0 \big| \mathbf{x}, z\right) = 0 \tag{3.27}$$

$$v_1 = g_1(\mathbf{x}) + e_1 \quad \text{with} \quad E\left(e_1 \big| \mathbf{x}, z\right) = 0 \tag{2.28}$$

By substituting these expressions for v_0 and v_1 into the POM for Y, we obtain that:

$$Y = \mu_0 + \alpha D + g_0(\mathbf{x}) + D[g_1(\mathbf{x}) - g_0(\mathbf{x})] + e_0 + D(e_1 - e_0) \qquad (3.29)$$

By assuming in the previous equation that $g_0(\mathbf{x}) = \mathbf{x}\boldsymbol{\beta}_0$, $g_1(\mathbf{x}) = \mathbf{x}\boldsymbol{\beta}_1$, and $\varepsilon = e_0 + D(e_1 - e_0)$ and by applying the same procedure as seen in Case 1, we obtain the following regression model:

$$Y = \mu_0 + \text{ATE} \cdot D + \mathbf{x}\boldsymbol{\beta}_0 + D(\mathbf{x} - \boldsymbol{\mu_x})\boldsymbol{\beta} + \varepsilon \qquad (3.30)$$

This model contains two endogenous variables, D and $D(\mathbf{x} - \boldsymbol{\mu_x})$. How can we deal with this additional endogenous variable? Intuitively, if $h = h(\mathbf{x}, z)$ is an instrument for D, then a suitable instrument for $D \cdot (\mathbf{x} - \boldsymbol{\mu_x})$ is $h \cdot (\mathbf{x} - \boldsymbol{\mu_x})$. Thus, IV estimation can still be implemented. Nevertheless, before applying IV as in Case 1, we need to distinguish between two further sub-cases related to Case 2:

Case 2.1 $e_1 = e_0$ (only observable heterogeneity)

Case 2.2 $e_1 \neq e_0$ (both observable and unobservable heterogeneities)

In what follows we examine the two cases separately.

Case 2.1 $e_1 = e_0$ (only observable heterogeneity)

This subcase assumes that unobservable heterogeneity is not at work and thus only observable heterogeneity matters. This is a quite strong assumption, but one that holds in many applications, especially when the analyst has access to a large set of observable variables and is sure that diversity in units' outcome response is driven by these (available) observable factors. In this case, therefore, we have that $\varepsilon = e_0$. Recalling that $E(e_0 \mid \mathbf{x}, z) = 0$, we can immediately conclude that:

$$Y = \mu_0 + \alpha D + \mathbf{x}\boldsymbol{\beta}_0 + D(\mathbf{x} - \boldsymbol{\mu_x})\boldsymbol{\beta} + e_0 \qquad (3.31)$$

with $E(e_0 \mid \mathbf{x}, z, D) = E(e_0 \mid D)$. Thus what remains in the model is simply the endogeneity due to D and $D(\mathbf{x} - \boldsymbol{\mu_x})$. The following procedure is therefore suitable in order to obtain a consistent estimation of the parameters in (3.31):

- Apply a probit of D on $\mathbf{x}$ and z, obtaining p_D, i.e., the "predicted probability of D."
- Estimate the following equation: $Y_i = \mu_0 + \alpha D_i + \mathbf{x}_i\boldsymbol{\beta}_0 + D_i(\mathbf{x}_i - \boldsymbol{\mu_x})\boldsymbol{\beta} + error_i$ using as instruments: $1, p_D, \mathbf{x}_i, p_D(\mathbf{x}_i - \boldsymbol{\mu_x})$.

This procedure is equivalent to the Probit-2SLS estimator presented in the previous section. Of course, either Direct-2SLS or Probit-OLS procedure can, as above, be applied here with minimal changes.[1]

---

[1] For the sake of brevity, we do not report the implementation of these procedures for this case, although it is evident how they can be performed.

A particularly attractive property of a model with heterogeneity is that various functions and interactions of $(\mathbf{x}, z)$ can be used to generate additional instruments, in order to obtain an *overidentified* setting and thus test the (joint) exogeneity of the instruments.

Case 2.2 $e_1 \neq e_0$ (both observable and unobservable heterogeneities)

When the unobservable component affecting the outcome for a given unit is different when such a unit is treated or untreated, unobservable heterogeneity occurs. In this case, as seen above, the full and more general regression model associated with the POM is:

$$Y = \mu_0 + \alpha D + g_0(\mathbf{x}) + D[g_1(\mathbf{x}) - g_0(\mathbf{x})] + e_0 + D(e_1 - e_0) \qquad (3.32)$$

In this case, the error term contains the endogenous variable D so that the mean of $D(e_1 - e_0)$ conditional on $\mathbf{x}$ and z is not equal to zero. Thus, to restore consistent estimation, we need to assume some additional conditions.

One possible solution could be that of assuming that $E[D(e_1 - e_0) \mid \mathbf{x}, z] = E[D(e_1 - e_0)]$. Applying previous algebra yields the following form of the outcome equation:

$$Y = \mu_0 + \alpha D + \mathbf{x}\boldsymbol{\beta}_0 + D(\mathbf{x} - \boldsymbol{\mu}_\mathbf{x})\boldsymbol{\beta} + e_0 + D(e_1 - e_0) \qquad (3.33)$$

By defining:

$$r = D(e_1 - e_0) - E[D(e_1 - e_0)]$$

and by adding and subtracting $E[D(e_1 - e_0)]$ in (3.18), we obtain:

$$Y = \eta + \alpha D + \mathbf{x}\boldsymbol{\beta}_0 + D(\mathbf{x} - \boldsymbol{\mu}_\mathbf{x})\boldsymbol{\beta} + e_0 + r \qquad (3.34)$$

where $\eta = \mu_0 + E[D(e_1 - e_0)]$. It is immediate to see that $E(e_0 + r \mid \mathbf{x}, z) = 0$. Thus, any function of $(\mathbf{x}, z)$ can be used as instrument in the outcome equation. One can, therefore, apply an IV procedure identical to that of Case 2.1, that is, one based on estimating:

$$Y_i = \eta + \alpha D_i + \mathbf{x}_i\boldsymbol{\beta}_0 + D_i(\mathbf{x}_i - \boldsymbol{\mu}_\mathbf{x})\boldsymbol{\beta} + error_i \qquad (3.35)$$

using as instruments 1, p_D, $\mathbf{x}_i$, and $p_D(\mathbf{x}_i - \boldsymbol{\mu}_\mathbf{x})$. This IV estimator is consistent but generally not efficient. In order to obtain an efficient estimation, one needs to introduce some additional hypotheses. In what follows, we focus on the Heckman (1978) Selection-model (known as "Heckit") with *unobservable heterogeneity*. It is a strong parametric model, but it can be useful in empirical applications to obtain efficient estimation of ATEs.

It is also worth noting that a consistent estimation of ATET and ATENT can be obtained using formulas analogous to those in (2.33)–(2.38) by replacing the unknown parameters of those formulas with those obtained from previous IV estimation procedures. The IV estimations of ATEs therefore are:

$$\widehat{ATE} = \widehat{\alpha}_{IV} \tag{3.36}$$

$$\widehat{ATE}(\mathbf{x}) = \widehat{\alpha}_{IV} + (\mathbf{x} - \overline{\mathbf{x}})\widehat{\boldsymbol{\beta}}_{IV} \tag{3.37}$$

$$\widehat{ATET} = \widehat{\alpha}_{IV} + (N_1)^{-1}\sum_{i=1}^{N} D_i(\mathbf{x}_i - \overline{\mathbf{x}})\widehat{\boldsymbol{\beta}}_{IV} \tag{3.38}$$

$$\widehat{ATET}(\mathbf{x}) = \left[\widehat{\alpha}_{IV} + (\mathbf{x} - \overline{\mathbf{x}})\widehat{\boldsymbol{\beta}}_{IV}\right]_{(D=1)} \tag{3.39}$$

$$\widehat{ATENT} = \widehat{\alpha}_{IV} + (1/N_0)^{-1}\sum_{i=1}^{N}\left(1 - D_i\right)(\mathbf{x}_i - \overline{\mathbf{x}})\widehat{\boldsymbol{\beta}}_{IV} \tag{3.40}$$

$$\widehat{ATENT}(\mathbf{x}_i) = \left[\widehat{\alpha}_{IV} + (\mathbf{x}_i - \overline{\mathbf{x}})\widehat{\boldsymbol{\beta}}_{IV}\right]_{(D=0)} \tag{3.41}$$

As in the Control-function regression case, standard errors for ATET and ATENT can be obtained via bootstrap procedures.

3.2.4 Problems with IV Estimation

IV estimation is a powerful tool to deal with treatment endogeneity produced by selection on unobservables. As seen, in fact, IV methods are able to restore consistent estimation of average treatment effects on the target variable without taking on excessively strong parametric assumptions like, for instance, specific distributional forms of the errors. Nevertheless, IV have a number of non-negligible limitations; thus, the implementation of this approach is sometimes questionable in empirical applications. In what follows, we consider three main drawbacks possibly arising from the use of IV: (1) inconsistency; (2) lower efficiency; (3) small-sample bias. See Cameron and Trivedi (2005, pp. 98–112) for a detailed review.

The inconsistency and lower efficiency limitations are related to problems induced by so-called "weak" instruments (Bound et al. 1995), instruments that are either not fully exogenous for the outcome or not sufficiently well correlated with the treatment variable in a multivariate sense. If one of these two conditions is not met, the reliability of IV estimation can be questionable due to possible inconsistency and/or low precision (i.e., larger standard errors) of IV.

The third drawback refers to the bias of 2SLS when one cannot invoke the usual asymptotic results. In finite samples, in fact, it can be proven that IV may be inconsistent, with the bias possibly increasing with the number of instruments used and the weakness of these instruments. In what follows, each of these limitations are discussed separately.

3.2.4.1   Inconsistency of IV

To illustrate how a weak instrument can produce inconsistent IV estimates, take the case of a single-covariate/single-instrument linear regression of the type:

$$Y = \alpha D + u \tag{3.42}$$

where we assume that both Y and D are standardized with mean equal to zero and unit variance. This is identical to (3.1), except for the fact that with standardized variables the intercept is now zero. Adapting (3.7) and (3.12), we have that:

$$\alpha_{OLS} = \frac{\text{Cov}(Y;D)}{\text{Var}(D)} = \alpha + \frac{\text{Cov}(D;u)}{\text{Var}(D)} \tag{3.43}$$

$$\alpha_{IV} = \frac{\text{Cov}(Y;z)}{\text{Cov}(D;z)} = \alpha + \frac{\text{Cov}(z;u)}{\text{Cov}(z;D)} \tag{3.44}$$

implying that IV are also inconsistent when $\text{Cov}(z;u) \neq 0$, in other words, when z is no longer fully exogenous. Furthermore, the bias increases as the covariance of z and D decreases, showing that poor projection of D on z leads to a larger bias. Interestingly, we can also perform a ratio between the OLS and IV bias to see that:

$$\frac{\text{plim}\{\widehat{\alpha}_{IV} - \alpha\}}{\text{plim}\{\widehat{\alpha}_{OLS} - \alpha\}} = \frac{\text{Cov}(z;u)}{\text{Cov}(D;u)} \times \frac{1}{\text{Cov}(z;D)} \tag{3.45}$$

since $\text{Var}(D) = 1$ by definition. The previous ratio does not exclude the possibility that the IV bias is greater than the OLS bias. For instance, if one supposes that $\text{Cov}(z;u) = \text{Cov}(D;u) = 0.1$, but that $\text{Cov}(D;u) = 0.20$, then the IV bias is five times that of the OLS bias, and this result is obtained with a very low degree of endogeneity of only 0.1. Unless we can rely on a "pure" exogenous instrument, IV are strongly sensitive to departures from this hypothesis. Moreover, the lower the covariance between z and D, the more the IV bias outweigh of the OLS; finally, introducing exogenous covariates in (3.42) does not change this result.

3.2.4.2   Lower Efficiency of IV

Even when the instrument z is purely exogenous, so that IV is by definition consistent, the presence of a weak instrument, one poorly correlated with the endogenous D, creates further problems. In particular, poorly correlated instruments result in inflated standard errors of the IV estimator that may become significantly larger than those obtained with OLS. To illustrate this, take the usual formula for the asymptotic variance of the IV estimator:

$$V(\widehat{\alpha}_{IV}) = \sigma^2 \left(\mathbf{D'z}\right)^{-1} \left(\mathbf{z'z}\right) \left(\mathbf{z'D}\right)^{-1} \tag{3.46}$$

Since we are assuming standardized variables and only one endogenous variable and one instrument, we can write that:

$$V(\widehat{\alpha}_{IV}) = \sigma^2 \left(\mathbf{D'D}\right)^{-1} \left(\mathbf{D'D}\right) \left\{ \left(\mathbf{D'z}\right)^{-1} \left(\mathbf{z'z}\right) \left(\mathbf{z'D}\right)^{-1} \right\}$$

$$= V(\widehat{\alpha}_{OLS}) \left(\mathbf{D'D}\right) \left\{ \left(\mathbf{D'z}\right)^{-1} \left(\mathbf{z'z}\right) \left(\mathbf{z'D}\right)^{-1} \right\}$$

$$= V(\widehat{\alpha}_{OLS}) \cdot N$$

$$\cdot \operatorname{Var}(D) \left\{ \frac{1}{N \cdot \operatorname{Cov}(D;z)} \cdot N \cdot \operatorname{Var}(z) \cdot \frac{1}{N \cdot \operatorname{Cov}(D;z)} \right\}$$

$$= V(\widehat{\alpha}_{OLS}) \cdot \left\{ \frac{1}{[\operatorname{Cov}(D;z)]^2} \right\} = \frac{V(\widehat{\alpha}_{OLS})}{\rho_{D,z}^2} \tag{3.47}$$

By assumption $\operatorname{Var}(D) = \operatorname{Var}(z) = 1$, thus the covariance between D and z is equivalent to the coefficient of correlation $\rho_{D,z}$. Simply rewriting previous expression, we therefore obtain:

$$V(\widehat{\alpha}_{IV}) = \frac{V(\widehat{\alpha}_{OLS})}{\rho_{D,z}^2} \tag{3.48}$$

implying that the variance of IV is always higher than that of OLS, since $1/\rho_{D,z}^2$ is higher or at most equal to one. More specifically, assuming that the variance of the OLS estimator is equal to one, and the correlation between D and z equal to 0.2, implies that the variance of IV is 25 times larger than that of OLS. As a consequence, a weak instrument (weak correlation between D and z) may result in a very low precision in estimating α. This result can be extended in the case in which additional (exogenous) covariates are added, provided that the one-endogenous/one-instrument setting is maintained.

The previous result implies, somewhat strikingly, that in a situation in which the instrument is exogenous (and thus IV consistent) but poorly correlated with the endogenous variable, the loss in efficiency of IV can outweigh gain in bias-reduction vis-a-vis OLS. Thus, in terms of the mean square error (MSE), the OLS might actually be superior to the IV estimator. More specifically, the MSE of a generic estimator $\widehat{\theta}$ is equal to:

$$\operatorname{MSE}\left(\widehat{\theta}\right) = V\left(\widehat{\theta}\right) + B\left(\widehat{\theta}\right)^2$$

where $V(\cdot)$ is the variance and $B(\cdot)$ the bias. Thus, we might obtain that:

Fig. 3.2 Example of a
consistent IV estimate of α
having a large variance (due
to the use of a weak
instrument), compared with
an inconsistent OLS having
smaller variance. The value
of the true parameter is
$\alpha = 7$; OLS is centered
around $\alpha = 3$

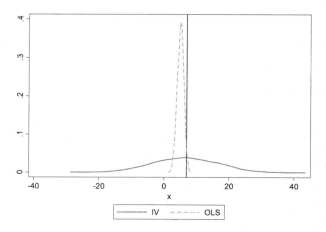

$$MSE(\widehat{\alpha}_{IV}) > MSE(\widehat{\alpha}_{OLS})$$

in which case OLS is more appealing than IV as an estimator of the true population
parameter α. Figure 3.2 provides a graphical example of previous situation by
plotting the distribution of the IV and OLS estimators.

It is immediate to see that—with α equal to 7 and the OLS centered in $\alpha = 3$—IV
is not a reliable estimator, as it presents very larger tails compared to those of OLS.
The probability mass of the OLS is, however, much more concentrated around the
true α, although this estimator shows a bias equal to 4. In such cases, OLS seems,
therefore, undoubtedly more reliable than IV.

3.2.4.3   Small-Sample Bias of IV

It is a well-known result that 2SLS are biased in finite samples (Nelson and Startz
1990a, b; Phillips 1983). This bias is cumbersome to calculate and may be large;
thus, the behavior of an IV estimator when the sample size is small may be
problematic. Following the paper by Murray (2006), we limit our attention here
to the case in which we have only one endogenous variable in a univariate
regression model and a number L of instrumental-variables. The model is therefore:

$$Y = \mu + \alpha D + u$$
$$D = \mu + \mathbf{z}\boldsymbol{\gamma} + u$$

with $\mathbf{z}$ equal to a row vector of L instruments. Hahn and Hausman (2005) have
showed that, for a model of this kind, the 2SLS bias is approximately equal to:

$$E(\widehat{\alpha}_{2SLS}) - \alpha \approx \frac{L \cdot \rho \cdot (1 - R^2)}{N \cdot R^2} \tag{3.49}$$

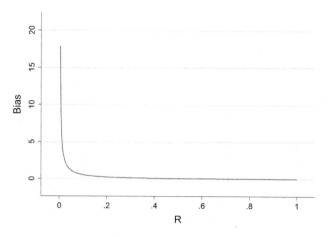

Fig. 3.3 2SLS bias as function of R, when $L = 10$, $\rho = 0.6$, and $N = 100$

where: L is the number of instrumental-variables; ρ is the correlation between D and u, i.e., the degree of D's endogeneity; and R^2 is the share of D's variance explained by the instruments $\mathbf{z}$, i.e., the multivariate correlation between D and $\mathbf{z}$.

It is clear that, as soon as L and/or ρ increases, the bias increases accordingly. This means that adding additional instruments without obtaining a higher R^2 rate actually worsens the extent of the bias. The simple addition of poorly explicative instruments can therefore lead to further bias. Of course, as N increases, the bias disappears. Figure 3.3 shows the 2SLS bias as function of R^2, when $L = 10$, $\rho = 0.6$, and $N = 100$; it is easy to see that, as function of R^2, the bias take a hyperbolic shape with the bias disappearing when $R^2 = 1$.

Finally, Hahn and Hausman (2005) show that the ratio between the 2SLS's and OLS's bias is approximately equal to:

$$\frac{\text{Bias}(\widehat{\alpha}_{2\text{SLS}})}{\text{Bias}(\widehat{\alpha}_{\text{OLS}})} \approx \frac{L}{N \cdot R^2} \tag{3.50}$$

implying that, as soon as the denominator is higher than the number of instruments, the 2SLS bias is lower than that of OLS. For instance, suppose that the OLS bias is 100 and that $L = 3$, $N = 20$, and $R^2 = 0.3$; in this case, the bias of 2SLS is 50. When we have few observations and a relatively weak instrument, the bias of 2SLS is, therefore, smaller than that of OLS. Moreover, as L/NR^2 is positive, the bias of 2SLS has the same sign of the OLS bias[2].

---

[2] Stock and Yogo (2002) have proposed a test to establish when an instrument is good enough to produce a 2SLS bias that is lower than a certain share of the OLS bias. With one single endogenous variable, this test follows a standard F-statistics, while for more than one endogenous regressor, the authors have tabulated the critical values. Performing this test, however, requires an overidentified setting.

To conclude, as it is difficult to find relatively good instruments in practice (i.e., variables capable of explaining the selection-into-program, while at the same time being not directly related to the outcome), the evaluator has to weigh up the advantages/disadvantages of using IV approaches. Recall, for example, that it can sometimes be better to use a biased OLS than a consistent IV with weak instruments.

Finally note that even when a relatively strong instrument (in terms of correlation with the endogenous variable) is available, its exogeneity cannot be assured. Testing the exogeneity of instruments requires an overidentified setting, that is, a setting where the analyst has access to more than one instrument for the endogenous treatment D. In typical micro-econometric studies, finding more than one instrument is rather hard, given the particular properties that such variables have to possess. Moreover, to further complicate things, with more than one instrument at hand, the analyst can statistically test only the joint exogeneity of "all" instruments used and not that of each single instrument separately. In the case of just-identified settings (i.e., only one instrument for D), testing the exogeneity of the instrument is not possible and analysts normally have to provide convincing arguments in order to support the suitability of the (single) instrument chosen, especially with regard to its assumed exogeneity. In fact, the multivariate correlation of a potential instrument with the treatment variable can be properly tested through a first-step Probit regression. Justifying instrument's exogeneity, on the other hand, is a much more subtle task than simply demanding an acceptable correlation with the treatment variable.

3.3 Selection-Model

In this section, we present the Selection-model (SM) approach to estimate ATEs, originally developed by Heckman (1978, 1979). Although initially proposed for regression models using datasets with truncated (unobservable) outcomes due to some form of unit selection process (tobit-type settings), this approach has become increasingly popular in the applied program evaluation literature, where it is generally known as the "Heckit" model. By and large, such a model can be easily compared (if not included) with the IV approach to consistently estimate the parameters in system (3.21) without the necessity of including an instrument. Naturally, the cost of not having an instrument to rely on is the necessity for additional assumptions, in particular the joint normality of the error terms in system such as (3.21). Before proceeding to a formal treatment of the Selection-model, we give an account of the selection bias in models represented by (3.21), in order to show which is the direction of the OLS selection bias when one does not control for unobservable factors. This is useful, as in Selection-models the direction of the bias has a clear statistical interpretation, in that it is proportional to the correlation between the unobservables of the selection and the unobservables of the outcome equation in the joint normal distribution of errors.

3.3.1   Characterizing OLS Bias within a Selection-Model

In this subsection, we consider a simplified version of system (3.21), of the following type:

$$
\begin{aligned}
Y &= \mu_Y + \beta_Y x + \alpha D + u \quad &\text{Outcome equation} \\
D &= \mu_D + \beta_D x + \varepsilon &\text{Selection equation} \\
u &= \gamma_u Q + e_u \\
\varepsilon &= \gamma_\varepsilon Q + e_\varepsilon
\end{aligned}
\tag{3.51}
$$

where α is the ATE; x is a common observable control variable; Q a common unobservable component; and e_u and e_ε are two exogenous random shocks with zero unconditional mean. Since Q is unobservable, it is part of both error terms u and ε. In this type of model, it can be shown that the bias of the OLS estimator takes the following form:

$$
\alpha_{\text{OLS}} = \alpha + \frac{\text{Cov}(\varepsilon; u)}{\text{Var}(D)}
\tag{3.52}
$$

that is:

$$
\alpha_{\text{OLS}} = \alpha + \gamma_\varepsilon \gamma_u \frac{\text{Var}(Q)}{\text{Var}(D)}
\tag{3.53}
$$

Thus when:

- $\gamma_u \gamma_\varepsilon > 0$, then OLS has an upward bias.
- $\gamma_u \gamma_\varepsilon < 0$, then OLS has a downward bias.
- $\gamma_u \gamma_\varepsilon = 0$, then OLS is unbiased (consistent).

The proof of the previous expression is quite straightforward. The first problem to overcome is the presence of the covariate x. By defining $\widetilde{Y} = Y - \beta_Y x$, however, we can rewrite the outcome equation as:

$$
\widetilde{Y} = \mu_Y + \alpha D + u
$$

so that the OLS estimation of α is, by definition, equal to:

$$
\alpha_{\text{OLS}} = \frac{\text{Cov}\left(\widetilde{Y}; D\right)}{\text{Var}(D)}
$$

Now, we can develop further the numerator as follows:

$$\mathrm{Cov}\left(\widetilde{Y};D\right) = \mathrm{Cov}(Y;D) - \beta_Y \mathrm{Cov}(x;D)$$

$$
\begin{aligned}
&= \mathrm{Cov}(\mu_Y + \beta_Y x + \alpha D + u; \mu_D + \beta_Y + \varepsilon) - \beta_Y \mathrm{Cov}(x; \mu_D + \beta_D x + \varepsilon) \\
&= \{\beta_Y \beta_D \mathrm{Var}(x) + \beta_Y \mathrm{Cov}(x; \varepsilon) + \alpha \beta_D \mathrm{Cov}(D; x) + \alpha \mathrm{Cov}(D; \varepsilon) \\
&\quad + \beta_D \mathrm{Cov}(x; u) + \mathrm{Cov}(\varepsilon; u)\} - \{\beta_Y \beta_D \mathrm{Var}(x) + \beta_Y \mathrm{Cov}(x; \varepsilon)\}
\end{aligned}
$$

By simplifying, this implies that:

$$\mathrm{Cov}\left(\widetilde{Y};D\right) = \alpha \beta_D \mathrm{Cov}(D;x) + \alpha \mathrm{Cov}(D;\varepsilon) + \mathrm{Cov}(\varepsilon;u)$$

By developing further these covariates, we finally obtain:

$$\mathrm{Cov}\left(\widetilde{Y};D\right) = \alpha \beta_D^2 \mathrm{Var}(x) + \alpha \mathrm{Var}(\varepsilon) + \mathrm{Cov}(\varepsilon;u)$$

Since $\mathrm{Var}(D) = \mathrm{Var}(\mu_D + \beta_D x + \varepsilon) = \beta_D^2 \mathrm{Var}(x) + \mathrm{Var}(\varepsilon)$, we have that:

$$\alpha_{\mathrm{OLS}} = \frac{\mathrm{Cov}\left(\widetilde{Y};D\right)}{\mathrm{Var}(D)} = \frac{\alpha \beta_D^2 \mathrm{Var}(x) + \alpha \mathrm{Var}(\varepsilon) + \mathrm{Cov}(\varepsilon;u)}{\beta_D^2 \mathrm{Var}(x) + \mathrm{Var}(\varepsilon)} = \alpha + \frac{\mathrm{Cov}(\varepsilon;u)}{\mathrm{Var}(D)}$$

proving (3.52). At this point, we can develop further the previous equation by plugging in the equations of u and ε:

$$\alpha_{\mathrm{OLS}} = \alpha + \frac{\mathrm{Cov}(\gamma_\varepsilon Q + e_\varepsilon; \gamma_u Q + e_u)}{\mathrm{Var}(D)} = \alpha + \gamma_\varepsilon \gamma_u \frac{\mathrm{Var}(Q)}{\mathrm{Var}(D)}$$

proving (3.53). Of course, when more than one unobservable is included in the error terms, the bias has a different and more complicated formula: by assuming, for instance, to have two unobserved confounders, Q_1 and Q_2, we can show the OLS bias to be equal to:

$$
\begin{aligned}
\alpha_{\mathrm{OLS}} - \alpha &= \frac{\mathrm{Cov}(\gamma_{\varepsilon 1} Q_1 + \gamma_{\varepsilon 2} Q_2 + e_\varepsilon; \gamma_{u1} Q_1 + \gamma_{u2} Q_2 + e_u)}{\mathrm{Var}(D)} \\
&= \frac{\gamma_{\varepsilon 1} \gamma_{u1} \mathrm{Var}(Q_1) + \gamma_{\varepsilon 2} \gamma_{u2} \mathrm{Var}(Q_2) + [\gamma_{\varepsilon 1} \gamma_{u2} + \gamma_{\varepsilon 2} \gamma_{u1}] \mathrm{Cov}(Q_1; Q_2)}{\mathrm{Var}(D)}
\end{aligned}
$$

If the two unobservables are also uncorrelated, so that $\mathrm{Cov}(Q_1; Q_2) = 0$, we obtain:

$$\alpha_{\mathrm{OLS}} - \alpha = \frac{\gamma_{\varepsilon 1} \gamma_{u1} \mathrm{Var}(Q_1) + \gamma_{\varepsilon 2} \gamma_{u2} \mathrm{Var}(Q_2)}{\mathrm{Var}(D)} = \gamma_{\varepsilon 1} \gamma_{u1} \frac{\mathrm{Var}(Q_1)}{\mathrm{Var}(D)} + \gamma_{\varepsilon 2} \gamma_{u2} \frac{\mathrm{Var}(Q_2)}{\mathrm{Var}(D)}$$

thus the bias is a linear combination of the products of the two coefficients of Q_j ($j = 1, 2$) of both errors. Observe that:

- $\gamma_{e1}\gamma_{u1}\mathrm{Var}(Q_1) > \gamma_{e2}\gamma_{u2}\mathrm{Var}(Q_2)$, then OLS has an upward bias.
- $\gamma_{e1}\gamma_{u1}\mathrm{Var}(Q_1) < \gamma_{e2}\gamma_{u2}\mathrm{Var}(Q_2)$, then OLS has a downward bias.
- $\gamma_{e1}\gamma_{u1}\mathrm{Var}(Q_1) = \gamma_{e2}\gamma_{u2}\mathrm{Var}(Q_2)$, then OLS is unbiased (consistent).

Of course, with many unobservables, possibly also correlated, the conditions required to identify the direction of the OLS bias become much more complicated, no longer having a clear-cut meaning. One possible simplification is that of assuming a distributional behavior of the joint distribution of the error terms ε and u, independently of the number of unobservables they may contain. As pretty outlined above, this is the route taken by Selection-models, allowing one to correctly identify ATE without using IV methods. Furthermore, it is also straight-forward to estimate the OLS bias and determine whether it has a downward or upward direction. This still requires to assume the joint normality of errors that in many contexts may be heroic.

3.3.2   A Technical Exposition of the Selection-Model

In this section, we offer a detailed exposition of the Heckman Selection-model for the case in which both observable and unobservable heterogeneities are assumed. This is the most general Selection-model, simpler models being just peculiar sub-cases.

We begin by considering the Case 2.2 from the IV section; in such a case, we had the following form for the (observable) outcome equation:

$$Y = \mu_0 + \alpha D + g_0(\mathbf{x}) + D[g_1(\mathbf{x}) - g_0(\mathbf{x})] + e_0 + D(e_1 - e_0)$$

which, under some manipulations leads to:

$$Y = \mu_0 + \alpha D + \mathbf{x}\boldsymbol{\beta}_0 + D(\mathbf{x} - \boldsymbol{\mu}_\mathbf{x})\boldsymbol{\beta} + e_0 + D(e_1 - e_0)$$

This model contains both observable and unobservable heterogeneities, and a consistent estimation in this case requires ad-hoc assumptions (see the previous IV section). Nevertheless, a generalized Heckit model (Heckman 1979) can be implemented to obtain consistent and efficient estimates of the parameters. Estimation is based on these assumptions:

(a) $Y = \mu_0 + \alpha D + \mathbf{x}\boldsymbol{\beta}_0 + D(\mathbf{x} - \boldsymbol{\mu}_\mathbf{x})\boldsymbol{\beta} + u$
(b) $E(e_1|\mathbf{x}, z) = E(e_0|\mathbf{x}, z) = 0$
(c) $D = 1[\theta_0 + \mathbf{x}\boldsymbol{\theta}_1 + \theta_2 z + a \geq 0]$
(d) $E(a|\mathbf{x}, z) = 0$
(e) $(a, e_0, e_1) \sim {}^3N$
(f) $a \sim N(0, 1) \Rightarrow \sigma_a = 1$
(g) $u = e_0 + D(e_1 - e_0)$ (3.54)

where the most crucial hypothesis here is that of assuming a trivariate normal distribution of the error terms of the potential outcomes (e_1, e_0) and of the selection equation (a), respectively. Observe that, although z is reported in (3.54) as regressor, the identification of such a model does not require an instrumental-variable to be specified. The normality assumption is sufficient to obtain consistent results.

Estimating such a model requires to directly calculate $E(Y \mid \mathbf{x}, z, D)$. To this end, write the Y-equation (3.54a) as $Y = A + u$, with $A = \mu_0 + \alpha D + \mathbf{x}\boldsymbol{\beta}_0 + D(\mathbf{x} - \boldsymbol{\mu_x})\boldsymbol{\beta}$ and $u = e_0 + D(e_1 - e_0)$. Thus:

$$Y = A + E(u|\mathbf{x}, z, D) + \varepsilon$$

with $\varepsilon = [u - E(u \mid \mathbf{x}, z, D)]$. In this case, it is immediate to see that $E(Y \mid \mathbf{x}, z, D) = A + E(u \mid \mathbf{x}, z, D)$ since, by definition, $E(\varepsilon \mid \mathbf{x}, z, D) = 0$. Thus, once the expression of $E(u \mid \mathbf{x}, z, D)$ is known in a parametric way, one may apply an OLS regression to recover consistent estimates of the parameters. Therefore, to calculate what $E(u \mid \mathbf{x}, z, D)$ is equal to, we can write:

$$\begin{aligned} E(u|\mathbf{x},z,D) &= E(e_0 + D(e_1 - e_0)|\mathbf{x},z,D) \\ &= E(e_0|\mathbf{x},z,D) + DE(e_1|\mathbf{x},z,D) - DE(e_0|\mathbf{x},z,D) \\ &= (1-D)E(e_0|\mathbf{x},z,D) + DE(e_1|\mathbf{x},z,D) \end{aligned}$$

Since (e_1, e_0) are uncorrelated with ($\mathbf{x}$, z), we have that:

$$E(u|\mathbf{x},z,D) = (1-D)E(e_0|D) + DE(e_1|D)$$

Now, write the previous formula in the two states:

$$E(u|\mathbf{x},z,D) = \begin{cases} E(u|D=1) = E(e_1|D=1) & \text{if } D=1 \\ E(u|D=0) = E(e_0|D=0) & \text{if } D=0 \end{cases}$$

This means that:

$$E(u|\mathbf{x},z,D) = (1-D)E(e_0|D=0) + DE(e_1|D=1)$$

Since $D = 1[\theta_0 + \boldsymbol{\theta}_1\mathbf{x} + \theta_2 z + a \geq 0]$, then:

$$\begin{aligned} E(u|\mathbf{x},z,D) &= (1-D)E(e_0|a < -\theta_0 - \boldsymbol{\theta}_1\mathbf{x} - \theta_2 z) \\ &\quad + DE(e_1|a \geq -\theta_0 - \boldsymbol{\theta}_1\mathbf{x} - \theta_2 z) \end{aligned}$$

From the properties of the trivariate normal distribution, we have that:

$$\begin{cases} \mathrm{E}\big(e_0\big|a < \mathbf{q\theta}\big) = -\sigma_{e_0a}\dfrac{\phi(\mathbf{q\theta})}{1 - \Phi(\mathbf{q\theta})} \\[2mm] \mathrm{E}\big(e_1\big|a \ge \mathbf{q\theta}\big) = \sigma_{e_1a}\dfrac{\phi(\mathbf{q\theta})}{\Phi(\mathbf{q\theta})} \\[2mm] \mathbf{q\theta} = -\theta_0 - \theta_1\mathbf{x} - \theta_2 z \end{cases} \qquad (3.55)$$

where $\dfrac{\phi(\mathbf{q\theta})}{1-\Phi(\mathbf{q\theta})}$ and $\dfrac{\phi(\mathbf{q\theta})}{\Phi(\mathbf{q\theta})}$ are known as "inverse Mills ratios," sometimes also called "selection hazards." Thus, by putting:

$$\mathrm{E}\big(Y\big|\mathbf{x}, z, D\big) = A + \rho_1 D\frac{\phi(\mathbf{q\theta})}{\Phi(\mathbf{q\theta})} + \rho_0(1 - D)\frac{\phi(\mathbf{q\theta})}{1 - \Phi(\mathbf{q\theta})}$$

and by making explicit A, we finally get:

$$\mathrm{E}\big(Y\big|\mathbf{x}, z, D\big) = \overbrace{\mu_0 + \alpha D + \mathbf{x}\boldsymbol{\beta}_0 + w\,(\mathbf{x} - \boldsymbol{\mu}_\mathbf{x})\boldsymbol{\beta}}^{A} + \rho_1 D\frac{\phi(\mathbf{q\theta})}{\Phi(\mathbf{q\theta})}$$
$$+ \rho_0(1 - D)\frac{\phi(\mathbf{q\theta})}{1 - \Phi(\mathbf{q\theta})} \qquad (3.56)$$

A *two-step* procedure can be used to estimate this equation:

1. Run a Probit of D_i on $(1, \mathbf{x}_i, z_i)$ and get: $\big(\widehat{\phi}_i, \widehat{\Phi}_i\big)$
2. Run an OLS of Y_i on: $\left[1, D_i, \mathbf{x}_i, D_i(\mathbf{x}_i - \boldsymbol{\mu}_\mathbf{x})_i, D_i\dfrac{\widehat{\phi}_i}{\widehat{\Phi}_i}, (1 - D_i)\dfrac{\widehat{\phi}_i}{1-\widehat{\Phi}_i}\right]$

The previous procedure produces consistent estimations of the parameters of regression (3.56). Once these parameters' estimates are available, one can also test the null hypothesis:

$$H_0 : \rho_1 = \rho_0 = 0$$

that, if accepted, allows one to conclude that there is no selection on unobservables. By setting:

$$\lambda_1(\mathbf{q\theta}) = \frac{\phi(\mathbf{q\theta})}{\Phi(\mathbf{q\theta})} \quad \text{and} \quad \lambda_0(\mathbf{q\theta}) = \frac{\phi(\mathbf{q\theta})}{1 - \Phi(\mathbf{q\theta})}$$

we can also write previous regression as:

$$\mathrm{E}\big(Y\big|\mathbf{x}, z, w\big) = \mu_0 + \alpha D + \mathbf{x}\boldsymbol{\beta}_0 + D\,(\mathbf{x} - \boldsymbol{\mu}_\mathbf{x})\boldsymbol{\beta} + \rho_1 D\lambda_1(\mathbf{q\theta})$$
$$+ \rho_0(1 - D)\lambda_0(\mathbf{q\theta}) \qquad (3.57)$$

Once all the parameters in the previous equation are estimated by the two-step procedure, one can calculate the usual causal parameters ATEs. In this case, however, the formulas are slightly different to the case of the Control-function regression and IV. First, it is immediate to see that:

$$\text{ATE} = \alpha$$
$$\text{ATE}(\mathbf{x}) = \alpha + (\mathbf{x} - \bar{\mathbf{x}})\boldsymbol{\beta} \tag{3.58}$$

which is obtained following the same procedure seen in the Case 2 of Control-function regression. ATET($\mathbf{x}$), ATET, ATENT($\mathbf{x}$), and ATENT, however, assume a different form compared to that of the Control-function Case 2. We start by showing the formula for ATET($\mathbf{x}$) and ATET and then for ATENT($\mathbf{x}$) and ATENT. Under previous assumptions, we have that:

$$\text{ATET}(\mathbf{x}) = \text{E}(y_1 - y_0 | \mathbf{x}, D = 1)$$
$$= (\mu_1 - \mu_0) + [g_1(\mathbf{x}) - g_0(\mathbf{x})] + \text{E}(e_1 - e_0 | \mathbf{x}, D = 1)$$

We know that e_1 and e_0 are independent of $\mathbf{x}$, so that $\text{E}(e_1 - e_0 | \mathbf{x}, D = 1) = \text{E}(e_1 - e_0 | D = 1)$. The value of the last expectation is easy to determine. Setting:

$$e_1 - e_0 = \eta$$

we know that η follows a normal distribution. This means that:

$$\text{E}(\eta | D = 1) = \sigma_{\eta a} \frac{\phi}{\Phi}$$

From the linear property of the covariance, we have that:

$$\sigma_{\eta a} = \text{Cov}(\eta; a) = \text{Cov}(e_1 - e_0; a) = \text{Cov}(e_1; a) - \text{Cov}(e_0; a) = \sigma_{e_1 a} - \sigma_{e_0 a}$$
$$= \rho_1 + \rho_0$$

since $\rho_0 = -\sigma_{e_0 a}$ and $\rho_1 = \sigma_{e_1 a}$. This implies that:

$$\text{ATET}(\mathbf{x}) = [\alpha + (\mathbf{x} - \bar{\mathbf{x}})\beta + (\rho_1 + \rho_0) \cdot \lambda_1(\mathbf{q}\theta)]_{(D=1)}$$
$$\text{ATET} = \alpha + \frac{1}{\sum\limits_{i=1}^{N} D_i} \sum\limits_{i=1}^{N} D_i(\mathbf{x}_i - \bar{\mathbf{x}})\beta + (\rho_1 + \rho_0) \cdot \frac{1}{\sum\limits_{i=1}^{N} D_i} \sum\limits_{i=1}^{N} D_i \cdot \lambda_1(\mathbf{q}\theta) \tag{3.59}$$

In a similar way, it is immediate to show that:

$$\text{ATENT}(\mathbf{x}) = \left[\alpha + (\mathbf{x} - \bar{\mathbf{x}})\widehat{\boldsymbol{\beta}} + (\rho_1 + \rho_0) \cdot \lambda_0 \left(\mathbf{q}\widehat{\boldsymbol{\theta}} \right) \right]_{(D=1)}$$

$$\text{ATENT} = \alpha + \cfrac{1}{\displaystyle\sum_{i=1}^{N}(1 - D_i)} \sum_{i=1}^{N}(1 - D_i)\,(\mathbf{x}_i - \bar{\mathbf{x}})\boldsymbol{\beta} + (\rho_1 + \rho_0)$$

$$\cdot \cfrac{1}{\displaystyle\sum_{i=1}^{N}(1 - D_i)} \sum_{i=1}^{N}(1 - D_i) \cdot \lambda_{0i}(\mathbf{q}\boldsymbol{\theta}) \tag{3.60}$$

Having estimated $\{\alpha,\, \rho_1,\, \rho_0,\, \boldsymbol{\beta},\, \lambda_1,\, \lambda_0\}$ using the two-step procedure, one can substitute them into previous ATEs' formulas to recover all the causal effects of interest. Observe that standard errors for the ATET and the ATENT can be obtained by bootstrap procedures.

Finally, since under the joint-normality assumption, the model is fully parametric, a maximum likelihood estimation can be employed, thus not only yielding consistent but also efficient estimations of the causal parameters. Generally, however, maximum likelihood estimation can result in convergence problems, especially when many discrete control variables are used. In such cases, the two-step procedure is a valuable (although less efficient) alternative.

3.3.3 Selection-Model with a Binary Outcome

In many program evaluation applications, it is common to come across situations in which the outcome variable takes on a binary form. For a given set of individuals, for instance, one might be interested in knowing whether the likelihood of finding a job is increased by participating in a training program; in this case, the outcome Y presents only two values: "employed" and "unemployed." In such cases, by eliminating the interaction term and the instrument z for the sake of simplicity, system (3.54) becomes:

$$Y = 1[\mu + \alpha D + \mathbf{x}\boldsymbol{\beta} + u]$$
$$D = 1[\theta + \mathbf{x}\boldsymbol{\theta} + a \geq 0]$$

where $(Y; D)$ is still distributed as bivariate normal with mean zero, unit variance, and correlation equal to ρ. It is immediate to see that in this framework, the ATE is equal to:

$$\text{ATE} = \Phi(\mu + \alpha + \mathbf{x}\boldsymbol{\beta}) - \Phi(\mu + \mathbf{x}\boldsymbol{\beta})$$

Since Y is binary, assuming a linear probability model for the outcome equation would be incorrect and estimating the previous system using the Heckman two-step procedure, *as if* the outcome was continuous, would lead to biased results. As the model is fully parametric, however, a maximum likelihood (ML) estimation can be performed noting that the joint density distribution of $(Y; D)$ can be written as:

$$f(Y, D|\mathbf{x}) = f(Y|D, \mathbf{x}) f(D|\mathbf{x})$$

From this decomposition of the joint density of the endogenous variables conditional on the exogenous observables, it is not difficult to obtain the log likelihood; maximizing the log likelihood, however, requires nonstandard integrals computation (*quadrature methods*) and possibly may have a number of convergence problems (Wooldridge 2010, pp. 594–596). To avoid computational burden, Burnett (1997) proposed a simple two-step procedure which mimics the two-step approach adopted by Rivers and Vuong (1988) in the case of a binary outcome model with a continuous endogenous regressor. This procedure works as follows:

1. Estimate a probit of D_i on $\{1, \mathbf{x}_i\}$, and get an estimate of the probit residuals:
$$\widehat{r}_i = D_i - \Phi\left(\mathbf{x}_i\widehat{\boldsymbol{\theta}}\right)$$
2. Estimate a second probit of Y_i on $\{1, \mathbf{x}_i, D_i, \widehat{r}_i\}$ to get parameters estimates.

Unfortunately, this does not lead to consistent estimates of ATE and other parameters. Monte Carlo experiments conducted by Nicoletti and Peracchi (2001), however, have shown that the bias of such a two-step procedure, especially when taking heteroskedasticity into account, can be ignored and is not larger than the ML estimator bias. Moreover, this result holds even when the correlation coefficient between Y and D is remarkably high. Finally, note that while inconsistent, the previous two-step approach offers a valid test for the endogeneity of D. Indeed, under the null hypothesis of an exogenous D, the usual t statistic for $\widehat{r}_i$ is consistent (Wooldridge 2010, p. 597).

3.4 Difference-in-Differences

A powerful approach to deal with endogenous selection without the need for instrumental-variables or additional distributional assumptions is the so-called difference-in-differences (DID) method (Abadie 2005; Angrist and Pischke 2008, Chap. 5; Bertrand et al. 2004; Card and Krueger 2000; Donald and Lang 2007; Meyer et al. 1995).

DID is suitable in evaluation contexts where observational data for treated and untreated units are available both before and after treatment. It can be shown that causal effects, under such a data structure, can be identified and estimated consistently by DID.

Two types of DID estimators have been proposed in the literature, the choice of which depends on whether the data are a pure longitudinal dataset (panel data) or a repeated cross section. In the first case (panel), the same unit (either treated or

Table 3.2 Two-way table of the DID statistical setting

		Location s	
		Rome	Milan
Time t	t_0	*Untreated*	*Untreated*
	t_1	*Treated*	*Untreated*

untreated) is observed before and after a treatment occurred; in the second case (repeated cross section), the units observed before and after treatment (either treated or not) may be different. Identification assumptions of both types of DID are, however, the same. In what follows, we present the more conventional type of DID, which is used in repeated cross section of individuals, before going on to discuss DID in a longitudinal data structure.

3.4.1 DID with Repeated Cross Sections

In this section we illustrate the DID method using an example similar to that of Card and Krueger (1994)[3]. We will focus on the estimation of the ATE. Following those authors, suppose to have a dataset made of repeated cross sections of N different restaurants, located in both Rome and Milan. The restaurants are observed at time t_0 and, successively, at time t_1. Suppose that, in between t_0 and t_1, the restaurants in Rome benefitted from an incentive to increase employment, the target variable which we denote Y. It is clear, as indicated in Table 3.2, that only the restaurants observed in Rome at time t_1 are those actually treated.

We can define a binary variable s to identify the restaurant location, where $s_i = R$, if restaurant i is located in Rome, and $s_i = M$, if restaurant i is located in Milan. Likewise, we can define a time binary variable t taking the values $t_i = t_1$, if restaurant i is observed after policy implementation, and $t_i = t_0$, if restaurant i is observed before the implementation of the policy. Finally, let Y_i indicate the employment outcome of restaurant i after policy implementation occurrence. In such a context, we can define the average treatment effect as:

$$\text{ATE}(s,t) = \text{E}(Y_{1ist} - Y_{0ist}|s,t) = \delta = \text{constant} \tag{3.61}$$

where the location index $s = \{R, M\}$ and time index $t = \{t_0, t_1\}$, and Y_1 and Y_0 are the usual potential outcomes. It is immediate to see that this definition of ATE assumes a constant effect over s and t. Indeed, as the counterfactual logic suggests, in a two-period/two-location setting, one can define four average treatment effects defined as:

[3] Some econometrics of this section draws on Angrist and Pischke (2008, pp. 221–243).

$$E(Y_{1iRt_0} - Y_{0iRt_0}) = \delta_1$$
$$E(Y_{1iRt_1} - Y_{0iRt_1}) = \delta_2$$
$$E(Y_{1iMt_0} - Y_{0iMt_0}) = \delta_3 \quad\quad (3.62)$$
$$E(Y_{1iMt_1} - Y_{0iMt_1}) = \delta_4$$

Thus, the first assumption lying behind the traditional DID estimator is that $\delta_1 = \delta_2 = \delta_3 = \delta_4 = \delta = constant$. This means that the ATE conditional on s and t is equal to the unconditional ATE, i.e., ATE$(s, t) =$ ATE.

The second assumption for identifying the causal effect using DID is the so-called *common-trend* assumption, which states that:

$$E\left(Y_{0ist}|s,t\right) = \gamma_s + \lambda_t \quad\quad (3.63)$$

where γ_s is a location-specific effect and λ_t a time-specific effect. This assumption simply sets that the nontreatment employment time trend is in Rome (the treated location) and Milan (the non-treated one) as the same. Indeed, it is easy to see that this trend is equal to $\lambda_{t_1} - \lambda_{t_0}$ for both locations.

To see how these two assumptions identiy δ, we have to specify how the potential outcomes are modeled. In this sense, we assume that:

$$Y_{0ist} = \gamma_s + \lambda_t + e_{0ist}$$
$$Y_{1ist} = \gamma_s + \lambda_t + \delta + e_{1ist} \quad\quad (3.64)$$
$$Y_{ist} = Y_{0ist} + D_{st}(Y_{1ist} - Y_{0ist})$$

where $E(e_{0ist} \mid s,t) = E(e_{1ist} \mid s, t) = 0$, and $D_{st} = 1$ if $s = R$ and $t = t_0$, and $D_{st} = 0$ otherwise. Moreover, we also assume that $E(e_{0ist} \mid \mathbf{x}_{st}) = E(e_{1ist} \mid \mathbf{x}_{st}) = 0$, so that there is no need to control for state-time covariates in order to ensure consistency. Given (3.64), by simple substitution, we obtain:

$$Y_{ist} = \gamma_s + \lambda_t + D_{st}\delta + e_{ist} \qu\quad (3.65)$$

with $E\left(e_{ist}|s,t\right) = E\left[e_{0ist} + D_{st}(e_{1ist} - e_{0ist})|s,t\right] = 0$. Thus, a simple OLS regression of Y on a location and time variable and on D_{st} provides a consistent estimation of the ATE $= \delta$.

To understand better how the previous assumptions identify the ATE in DID, we first consider an analytical example and then its graphical representation (Fig. 3.4). By definition, ATE is equal to:

$$\beta = \underbrace{E(Y_{1iRt_1})}_{known} - \underbrace{E(Y_{0iRt_1})}_{unknown} \quad\quad (3.66)$$

Suppose that $E(Y_{1iRt_1}) = \gamma_R + \lambda_{t_1} + \delta = 3$, whereas $E(Y_{0iRt_1}) = \gamma_R + \lambda_{t_1} = ?$. Thus:

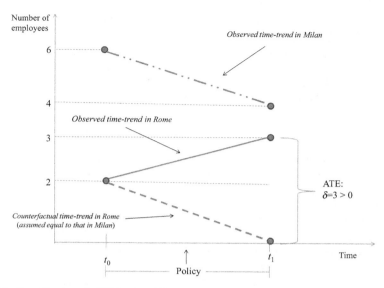

Fig. 3.4 Identification of ATE by the difference-in-differences (DID) estimator

$$\delta = 3 - (\gamma_R + \lambda_{t_1}) = 3 - ?$$

so δ is not identified. Nevertheless, by observation, we know both these quantities:

$$E(Y_{0iRt_0}) = \gamma_R + \lambda_{t_0} = \text{known} = 2$$
$$E(Y_{1iRt_1}) = \gamma_R + \lambda_{t_1} + \delta = \text{known} = 3$$

entailing that $\delta = 1 - (\lambda_{t_1} - \lambda_{t_0})$. Using the data for $s = R$, we cannot, however, calculate $(\lambda_{t_1} - \lambda_{t_0})$. We can nevertheless exploit data from $s = M$, in order to estimate quantity $(\lambda_{t_1} - \lambda_{t_0})$. In fact:

$$E(Y_{0iMt_0}) = \gamma_M + \lambda_{t_0} = \text{known} = 6$$
$$E(Y_{1iMt_1}) = \gamma_M + \lambda_{t_1} = \text{known} = 3$$

implying that $(\lambda_{t_1} - \lambda_{t_0}) = 4 - 6 = 2$; subsequently, we have that:

$$\delta = 1 - (\lambda_{t_1} - \lambda_{t_0}) = 1 - (-2) = 3$$

and the ATE is identified and equal to 3. Note that this result is possible since we assume that $\lambda_{t_1} - \lambda_{t_0}$, i.e., the time trend is the same in both Rome and Milan. If the trend was not equal, the ATE would have not been identified.

Figure 3.4 shows a graphical representation of DID, from which it is evident that the common-trend assumption is a necessary one in order to identify ATE. If this were not the case, the counterfactual trend in Rome would be different from that of

Milan, thus implying a different value of ATE (e.g., ATE $= 2$), while we errone-ously set the ATE $= 3$.

Correcting for possible differences in time trends across the two cities is necessary in order for DID to remain unbiased. One way to relax the common-trend assumption would be to allow the DID equation to contain a location-specific trend coefficient, in other words:

$$Y_{ist} = \gamma_s + \lambda_t + \theta_{st} + D_{st}\delta + e_{ist} \tag{3.67}$$

To estimate a model with an s-specific trend as (3.67), one needs unfortunately at least three periods; using just three periods to infer the difference in pre- and post-trend may, however, be questionable. Additional pre-and post-treatment observa-tions are thus needed to obtain more reliable estimates. A second possibility may be to add covariates as a source of omitted location-specific trends (an option which is discussed in the next section). In fact, although (3.65) can be correctly used for estimating the ATE by DID, in empirical work researchers usually adopt a slightly different regression-type model, resulting in the same form as (3.67)[4]:

$$Y_i = \mu + \beta s_i + \gamma t_i + \delta(s_i \cdot t_i) + \varepsilon_i \tag{3.68}$$

where $E(\varepsilon_i \mid s_i, t_i, s_i \cdot t_i,) = 0$, so that an OLS of (3.68) yields a consistent estimation of the parameters. Note once again that the treatment variable is in this case $D_i = s_i \cdot t_i$. We can show which parameters in (3.68) are equal to and also what is their relationship to the parameters in (3.65). Since:

$$\begin{aligned}
E(Y|s=1,t=0) &= E(Y_0^T) = \mu + \beta \\
E(Y|s=1,t=1) &= E(Y_1^T) = \mu + \beta + \gamma + \delta \\
E(Y|s=0,t=0) &= E(Y_0^C) = \mu \\
E(Y|s=0,t=1) &= E(Y_1^C) = \mu + \gamma
\end{aligned} \tag{3.69}$$

we can immediately see that:

$$\begin{aligned}
\mu &= \gamma_R + \lambda_{t_0} \\
\beta &= \gamma_M - \lambda_R \\
\gamma &= \lambda_{t_1} - \lambda_{t_0}
\end{aligned} \tag{3.70}$$

Given this result, it seems worth proving what exactly a consistent estimation of δ is equal to, starting first from the two biased estimators:

1. *Before/After estimator*

     This estimator is equal to the difference between the average of the outcome of the treated units, *before* and *after* the policy:

---

[4] Observe that in (3.68) we consider these codifications of s and t: $s = \{R=1; M=0\}$ and $t = \{t_1 = 1; t_0 = 0\}$.

$$\delta_{BA} = E(Y_1^T) - E(Y_0^T) = \gamma + \delta \qquad (3.71)$$

which is *biased* as soon as $\gamma \neq 0$. It can be obtained by the following OLS regression estimated on treated units ($s_i = 1$) only:

$$\begin{cases} Y_i = \mu_1 + \delta_{BA} \cdot t_i + error_i \\ s_i = 1 \end{cases} \qquad (3.72)$$

2. *Treatment/Control estimator*

   It is equal to the difference between the average of the outcome of *treated* units and that of *control* units, once the policy intervention has taken place ($t_i = 1$):

$$\delta_{TC} = E(Y_1^T) - E(Y_1^C) = \beta + \delta \qquad (3.73)$$

which is *biased* as soon as $\beta \neq 0$. An estimation of δ_{TC} can be obtained by the following OLS regression, performed only on units observed after policy ($t_i = 1$):

$$\begin{cases} Y_i = \mu_2 + \delta_{TC} \cdot s_i + error_i \\ t_i = 1 \end{cases} \qquad (3.74)$$

3. *DID estimator*

   Finally, DID is defined as:

$$\begin{aligned} \delta_{DID} &= \left[E(Y_1^T) - E(Y_0^T)\right] - \left[E(Y_1^C) - E(Y_0^C)\right] \\ &= \left[(\mu + \beta + \gamma + \delta) - (\mu + \beta)\right] - \left[(\mu + \gamma) - \mu\right] = \delta \end{aligned} \qquad (3.75)$$

thus proving that δ_{DID} is an unbiased estimator of the average treatment effect δ.

3.4.1.1   Generalizing DID in Repeated Cross Sections

We saw that one way of relaxing the common-trend assumption may be that of adding further covariates to the DID regression. This characteristic is in fact a significant advantage of DID compared with other methods. Even when the common-trend is not violated, including additional covariates (either t-invariant or s-invariant or unit specific) helps to increase the precision of the ATE's estimation (efficiency) provided, of course, that the model is correctly specified (i.e., the covariates are the correct predictors of outcome's DGP). In such a case, the DID assumes the usual regression form (Card 1992):

$$Y_{ist} = \gamma_s + \lambda_t + D_{st}\delta + \boldsymbol{\beta}\mathbf{x}_{ist} + e_{ist} \qquad (3.76)$$

where $\boldsymbol{\beta}$ is a vector of additional covariates parameters.

An additional interesting generalization of the DID estimator is required when D_{st} changes over time in the different locations. This is a generalization of the two-location/two-time DID to multiple-location/multiple-time case. It could, for example, be the case that a similar policy is implemented in various locations at different times. Angrist and Pischke (2008), following Autor (2003), suggest one should use in this case the following regression with lags and leads of the treatment variable D_{st}:

$$Y_{ist} = \gamma_s + \lambda_t + \sum_{\tau=0}^{m} D_{s,t-\tau}\delta_{-\tau} + \sum_{\tau=1}^{q} D_{s,t+\tau}\delta_{+\tau} + \boldsymbol{\beta}\mathbf{x}_{ist} + e_{ist} \qquad (3.77)$$

Equation (3.77) allows for a dynamic interpretation of the policy effect. As we will see in Sect. 3.4.4, it is possible to graph the pattern of the dynamic causal effects by plotting over time coefficients point estimation and confidence intervals. Using lags and leads can provide an interesting test to determine whether past treatments affect current outcome, or for the presence of anticipatory effects, thus challenging the conventional idea that causality works only "from the past to the present" (Granger 1969).

Anticipatory effects can also have a causal interpretation, once it is accepted that individuals make decisions not only on the basis of past events but also by formulating expectations of the future. This forward looking feature of the human decision-making process can be seen to be rational; for example, if one expects to become treated in 2 years from now, he (or she) could modify his (or her) current behavior in order to be able to exploit the opportunity he (or she) will get. Consider, for instance, a company expecting to receive support for R&D activity in 2 years time; in this situation, the firm immediately increases its portfolio of innovative projects so as they could potentially receive support in the future. An unemployed worker, on the other hand, could be less keen to search for a new job if he (or she) expects to be involved in a training course in the near future. Thus, future treatments can have, as past treatments, a significant impact on the present outcome.

3.4.2   DID with Panel Data

The DID estimator can also be identified using longitudinal datasets, where the same unit i can be observed before and after treatment (see, for instance, Lach (2002)). Assume we have data for two points in time $t = \{0, 1\}$ as in the cross-section case. In a panel data setup, DID is defined as the OLS estimator of α in the following regression:

$$\begin{cases} t = 1 : Y_{i1} = \mu_1 + \alpha D_{i1} + u_{i1} \\ t = 0 : Y_{i0} = \mu_0 + \alpha D_{i0} + u_{i0} \\ D_{i0} = 0 \end{cases} \qquad (3.78)$$

where estimation is only carried out for those units which are untreated in $t=0$. By subtracting, we then obtain:

$$\begin{cases} \Delta Y_{i1} = \mu + \alpha \Delta D_{i1} + \Delta u_{i1} \\ D_{i0} = 0 \end{cases} \qquad (3.79)$$

with $\mu=\mu_1-\mu_0$, which is equivalent to:

$$\begin{cases} \Delta Y_{i1} = \mu + \alpha D_{i1} + \Delta u_{i1} \\ D_{i0} = 0 \end{cases} \qquad (3.80)$$

The previous relationship can be written in matrix form as follows:

$$\Delta \mathbf{y}_1 = [\mathbf{1}; \mathbf{D}] \begin{pmatrix} \mu \\ \alpha \end{pmatrix} + \Delta \mathbf{u}_1 \qquad (3.81)$$

By definition, the OLS estimation of the previous regression is:

$$\begin{pmatrix} \widehat{\mu} \\ \widehat{\alpha} \end{pmatrix}_{\text{OLS}} = \left[\begin{pmatrix} \mathbf{1}' \\ \mathbf{D}_1' \end{pmatrix} (\mathbf{1}; \mathbf{D}_1) \right]^{-1} \cdot \begin{pmatrix} \mathbf{1}' \\ \mathbf{D}_1' \end{pmatrix} \cdot \Delta \mathbf{y}_1 = \begin{bmatrix} \mathbf{1}'\mathbf{1} & \mathbf{1}'\mathbf{D}_1 \\ \mathbf{D}_1'\mathbf{1} & \mathbf{D}_1'\mathbf{D}_1 \end{bmatrix}^{-1} \cdot \begin{pmatrix} \mathbf{1}' \\ \mathbf{D}_1' \end{pmatrix} \cdot \Delta \mathbf{y}_1 =$$

$$= \begin{bmatrix} N & N_T \\ N_T & N_T \end{bmatrix}^{-1} \cdot \begin{pmatrix} \sum_{i=1}^{N} \Delta Y_{i1} \\ \sum_{i=1}^{N_T} \Delta Y_{i1} \end{pmatrix} = \frac{1}{N_T \cdot N_C} \cdot \begin{bmatrix} N_T & -N_T \\ -N_T & N \end{bmatrix} \cdot \begin{pmatrix} \sum_{i=1}^{N} \Delta Y_{i1} \\ \sum_{i=1}^{N_T} \Delta Y_{i1} \end{pmatrix} =$$

$$\frac{1}{N_T \cdot N_C} \cdot \begin{bmatrix} N_T \sum_{i=1}^{N} \Delta Y_{i1} - N_T \sum_{i=1}^{N_T} \Delta Y_{i1} \\ -N_T \sum_{i=1}^{N} \Delta Y_{i1} + N \sum_{i=1}^{N_T} \Delta Y_{i1} \end{bmatrix} = \frac{1}{N_T \cdot N_C} \cdot \begin{bmatrix} N_T \sum_{i=1}^{N_C} \Delta Y_{i1} \\ -N_T \sum_{i=1}^{N} \Delta Y_{i1} + N \sum_{i=1}^{N_T} \Delta Y_{i1} \end{bmatrix} =$$

$$= \frac{1}{N_T \cdot N_C} \cdot \begin{bmatrix} N_T \sum_{i=1}^{N_C} \Delta Y_{i1} \\ -N_T \sum_{i=1}^{N} \Delta Y_{i1} + N_T \sum_{i=1}^{N_T} \Delta Y_{i1} + N_C \sum_{i=1}^{N_T} \Delta Y_{i1} \end{bmatrix} =$$

$$\begin{bmatrix} \frac{1}{N_C} \sum_{i=1}^{N_C} \Delta Y_{i1} \\ \frac{1}{N_T} \sum_{i=1}^{N_T} \Delta Y_{i1} - \frac{1}{N_C} \sum_{i=1}^{N_C} \Delta Y_{i1} \end{bmatrix} = \begin{bmatrix} \left(\overline{Y}_{i1} - \overline{Y}_{i0} \right)_{\text{control}} \\ \left(\overline{Y}_{i1} - \overline{Y}_{i0} \right)_{\text{treated}} - \left(\overline{Y}_{i1} - \overline{Y}_{i0} \right)_{\text{control}} \end{bmatrix}$$

proving that:

$$\widehat{\alpha}_{\text{DID}} = \left(\overline{Y}_{i1} - \overline{Y}_{i0} \right)_{\text{treated}} - \left(\overline{Y}_{i1} - \overline{Y}_{i0} \right)_{\text{control}} \qquad (3.82)$$

Rearranging the previous expression, we obtain:

$$\widehat{\alpha}_{\text{DID}} = \underbrace{\left(\overline{Y}_{i1}^{T} - \overline{Y}_{i0}^{T}\right)}_{\substack{\text{Before/After}\\\text{estimator for}\\\text{Treated}}} - \underbrace{\left(\overline{Y}_{i1}^{C} - \overline{Y}_{i0}^{C}\right)}_{\substack{\text{Before/After}\\\text{estimator for}\\\text{Untreated}}} \tag{3.83}$$

or equivalently:

$$\widehat{\alpha}_{\text{DID}} = \left(\overline{Y}_{i1}^{T} - \overline{Y}_{i1}^{C}\right) - \left(\overline{Y}_{i0}^{T} - \overline{Y}_{i0}^{C}\right) \tag{3.84}$$

where we have that:

$$\overline{Y}_{i1}^{T} = \text{average of } Y \text{ on treated at } t = 1$$
$$\overline{Y}_{i1}^{C} = \text{average of } Y \text{ on untreated at } t = 1$$
$$\overline{Y}_{i0}^{T} = \text{average of } Y \text{ on treated at } t = 0$$
$$\overline{Y}_{i0}^{C} = \text{average of } Y \text{ on untreated at } t = 0$$

Now, since:

$$\widehat{\alpha}_{\text{DID}} = \underbrace{\left(\overline{Y}_{i1}^{T} - \overline{Y}_{i0}^{T}\right)}_{\substack{\text{Before/After}\\\text{estimator for}\\\text{Treated}}} - \underbrace{\left(\overline{Y}_{i1}^{C} - \overline{Y}_{i0}^{C}\right)}_{\substack{\text{Before/After}\\\text{estimator for}\\\text{Untreated}}} = \widehat{\alpha}_{\text{BA}}^{T} - \widehat{\alpha}_{\text{BA}}^{C} \tag{3.85}$$

it follows that the before/after estimator on treated units is biased and that bias is equal to:

$$\text{Bias}\left(\widehat{\alpha}_{\text{BA}}^{T}\right) = \widehat{\alpha}_{\text{DID}} - \left(\widehat{\alpha}_{\text{DID}} + \widehat{\alpha}_{\text{BA}}^{C}\right) = -\widehat{\alpha}_{\text{BA}}^{C} \tag{3.86}$$

Nevertheless, note that DID is consistent as soon as:

$$\text{Cov}(D_{i1}; \Delta u_{i1}) = 0 \tag{3.87}$$

which is a stronger version of the CMI. Condition (3.87) is a shortcoming of DID, although, as in the repeated cross-section case, one can control also for time and individual effects in order to preserve exogeneity. Finally, DID with panel data can also be easily extended to the case of dynamic treatment by introducing lags and leads as we did in the cross-section case:

$$Y_{it} = \gamma_i + \lambda_t + \sum_{\tau=0}^{m} D_{t-\tau}\delta_{-\tau} + \sum_{\tau=1}^{q} D_{t+\tau}\delta_{+\tau} + \boldsymbol{\beta}\mathbf{x}_{it} + e_{it} \qquad (3.88)$$

Equation (3.88) is equivalent to that of (3.77), except from the omission of the location dimension s. In this case, building lags and leads reduces the sample size as missing values are generated over time. However, an OLS regression of the previous regression provides consistent estimation of the causal effects. In Sect. 3.4.4, we will focus more in detail on DID within a time-varying treatment setting.

3.4.2.1 A Comparison Between DID and FE Estimator

In many program evaluation applications using longitudinal setting, *fixed effects* (FE) estimation of the outcome equation, possibly augmented by treatment-lagged variables, is used.

How does the FE estimation differ from that of the DID? Does the choice between FE and DID matter in terms of the precision of the estimates? Intuitively, DID estimator should be more robust than FE since, by definition, DID takes into account a *ceteris paribus* condition that the FE estimator overlooks. To see this, we write the two regressions for DID and FE:

$$\text{DID} : \begin{cases} Y_{it} = \theta_i + \lambda_t + D_{it}\alpha + \mathbf{x}_{it}\boldsymbol{\beta} + u_{it} \\ D_{i,t-1} = 0 \end{cases} \qquad (3.89)$$

$$\text{FE} : \{ Y_{it} = \theta_i + \lambda_t + D_{it}\alpha + \mathbf{x}_{it}\boldsymbol{\beta} + u_{it} \qquad (3.90)$$

where, by substitution and by differencing, we obtain (omitting $\Delta\mathbf{x}_{it}$ and $\Delta\lambda_t$ for simplicity):

$$\text{DID} : \Delta Y_{it} = \alpha D_{it} + \Delta u_{it} \qquad (3.91)$$

$$\text{FE} : \Delta Y_{it} = \alpha \Delta D_{it} + \Delta u_{it} \qquad (3.92)$$

thus yielding two different conditions for consistency. For the DID equation we need that:

$$\text{Cov}(D_{it}; u_{it} - u_{i,t-1}) = \text{Cov}(D_{it}; u_{it}) - \text{Cov}(D_{it}; u_{i,t-1}) = 0 \qquad (3.93)$$

that is:

$$\text{Cov}(D_{it}; u_{it}) = \text{Cov}(D_{it}; u_{i,t-1}) \qquad (3.94)$$

and for the FE equation, we require:

$$\text{Cov}(D_{it} - D_{i,t-1}; u_{it} - u_{i,t-1}) = [\text{Cov}(D_{it}; u_{it}) - \text{Cov}(D_{it}; u_{i,t-1})]$$
$$+ [\text{Cov}(D_{i,t-1}; u_{i,t-1}) - \text{Cov}(D_{i,t-1}; u_{it})]$$
$$= 0 \qquad (3.95)$$

that is:

$$[\text{Cov}(D_{it}; u_{it}) - \text{Cov}(D_{it}; u_{i,t-1})] = [\text{Cov}(D_{i,t-1}; u_{i,t-1}) - \text{Cov}(D_{i,t-1}; u_{it})] \quad (3.96)$$

We observe immediately that when DID is consistent—i.e., (3.94) holds—(3.96) becomes:

$$\text{Cov}(D_{i,t-1}; u_{i,t-1}) - \text{Cov}(D_{i,t-1}; u_{it}) = 0 \Rightarrow \text{Cov}(D_{i,t-1}; u_{i,t-1})$$
$$= \text{Cov}(D_{i,t-1}; u_{it}) \qquad (3.97)$$

Equation (3.97) implies that a second and more restrictive requirement with respect to the correlation between D and u at different points in time is required by the FE estimator. The condition under which the consistency of DID is achieved is therefore less restrictive than that required for the FE estimator. In this sense, DID is preferable to the FE estimator.

Nevertheless, even if estimation by DID entails less restrictive identification conditions than FE, implementing DID reduces the number of observations required to estimate the ATE due to the pre-period zero-treatment condition. When reduction in observations is significant, the relative attractiveness of DID vis-a-vis FE may reduce and a *trade-off* between identification requirements and inferential precision can arise. If the number of observations falls dramatically, it is likely that FE may produce a more robust estimation of the effect of the policy to be evaluated than that obtained using DID.

3.4.3 DID with Matching

Hybrid program evaluation methods are generally more robust than stand-alone approaches. In Sect. 2.5, we presented the case of the Doubly-robust estimator, combining Reweighting on inverse-probability with Regression-adjustment.

Another type of hybrid method is the Matching-DID (M-DID), a combination of DID with a propensity-score Matching (Heckman et al. 1998; Smith and Todd 2005). This estimator is similar to the DID estimator presented in Sects. 3.4.1 and 3.4.2, but it has the advantage that it does not require the imposition of the linear-in-parameters form of the outcome equation. As such, it can be seen as a nonparametric DID, reweighting observations according to a weighting function dependent on the specific Matching approach adopted. As in the standard DID, there are two types of M-DID: one for panel and one for repeated cross-section data. Both formulas are provided below, where our discussion is limited to the estimation of ATET (the estimation of the ATENT follows a similar procedure).

In the case of panel data, the M-DID formula takes the following form:

$$\widehat{\text{ATET}}_{\text{M-DID}} = \frac{1}{N_1} \sum_{i \in \{T\}} \left((Y_{i1}^T - Y_{i0}^T) - \sum_{j \in C(i)} h(i, j) \left(Y_{j1}^C - Y_{j0}^C \right) \right)$$

where $t = 1$ is the after-policy time, and $t = 0$ is the before-policy time; T is the treated set; C is the untreated set of units; $h(i, j)$ the (specific) matching weights; and $C(i)$ is the neighborhood of the treated unit i.

For the repeated cross-section case, we have, respectively:

$$\widehat{\text{ATET}}_{\text{M-DID}} = \frac{1}{N_{T,1}} \sum_{i \in \{T_1\}} \left(Y_{i1}^T - \sum_{j \in C_1(i)} h(i, j) Y_{j1}^C \right)$$

$$- \frac{1}{N_{T,0}} \sum_{i \in \{T_0\}} \left(Y_{i0}^T - \sum_{j \in C_0(i)} h(i, j) Y_{j0}^C \right)$$

where $N_{T,1}$ is the number of treated units (T) at time $t = 1$; $N_{T,0}$ is the number of treated units (T) at time $t = 0$; T_1 is the set of treated at time $t = 1$; T_0 is the set of treated at time $t = 0$; $C_1(i)$ is the neighborhood of unit i in time $t = 1$; and $C_0(i)$ is the neighborhood of unit i in time $t = 0$ (see also Blundell and Costa Dias 2000).

As is usual with Matching, the advantage of using this nonparametric approach should be reconsidered when the reduction in sample size, as a result of the Matching trimming mechanism, is significant.

3.4.4   Time-Variant Treatment and Pre–Post Treatment Analysis

In this section, we focus on treatment effect estimation in the presence of *time-variant* treatment. Such a setting frequently characterizes numerous economic and social phenomena, which generally change over time. One could, for example, be interested in ascertaining both whether a certain treatment has had an impact on a given target with some delays and whether there are possible anticipatory effects. To begin with, consider a binary treatment indicator for individual i at time t:

$$D_{it} = \begin{cases} 1 & \text{if unit } i \text{ is treated at time } t \\ 0 & \text{if unit } i \text{ is untreated at time } t \end{cases}$$

and assume an outcome equation with one lag and one lead:

$$Y_{it} = \mu_{it} + \beta_{-1}D_{it-1} + \beta_0 D_{it} + \beta_{+1}D_{it+1} + \gamma \mathbf{x}_{it} + u_{it}$$

In this setup, we have then the following *sequence of treatments*:

$$\{w^j\} = \{D_{it-1}, D_{it}, D_{it+1}\} = \begin{cases} w^1 = (0,0,0) \\ w^2 = (1,0,0) \\ w^3 = (0,1,0) \\ w^4 = (0,0,1) \end{cases}$$

Where the sequence w^1 is the usual benchmark of non-treatment over time. The generic treatment sequence is indicated by w^j (with $j = 1, \ldots, 4$) and the associated potential outcome as $Y(w^j)$. In this setting, we can easily define the "average treatment effect between the two potential outcomes $Y(w^j)$ and $Y(w^k)$" as:

$$\text{ATE}_{jk} = \text{E}[Y_{it}(w^j) - Y_{it}(w^k)] \quad \forall\, (i,t)$$

Under CMI, we have that:

$$\begin{aligned} \text{ATE}_{jk} &= \text{E}_{\mathbf{x}}\{\text{ATE}_{jk}(\mathbf{x})\} = \text{E}_{\mathbf{x}}\{\text{E}[Y_{it}(w^j, \mathbf{x}) - Y_{it}(w^k, \mathbf{x})]\} \\ &= \text{E}_{\mathbf{x}}\{\text{E}[(Y_{it}|w^j, \mathbf{x}) - \text{E}(Y_{it}|w^k, \mathbf{x})]\} \end{aligned}$$

In such a model with one lag and one lead, we can define and collect six ATEs as follows:

$$\begin{bmatrix} & w_1 & w_2 & w_3 & w_4 \\ w_1 & - & & & \\ w_2 & \text{ATE}_{21} & - & & \\ w_3 & \text{ATE}_{31} & \text{ATE}_{32} & - & \\ w_4 & \text{ATE}_{41} & \text{ATE}_{42} & \text{ATE}_{43} & - \end{bmatrix}$$

Using the Y-equation we can also show that:

$$\begin{aligned} \text{ATE}_{21} &= \text{E}[(Y_{it}|w_2) - \text{E}(Y_{it}|w_1)] = (\bar{\mu} + \beta_{-1} + \gamma\bar{\mathbf{x}}) - (\bar{\mu} + \gamma\bar{\mathbf{x}}) = \beta_{-1} \\ \text{ATE}_{31} &= \text{E}[(Y_{it}|w_3) - \text{E}(Y_{it}|w_1)] = \beta_0 \\ \text{ATE}_{41} &= \text{E}[(Y_{it}|w_4) - \text{E}(Y_{it}|w_1)] = \beta_{+1} \\ \text{ATE}_{32} &= \text{E}[(Y_{it}|w_3) - \text{E}(Y_{it}|w_2)] = \beta_0 - \beta_{-1} \\ \text{ATE}_{42} &= \text{E}[(Y_{it}|w_4) - \text{E}(Y_{it}|w_2)] = \beta_{+1} - \beta_{-1} \\ \text{ATE}_{43} &= \text{E}[(Y_{it}|w_4) - \text{E}(Y_{it}|w_3)] = \beta_{+1} - \beta_0 \end{aligned}$$

In general, we obtain a number of ATEs equal to $(M^2 - M)/2$, where M is the number of binary treatments considered in the dynamic treatment setting. An important advantage of a dynamic treatment model of this kind is the possibility to plot graphically the results, i.e., the estimated potential outcomes and the effects over time. To this end, define the predictions of Y_{it} given the sequence of treatment as:

$$\mathrm{E}\left(Y_{it}\middle|D_{it-1},D_{it},D_{it+1},\mathbf{x}_{it}\right) = \bar{\mu}_t + \beta_{-1}D_{it-1} + \beta_0 D_{it} + \beta_{+1}D_{it+1} + \boldsymbol{\gamma}\bar{\mathbf{x}}_t$$

Consider now only these two specific sequences of treatment:

$$w^T = \{D_{it-1} = 0, D_{it} = 1, D_{it+1} = 0\}$$
$$w^C = \{D_{it-1} = 0, D_{it} = 0, D_{it+1} = 0\}$$

where:

$$w^T : \text{treatment only at the } t$$
$$w^C : \text{never treated over } t$$

Define the prediction of Y at $t-1$, t, and $t+1$:

$$\mathrm{E}\left(Y_{it-1}\middle|D_{it-1},D_{it},D_{it+1}\right) = \bar{\mu}_{t-1} + \beta_{-1}D_{it-2} + \beta_0 D_{it-1} + \beta_1 D_{it} + \boldsymbol{\gamma}\bar{\mathbf{x}}_{t-1}$$
$$\mathrm{E}\left(Y_{it}\middle|D_{it-1},D_{it},D_{it+1}\right) = \bar{\mu}_t + \beta_{-1}D_{it-1} + \beta_0 D_{it} + \beta_{+1}D_{it+1} + \boldsymbol{\gamma}\bar{\mathbf{x}}_t$$
$$\mathrm{E}\left(Y_{it+1}\middle|D_{it-1},D_{it},D_{it+1}\right) = \bar{\mu}_{t+1} + \beta_{-1}D_{it} + \beta_0 D_{it+1} + \beta_{+1}D_{it+2} + \boldsymbol{\gamma}\bar{\mathbf{x}}_{t+1}$$

which can be used to calculate the expected outcome over $\{t-1, t, t+1\}$ of the previous two sequences. Thus:

(i) For w^T, we have that:

$$\mathrm{E}\left(Y_{it-1}\middle|w^T = 0, 1, 0\right) = \bar{\mu}_{t-1} + \beta_{+1} + \boldsymbol{\gamma}\bar{\mathbf{x}}_{t-1}$$
$$\mathrm{E}\left(Y_{it}\middle|w^T = 0, 1, 0\right) = \bar{\mu}_t + \beta_0 + \boldsymbol{\gamma}\bar{\mathbf{x}}_t$$
$$\mathrm{E}\left(Y_{it+1}\middle|w^T = 0, 1, 0\right) = \bar{\mu}_{t+1} + \beta_{-1} + \boldsymbol{\gamma}\bar{\mathbf{x}}_{t+1}$$

(ii) For w^C, we have that:

$$\mathrm{E}\left(Y_{it-1}\middle|w^C = 0, 0, 0\right) = \bar{\mu}_{t-1} + \boldsymbol{\gamma}\bar{\mathbf{x}}_{t-1}$$
$$\mathrm{E}\left(Y_{it}\middle|w^C = 0, 0, 0\right) = \bar{\mu}_t + \boldsymbol{\gamma}\bar{\mathbf{x}}_t$$
$$\mathrm{E}\left(Y_{it+1}\middle|w^C = 0, 0, 0\right) = \bar{\mu}_{t+1} + \boldsymbol{\gamma}\bar{\mathbf{x}}_{t+1}$$

We can plot these predictions over time (Fig. 3.5) and depict these situations:

- $\beta_{+1} > 0$ and significant. In this case, there is a positive effect of the treatment at t on the outcome at $t-1$. This means that the *current* treatment had an effect on *past* outcome (*anticipatory effect*). Therefore, the pretreatment period is characterized by a positive effect of current treatment.
- $\beta_0 > 0$ and significant. In this case, there is a positive effect of the treatment at t on the outcome at t. This means that the *current* treatment had an effect on

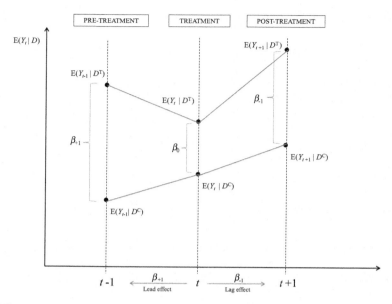

Fig. 3.5 Pre $(t-1)$- and post $(t+1)$-treatment effect of a policy performed at t

current outcome (*simultaneous effect*). Therefore, the treatment period is characterized by a positive effect of the treatment administered in the same period.

- $\beta_{-1} > 0$ and significant. In this case, there is a positive effect of the treatment at t on the outcome at $t+1$. This means that the *current* treatment had an effect on *future* outcomes (*lagged effect*). Therefore, the post treatment period is characterized by a positive effect of current treatment.

This approach can naturally be extended to multiple lags and leads. See Autor (2003) and Cerulli (2012) for more details.

3.5 Implementation and Application of IV and Selection-Model

This section offers an application of the IV methods and Selection-model presented in the theoretical sections. We begin by presenting the Stata user-written command `ivtreatreg` (Cerulli 2014), performing IV and (generalized) Heckman Selection-model estimations. Next, we illustrate a Monte Carlo exercise to assess whether the theoretical properties of IV and Selection-model are confirmed in practice. A subsection is dedicated to an application of IV and Heckit on real data. Finally, an implementation of the Selection-model using the built-in Stata routine `etregress` is also discussed.

3.5.1 The Stata Command *ivtreatreg*

The Stata routine ivtreatreg (Cerulli 2014) estimates the four binary treatment models presented in previous sections, i.e., Direct-2SLS, Probit-OLS, Probit-2SLS, and Heckit, with and without idiosyncratic (or heterogeneous) average treatment effects. As noted in Chap. 2, an older version of this command also estimated the Control-function regression (CFR) model using the option model(cf-ols), which can be now estimated using the built-in Stata13 command teffects ra.

Depending on the specified model, ivtreatreg provides consistent estimation of ATEs either under the hypothesis of "selection on observables" (using, as said, the option model(cf-ols), but only in the older version) or "selection on unobservables" (using one of the three Instrumental-variables (IV) models or the Heckman Selection-model reviewed in previous sections). Conditional on a prespecified subset of exogenous variables—those driving the heterogeneous response to treatment—ivtreatreg calculates for each specific model, the average treatment effect (ATE), the average treatment effect on treated (ATET), and the average treatment effect on non-treated (ATENT), in addition to the estimates of these parameters conditional on the observable factors **x** (i.e., ATE(**x**), ATET(**x**), and ATENT(**x**)).

The syntax of the command is fairly simple:

Syntax of ivtreatreg

```
ivtreatreg outcome treatment [varlist] [if] [in] [weight], model(modeltype)
    [hetero(varlist_h) iv(varlist_iv) conf(number) graphic vce(robust)
    const(noconstant) head(noheader)]
```

where outcome specifies the target variable that is the object of the evaluation; treatment specifies the binary (i.e., taking 0 = treated or 1 = untreated) treatment variable; varlist defines the list of exogenous variables that are considered as observable confounders.

ivtreatreg allows for specifying a series of convenient options of different importance:

```
----------------------------------------------------------------
Required options
----------------------------------------------------------------
model(modeltype) specifies the treatment model to be estimated, where modeltype must be
    one of the following (and abovementioned) four models: "direct-2sls", "probit-2sls",
    "probit-ols", "heckit". It is always required to specify one model.
----------------------------------------------------------------
modeltype        description
----------------------------------------------------------------
direct-2sls      IV regression estimated by direct two-stage least squares
probit-2sls      IV regression estimated by Probit and two-stage least squares
probit-ols       IV two-step regression estimated by Probit and OLS
heckit           Heckman two-step selection-model
```

```
----------------------------------------------------------------
Optional options
----------------------------------------------------------------
```

hetero(varlist_h) specifies the variables over which to calculate the idyosincratic Average
  Treatment Effect ATE(x), ATET(x) and ATENT(x), where x=varlist_h. It is optional for all
  models. When this option is not specified, the command estimates the specified model without
  heterogeneous average effect. Observe that varlist_h should be the same set or a subset of
  the variables specified in varlist.

iv (varlist_iv) specifies the variable(s) to be used as instruments. This option is
  strictly required only for "direct-2sls", "probit-2sls" and "probit-ols", while it
  is optional for "heckit".

graphic allows for a graphical representation of the density distributions of ATE(x),
  ATET(x) and ATENT(x). It is optional for all models and gives an outcome only if
  variables into hetero() are specified.

vce(robust) allows for robust regression standard errors. It is optional for all
  models.

beta reports standardized beta coefficients. It is optional for all models.

const(noconstant) suppresses regression constant term. It is optional for all models.

conf(number) sets the confidence level equal to the specified number. The default is
  number=95.

```
----------------------------------------------------------------
```

The routine also creates a number of variables which can be used to analyze the
data further:

_ws_varname_h are the additional regressors used in model's regression when hetero
  (varlist_h) is specified. They are created for all models.
_z_varname_h are the instrumental-variables used in model's regression when hetero
  (varlist_h) and iv(varlist_iv) are specified. They are created only in IV models.
ATE(x) is an estimate of the idiosyncratic Average Treatment Effect.
ATET(x) is an estimate of the idiosyncratic Average Treatment Effect on treated.
ATENT(x) is an estimate of the idiosyncratic Average Treatment Effect on Non-Treated.
G_fv is the predicted probability from the Probit regression, conditional on the
  observable confounders used.
_wL0, wL1 are the Heckman correction-terms.

Interestingly, ivtreatreg also returns some useful scalars:

e(N_tot) is the total number of (used) observations.
e(N_treated) is the number of (used) treated units.
e(N_untreated) is the number of (used) untreated units.
e(ate) is the value of the Average Treatment Effect.
e(atet) is the value of the Average Treatment Effect on Treated.
e(atent) is the value of the Average Treatment Effect on Non-treated.

Further information on `ivtreatreg` can be found in the help file of this command.

3.5.2   A Monte Carlo Experiment

In this section, we offer a Monte Carlo experiment to ascertain whether the IV and Selection-models are consistent with theoretical predictions. Performing a Monte Carlo simulation is also an essential robustness check to assess the reliability of any user-written command.

The first step is to define a data generating process (DGP) as follows:

$$\begin{cases} D = 1 \left[0.5 + 0.5x_1 + 0.3x_2 + 0.6z + a > 0 \right] \\ Y_0 = 0.1 + 0.2x_1 + 0.2x_2 + e_0 \\ Y_1 = 0.3 + 0.3x_1 + 0.3x_2 + e_0 \end{cases}$$

where:

$$\begin{cases} x_1 \sim \ln(h_1) \\ x_2 \sim \ln(h_2) \\ z \sim \ln(h_3) \\ h_1 \sim \chi^2(1) + c \\ h_2 \sim \chi^2(1) + c \\ h_3 \sim \chi^2(1) + c \\ c \sim \chi^2(1) \end{cases}$$

and

$$(a, e_0, e_1) \sim N(\mathbf{0}; \mathbf{\Omega})$$

$$\mathbf{\Omega} = \begin{pmatrix} \sigma_a^2 & \sigma_{a,e_0} & \sigma_{a,e_1} \\ & \sigma_{e_0}^2 & \sigma_{a,e_1} \\ & & \sigma_{e_1}^2 \end{pmatrix} = \begin{pmatrix} \sigma_a^2 & \rho_{a,e_0}\sigma_a\sigma_{e_0} & \rho_{a,e_1}\sigma_a\sigma_{e_1} \\ & \sigma_{e_0}^2 & \rho_{e_0,e_1}\sigma_{e_0}\sigma_{e_1} \\ & & \sigma_{e_1}^2 \end{pmatrix}$$

$$\sigma_a^2 = 1, \quad \sigma_{e_0}^2 = 3, \quad \sigma_{e_1}^2 = 6.5,$$
$$\rho_{a,e_0} = 0.5, \quad \rho_{a,e_1} = 0.3, \quad \rho_{e_0,e_1} = 0$$

Assuming that the correlation between a and e_0 (i.e., ρ_{a,e_0}) and the correlation between a and e_1 (i.e., ρ_{a,e_1}) are different from zero implies that D—the selection binary indicator—is endogenous. The variable z denotes an instrument, which is directly correlated with D but (directly) uncorrelated with Y_1 and Y_0. Given these assumptions, the DGP is completed by the POM, $Y_i = Y_{0i} + D_i (Y_{1i} - Y_{0i})$, generating the observable outcome Y.

The DGP is simulated 500 times using a sample size of 10,000. For each simulation, we obtain a different data matrix (x_1, x_2, Y, D, z) on which we apply the four models implemented by `ivtreatreg` and the CFR model.

Table 3.3 Simulation output. Unbiasedness of ATE estimators

	No. of simulations	Mean of ATE	Std. dev.	Min	Max
Probit-OLS	500	0.229	0.098	−0.050	0.520
Direct-2SLS	500	0.250	0.112	−0.081	0.560
Heckit	500	0.216	0.090	−0.045	0.475
Probit-2SLS	500	0.235	0.092	−0.053	0.523
CFR (or CF-OLS)	500	1.371	0.045	1.242	1.504

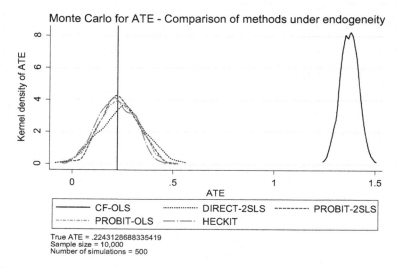

Fig. 3.6 Distributions of ATE under the five models implemented by `ivtreatreg`

Table 3.3 and Fig. 3.6 present our simulation results. The true ATE value from the DGP is 0.224. As expected, all the IV procedures provide consistent estimation of the true ATE, a slight bias only being obtained with the Direct-2SLS model.

The CFR results are clearly biased, with a mean of 1.37, confirming that with endogeneity, the implementation of CFR might lead to very unreliable conclusions. Figure 3.6 confirms these findings, plotting the distributions of ATE obtained by each single method over the 500 DGP simulations. This clearly emphasizes the very different pattern of the CFR estimator.

Figure 3.7 shows the distributions of ATE using the IV methods. All methods perform rather similarly, with the exception of Direct-2SLS which has a slightly different shape with a larger right tail, thus suggesting we should look at the estimation precision a bit more closely. Under our DGP assumptions, we expect the Heckit model to be the most efficient method, followed by Probit-OLS and Probit-2SLS, with Direct-2SLS being the worst performing. In fact, our DGP follows exactly the same assumptions under which the Heckit is based (in particular, the joint normality of a, e_0, and e_1).

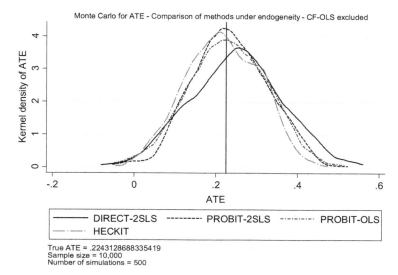

Fig. 3.7   Distributions of ATE. Only instrumental-variables (IV) methods

The result in Table 3.4 confirms these theoretical predictions: the lowest standard error is obtained by Heckit (0.087) and the highest by Direct-2SLS (0.116), the other methods falling in between. Note that the mean test presented in this table indicates that standard errors values are precisely estimated, all being included within the 95 % confidence interval. CFR, in particular, is very precisely estimated, although it is severely biased. Table 3.4 contains simulation results also on t-statistics and test size. The size of a test is the probability of rejecting a hypothesis H_0 when H_0 is true. In our DGP, we have set a two-sided test, where H_0: ATE $= 0.224$ against the alternative H_1: ATE $\neq 0.224$.

The results presented under the heading Test size in Table 3.4 represent the proportion of simulations which lead us to reject the H_0. These values are the "rejection rates" and have to be interpreted as the simulation estimate of the true test size. As it is immediate to see, the rejection rates are all lower than the usual 5 % significance, and the values are precisely estimated, since they are contained within the 95 % confidence interval in the simulation mean test. The only exception being, as expected, the CFR, whose test size is equal to 1: the two-sided test considered always leads to reject H_0 in this case.

Finally, it can be showed (although not reported) that under treatment exogeneity, CFR proves to be the most efficient unbiased estimator of ATE among the methods considered.

Table 3.4 Simulation output. Standard errors, t-statistic, and test size of ATE estimators

	Mean	Std. err.	[95 % Conf. interval]	
Standard errors				
Probit-OLS	0.0977	0.0001	0.0975	0.0979
Direct-2SLS	0.1159	0.0001	0.1156	0.1162
HECKIT	0.0874	0.0001	0.0872	0.0875
Probit-2SLS	0.0971	0.0001	0.0969	0.0973
CFR	0.0419	0.0000	0.0419	0.0419
T-statistic				
Probit-OLS	0.0553	0.0429	−0.0289	0.1395
Direct-2SLS	0.2371	0.0430	0.1526	0.3216
HECKIT	−0.0757	0.0441	−0.1624	0.0110
Probit-2SLS	0.1245	0.0419	0.0420	0.2069
CFR	27.3690	0.0403	27.2897	27.4482
Test size				
Probit-OLS	0.0380	0.0086	0.0212	0.0548
Direct-2SLS	0.0440	0.0092	0.0260	0.0620
HECKIT	0.0400	0.0088	0.0228	0.0572
Probit-2SLS	0.0420	0.0090	0.0244	0.0596
CFR	1	0		

3.5.3 An Application to Determine the Effect of Education on Fertility

In order to provide an application of IV and Selection-model to real data, we consider an illustrative dataset called FERTIL2.DTA, which contains cross-sectional data on 4,361 women of childbearing age in Botswana[5].

This dataset contains 28 variables relating to various individual and family characteristics. We are particularly interested in evaluating the impact of the variable "educ7" (taking value 1 if a woman has more than or exactly 7 years of education and 0 otherwise) on the number of children in the family ("children"). Several conditioning (or confounding) observable factors are included in the dataset, such as the age of the woman ("age"), whether or not the family owns a TV ("tv"), whether or not the woman lives in a city ("urban"), and so forth. In order to investigate the relationship between education and fertility, we estimate the following specification for each of the four models implemented by `ivtreatreg`:

```
. set more off

. xi: ivtreatreg children educ7 age agesq evermarr urban electric tv , ///
hetero(age agesq evermarr urban) iv(frsthalf) model(modeltype) graphic
```

---

[5] This dataset is used in a number of examples in *Introductory Econometrics: A Modern Approach* by Wooldridge (2008). It can be freely downloaded here: http://fmwww.bc.edu/ec-p/data/wooldridge/FERTIL2.dta.

Following Wooldridge (2001, example 18.3, p. 624), this specification adopts— as an instrumental-variable—the covariate "frsthalf" which takes a value equal to 1 if the woman was born in the first 6 months of the year and zero otherwise. This variable is (partially) correlated with "educ7," but should not be related to the number of children in the family. The choice of "frsthalf" as an instrument follows the same rationale of the choice of "quarter-of-birth" used as an instrument for years of education in Angrist and Krueger (1991) discussed in Sect. 3.2.

Table 3.7 shows that the simple Difference-in-means (DIM) estimator (the mean of children in the group of more educated women, the treated ones, minus the mean of children in the group of less educated women, the untreated ones) equals -1.77 with a t-value of -28.46. Thus the more educated women tend to have—without *ceteris paribus* conditions—about two fewer children than the less educated ones. Adding confounding factors in the regression specification, we obtain the OLS estimate of the ATE that, in the absence of heterogeneous treatment, is equal to -0.394 with a t-value of -7.94; although significant, the magnitude, as expected, is considerably lower compared to that of the Difference-in-means estimation, indicating, therefore, that confounders are relevant. When we consider OLS estimation with heterogeneity, we obtain an ATE equal to -0.37, significant at 1 % (column CFR in Table 3.7).

When the IV estimation is considered, the results change, however, dramatically. We estimate the previous specification for Probit-2SLS using `ivtreatreg` with heterogeneous treatment response. Results are reported in Table 3.5, which contains both results from the probit first step and from the IV regression of the second step. The probit results indicate that "frsthalf" is sufficiently (partially) correlated with "educ7"; thus, it can be reliably used as an instrument for this variable. Step 2 shows that the ATE (again, the coefficient of "educ7") is no longer significant and, above all, it changes sign becoming positive and equal to 0.30.

The results are in line with the IV estimations obtained by Wooldridge (2010). Nevertheless, having assumed heterogeneous response to treatment allows us to now calculate also the ATET and ATENT and to investigate the cross-unit distribution of these effects. `ivtreatreg` returns these parameters as scalars (along with treated and untreated sample size):

```
. ereturn list

    scalars:

        e(N_untreat) =   1937
         e(N_treat) =   2421
           e(N_tot) =   4358
           e(atent) =  -.4468834318603838
            e(atet) =   .898290019555276
             e(ate) =   .3004007408742051
```

In order to obtain the standard errors for testing the significance of both ATET and ATENT, a bootstrap procedure can be easily implemented in the following manner:

Table 3.5 Results form `ivtreateg` when Probit-2SLS is the specified model and treatment heterogeneous response is assumed

```
--------------------------------------------------------------------------------
Step 1. Probit regression                          Number of obs   =      4358
                                                   LR chi2(7)      =   1130.84
                                                   Prob > chi2     =    0.0000
Log likelihood = -2428.384                         Pseudo R2       =    0.1889
--------------------------------------------------------------------------------
      educ7 |      Coef.   Std. Err.       z    P>|z|     [95% Conf. Interval]
------------+-------------------------------------------------------------------
   frsthalf | -.2206627   .0418563    -5.27   0.000    -.3026995   -.1386259
        age | -.0150337   .0174845    -0.86   0.390    -.0493027    .0192354
      agesq | -.0007325   .0002897    -2.53   0.011    -.0013003   -.0001647
    evermarr | -.2972879   .0486734    -6.11   0.000     -.392686   -.2018898
      urban |  .2998122   .0432321     6.93   0.000     .2150789    .3845456
    electric |  .4246668   .0751255     5.65   0.000     .2774235     .57191
         tv |  .9281707   .0977462     9.50   0.000     .7365915    1.11975
      _cons |   1.13537   .2440057     4.65   0.000     .6571273    1.613612
--------------------------------------------------------------------------------

Step 2. Instrumental variables (2SLS) regression

      Source |       SS           df       MS           Number of obs  =      4358
-------------+------------------------------           F( 11,  4346)  =    448.51
       Model |  10198.4139       11   927.128534        Prob > F       =    0.0000
    Residual |  11311.6182     4346   2.60276536        R-squared      =    0.4741
-------------+------------------------------           Adj R-squared  =    0.4728
       Total |  21510.0321     4357   4.93689055        Root MSE       =    1.6133

--------------------------------------------------------------------------------
    children |      Coef.   Std. Err.       t    P>|t|     [95% Conf. Interval]
------------+-------------------------------------------------------------------
       educ7 |  .3004007   .4995617     0.60   0.548    -.6789951    1.279797
     _ws_age | -.8428913   .1368854    -6.16   0.000    -1.111256   -.5745262
   _ws_agesq |   .011469   .0019061     6.02   0.000      .007732    .0152059
 _ws_evermarr | -.8979833   .2856655    -3.14   0.002    -1.458033   -.3379333
   _ws_urban |  .4167504   .2316103     1.80   0.072     -.037324    .8708247
         age |   .859302   .0966912     8.89   0.000      .669738    1.048866
       agesq |   -.01003   .0012496    -8.03   0.000    -.0124799   -.0075801
    evermarr |  1.253709   .1586299     7.90   0.000     .9427132    1.564704
       urban | -.5313325   .1379893    -3.85   0.000     -.801862    -.260803
    electric | -.2392104   .1010705    -2.37   0.018      -.43736   -.0410608
         tv | -.2348937   .1478488    -1.59   0.112    -.5247528    .0549653
      _cons |  -13.7584   1.876365    -7.33   0.000    -17.43704   -10.07977
--------------------------------------------------------------------------------
Instrumented:  educ7 _ws_age _ws_agesq _ws_evermarr _ws_urban
Instruments:   age agesq evermarr urban electric tv G_fv _z_age _z_agesq
               _z_evermarr _z_urban
--------------------------------------------------------------------------------
```

```
. xi: bootstrap atet=r(atet) atent=r(atent), rep(100): ///
ivtreatreg children  educ7 age agesq evermarr urban electric tv  , ///
hetero(age agesq evermarr urban) iv(frsthalf) model(probit-2sls)
```

The results obtained are reported in Table 3.6. As it can be seen, both ATET and ATENT are insignificant, indicating values not that substantially different from the ATE. A simple check should show that ATE = ATET $p(D = 1)$ + ATENT $p(D = 0)$:

```
. di "ATE= " (e(N_treat)/e(N_tot))*e(atet)+(e(N_untreat)/e(N_tot))*e(atent)
ATE= .30040086
```

Table 3.6 Bootstrap standard errors for ATET(**x**) and ATENT(**x**) using `ivtreatreg` with model Probit-2SLS

```
-----------------------------------------------------------------------------
Bootstrap results                              Number of obs      =       4358
                                               Replications       =        100
-----------------------------------------------------------------------------
command: ivtreatreg children educ7 age agesq evermarr urban electric tv,
         hetero(age agesq evermarr urban) iv(frsthalf) model(probit-2sls)

           atet:  r(atet)
           atent: r(atent)
-----------------------------------------------------------------------------
         |   Observed    Bootstrap                          Normal-based
         |      Coef.    Std. Err.      z     P>|z|     [95% Conf. Interval]
---------+-------------------------------------------------------------------
    atet |    .89829    .5488267     1.64    0.102     -.1773905     1.973971
   atent |  -.4468834   .4124428    -1.08    0.279     -1.255257     .3614897
-----------------------------------------------------------------------------
```

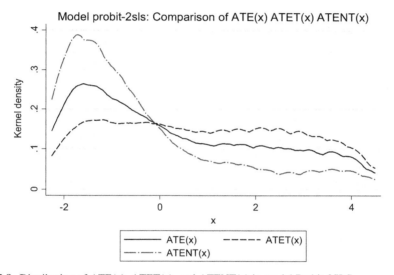

Fig. 3.8 Distribution of ATE(**x**), ATET(**x**), and ATENT(**x**) in model Probit-2SLS

which confirms the expected result. Finally, Fig. 3.8 plots the distributions of ATE(**x**), ATET(**x**), and ATENT(**x**).

What emerges from this analysis is that ATET(**x**) shows a substantially uniform distribution, while both the ATE(**x**) and the ATENT(**x**) distributions are more concentrated on negative values. In particular, ATENT(**x**) shows the highest modal value of approximately -2.2 children; thus, less educated women would have been less fertile if they had been more educated.

Table 3.7 shows the ATE results obtained for all the models and also for the simple Difference-in-means (DIM). The ATE obtained by IV methods is not always significant and is positive only in the Probit-2SLS estimation. The rest of ATEs are

Table 3.7 Estimation of the ATE for the five models estimated by `ivtreatreg`

Variable	DIM	CFR	PROBIT-OLS	DIRECT-2SLS	PROBIT_2SLS	HECKIT
educ7	-1.770***	-0.372***		-1.044	0.300	-1.915***
	0.06219	0.05020		0.66626	0.49956	0.39871
	-28.46	-7.42		-1.57	0.60	-4.80
G_fv			-0.11395			
			0.50330			
			-0.23			

legend: b/se/t

always negative: thus more educated women would have been more fertile if they had been less educated. The case of Heckit is a little more puzzling, as the result is significant and very close to the DIM estimation, which is suspected to be biased; this result could be due to the fact that the identification conditions of Heckit are not satisfied in this dataset.

Figure 3.9, finally, plots the average treatment effect distribution for each method. By and large, these distributions follow a similar pattern, although Direct-2SLS and Heckit estimations show some appreciable differences. The Heckit, in particular, exhibits a very different pattern, with a strong demarcation between the plot of treated and untreated units. As such, it does not seem to be a reliable estimation procedure in this example, and this result deserves further investigation[6].

Finally, note that the distribution for Direct-2SLS is on the whole more uniform than in the other cases where a strong left-side inflation dominates, with the ATENT (x) being more concentrated on negative values than ATET(x) on positive ones. What might this mean? It seems that the counterfactual condition of these women is not the same: on average, if a less educated woman became more educated, then her fertility would decrease more than the increase in fertility of more educated women becoming (in a virtual sense) less educated.

3.5.4 Applying the Selection-Model Using *etregress*

Although `ivtreatreg` encompasses also the Heckman Selection-model presented in Sect. 3.3.2, it seems useful to discuss the use of the Stata built-in command `etregress`. In common with `ivtreatreg`, this command estimates the ATE in a linear regression model with an endogenous binary treatment variable. In contrast to `ivtreatreg`, the `etregress` module assumes a homogenous

---

[6] A possible explanation for understanding this poor behavior of the Heckit may be that "children" is a count variable, thus presenting a strong asymmetric shape in its distribution with a high probability mass where the number of children is small. As such, it does not comply with the normality assumption of the outcome required by the Heckit model; a logarithmic transformation of "children" is likely to be correct for this problem.

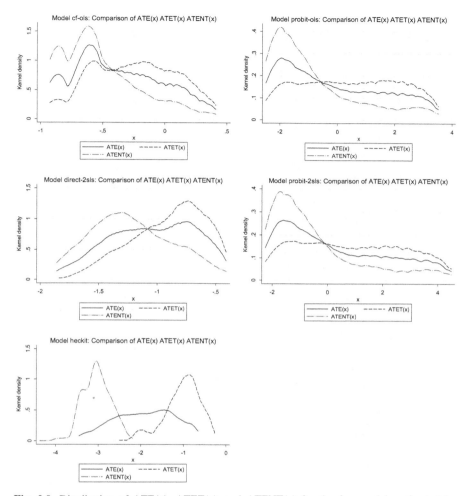

Fig. 3.9 Distribution of ATE(**x**), ATET(**x**), and ATENT(**x**) for the five models estimated by `ivtreatreg`

reaction of potential outcomes to confounders, but it offers the advantage of exploiting a full maximum likelihood approach besides the two-step consistent estimator. The basic syntax of this command is:

```
etregress depvar [indepvars], treat(depvar_t = indepvars_t) [twostep]
```

where `depvar` is the outcome; `indepvars` the exogenous covariates explaining the outcome equation; `depvar_t` is the endogenous treatment; and `indepvars_t` the confounders explaining the selection equation. This command, therefore, estimates the system represented in (3.51). The two-step procedure follows the one provided by `ivtreatreg`; the ML approach is an original option of this model.

Suppose that fertility depends not only on observable factors (those already present in the dataset) but also—let's say—on one unobservable component, that we call Q_i, representing a woman's genetic ability to have children more easily. Suppose that this genetic factor has also some explicative power on women's predisposition to education. Since Q_i is not observable in both the outcome and selection equations, then it will be a part of the error terms in the two equations. We saw in Sect. 3.3.1 that because of the presence of a common unobservable factor, the covariance between u and ε in system (3.51) will be different from zero. There, we assumed that $u = \gamma_u \cdot Q + e_u$ and $\varepsilon = \gamma_\varepsilon \cdot Q + e_\varepsilon$, where γ_u and γ_ε denote the effect of Q on u and ε, respectively, with e_u and e_ε being two purely exogenous random shocks; these assumptions imply that $\mathrm{Cov}(u;\ \varepsilon) = \gamma_u \gamma_\varepsilon \mathrm{Var}(Q)$, indicating that the sign of the covariance between the two error terms depends on the sign of the product $\gamma_u \gamma_\varepsilon$. This sign can also provide us with an idea of the direction of the OLS bias. We also saw in (3.53) that:

$$\alpha_{\mathrm{OLS}} = \alpha_{\mathrm{SM}} + \gamma_\varepsilon \gamma_u \frac{\mathrm{Var}(Q)}{\mathrm{Var}(D)}$$

implying that when:

- $\gamma_u \gamma_\varepsilon > 0$, then OLS has an upward bias.
- $\gamma_u \gamma_\varepsilon < 0$, then OLS has a downward bias.
- $\gamma_u \gamma_\varepsilon = 0$, then OLS is unbiased (consistent).

We can easily estimate and compare the SM and the OLS treatment effects in this example. We set out by estimating α_{SM} typing:

```
. xi: etregress children age agesq evermarr urban electric tv  ,   ///
treat(educ7 = age agesq evermarr urban electric tv)

Linear regression with endogenous treatment          Number of obs   =      4358
Estimator: maximum likelihood                         Wald chi2(7)    =   5032.82
Log likelihood = -10134.112                           Prob > chi2     =    0.0000

-----------------------------------------------------------------------------------
             |     Coef.    Std. Err.      z      P>|z|     [95% Conf. Interval]
-------------+---------------------------------------------------------------------
children     |
        age  |   .2479356   .0198391     12.50    0.000     .2090517    .2868195
       agesq |  -.0021111   .0003189     -6.62    0.000    -.0027362    -.001486
     evermarr|   .4919836   .06138898      .010    .000     .3716635    .6123036
       urban |  -.0448949   .0540729     -0.83    0.406    -.1508758    .061086
     electric|  -.0706167   .0882316     -0.80    0.424    -.2435475    .1023141
          tv |   .1649312   .1063599      1.55    0.121    -.0435303    .3733927
```

```
      educ7 |   -2.310078    .1046295    -22.08    0.000    -2.515148    -2.105008
      _cons |   -1.715568    .2956674     -5.80    0.000    -2.295065     -1.13607
------------+----------------------------------------------------------------------
educ7       |
        age |    .0060915     .016699      0.36    0.715    -.0266379     .0388209
      agesq |    -.001163    .0002743     -4.24    0.000    -.0017007    -.0006254
    evermarr |   -.2720595    .0477597     -5.70    0.000    -.3656669    -.1784521
       urban |     .293575    .0420911      6.97    0.000      .211078     .3760721
    electric |    .4497788    .0733312      6.13    0.000     .3060524     .5935053
          tv |     .965347    .0938972     10.28    0.000     .7813118     1.149382
      _cons |    .7168491    .2339981      3.06    0.002     .2582213     1.175477
------------+----------------------------------------------------------------------
     /athrho |    .8739284    .0487247     17.94    0.000     .7784298      .969427
    /lnsigma |    .5049432    .0176032     28.68    0.000     .4704415     .5394449
------------+----------------------------------------------------------------------
         rho |    .7033646    .0246195                        .6518045     .7484524
       sigma |    1.656891    .0291666                        1.600701     1.715055
      lambda |    1.165399     .058385                        1.050966     1.279831
----------------------------------------------------------------------------------
LR test of indep. eqns. (rho = 0):   chi2(1) =     96.92    Prob > chi2 = 0.0000
----------------------------------------------------------------------------------
```

The results obtained indicate that the estimated correlation (rho) between the treatment ("educ7") and the outcome ("children") errors is 0.7, thus offering evidence that when the unobservable factor Q raises the observed number of children, it increases contemporaneously a woman's propensity to get educated (and vice versa). The estimated ATE (that is α_{SM}) is equal to around -2.31.

Since the errors' correlation is positive and quite high, we suspect that OLS estimation is significantly upward biased. We estimate α_{OLS} typing:

```
. reg children educ7 age agesq evermarr urban electric tv
      Source |       SS       df       MS              Number of obs =     4358
-------------+------------------------------            F(  7,  4350) =   880.03
       Model |  12607.4006       7  1801.05723          Prob > F      =   0.0000
    Residual |  8902.63153    4350  2.04658196          R-squared     =   0.5861
-------------+------------------------------            Adj R-squared =   0.5855
       Total |  21510.0321    4357  4.93689055          Root MSE      =   1.4306

----------------------------------------------------------------------------------
    children |      Coef.   Std. Err.      t    P>|t|     [95% Conf. Interval]
-------------+--------------------------------------------------------------------
       educ7 |   -.3935524    .0495534     -7.94    0.000    -.4907024    -.2964025
         age |    .2719307    .0171033     15.90    0.000     .2383996     .3054618
       agesq |    -.001896    .0002752     -6.89    0.000    -.0024356    -.0013564
    evermarr |    .6947417    .0523984     13.26    0.000     .5920142     .7974691
       urban |   -.2437082    .0460252     -5.30    0.000     -.333941    -.1534753
```

```
electric |   -.336644    .0754557    -4.46    0.000    -.4845756    -.1887124
      tv |  -.3259749    .0897716    -3.63    0.000    -.501973    -.1499767
   _cons |  -3.526605    .2451026   -14.39    0.000    -4.007131    -3.046079
```

We immediately see that $\alpha_{OLS} = -0.393$ is in fact higher than $\alpha_{SM} = -2.31$, with a bias calculated as α_{OLS} minus α_{SM} of 1.917. We can conclude that using OLS provides an inconsistent estimate of ATE; of course, the results obtained are acceptable, provided that the true data generating process is exactly the one provided by the Selection-model's assumptions.

3.6 Implementation and Application of DID

In this section, we implement the DID estimator in a repeated cross section and in a longitudinal data structure. In repeated cross sections, each subject appears only once in the dataset, either before or after treatment. In longitudinal data (panel), the same subject is observed before and after the treatment occurs. In what follows, we start illustrating first how to estimate DID in a repeated cross sections setting and then in a longitudinal dataset by exploiting two ad-hoc artificial datasets built only for illustrative purposes.

3.6.1 DID with Repeated Cross Sections

In this exercise, we make use of the dataset "DID_1.dta," an artificial dataset very similar to that analyzed in Card and Krueger (1994). Our aim is to measure the effect of incentives offered to a number of restaurants in Rome, Milan being the comparison location. More specifically, we are interested in measuring the incentives' effect on employment. The dataset, containing 20 restaurants, is reported below:

Restaurant identifier	Number of employees	Location	Time	Interaction location/time
ID	Y	S	T	$S \cdot T$
1	34	1	0	0
2	67	0	0	0
3	5	0	0	0
4	150	1	1	1
5	78	0	1	0
6	98	0	0	0
7	200	1	1	1
8	45	0	0	0

(continued)

Restaurant identifier	Number of employees	Location	Time	Interaction location/time
ID	Y	S	T	S · T
9	33	0	0	0
10	45	0	1	0
11	22	1	0	0
12	12	0	0	0
13	34	0	1	0
14	180	1	1	1
15	88	0	1	0
16	9	0	0	0
17	56	1	0	0
18	4	0	0	0
19	3	0	0	0
20	190	1	1	1

The variable ID is the restaurant identifier; Y is the number of employees; S is the location variable taking value 1 for "Rome" and 0 for "Milan"; T is the time indicator equal to 0 if the restaurant is observed before the incentives are introduced and 1 after incentives; and finally, $S \cdot T$ is the interaction variable between S and T. We can run regression (3.68) to obtain an estimate of the DID:

```
. regress Y S T ST

      Source |       SS       df       MS                  Number of obs =      20
-------------+------------------------------               F(  3,    16) =   26.93
       Model |  65721.1333        3  21907.0444            Prob > F      =  0.0000
    Residual |  13015.4167       16  813.463542            R-squared     =  0.8347
-------------+------------------------------               Adj R-squared =  0.8037
       Total |    78736.55       19  4144.02895            Root MSE      =  28.521

------------------------------------------------------------------------------
           Y |      Coef.   Std. Err.      t    P>|t|     [95% Conf. Interval]
-------------+----------------------------------------------------------------
           S |   6.666667   19.01419     0.35   0.730    -33.64161    46.97494
           T |   30.58333   17.13916     1.78   0.093    -5.750058    66.91672
          ST |   112.0833    27.7177     4.04   0.001     53.32443    170.8422
       _cons |   30.66667   9.507094     3.23   0.005     10.51253    50.82081
------------------------------------------------------------------------------
```

We see the DID estimation of the ATE is equivalent to the coefficient of the variable $S \cdot T$, which is significant and equal to about 112. As shown in Sect. 3.4.1, however, we can also calculate DID by hand, by firstly estimating the Before/After estimator of (3.72) as follows:

```
. regress Y T if S==1

------------------------------------------------------------------------------
          Y |      Coef.   Std. Err.      t    P>|t|     [95% Conf. Interval]
------------+-----------------------------------------------------------------
          T |   142.6667   15.25487     9.35   0.000     103.4528    181.8806
      _cons |   37.33333    11.5316     3.24   0.023     7.690414    66.97625
------------------------------------------------------------------------------
```

This estimate returns a coefficient equal to around 142. Thus, the comparison within the group of treated subjects (restaurants located in Rome) before and after support would lead to an overestimation ($142 - 112 = 30$ more employees!) of the treatment effect. This happens because the Before/After estimator fails to take into account the counterfactual situation. Indeed, we saw that $\delta_{BA} = \gamma + \delta$, so that we get that $\gamma = 30$.

In a similar way, we can compute the Treatment/Control estimator of (3.74):

```
. regress Y S if T==1
      Source |       SS       df       MS              Number of obs =       8
-------------+------------------------------           F(  1,     6) =   49.73
       Model |  28203.125        1   28203.125         Prob > F      =  0.0004
    Residual |    3402.75        6     567.125         R-squared     =  0.8923
-------------+------------------------------           Adj R-squared =  0.8744
       Total |  31605.875        7    4515.125         Root MSE      =  23.814

------------------------------------------------------------------------------
          Y |      Coef.   Std. Err.      t    P>|t|     [95% Conf. Interval]
------------+-----------------------------------------------------------------
          S |     118.75   16.83931     7.05   0.000     77.54568    159.9543
      _cons |      61.25   11.90719     5.14   0.002     32.11415    90.38585
------------------------------------------------------------------------------
```

This comparison between the treated (restaurants in Rome) and non-treated (restaurants in Milan) after treatment leads to a level of treatment equal to around 118, which still overestimates the actual effect given by DID, i.e., 112. We saw that $\delta_{TC} = \beta + \delta$, thus $\beta = 6$. We can obtain the same result "by hand" by typing:

- Average over treated units in $T = 0$: $\mu + \beta$

```
. sum Y if S==1 & T==0
37.33333
```

- Average over treated units in $T = 1$: $\mu + \beta + \gamma + \delta$

```
. sum Y if S==1 & T==1
180
```

- Average over untreated units in $T = 0$: μ

```
. sum Y if S==0 & T==0
30.6
```

- Average over untreated units in $T = 1$: $\mu + \gamma$

```
. sum Y if S==0 & T==1
61.25
```

The same results can also be obtained using the user-written command diff (Villa 2014). The Stata help-file of this command is displayed by typing:

```
. help diff
Title
        diff - Differences in differences estimation
Syntax
        diff outcome_var [if] [in] [weight] ,[ options]
Description
-----------------------------------------------------------------------------------
diff performs several differences in differences (diff-in-diff) estimations of the
    treatment effect of a given outcome variable from a pooled base line and follow up
    dataset: Single Diff-in-Diff, Diff-in-Diff controlling for covariates, Kernel-based
    Propensity Score Matching diff-in-diff, and the Quantile Diff-in-Diff.
Options
-----------------------------------------------------------------------------------
        required
-----------------------------------------------------------------------------------
period(varname) Indicates the dummy period variable (0: baseline; 1: follow up).
treated(varname) Indicates the dummy treated variable (0: controls; 1:treated).
-----------------------------------------------------------------------------------
        optional
-----------------------------------------------------------------------------------
cov (varlist) Specifies the pre-treatment covariates of the model. When option kernel
    is selected these variables are used to generate the propensity score.

kernel Performs the Kernel-based Propensity Score Matching diff-in-diff. This option
    generates _weights that contains the weights derived from the kernel density func-
    tion, _ps when the Propensity Score is not specified in pscore(varname). This option
    requires the id(varname) of each individual.

id(varname) Option kernel requires the supply of the identification variable.

bw (#) Supplied bandwidth of the kernel. The default is the optimum bw estimated by
    Stata. See [R] kdensity
```

ktype(kernel) Specifies the kernel function; the default is epanechnikov. See
    [R] kdensity

qdid(quantile) Performs the Quantile Difference in Differences estimation at the spec-
    ified quantile from 0.1 to 0.9 (quantile 0.5 performs the QDID at the medeian). You
    may combine this option with kernel and cov options. qdid does not support weights
    nor robust standard errors. This option uses [R] qreg and [R] bsqreg for
    bootstrapped standard errors.

pscore(varname) Supplied Propensity Score.

logit Specifies logit estimation of the Propensity Score. The default is Probit.

support Performs diff on the common support of the propensity score given the
    option kernel.

SE/Robust
    ----
cluster(varname) Calculates clustered Std. Errors by varname.
robust Calculates robust Std. Errors.
bs performs a Bootstrap estimation of coefficients and standard errors.
reps(int) Specifies the number of repetitions when the bs is selected. The
    default are 50 repetitions.

Balancing test
    ----
test Performs a balancing t-test of difference in means of the specified
    covariates between control treated groups in period == 0. The option test
    combined with kernel performs the balancing t-test with the weighted
    covariates. See [R] ttest.

Reporting
    ----
report Displays the inference of the included covariates or the estimation of
    the Propensity Score when option kernel is specified.
nostar Removes the inference stars from the p-values.

In order to run such a command, at least two options are required: period
(varname) indicating the dummy period variable (0: baseline; 1: follow up) and
treated(varname) indicating the dummy treated variable (0: controls; 1:
treated). Thus, we have all the ingredients to estimate our DID by diff, that is:

```
. diff Y, treated(D) period(T)
--------------------------------------------------------------------------------

 Number of observations: 20

           Baseline        Follow-up
   Control: 9              4            13
   Treated: 3              4             7
           12              8
 R-square:   0.83470
                        DIFFERENCE IN DIFFERENCES ESTIMATION
----------------------------- BASE LINE ------------------- FOLLOW UP ----------
Outcome Variable(s)| Control| treated| Diff(BL)| Control| treated| Diff(FU)| DID
-------------------+--------+--------+---------+--------+--------+---------+--------
Y                  | 30.667 | 37.333 | 6.667   | 61.250 | 180.000| 118.750 | 112.083
Std. Error         | 9.507  | 16.467 | 19.014  | 14.261 | 14.261 | 20.168  | 27.718
t                  | 3.23   | 31.07  | 0.35    | 32.81  | 75.78  | 12.22   | 4.04
P>|t|              | 0.005  | 0.038  | 0.730   | 0.001  | 0.000  | 0.000***| 0.001***
--------------------------------------------------------------------------------
* Means and Standard Errors are estimated by linear regression
**Inference: *** p<0.01; ** p<0.05; * p<0.1
--------------------------------------------------------------------------------
```

Although the results presented in the `diff` output table are identical to those obtained previously, they are much better summarized and displayed. Note that `diff` also performs DID adjusted for covariates and "DID with Matching" (M-DID). As such, it is a valuable command for dealing with both observable and unobservable selection in both the parametric and nonparametric case.

3.6.2 DID Application with Panel Data

In this section, we use the "DID_2.dta" dataset, an artificial longitudinal dataset of 12 units observed for 2 years: 2000 and 2001. The sample size is 24. We consider a generic outcome Y, a binary treatment d, and two covariates x_1 and x_2. As usual, we are interested in measuring the causal effect of d on Y. The dataset needed to calculate DID according to (3.80) is reported below:

Id	Year	d_{it}	y_{it}	$x_{1,it}$	$x_{2,it}$	y_{it-1}	d_{it-1}	$x_{1,it-1}$	$x_{2,it-1}$	Δy_{it}	$\Delta x_{1,it}$	$\Delta x_{2,it}$	Δd_{it}
1	2000	1	17	73	13	–	–	–	–	–	–	–	–
1	2001	1	32	46	65	17	1	73	13	15	–27	52	0
2	2000	0	79	93	69	–	–	–	–	–	–	–	–
2	2001	1	72	66	36	79	0	93	69	–7	–27	–33	1
3	2000	0	54	57	69	–	–	–	–	–	–	–	–
3	2001	1	98	55	13	54	0	57	69	44	–2	–56	1

(continued)

Id	Year	d_{it}	y_{it}	$x_{1,it}$	$x_{2,it}$	y_{it-1}	d_{it-1}	$x_{1,it-1}$	$x_{2,it-1}$	Δy_{it}	$\Delta x_{1,it}$	$\Delta x_{2,it}$	Δd_{it}
4	2000	1	5	22	48	–	–	–	–	–	–	–	–
4	2001	0	34	30	15	5	1	22	48	29	8	−33	−1
5	2000	0	41	0	40	–	–	–	–	–	–	–	–
5	2001	1	20	60	17	41	0	0	40	−21	60	−23	1
6	2000	0	46	40	69	–	–	–	–	–	–	–	–
6	2001	1	7	13	61	46	0	40	69	−39	−27	−8	1
7	2000	0	39	73	66	–	–	–	–	–	–	–	–
7	2001	0	91	41	91	39	0	73	66	52	−32	25	0
8	2000	0	59	29	94	–	–	–	–	–	–	–	–
8	2001	0	100	51	97	59	0	29	94	41	22	3	0
9	2000	1	77	70	23	–	–	–	–	–	–	–	–
9	2001	0	33	69	85	77	1	70	23	−44	−1	62	−1
10	2000	0	75	61	6	–	–	–	–	–	–	–	–
10	2001	1	24	75	5	75	0	61	6	−51	14	−1	1
11	2000	0	20	68	39	–	–	–	–	–	–	–	–
11	2001	0	75	3	71	20	0	68	39	55	−65	32	0
12	2000	1	53	69	65	–	–	–	–	–	–	–	–
12	2001	0	97	16	28	53	1	69	65	44	−53	−37	−1

In order to calculate DID, we first generate one-lag variables for the outcome Y and the covariates x_1 and x_2 (reported in the previous table):

```
. sort id year
. by id: gen Y_1 = Y[_n-1]
. by id: gen d_it_1 = d_it[_n-1]
. by id: gen x1_1 = x1[_n-1]
. by id: gen x2_1 = x2[_n-1]
```

We then generate the first-differences for Y, x_1 and x_2, and D:

```
. sort id year
. gen delta_Y = Y-Y_1
. gen delta_x1 = x1-x1_1
. gen delta_x2 = x2-x2_1
. gen delta_d = d_it-d_it_1
```

Thus, we have all the components necessary to calculate the simple DID estimator with no covariates presented in (3.80):

```
. reg delta_Y d_it if d_it_1==0
      Source |       SS        df       MS              Number of obs =        8
-------------+------------------------------            F(  1,     6) =     8.32
       Model |  7712.03333      1  7712.03333           Prob > F      =   0.0279
    Residual |  5561.46667      6  926.911111           R-squared     =   0.5810
-------------+------------------------------            Adj R-squared =   0.5112
       Total |     13273.5      7  1896.21429           Root MSE      =   30.445

------------------------------------ ------------------------------------------
     delta_Y |     Coef.   Std. Err.      t    P>|t|     [95% Conf. Interval]
-------------+---------------------------- ------------------------------------
        d_it |  -64.13333   22.23404    -2.88   0.028    -118.5381   -9.728594
       _cons |   49.33333   17.57755     2.81   0.031     6.322611    92.34406
------------------------------------ ------------------------------------------
```

We obtain a DID estimate of approximately −64, significant at 5 %. Observe that the sample size passes from 24 to 8 due to the lagged variables and the *ceteris paribus* condition implied by "d_it_1==0." The same result can also be obtained running alternative regressions:

```
. reg delta_Y d_it if delta_d==d_it
```

or:

```
. reg delta_Y delta_d if d_it_1==0
```

It seems worth also looking at the OLS estimates for this dataset:

```
* OLS model (standard)
. reg Y d_it
      Source |       SS        df       MS              Number of obs =       24
-------------+------------------------------            F(  1,    22) =     2.73
       Model |  2267.14286      1  2267.14286           Prob > F      =   0.1127
    Residual |  18266.8571     22  830.311688           R-squared     =   0.1104
-------------+------------------------------            Adj R-squared =   0.0700
       Total |       20534     23  892.782609           Root MSE      =   28.815

------------------------------------ ------------------------------------------
           Y |     Coef.   Std. Err.      t    P>|t|     [95% Conf. Interval]
-------------+---------------------------- ------------------------------------
        d_it |  -19.71429    11.9306    -1.65   0.113    -44.45683    5.028258
       _cons |   60.21429   7.701167     7.82   0.000     44.24304    76.18553
------------------------------------ ------------------------------------------
```

OLS estimation returns a negative effect of the policy (roughly −20) but which is no longer significant. When compared to DID, the OLS bias is approximately

44 in absolute value (quite high and around 69 %). Looking at the results of the First-difference (FD) model, we have:

```
* FD model (First-differences)
. reg delta_Y delta_d , noconst
      Source |       SS       df       MS               Number of obs =      12
-------------+------------------------------           F(  1,   11) =    0.83
       Model |    1326.125    1    1326.125            Prob > F      =  0.3817
    Residual |   17569.875   11  1597.26136            R-squared     =  0.0702
-------------+------------------------------           Adj R-squared = -0.0143
       Total |       18896   12  1574.66667            Root MSE      =  39.966

     delta_Y |     Coef.   Std. Err.      t    P>|t|     [95% Conf. Interval]
-------------+----------------------------------------------------------------
     delta_d |   -12.875   14.13003    -0.91   0.382    -43.97498    18.22498
```

We see that FD shows a negative effect smaller than DID and OLS (about -13) but is insignificant. Finally, we can estimate the previous model also by a Fixed-effect (FE) regression:

```
* FE model (Fixed effects)
. tsset id year
       panel variable:  id (strongly balanced)
        time variable:  year, 2000 to 2001
                delta:  1 unit
 . xtreg Y d_it , fe
Fixed-effects (within) regression           Number of obs      =        24
Group variable: id                          Number of groups   =        12
R-sq:  within  = 0.0702                      Obs per group: min =         2
       between = 0.1984                                     avg =       2.0
       overall = 0.1104                                     max =         2
                                            F(1,11)            =      0.83
corr(u_i, Xb)  = 0.1672                      Prob > F           =    0.3817

           Y |     Coef.   Std. Err.      t    P>|t|     [95% Conf. Interval]
-------------+----------------------------------------------------------------
        d_it |   -12.875   14.13003    -0.91   0.382    -43.97498    18.22498
       _cons |  57.36458   8.242516     6.96   0.000     39.22293    75.50624
-------------+----------------------------------------------------------------
     sigma_u |  21.057042
     sigma_e |  28.260055
         rho |  .35699551   (fraction of variance due to u_i)
-----------------------------------------------------------------------------
F test that all u_i=0:     F(11, 11) =     1.08             Prob > F = 0.4508
```

As expected, the FE estimator is equivalent to the FD, since we are only considering 2 years. Indeed, it is known that when $t = 2$, then FE and FD return the same result.

We can also calculate DID by hand to check whether the regression approach is correct:

- Average Y over those treated units that were untreated in $t = 2000$:

```
. sum delta_Y if d_it == 1 & d_it_1==0
. scalar mean_t = r(mean)
. di mean_t
```

- Average Y over those untreated units that were also untreated in $t = 2000$:

```
. sum delta_Y if d_it == 0 & d_it_1==0
. return list
. scalar mean_c = r(mean)
. di mean_c
. scalar did = mean_t - mean_c
. di "DID = " did
DID = -64.133333
```

showing that the previous regression provides the correct causal parameter. Finally, we calculate the DID conditional on the covariates:

```
. reg delta_Y d_it delta_x1 delta_x2
      Source |       SS          df       MS              Number of obs =      12
-------------+------------------------------             F(  3,     8) =    2.33
       Model |  8270.00495        3   2756.66832         Prob > F      =  0.1507
    Residual |  9465.66172        8   1183.20771         R-squared     =  0.4663
-------------+------------------------------             Adj R-squared =  0.2662
       Total |  17735.6667       11   1612.33333         Root MSE      =  34.398

-------------+------------------------------------------------------------------
     delta_Y |      Coef.   Std. Err.      t    P>|t|     [95% Conf. Interval]
-------------+------------------------------------------------------------------
        d_it |  -39.89922   21.30604    -1.87   0.098    -89.03104      9.2326
    delta_x1 |  -.4002804   .3151978    -1.27   0.240    -1.127128     .3265671
    delta_x2 |  -.3985679   .2910458    -1.37   0.208    -1.069721     .2725849
       _cons |   24.88193   15.47731     1.61   0.147    -10.80882     60.57268
--------------------------------------------------------------------------------
```

The conditional-DID is around 40, but still significant at 1 %. Introducing covariates has therefore resulted in some reduction in both the magnitude and significance of the causal effect, but it has preserved the reliability of the simple DID result.

References

Abadie, A. (2005). Semiparametric difference-in-differences estimators. *Review of Economic Studies, 72*, 1–19. doi:10.1111/0034-6527.00321.

Abadie, A., Angrist, J., & Imbens, G. (2002). Instrumental variables estimates of the effect of subsidized training on the quantiles of trainee earnings. *Econometrica, 70*, 91–117. doi:10.1111/1468-0262.00270.

Angrist, J. D. (1991). *Instrumental variables estimation of average treatment effects in econometrics and epidemiology* (Working Paper No. 115). National Bureau of Economic Research.

Angrist, J. D., & Imbens, G. W. (1995). Two-stage least squares estimation of average causal effects in models with variable treatment intensity. *Journal of the American Statistical Association, 90*, 431–442. doi:10.1080/01621459.1995.10476535.

Angrist, J. D., Imbens, G. W., & Rubin, D. B. (1996). Identification of causal effects using instrumental variables. *Journal of the American Statistical Association, 91*, 444–455. doi:10.1080/01621459.1996.10476902.

Angrist, J. D., & Krueger, A. B. (1991). Does compulsory school attendance affect schooling and earnings? *Quarterly Journal of Economics, 106*, 979–1014.

Angrist, J. D., & Krueger, A. B. (2001). Instrumental variables and the search for identification: From supply and demand to natural experiments. *Journal of Economic Perspectives, 15*, 69–85.

Angrist, J. D., & Pischke, J.-S. (2008). *Mostly harmless econometrics: An empiricist's companion.* Princeton, NJ: Princeton University Press.

Autor, D. H. (2003). Outsourcing at will: The contribution of unjust dismissal doctrine to the growth of employment outsourcing. *Journal of Labor Economics, 21*, 1–42.

Bertrand, M., Duflo, E., & Mullainathan, S. (2004). How much should we trust differences-in-differences estimates? *Quarterly Journal of Economics, 119*, 249–275. doi:10.1162/003355304772839588.

Blundell, R., & Costa Dias, M. (2000). Evaluation methods for non-experimental data. *Fiscal Studies, 21*, 427–468. doi:10.1111/j.1475-5890.2000.tb00031.x.

Bound, J., Jaeger, D. A., & Baker, R. M. (1995). Problems with instrumental variables estimation when the correlation between the instruments and the endogenous explanatory variable is weak. *Journal of the American Statistical Association, 90*, 443–450. doi:10.1080/01621459. 1995.10476536.

Burnett, N. J. (1997). Gender economics courses in liberal arts colleges. *Journal of Economic Education, 28*, 369–376. doi:10.1080/00220489709597940.

Cameron, A. C., & Trivedi, P. K. (2005). *Microeconometrics: Methods and applications.* Cambridge: Cambridge University Press.

Card, D. (1992). Using regional variation in wages to measure the effects of the federal minimum wage. *Industrial & Labor Relations Review, 46*, 22–37.

Card, D., & Krueger, A. B. (1994). Minimum wages and employment: A case study of the fast-food industry in New Jersey and Pennsylvania. *American Economic Review, 84*, 772–793.

Card, D., & Krueger, A. B. (2000). Minimum wages and employment: A case study of the fast-food industry in New Jersey and Pennsylvania: Reply. *American Economic Review, 90*, 1397–1420.

Cerulli, G. (2012). An assessment of the econometric methods for program evaluation and a proposal to extend the difference-in-differences estimator to dynamic treatment. In S. A. Mendez & A. M. Vega (Eds.), *Econometrics: New research.* New York: Nova. Chapter 1.

Cerulli, G. (2014). ivtreatreg: A command for fitting binary treatment models with heterogeneous response to treatment and unobservable selection. *Stata Journal, 14*, 453–480.

Donald, S. G., & Lang, K. (2007). Inference with difference-in-differences and other panel data. *Review of Economics and Statistics, 89*, 221–233. doi:10.1162/rest.89.2.221.

Granger, C. W. J. (1969). Investigating causal relations by econometric models and cross-spectral methods. *Econometrica, 37*(3), 424–438.

Hahn, J., & Hausman, J. (2005). Estimation with valid and invalid instruments. *Annales d'Economie et de Statistique, 79–80*, 25–57.

Heckman, J. J. (1978). Dummy endogenous variables in a simultaneous equation system. *Econometrica, 46*, 931–959.

Heckman, J. J. (1979). Sample selection bias as a specification error. *Econometrica: Journal of the Econometric Society, 47*, 153–161.

Heckman, J. (1997). Instrumental variables: A study of implicit behavioral assumptions used in making program evaluations. *Journal of Human Resources, 32*, 441. doi:10.2307/146178.

Heckman, J., Ichimura, H., Smith, J., & Todd, P. (1998). *Characterizing selection bias using experimental data* (Working paper N. w6699). Cambridge: National Bureau of Economic Research.

Heckman, J., & Vytlacil, E. (1998). Instrumental variables methods for the correlated random coefficient model: Estimating the average rate of return to schooling when the return is correlated with schooling. *Journal of Human Resources, 33*, 974. doi:10.2307/146405.

Heckman, J. J., & Vytlacil, E. J. (2001). Instrumental variables, selection models, and tight bounds on the average treatment effect. In P. D. M. Lechner & D. F. Pfeiffer (Eds.), *Econometric evaluation of labour market policies* (ZEW economic studies, pp. 1–15). Heidelberg: Physica.

Imbens, G. W., & Angrist, J. D. (1994). Identification and estimation of local average treatment effects. *Econometrica, 62*, 467–475. doi:10.2307/2951620.

Lach, S. (2002). Do R&D subsidies stimulate or displace private R&D? Evidence from Israel. *Journal of Industrial Economics, 50*, 369–390.

Lee, M. (2005). *Micro-econometrics for policy, program and treatment effects (OUP catalogue)*. Oxford: Oxford University Press.

Meyer, B. D., Viscusi, W. K., & Durbin, D. L. (1995). Workers' compensation and injury duration: Evidence from a natural experiment. *American Economic Review, 85*, 322–340.

Murray, M. P. (2006). Avoiding invalid instruments and coping with weak instruments. *Journal of Economic Perspectives, 20*, 111–132. doi:10.1257/jep.20.4.111.

Nelson, C. R., & Startz, R. (1990a). Some further results on the exact small sample properties of the instrumental variable estimator. *Econometrica, 58*, 967–976.

Nelson, C. R., & Startz, R. (1990b). The distribution of the instrumental variables estimator and its t-ratio when the instrument is a poor one. *Journal of Business, 63*, S125–S140.

Nicoletti, C., & Peracchi, F. (2001). Two-step estimation of binary response models with sample selection. Fac. Econ. Tor Vergata Univ. Rome.

Phillips, P. C. B. (1983). Exact small sample theory in the simultaneous equations model. In Z. Griliches & M. D. Intriligator (Eds.), *Handbook of econometrics* (1st ed., Vol. 1, Chap. 8, pp. 449–516). Amsterdam: Elsevier.

Rivers, D., & Vuong, Q. H. (1988). Limited information estimators and exogeneity tests for simultaneous probit models. *Journal of Econometrics, 39*, 347–366.

Sargan, J. D. (1958). The estimation of economic relationships using instrumental variables. *Econometrica, 26*, 393–415. doi:10.2307/1907619.

Smith, J. A., & Todd, P. E. (2005). Does matching overcome LaLonde's critique of nonexperimental estimators? *Journal of Econometrics, 125*, 305–353. doi:10.1016/j.jeconom.2004.04.011.

Stock, J. H., & Yogo, M. (2002). *Testing for weak instruments in linear IV regression* (NBER Technical Working Paper No. 0284). National Bureau of Economic Research, Inc.

Villa, J. M. (2014). DIFF: Stata module to perform differences in differences estimation, Statistical software components. Boston College Department of Economics.

Wooldridge, J. M. (2001). *Econometric analysis of cross section and panel data*. Cambridge, MA: MIT Press.

Wooldridge, J. (2008). *Introductory econometrics: A modern approach*. Florence, KY: Cengage Learning.

Wooldridge, J. M. (2010). *Econometric analysis of cross section and panel data*. Cambridge, MA: MIT Press.

Chapter 4
Local Average Treatment Effect and Regression-Discontinuity-Design

Contents

4.1   Introduction

This chapter addresses two different but related subjects, both widely developed and used within the literature on the econometrics of program evaluation: the Local average treatment effect (LATE) and the Regression-discontinuity-design (RDD). Considered as nearly quasi-experimental methods, these approaches have recently been the subject of a vigorous interest as tools for detecting causal effects of treatment on given target variables within a special statistical setting.

© Springer-Verlag Berlin Heidelberg 2015
G. Cerulli, *Econometric Evaluation of Socio-Economic Programs*,
Advanced Studies in Theoretical and Applied Econometrics 49,
DOI 10.1007/978-3-662-46405-2_4

A pioneering application of LATE can be found in the work by Angrist (1990) seeking to detect the effect of Vietnam veteran status on civilian earnings. In his work, the author makes explicit that LATE is equivalent to an Instrumental-variables (IV) estimation (see Chap. 3), with the instrument taking a binary form and assuming an explicit random nature. More importantly, Angrist proves that—in an endogenous treatment setting—the whole population average treatment effect cannot be identified; what is identified by IV is the treatment effect on a specific subpopulation, the so-called *compliers*, defined as those individuals whose treatment assignment complies with instrument inducement. In the specific case of Angrist (1990), the assignment risk of military service associated to draft lottery served as an instruments' generator to produce a Wald (1940) type IV estimation of the causal effect. Compliers are not observable but, quite surprisingly, Abadie (2003) provided a powerful reweighting approach (*Abadie's kappas*) to character-ize the distribution of the treatment effect within this group, as only the average treatment effect on compliers owns a causal interpretation.

The analysis of LATE is organized in the following manner: Sect. 4.2 presents the theory behind LATE, illustrating how such approach can be embedded within the setting of a randomized experiment with imperfect compliance (Sect. 4.2.1). The discussion then goes on to present the Wald estimator and show its relation to LATE (Sect. 4.2.2); then, Sect. 4.2.3 is dedicated to the sample estimation of LATE, and Sect. 4.2.4 to the definition and estimation of average response for compliers; Sect. 4.2.5 addresses the possibility of characterizing in the LATE model the compliers' subpopulation. Finally, Sect. 4.2.6 extends LATE in the case of multiple instruments and multiple treatments. Section 4.4.1 presents two LATE applications, one on real data and the other on simulated data: the former makes use of the dataset CHILDREN.DTA containing a subset of data used in Angrist and Evans (1998) to investigate the effect of childbearing on female labor market participation; the latter exercise simulates a specific data generating process (DGP) for LATE in order to assess the reliability of the Stata code developed in the application on previous real data. Building such a DGP also provides a useful laboratory experiment to help us better understand the findings presented in the theoretical part of this chapter.

The Regression-discontinuity-design (RDD) is another powerful quasi-experimental method to consistently estimate causal effects in program evaluation. RDD can be applied when the selection-into-program is highly determined by the level assumed by a specific variable (called the *forcing* variable) which is used to define a threshold separating—either sharply or fuzzily—treated and untreated units. What characterizes RDD is the fact that the treatment probability varies in a discontinuous way at the threshold, thus producing conditions for correctly identifying the effect of a given treatment. Basically, the idea is that, in a neigh-borhood of the threshold, conditions for a natural experiment (i.e., random assign-ment) are restored. Thus, as long as the threshold is well identified, and treatment depends on the forcing variable, one can retrieve the effect of the policy simply by comparing the mean outcome of individuals laying on the left and right of the threshold (Van Der Klaauw 2008).

As suggested by Cook (2008) in his survey paper, RDD was firstly conceptually developed and applied by Thistlethwaite and Campbell (1960) in a paper studying the effect of receiving scholarships on individual career. With no use of sophisticated statistics, these authors proved that a correct identification of the actual causal effect of receiving a scholarship on one's career might be possible by exploiting information about the selection criterion used by the institutions awarding scholarships. As scholarships were awarded if a specific test score exceeded a certain threshold, they suggested comparing the outcome of people on the right with that of those on the left of such a threshold, assuming that—around a reasonable interval around the threshold—the two groups might have been considered pretty similar. Interestingly, it is only from about 1995 that the RDD approach was reconsidered as a valuable estimation strategy for causal effects, while before that time its use was relatively modest.

RDD has a remarkable potential to be applied in those social and economic contexts where the rules underlying the program application can sometimes provide certain types of discontinuities in the assignment to treatment. One example is the Van Der Klaauw (2002) estimation of the impact of financial aid offers on college enrolment, where the author relies on the discontinuity in students' grade point average and SAT score. Another example comes from the Angrist and Lavy (1999) study, where the authors try to assess the impact of class size on students' test scores exploiting the rule which states that a classroom is added when the average class size rises beyond a given cutoff.

Two types of RDD have been proposed in the literature: sharp RDD, used when the relation between treatment and forcing variable is deterministic; and fuzzy RDD, used when this relation is stochastic, thus subject to some uncertainty. Interestingly, as we will see, the average treatment effect (ATE) estimation in the case of a fuzzy RDD is simply a Wald estimator and thus equivalent to LATE.

The part of this chapter dedicated to RDD is organized as follows: Sect. 4.3 presents the RDD econometric theoretical background; in particular, Sect. 4.3.1 discusses sharp RDD and Sect. 4.3.2 fuzzy RDD; Sect. 4.3.3 and subsections discuss the choice of the bandwidth and of the polynomial order when nonparametric RDD is applied, while Sect. 4.3.4 provides some insights into the case in which additional covariates are considered; Sect. 4.3.5 examines a number of tests for assessing the validity of an RDD experiment, while Sect. 4.3.6 suggests a protocol for the empirical implementation of such approach. As applied example, Sect. 4.4.2 presents a simulation model both for sharp RDD and fuzzy RDD: the use of a simulation approach clearly illustrates the role played by each assumption lying behind the applicability of RDD and provides a virtual laboratory to assess the performance of such estimation approach in different settings.

4.2　Local Average Treatment Effect

The following subsections present and discuss at length the econometrics of LATE. They start from a discussion of a setting characterized by "randomization under imperfect compliance," and conclude with an examination of the form and properties of LATE with multiple instruments and multiple treatments[1].

4.2.1　Randomization Under Imperfect Compliance

A straightforward way in order to understand what LATE actually identifies can be seen by referring to a randomized experiment (or trial) where individuals do not necessarily comply with assignment to treatment. For example: suppose one has an experiment in which individuals are randomly assigned either to a treatment (a given medicine, for instance) or to a placebo; moreover, assume the outcome of this random draw is recorded in a variable z, which takes value one for those treated and zero for those taking the placebo; assume, nonetheless, that individuals can arbitrarily decide whether or not to comply with the value assumed by z; in this case then, we can have a situation in which a person with z equal to one—that is, one drawn to be part of the treated set—may refuse to be treated, thus becoming an untreated individual; on the contrary, a person with z equal to zero—that is, one drawn to be part of the untreated set—may refuse to stay untreated and decide to take the drug, thus becoming eventually a treated subject. Finally, suppose that the actual final treated/untreated status of individuals are recorded into the treatment variable D, composed of ones and zeros: as long as $D \neq z$ such an experiment suffers from *imperfect compliance* on the part of individuals, and the classical Difference-in-means (DIM) estimator, contrasting the average outcome Y on treated with that on untreated, is likely to be biased. Why? If we assume that the "choice to comply" is not random itself, but rather driven by individual motivations and strategies that are not all observable to the analyst, we then find ourselves in a hidden bias setting (*selection on unobservables*), the consequences and solutions of which have been extensively discussed in Chaps. 1 and 3.

Under imperfect compliance, a single individual i can be classified in specific subsets of units according to the realization of z and the perfect/imperfect compliance to the treatment. By defining D_1 as the unit i's treatment status when $z = 1$, and D_0 as the unit i's treatment status when $z = 0$ (with both D_1 and D_0 taking value one or zero), we can build the following taxonomy of individual potential statuses in such a setting, thus identifying four exclusive groups:

- *Never-takers*: individuals who, either if $z = 1$ or $z = 0$, decide not to get treated.
- *Defiers*: individuals who get treated when $z = 0$ and are untreated when $z = 1$.
- *Compliers*: individuals who get treated when $z = 1$ and are untreated when $z = 0$.
- *Always-takers*: individuals who, either if $z = 0$ or $z = 1$, decide to get treated.

---

[1] The econometrics of LATE provided in these subsections draws mainly on: Imbens and Angrist (1994); Angrist and Imbens (1995); Angrist and Pischke (2008, Chap. 4); Wooldridge (2010, Chap. 21).

It is worth stressing that, by observation, it is not possible to know whether a given individual in the sample is a *never-taker, defier, complier,* or *always-taker.* Since we only observe the realization of the vector $\{Y_i, D_i, z_i\}$ for each unit i, we cannot observe the realization of D_{0i} and D_{1i} which remain missing values (more precisely, only one of these two variables is observed for the same individual). For example, for an individual with $z = 1$ and $D = 1$, we cannot know what realization of D he would have chosen if he had received $z = 0$. In this sense, if the choice of this individual under $z = 0$ was $D = 1$, then he would be an *always-taker*; but if his choice under $z = 0$ was $D = 0$, then he would be a *complier*. This argument is similar to the missing observation problem presented at the outset of Chap. 1.

4.2.2 Wald Estimator and LATE

In light of the previous example, it seems interesting to derive the usual causal parameters within such a framework. It is clear that, as long as z is taken as random and thus strictly exogenous, it can be used as an instrument for D, D being endogenous because of the presence of a hidden bias. An IV approach would therefore seem appropriate. In such a context, characterized by a binary instrument, however, we can go a bit further by giving to the IV estimation a more precise causal interpretation. Consider the following definitions and assumptions: let Y be an outcome of interest, D a binary treatment indicator, and z a binary instrumental variable. Y may be earnings, D the event of having or not attended a high school, and z the event of having received a scholarship by lottery. The following assumption justifies z as an instrument:

Assumption 4.1 Suppose that z was assigned randomly, but that D depends on z, that is, D and z are correlated to some extent; one can then think about D as a function of z, that is $D = D(z)$ of this kind:

$$D(1) = D_1 = \text{treatment status when } z = 1$$
$$D(0) = D_0 = \text{treatment status when } z = 0$$

where both D_1 and D_0 can take values 0 or 1, given that for each unit we can only observe one of these two variables and never both. This leads to the taxonomy of potential statuses set out in Table 4.1.

For each individual, it is therefore possible to observe only his final status. Thus, D is what is ultimately observed exactly in the same way as Y is the observable counterpart in the potential outcome model encountered on numerous occasions in our discussions above. Given its nature, we can make two assumptions about z:

Assumption 4.2 z is randomly assigned, that is, z is exogenous and uncorrelated with potential outcome and potential treatments indicators:

Table 4.1 Classification of unit i when z is random and compliance to treatment is imperfect			$z_i = 0$	
			$D_{0i} = 0$	$D_{0i} = 1$
$z_i = 1$	$D_{1i} = 0$		*Never-taker*	*Defier*
	$D_{1i} = 1$		*Complier*	*Always-taker*

$$\{(Y_{01}, Y_{00}, Y_{10}, Y_{11}), D_1, D_0\} \perp z$$

where $(Y_{01}, Y_{00}, Y_{10}, Y_{11})$ are the four potential outcomes corresponding to combining the values assumed by D_1 and D_0.

Assumption 4.3 z is correlated with D:

$$p[D(z = 1) = 1] \neq p[D(z = 0) = 1]$$

that is, z has some predictive power on D.

The objective of this section is to provide an estimation of the average treatment effect, by characterizing its causal interpretation under Assumptions 4.1 and 4.2 and 4.3. Before going ahead, however, it is worthwhile presenting a peculiar IV estimator known in the literature as the Wald estimator (Wald 1940), taking on this form:

$$b = \frac{E(Y \mid z = 1) - E(Y \mid z = 0)}{E(D \mid z = 1) - E(D \mid z = 0)} = \frac{A}{B} \qquad (4.1)$$

This estimator has an immediate causal interpretation, as the numerator A is the difference of the mean of Y in the group of individuals with $z = 1$ and the group with $z = 0$, thus measuring the causal effect of z on Y. Part of this effect is due to the effect of z on D, that is measured by the numerator B. Since both A and B can be obtained by an OLS regression of Y on z and D on z (the two reduced forms), respectively, one can also write that:

$$b = \frac{\mathrm{Cov}(Y, z)}{\mathrm{Var}(z)} : \frac{\mathrm{Cov}(D, z)}{\mathrm{Var}(z)} = \frac{\mathrm{Cov}(Y, z)}{\mathrm{Cov}(D, z)} \qquad (4.2)$$

Thus, it is clear that, in order to extract a correct measure of the effect of D on Y, we need to divide A by B, as is represented graphically in Fig. 4.1, where the dotted line between z an Y indicates that the relation between these two variables is only indirect, that is, passing through the direct relation between z and D; as such, this offers a graphical representation of the exclusion restriction of this specific IV estimator.

The effect of z on Y is the product of the effect of z on D (i.e., B) and of D on Y (i.e., b), that is: A = B · b. Hence, the Wald estimator measures the causal effect of D on Y. As an estimator of b, we can rely on its sample equivalent, i.e.:

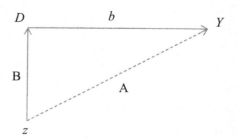

Fig. 4.1 Path-diagram representation of the causal link between z, D, and Y

$$\widehat{b} = \frac{\dfrac{\displaystyle\sum_i Y_i z_i}{\displaystyle\sum_{i=1} z_i} - \dfrac{\displaystyle\sum_i Y_i(1 - z_i)}{\displaystyle\sum_{i=1}(1 - z_i)}}{\dfrac{\displaystyle\sum_i D_i z_i}{\displaystyle\sum_i z_i} - \dfrac{\displaystyle\sum_i D_i(1 - z_i)}{\displaystyle\sum_i (1 - z_i)}} = \tag{4.3}$$

For the law of large numbers (LLN), being (4.3) function of sums, we have that:

$$\widehat{b} \xrightarrow{p} b$$

i.e., $\widehat{b}$ is a consistent estimation of b. It is possible to show under which conditions $\widehat{b}$ is a consistent estimator of ATE, and to this aim we distinguish two cases:

Case 1. The treatment effect is *constant* over observations.
Case 2. The treatment effect is *heterogeneous* over observations.

Case 1 The treatment effect is constant over observations.

In this case, we assume that $Y_{1i} - Y_{0i} = \alpha = constant$ for each unit i, and $\widehat{b}$ estimates consistently ATE $= \alpha$. In order to prove this proposition, we start by developing further the numerator A in (4.1). First, however, it is worth writing both the potential outcome and the potential treatment equations, i.e.:

$$\begin{cases} Y = D \cdot Y_1 + (1 - D) \cdot Y_0 \\ D = z \cdot D_1 + (1 - z) \cdot D_0 \end{cases} \tag{4.4}$$

Substituting the second into the first equation and using some simple algebra gives us:

$$Y = Y_0 + D_0 \cdot (Y_1 - Y_0) + z \cdot (D_1 - D_0) \cdot (Y_1 - Y_0) \tag{4.5}$$

Consider now the expectation of Y conditional on $z = 1$ and $z = 0$, thus:

$$\begin{aligned} E(Y \mid z = 1) &= E(Y_0) + E[D_0 \cdot (Y_1 - Y_0)] + E[(D_1 - D_0) \cdot (Y_1 - Y_0)] \\ E(Y \mid z = 0) &= E(Y_0) + E[D_0 \cdot (Y_1 - Y_0)] \end{aligned} \tag{4.6}$$

Since by definition:

$$\begin{aligned} A &= E(Y \mid z = 1) - E(Y \mid z = 0) = E[(D_1 - D_0)(Y_1 - Y_0)] = \alpha \cdot E[(D_1 - D_0)] \\ B &= E(D \mid z = 1) - E(D \mid z = 0) = E[(D_1 - D_0)] \end{aligned}$$

$$\tag{4.7}$$

this implies that:

$$b = \frac{A}{B} = \frac{\alpha \cdot E(D_1 - D_0)}{E(D_1 - D_0)} = \alpha \qquad (4.8)$$

proving that b identifies ATE and thus $\hat{b}$, the sample analog, consistently estimates ATE.

Case 2 The treatment effect is heterogeneous over observations

In this case we have that $Y_{1i} - Y_{0i} \neq \alpha$ and each observation i owns its own treatment effect. In this case, it can be proved that the Wald estimator does not consistently estimate the ATE, but another parameter called Local average treatment effect (LATE), which is equal to ATE calculated for a specific subpopulation of individuals, i.e., the *compliers*. In general, ATE cannot be identified.

In order to show what LATE is equal to, we start again from the numerator A in (4.1). We saw that:

$$A = E(Y \mid z = 1) - E(Y \mid z = 0) = E[(D_1 - D_0)(Y_1 - Y_0)] \qquad (4.9)$$

By defining $h = (D_1 - D_0)(Y_1 - Y_0)$, we have that:

$$A = E[h] \qquad (4.10)$$

From the law of iterated expectation (LIE) we know that, if x is a generic discrete variable assuming values $x = (x_1, x_2, \ldots, x_M)$ with probabilities $p = (p_1, p_2, \ldots, p_M)$, then $E(h) = p_1 E(h \mid x_1) + p_2 E(h \mid x_2) + \ldots + p_M E(h \mid x_M)$. By defining h as in (4.10), and $x = (D_1 - D_0) = [1, 0, -1]$ with probabilities $p = (p_1, p_0, p_{-1})$, then:

$$\begin{aligned} A &= E(h) \\ &= p_1 E[(D_1 - D_0)(Y_1 - Y_0) \mid D_1 - D_0 = 1] \\ &\quad + p_0 E[(D_1 - D_0)(Y_1 - Y_0) \mid D_1 - D_0 = 0] \\ &\quad + p_{-1} E[(D_1 - D_0)(Y_1 - Y_0) \mid D_1 - D_0 = -1] \end{aligned} \qquad (4.11)$$

that is:

$$\begin{aligned} A &= E[(Y_1 - Y_0) \mid D_1 - D_0 = 1] p(D_1 - D_0 = 1) \\ &\quad - E[(Y_1 - Y_0) \mid D_1 - D_0 = -1] p(D_1 - D_0 = -1) \end{aligned} \qquad (4.12)$$

It is easy to see in (4.12) that as soon as the two addends are equal, then $A = 0$ and $b = 0$ although there could be, for instance, a positive treatment effect for all the individuals considered. This is sufficient to show that, in the case of heterogeneous treatment, the ATE is not identified. In order to identify the causal effect of D on Y, we have to rely on the so-called *monotonicity assumption*, which states that $p(D_1 - D_0 = -1) = 0$; it occurs when:

$$D_1 \geq D_0 \qquad (4.13)$$

Under monotonicity, we get that:

$$A = E(Y \mid z = 1) - E(Y \mid z = 0)$$
$$= E[(Y_1 - Y_0) \mid D_1 - D_0 = 1]p(D_1 - D_0 = 1) \quad (4.14)$$

since the second addend becomes equal to zero. As for the denominator B, we had that:

$$B = E(D \mid z = 1) - E(D \mid z = 0) = E(D_1 - D_0) \quad (4.15)$$

Given monotonicity, $(D_1 - D_0)$ is a binary variable taking value zero or one; we can thus conclude that:

$$E(D_1 - D_0) = p(D_1 - D_0 = 1) \quad (4.16)$$

thus implying that:

$$b = \frac{A}{B} = \frac{E(Y_1 - Y_0 \mid D_1 - D_0 = 1) \cdot p(D_1 - D_0 = 1)}{p(D_1 - D_0 = 1)}$$
$$= E(Y_1 - Y_0 \mid D_1 - D_0 = 1) \quad (4.17)$$

To conclude, in Case 2 the Wald estimator of b is equal to the LATE, defined as the ATE in the subgroup of compliers, those individuals having $D_1 = 1$ and $D_0 = 0$ or equivalently $D_1 > D_0$:

$$b = \text{LATE} = E(Y_1 - Y_0 \mid D_1 - D_0 = 1) \quad (4.18)$$

It is important to observe that monotonicity, by assuming that $D_1 \geq D_0$, rules out the possible presence of *defiers* within the population; this assumption is however not empirically testable.

4.2.3   LATE Estimation

This section illustrates the steps required in order to estimate LATE empirically and to obtain usual standard errors for testing hypotheses. For the numerator A, we saw that:

$$A = E(Y \mid z = 1) - E(Y \mid z = 0) = E[(Y_1 - Y_0) \mid D_1 - D_0 = 1]p(D_1 - D_0 = 1)$$
$$= \text{LATE} \cdot p(D_1 - D_0 = 1)$$

that implies:

$$\text{LATE} = \frac{E(Y \mid z = 1) - E(Y \mid z = 0)}{p(D_1 - D_0 = 1)} \qquad (4.19)$$

To estimate LATE, we need to have the denominator of the previous ratio in terms of observables, that is:

$$\begin{aligned}
p(D_1 - D_0 = 1) &= E(D_1 - D_0) = E(D_1) - E(D_0) \\
&= E(D \mid z = 1) - E(D \mid z = 0) \\
&= p(D = 1 \mid z = 1) - p(D = 1 \mid z = 0)
\end{aligned} \qquad (4.20)$$

From this we get:

$$\text{LATE} = \frac{E(Y \mid z = 1) - E(Y \mid z = 0)}{p(D = 1 \mid z = 1) - p(D = 1 \mid z = 0)} \qquad (4.21)$$

which is expressed in terms of all observable components. Given the previous population formula, a simple (consistent) estimation in the sample is:

$$\widehat{\text{LATE}} = \frac{\bar{Y}_1 - \bar{Y}_0}{\bar{D}_1 - \bar{D}_0} \qquad (4.22)$$

which is equivalent to $\hat{b}$ in (4.3). Observe that the numerator in (4.22) is the difference between the average of Y in the subsample with $z = 1$ and that in the subsample with $z = 0$, whereas the denominator is the difference between the frequency of individuals with $D = 1$ in the subsample having $z = 1$ and the frequency of individuals with $D = 0$ in the subsample having $z = 0$.

It is immediate to see from (4.2) that a consistent estimation of LATE can be obtained from an IV estimation of α in the following regression:

$$Y = \mu + \alpha D + error \qquad (4.23)$$

using z as instrument for D. In this case, we can directly get the standard error for LATE.

Observe, finally, that there is a special case in which LATE is equal to the average treatment effect on treated (ATET): this occurs when $E(D_i \mid z_i = 0) = p(D_i = 1 \mid z_i = 0) = 0$, i.e., when individuals that were not drawn for treatment are prevented from choosing to become treated. In such a case, D_{0i} can only take one value equal to zero, as shown by Table 4.2.

The proof is straightforward (Bloom 1984). Using POM, we have that $E(Y \mid z = 1) = E(Y_0 \mid z = 1) + E(D(Y_1 - Y_0) \mid z = 1)$, but $E(Y \mid z = 0) = E(Y_0 \mid z = 0)$, since $E(D(Y_1 - Y_0) \mid z = 0) = 0$ given that $D = 0$ when $z = 0$. As a result, we have that $E(Y \mid z = 1) - E(Y \mid z = 0) = E(D(Y_1 - Y_0) \mid z = 1)$ since, by independence of z, $E(Y_0 \mid z = 1) = E(Y_0 \mid z = 0)$. However, $E(D(Y_1 - Y_0) \mid z = 1) = E(Y_1 - Y_0 \mid z = 1, D = 1) \, p(D = 1 \mid z = 1) + E(0 \cdot (Y_1 - Y_0) \mid z = 1, D = 0) \, p(D = 0 \mid z = 1) = E(Y_1 - Y_0 \mid$

Table 4.2 Classification of unit i when z is random, compliance to treatment is imperfect, but individuals that were not drawn for treatment are prevented from being treated

		$z_i = 0$
		$D_{0i} = 0$
$z_i = 1$	$D_{1i} = 0$	Never-taker
	$D_{1i} = 1$	Complier

$z = 1, D = 1)\, p(D = 1 \mid z = 1) = E(Y_1 - Y_0 \mid D = 1)\, p(D = 1 \mid z = 1)$, where the last equality derives from independence of z. Thus, we have that:

$$E(Y \mid z = 1) - E(Y \mid z = 0) = E(Y_1 - Y_0 \mid D = 1)\, p(D = 1 \mid z = 1)$$

Since, by assumption, $p(D = 1 \mid z = 0) = 0$, we obtain that:

$$
\begin{aligned}
\text{LATE} &= \frac{E(Y \mid z = 1) - E(Y \mid z = 0)}{p(D = 1 \mid z = 1) - p(D = 1 \mid z = 0)} \\
&= \frac{E(Y_1 - Y_0 \mid D = 1)\, p(D = 1 \mid z = 1)}{p(D = 1 \mid z = 1)} = E(Y_1 - Y_0 \mid D = 1) \quad (4.24)
\end{aligned}
$$

that is what we aimed at proving.

4.2.4 Estimating Average Response for Compliers

So far, we have considered identification and estimation of LATE without conditioning on the covariates $\mathbf{x}$. The previous framework, however, can be generalized by assuming that the independence of z is conditional on $\mathbf{x}$:

Assumption 4.4 Conditional independence of z. We assume that:

$$\{(Y_{01}, Y_{00}, Y_{10}, Y_{11}), D_1, D_0\} \perp z \mid \mathbf{x}$$

Of course, it is also possible to define LATE conditional on $\mathbf{x}$, that is:

$$\text{LATE}(\mathbf{x}) = E(Y_1 - Y_0 \mid \mathbf{x}, D_1 > D_0) \quad (4.25)$$

An interesting property of LATE($\mathbf{x}$) is that it is possible to show that:

$$\text{LATE}(\mathbf{x}) = E(Y \mid \mathbf{x}, D = 1, D_1 > D_0) - E(Y \mid \mathbf{x}, D = 0, D_1 > D_0) \quad (4.26)$$

The relationship in (4.26) comes from the POM using the fact that for compliers $z = D$ and exploiting conditional independence of z, so that:

$$E(Y \mid \mathbf{x}, D = 0, D_1 > D_0) = E(Y_0 \mid \mathbf{x}, z = 0, D_1 > D_0) = E(Y_0 \mid \mathbf{x}, D_1 > D_0)$$
$$E(Y \mid \mathbf{x}, D = 1, D_1 > D_0) = E(Y_1 \mid \mathbf{x}, z = 1, D_1 > D_0) = E(Y_1 \mid \mathbf{x}, D_1 > D_0)$$

Abadie (2003) calls $E(Y \mid \mathbf{x}, D, D_1 > D_0)$ as the local average response function (LARF). By assuming to know the true form of previous expectations, one could estimate LATE($\mathbf{x}$) by contrasting the result of an OLS regression of Y on $\mathbf{x}$ in the subgroup of compliers with $D = 0$, with that of compliers with $D = 1$. Although interesting, it is not possible as we cannot know from the observations theirselves which unit is a complier and which is not.

Abadie (2003) does however provide a fundamental theorem that allows us to estimate previous expectations without knowing as to which units are compliers.

Ababie theorem Suppose that all previous LATE identification assumptions (including monotonicity) hold conditional on $\mathbf{x}$; let $g(Y, D, \mathbf{x})$ be any measurable function of $(Y, D, \mathbf{x})$ with finite expectation; define:

$$k_0 = (1 - D)\frac{(1 - z) - p(z = 0 \mid \mathbf{x})}{p(z = 0 \mid \mathbf{x})\, p(z = 1 \mid \mathbf{x})} \tag{4.27}$$

$$k_1 = D\frac{z - p(z = 1 \mid \mathbf{x})}{p(z = 0 \mid \mathbf{x})\, p(z = 1 \mid \mathbf{x})} \tag{4.28}$$

$$k = k_0\, p(z = 0 \mid \mathbf{x}) + k_1\, p(z = 1 \mid \mathbf{x}) = 1 - \frac{D(1 - z)}{p(z = 0 \mid \mathbf{x})} - \frac{(1 - D)z}{p(z = 1 \mid \mathbf{x})} \tag{4.29}$$

Then we can prove that:

$$E[g(Y, D, \mathbf{x}) \mid D_1 > D_0] = \frac{1}{p(D_1 > D_0)} E[k \cdot g(Y, D, \mathbf{x})] \tag{4.30}$$

$$E[g(Y_0, \mathbf{x}) \mid D_1 > D_0] = \frac{1}{p(D_1 > D_0)} E[k_0 \cdot g(Y, \mathbf{x})] \tag{4.31}$$

$$E[g(Y_1, \mathbf{x}) \mid D_1 > D_0] = \frac{1}{p(D_1 > D_0)} E[k_1 \cdot g(Y, \mathbf{x})] \tag{4.32}$$

where we saw that $p(D_1 > D_0) = E(D \mid z = 1) - E(D \mid z = 0)$; thus all previous formulas are functions of observable quantities. Furthermore, the last three relations also hold conditional on $\mathbf{x}$. Observe also that $p(D_1 > D_0) = E(k)$.

This theorem is extremely useful, as it allows to compare the characteristics of treated and untreated individuals within the compliers' subset, without knowing who is and who is not a complier. In the case of LARF estimation, if we have a sample of i.i.d. observations $\{Y_i, D_i, z_i, \mathbf{x}_i,\}$ and define the LARF as $h(D, \mathbf{x}; \boldsymbol{\theta}_0) = \mathrm{E}(Y \mid \mathbf{x}, D, D_1 > D_0)$ where:

$$\boldsymbol{\theta}_0 = \mathrm{argmin}_{\boldsymbol{\theta} \in \Theta} \mathrm{E}\left\{ (Y - h(D, \mathbf{x}; \boldsymbol{\theta}))^2 \mid D_1 > D_0 \right\}$$

then, by applying the Abadie theorem, we can write that:

$$\boldsymbol{\theta}_0 = \mathrm{argmin}_{\boldsymbol{\theta} \in \Theta} \mathrm{E}\left\{ k(Y - h(D, \mathbf{x}; \boldsymbol{\theta}))^2 \right\}$$

which is now expressed in terms of all observable quantities. Notice that, in defining $\boldsymbol{\theta}_0$ as the solution, we eliminate $p(D_1 > D_0)$ as this term does not affect the population objective function of the previous minimization problem. Moreover, since $h(\cdot)$ has the form of a minimum square errors estimator, one can also think about LARF as the best least square approximation under functional form misspecification. If we assume a linear parametric form for $h(\cdot)$ we obtain:

$$(\mu_0, \alpha_0, \boldsymbol{\delta}_0) = \mathrm{argmin}_{(\mu, \alpha, \delta)} \mathrm{E}\left\{ k(Y - \mu - \alpha D - \mathbf{x}\boldsymbol{\delta})^2 \right\} \qquad (4.33)$$

thus we can provide the following two-step procedure for estimating LARF:

1. Calculate the weights k by first estimating parametrically (or nonparametrically) $p(z = 1 \mid \mathbf{x})$;
2. Estimate $(\mu_0, \alpha_0, \boldsymbol{\delta}_0)$ by a Weighted least square (WLS) with weights equal to k and estimate the LARF.

Two problems arise with such a procedure: (1) the weights in step 1 are generated variables to be used in the second step; thus, asymptotic standard errors should be corrected for this; (2) the estimated weights can be negative, thus the usual WLS cannot be feasible.

Regarding point (1), Abadie (2003) has provided analytical formulas for standard errors and also showed that bootstrap can be a valuable alternative; moreover, Abadie et al. (2002) have provided a solution to the negative estimated weights issue, suggesting to use the following weights:

$$\mathrm{E}(k \mid Y, D, \mathbf{x}) = 1 - \frac{D[1 - \mathrm{E}(z \mid Y, D = 1, \mathbf{x})]}{1 - p(z = 1 \mid \mathbf{x})}$$
$$- \frac{(1 - D)\mathrm{E}(z \mid Y, D = 0, \mathbf{x})}{p(z = 1 \mid \mathbf{x})} \qquad (4.34)$$

instead of the weights expressed as in (4.29). The most important advantage of using weights as in (4.34) is that:

$$E(k \mid Y, D, \mathbf{x}) = p(D_1 - D_0 \mid Y, D, \mathbf{x}) \qquad (4.35)$$

which is a probability and thus constrained to vary between zero and one. Using such a weighting scheme, therefore, leads to the following modified procedure for estimating LARF:

1. Calculate the weights $E(k \mid Y, D, \mathbf{x})$ by first estimating parametrically (or nonparametrically) $E(z \mid Y, D = 1, \mathbf{x})$, $E(z \mid Y, D = 0, \mathbf{x})$, and $p(z = 1 \mid \mathbf{x})$ in (4.34). In the parametric case, this involves:

   • Estimating a probit of z on $\{Y, D, \mathbf{x}\}$ for $D = 1$ and $D = 0$, then saving the fitted values
   • Estimating a probit of z only on $\mathbf{x}$, then saving the fitted values

2. Calculate $E(k \mid Y, D, \mathbf{x})$ by plugging the previously fitted values into formula (4.34), by replacing with one values that are larger than one and with zero values that are lower than zero.
3. Estimate $(\mu_0, \alpha_0, \delta_0)$ by a WLS with weights equal to the estimated $E(k \mid Y, D, \mathbf{x})$ and get standard errors using the analytical formulas provided by Abadie (2003, section 4.3) or by bootstrap to take into account the generated estimation from the second step.

Finally, it is worth stressing that if in the minimization (4.33) we adopt, in constructing k, a linear model for the probability of $z = 1$ given $\mathbf{x}$ of the type $p(z = 1 \mid \mathbf{x}) = \mathbf{x}\gamma$, then the parameters estimated by (4.33) coincide with the usual 2SLS estimation; this is no longer true, however, if $p(z = 1 \mid \mathbf{x})$ is estimated parametrically but nonlinearly or directly nonparametrically.

4.2.5 Characterizing Compliers

Previous analysis allows us for characterizing compliers, in the sense of making it possible to both count the overall number of compliers and their characteristics by treatment status. Indeed, under previous assumptions (including monotonicity), it is possible to estimate consistently the following quantities:

$$N \cdot p(D_1 > D_0) = \text{number of compliers}$$
$$N \cdot p(D_1 > D_0 \mid D = 1) = \text{number of treated compliers}$$
$$N \cdot p(D_1 > D_0 \mid D = 0) = \text{number of untreated compliers}$$

Indeed, we have already proven in (4.20) that:

$$p(D_1 > D_0) = p(D_1 - D_0 = 1) = p(D = 1 \mid z = 1) - p(D = 1 \mid z = 0)$$

which is a function of observable terms. We can also show how to express the quantity $p(D_1 > D_0 \mid D = 1)$ in terms of observables, namely:

$$p(D_1 > D_0 \mid D = 1) = \frac{p(D_1 > D_0) \cdot p(D = 1 \mid D_1 > D_0)}{p(D = 1)}$$

$$= \frac{[p(D = 1 \mid z = 1) - p(D = 1 \mid z = 0)] \cdot p(z = 1 \mid D_1 > D_0)}{p(D = 1)}$$

$$= \frac{[p(D = 1 \mid z = 1) - p(D = 1 \mid z = 0)] \cdot p(z = 1)}{p(D = 1)}$$

$$(4.36)$$

where the first equality uses the Bayes theorem, the second equality the fact that for compliers $D = z$, and the third equality exploits the independence of z.

A further attractive characterization of the compliers subgroup is that of comparing the distribution of the covariates for this set of individuals by treatment status. This is relevant, as differences in attributes for compliers have a causal interpretation. To this purpose, we can still use the Ababie theorem, using the k-weighting scheme for the variables of interest; for instance, suppose that we wish to compare the average value of a covariate x as taken in the treated and in the control group of compliers; by using the weights as reported in (4.27) and (4.28), and appropriately using formulas (4.31) and (4.32), we obtain:

$$E(x \mid D = 1; D_1 > D_0) = \frac{E(k_1 \cdot x)}{p(D_1 > D_0)}$$

$$= \frac{E(k_1 \cdot x)}{p(D = 1 \mid z = 1) - p(D = 1 \mid z = 0)} \qquad (4.37)$$

$$E(x \mid D = 0; D_1 > D_0) = \frac{E(k_0 \cdot x)}{p(D_1 > D_0)}$$

$$= \frac{E(k_0 \cdot x)}{p(D = 1 \mid z = 1) - p(D = 1 \mid z = 0)} \qquad (4.38)$$

whose sample equivalent is immediate. In such a way, it is possible to compare any attribute we are interested in within the compliers subgroup by treatment status. Computational implementation is also straightforward (see Sect. 4.4.1).

4.2.6 LATE with Multiple Instruments and Multiple Treatment

Previous analysis regarding LATE can be quite easily generalized to the case of: (1) multiple instruments and (2) multiple treatment.

In the case of multiple instruments, Imbens and Angrist (1994) and Angrist and Imbens (1995) have shown that LATE takes the form of a weighted average of single LATEs estimated using separately z_1 and z_2, these being two mutually exclusive instrumental dummies. In this framework, we can define the two LATEs as follows:

$$\text{LATE}(z_1) = \frac{\text{Cov}(Y; z_1)}{\text{Cov}(D; z_1)} \tag{4.39}$$

$$\text{LATE}(z_2) = \frac{\text{Cov}(Y; z_2)}{\text{Cov}(D; z_2)} \tag{4.40}$$

If we consider the first-stage fitted value as defined by:

$$\widehat{D} = \widehat{\lambda}_0 + \widehat{\lambda}_1 z_1 + \widehat{\lambda}_2 z_2 \tag{4.41}$$

we can immediately write down—as shown by Angrist and Pischke (2008, pp. 173–175)—that 2SLS estimator of LATE as:

$$
\begin{aligned}
\text{LATE} &= \frac{\text{Cov}\left(Y; \widehat{D}\right)}{\text{Cov}\left(D; \widehat{D}\right)} = \frac{\text{Cov}\left(Y; \widehat{\lambda}_0 + \widehat{\lambda}_1 z_1 + \widehat{\lambda}_2 z_2\right)}{\text{Cov}\left(D; \widehat{D}\right)} \\[2mm]
&= \frac{\widehat{\lambda}_1 \text{Cov}(Y; z_1) + \text{Cov}(Y; z_2)}{\text{Cov}\left(D; \widehat{D}\right)} \\[2mm]
&= \frac{\widehat{\lambda}_1 \text{Cov}(Y; z_1)}{\text{Cov}\left(D; \widehat{D}\right)} \cdot \frac{\text{Cov}(D; z_1)}{\text{Cov}(D; z_1)} + \frac{\widehat{\lambda}_2 \text{Cov}(Y; z_2)}{\text{Cov}\left(D; \widehat{D}\right)} \cdot \frac{\text{Cov}(D; z_2)}{\text{Cov}(D; z_2)} \\[2mm]
&= \left[\widehat{\lambda}_1 \frac{\text{Cov}(D; z_1)}{\text{Cov}\left(D; \widehat{D}\right)}\right] \cdot \frac{\text{Cov}(Y; z_1)}{\text{Cov}(D; z_1)} + \left[\widehat{\lambda}_2 \frac{\text{Cov}(D; z_2)}{\text{Cov}\left(D; \widehat{D}\right)}\right] \\
&\quad \cdot \frac{\text{Cov}(Y; z_2)}{\text{Cov}(D; z_2)} \\[2mm]
&= \phi \cdot \text{LATE}(z_1) + (1 - \phi) \cdot \text{LATE}(z_2) \tag{4.42}
\end{aligned}
$$

where:

$$\phi = \frac{\widehat{\lambda}_1 \text{Cov}(D; z_1)}{\widehat{\lambda}_1 \text{Cov}(D; z_1) + \widehat{\lambda}_2 \text{Cov}(D; z_2)} \tag{4.43}$$

is a weight ranging from zero to one depending on the first-stage importance of each single instrument in explaining the treatment D. Equation (4.42), hence, shows that the overall LATE is a weighting mean of the LATE obtained by exploiting one instrument at time.

In the case of multiple treatment, Angrist and Imbens (1995) have provided a fundamental theorem linking this case with the ordinary LATE estimator. To illustrate this, let the potential outcome take such a form:

$$Y_d = f(d) \qquad (4.44)$$

with $d \in \{0, 1, 2, \ldots, \bar{d}\}$ indicating a multinomial treatment variable taking ordinal values between 0 and $\bar{d}$: one could think about d as the number of years of education, the number of children some women had, and so forth.

As in the binary case, assume knowing an instrument z is randomly assigned, with d depending on z; as such, d is a function of z, such that:

$$d_1 = \text{treatment status when } z = 1$$
$$d_0 = \text{treatment status when } z = 0$$

where d_1 and d_0 can take values within $\{0, 1, 2, \ldots, \bar{d}\}$, and where for each unit we can only observe one of these two variables, never both. Given the corresponding independence assumption:

$$(Y_0, Y_1, \ldots, Y_{\bar{d}}), d_1, d_0 \perp z$$

and the corresponding first-stage condition:

$$E[d_1] \neq E[d_0]$$

which simply suggests that z has some predictive power on d, the monotonicity assumption in such a multinomial case takes on this (corresponding) form:

$$d_1 \geq d_0.$$

Given previous assumptions, it can be proved in such a setting that LATE takes on the following form:

$$\text{LATE} = \frac{E(Y \mid z = 1) - E(Y \mid z = 0)}{E(d \mid z = 1) - E(d \mid z = 0)}$$

$$= \sum_{k=1}^{\bar{d}} \theta_k \cdot E(Y_d - Y_{d-1} \mid d_0 < k \leq d_1) \qquad (4.45)$$

where we have that:

$$\theta_k = \frac{p(d_0 < k \le d_1)}{\sum\limits_{k=1}^{\bar{d}} p(d_0 < k \le d_1)} \tag{4.46}$$

represents a weighting scheme with weights by definition adding to one. Equation (4.45) suggests that with multinomial treatment, LATE is an average of single LATEs singularly defined as the *unit* average treatment effect calculated in the subpopulation of *compliers at k*. In other words, those individuals comply with the instrument, so that when $z = 0$ they get a treatment higher than d_0, and when $z = 1$ they get a treatment at most equal to d_1.

Within the entire population, the share of compliers at k can be calculated by observing that:

$$p(d_0 < k \le d_1) = p(k \le d_1) - p(k \le d_0)$$
$$= [1 - p(k > d_1)] - [1 - p(k > d_0)]$$
$$= p(k > d_0) - p(k > d_1) = p(d_0 < k) - p(d_1 < k) \tag{4.47}$$

Since by independence we have that:

$$p(d_0 < k) - p(d_1 < k) = p(d < k \mid z = 0) - p(d < k \mid z = 1) \tag{4.48}$$

we can calculate the share of compliers using observable data as showed by (4.48).

Finally, it is quite easy to show that:

$$E(d \mid z = 1) - E(d \mid z = 0) = \sum_{k=1\bar{d}} [p(d < k \mid z = 0) - p(d < k \mid z = 1)]$$
$$= \sum_{k=1\bar{d}} p(d_0 < k \le d_1) \tag{4.49}$$

thus the weights θ_k can be consistently estimated, and both the numerator and denominator can be computed using observable variables. The first equality of (4.49) comes from the property of the mean of a finite count variable. Indeed, for a finite count variable $d \in \{0, 1, 2, \ldots, \bar{d}\}$, it can be proven that:

$$E(d) = \sum_{d=0\bar{d}} d \cdot p(d) = \sum_{k=0\bar{d}} \left[1 - \sum_{d=0}^{k} p(d) \right] \tag{4.50}$$

where:

$$\sum_{d=0}^{k} p(d) = p(d \le k) = F(k) \tag{4.51}$$

is the cumulative distribution function of the stochastic variable d. To prove (4.50), consider the case of $\bar{d} = 2$; in this case:

$$\sum_{k=0}^{2} \left[1 - \sum_{d=0}^{k} p(d) \right] = [1 - p(0)] + [1 - p(0) - p(1)]$$

$$+ [1 - p(0) - p(1) - p(2)]$$

$$= 3 - 3p(0) - 2p(1) - p(2) \tag{4.52}$$

At the same time, the mean of d is equal to:

$$E(d) = \sum_{d=0}^{\bar{d}} d \cdot p(d) = 0p(0) + 1p(1) + 2p(2) = p(1) + 2p(2) \tag{4.53}$$

However, since by definition $p(0) = 1 - p(1) - p(2)$, then (4.52) becomes:

$$\sum_{k=0}^{2} \left[1 - \sum_{d=0}^{k} p(d) \right] = 3 - 3p(0) - 2p(1) - p(2)$$

$$= 3 - 3 + 3p(1) - 3p(2) - 2p(1) - p(2)$$

$$= p(1) + 2p(2) \tag{4.54}$$

which is equal to (4.53), thus proving relation (4.50). Observe that, since the first value taken by d is zero, we can start previous summations directly from $d = 1$ leading to the same result with:

$$E(d) = \sum_{d=1}^{\bar{d}} d \cdot p(d) = \sum_{k=1}^{\bar{d}} \left[1 - \sum_{d=1}^{k} p(d) \right] \tag{4.55}$$

where:

$$\sum_{d=1}^{k} p(d) = p(d < k) \tag{4.56}$$

Given (4.55) and (4.56), we finally get—by substitution—(4.49).

4.3   Regression-Discontinuity-Design

Regression-discontinuity-design (RDD) can be used when the selection-into-program (D) is highly determined by the level assumed by a specific variable s (sometimes called "forcing" variable), defining a threshold $\bar{s}$ separating treated and untreated units (Imbens and Lemieux 2008; Lee and Lemieux 2009). In the literature, two types of RDD have been proposed and studied:

- *Sharp* RDD: when the relation between D and s is *deterministic*, thus creating a strict "jump" in the probability of receiving the treatment at the threshold
- *Fuzzy* RDD: when this relation is *stochastic*, thus producing a milder jump at the threshold

The idea behind RDD is that, in a neighborhood of the threshold, conditions for a natural experiment (i.e., a random assignment to treatment) are restored. Therefore, as long as: (1) the threshold is well identified and (2) the treatment is dependent on s, the analyst can obtain the policy effect simply by comparing the mean outcome of individuals laying on the left and the mean outcome of individuals laying on the right of the threshold. In what follows, we separately present and examine the sharp and fuzzy RDD setting (Fig. 4.2).

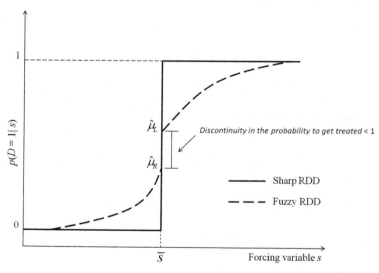

Fig. 4.2 Discontinuity in the probability to be treated in the sharp and fuzzy RDD

4.3.1 Sharp *RDD*

In sharp RDD, the selection-into-treatment follows a deterministic rule defined as:

$$D_i = 1[s \geq \bar{s}] \tag{4.57}$$

The idea behind such approach is that, in the threshold point $s = \bar{s}$, random assignment is in place so that independence assumption (IA) holds exactly in that point (i.e., locally).

A fundamental assumption in order for RDD to be able to identify the actual causal effect of interest is the so-called continuity of the mean potential outcomes at the threshold. Although not strictly necessary, this assumption is generally strengthened by requiring the continuity to hold over all the support of s:

Assumption 4.5 The two potential outcomes $E(Y_1 \mid s)$ and $E(Y_0 \mid s)$ are continuous functions over the support of s.

Under this assumption and using POM, i.e., $Y = Y_0 + D\,(Y_1 - Y_0)$, we have that:

$$E(Y_0 \mid s = \bar{s}) = \lim_{s \uparrow \bar{s}} E(Y_0 \mid S = s) = \lim_{s \uparrow \bar{s}} E(Y_0 \mid D = 0, S = s)$$

$$= \lim_{s \uparrow \bar{s}} E(Y \mid S = s) \tag{4.58}$$

$$E(Y_1 \mid s = \bar{s}) = \lim_{s \downarrow \bar{s}} E(Y \mid S = s) \tag{4.59}$$

Consequently, ATE is equal to the difference between (4.59) and (4.58), that is:

$$\begin{aligned} \text{ATE}_{\text{SRD}} &= E(Y_1 \mid s = \bar{s}) - E(Y_0 \mid s = \bar{s}) \\ &= \lim_{s \downarrow \bar{s}} E(Y \mid S = s) - \lim_{s \uparrow \bar{s}} E(Y \mid S = s) \end{aligned} \tag{4.60}$$

or equivalently:

$$\text{ATE}_{\text{SRD}} = m_R(\bar{s}) - m_L(\bar{s}) \tag{4.61}$$

where, for simplicity, $m_R(\bar{s}) = \lim_{s \downarrow \bar{s}} E(Y \mid S = s)$ and $m_L(\bar{s}) = \lim_{s \uparrow \bar{s}} E(Y \mid S = s)$.

Equation (4.61) implies that a simple Difference-in-means (DIM) of units laying on the right and on the left of a neighborhood of the threshold gives a consistent estimation of ATE.

In order to understand the relevance of Assumption 4.5 in the identification of ATE, assume that $E(Y_0 \mid s)$ is continuous while $E(Y_1 \mid s)$ is discontinuous in s at the threshold. Figure 4.3 presents such a situation; as clearly evident, $E(Y_1 \mid s)$ sets out a discontinuity at the threshold, implying that its right side limit C is different from its left side limit B. This means that the actual value of ATE is uncertain, equal to

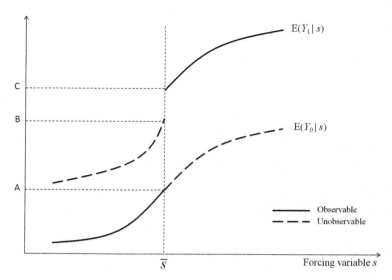

Fig. 4.3 Ambiguity in identifying ATE when mean potential outcomes are discontinuous in s at the threshold

(B-A) when seen from the left and equal to (C-A) when seen from the right. This uncertainty is ruled out if the function $E(Y_1 \mid s)$ crosses the vertical threshold line only in one point: this is equivalent to assuming that $E(Y_1 \mid s)$ is continuous.

By assuming that Assumption 4.5 holds, one can estimate (4.60) nonparametrically, once a given interval around the threshold of width h has been selected beforehand; for the moment, let us assume a given value for h so that the estimation is restricted to observations in the interval $(\bar{s} - h; \bar{s} + h)$. As a suitable nonparametric estimation technique, one could use a kernel weighted average, thus estimating (4.60) as:

$$\widehat{ATE}_{SRD} = \frac{\sum\limits_{i \in \{R\}} K\left(\frac{s_i - \bar{s}}{h}\right) Y_i}{\sum\limits_{i \in \{R\}} K\left(\frac{s_i - \bar{s}}{h}\right)} - \frac{\sum\limits_{i \in \{L\}} K\left(\frac{s_i - \bar{s}}{h}\right) Y_i}{\sum\limits_{i \in \{L\}} K\left(\frac{s_i - \bar{s}}{h}\right)} \quad (4.62)$$

where $K(\cdot)$ is a specific kernel function and $\{R\}$ and $\{L\}$ the set of units laying on the right and on the left of the cutoff, respectively. By choosing a uniform (or rectangular) kernel, (4.62) becomes:

$$\widehat{\text{ATE}}_{\text{SRD}} = \frac{\sum_{i \in \{R\}} \mathbf{1}\left(\frac{s_i - \bar{s}}{h} < 1\right) Y}{\sum_{i \in \{R\}} \mathbf{1}\left(\frac{s_i - \bar{s}}{h} < 1\right)} - \frac{\sum_{i \in \{L\}} \mathbf{1}\left(\frac{s_i - \bar{s}}{h} < 1\right) Y}{\sum_{i \in \{L\}} \mathbf{1}\left(\frac{s_i - \bar{s}}{h} < 1\right)} = \overline{Y}_{R,h} - \overline{Y}_{L,h} \quad (4.63)$$

where the index function $\mathbf{1}(a)$ is equal to one when expression a is true and zero otherwise. Equation (4.63) shows that the use of a rectangular kernel simply returns the difference between the mean of Y on the right and the mean of Y on the left of the threshold, where only observations within $(\bar{s} - h; \bar{s} + h)$ are used.

As other nonparametric methods, the estimator proposed in (4.62) presents some problems when used at boundaries. It can be shown that the bias of such estimator at boundary is $O(h)$, whereas typical kernel regressions have a bias that is $O(h^2)$. Porter (2003) shows that the limiting distribution of the Nadaraya–Watson estimator at the boundary point $\bar{s}$ is:

$$\sqrt{Nh} \cdot \left(\widehat{\text{ATE}}_{\text{SRD}} - \text{ATE}\right) \sim N\left[2 \cdot C \cdot K_1(0) \cdot \left[m_R'(\bar{s}) - m_L'(\bar{s})\right]; 4\delta_0 \frac{\sigma_R^2(\bar{s}) - \sigma_L^2(\bar{s})}{f_0(\bar{s})}\right]$$

$$(4.64)$$

where $K_1(0)$ and δ_0 depend on the kernel, and C is a finite number defined as the following limit: $h\sqrt{Nh} \to C$, when $h \to 0$ and $Nh \to \infty$. Therefore, given (4.64) we have that asymptotically:

$$\text{E}\left[\sqrt{Nh} \cdot \left(\widehat{\text{ATE}}_{\text{SRD}} - \text{ATE}\right)\right] \cong 2 \cdot h\sqrt{Nh} \cdot K_1(0) \cdot \left[m_R'(\bar{s}) - m_L'(\bar{s})\right]$$

thus:

$$\text{Bias}\left(\widehat{\text{ATE}}_{\text{SRD}}\right) = \text{ATE} + 2 \cdot h \cdot K_1(0) \cdot \left[m_R'(\bar{s}) - m_L'(\bar{s})\right] \quad (4.65)$$

which increases linearly with h.

Since the rate of convergence of the bias to zero, as N approaches infinity, is quite slow compared to other parametric methods, it seems convenient to search for some alternatives such as local linear regressions, which have the advantage of a bias $O(h^2)$ also at boundaries (Fan and Gijbels 1996; Lee et al. 2004)[2].

---

[2] For kernel regressions, the optimal bandwidth in interior points is $O(h^2)$ and is proportional to $N^{-1/5}$ (Härdle and Marron 1985), so that $1/5 = 0.2$ is the speed of convergence of the bias to zero; at boundaries, however, we saw that such convergence rate becomes $O(h)$ that is proportional to $(N^{-1/5})^{1/2}$, that is, half time the usual rate of convergence in interior points. This questions seriously the use of kernel regressions at boundaries.

The local linear regression simply requires us to run the following two regressions, estimated via standard OLS, on the left (L) and on the right (R) side of the threshold:

$$Y_i = \alpha_L + \delta_L(s_i - \bar{s}) + \varepsilon_{L,i} \tag{4.66}$$

$$Y_i = \alpha_R + \delta_R(s_i - \bar{s}) + \varepsilon_{R,i} \tag{4.67}$$

using only units belonging to $(\bar{s} - h; \bar{s})$ in regression (4.66) and only units belonging to $(\bar{s}; \bar{s} + h)$ in regression (4.67). Note that $\varepsilon_{L,i}$ and $\varepsilon_{R,i}$ are two pure random errors with unconditional mean equal to zero. The conditional expectations are therefore:

$$E(Y_i \mid s_i) = \alpha_L + \delta_L(s_i - \bar{s}) \tag{4.68}$$

$$E(Y_i \mid s_i) = \alpha_R + \delta_R(s_i - \bar{s}) \tag{4.69}$$

By combining the previous two equations into a unique local pooled linear regression, we obtain:

$$Y_i = \alpha_L + \text{ATE} \cdot D_i + \delta_L(s_i - \bar{s}) + (\delta_R - \delta_L) \cdot D_i \cdot (s_i - \bar{s}) + \varepsilon_i \tag{4.70}$$

where $\text{ATE}_{SRD} = (\alpha_R - \alpha_L)$ and $\varepsilon_i = \varepsilon_{L,I} + D_i(\varepsilon_{R,i} - \varepsilon_{L,i})$. This equation can in turn be estimated by OLS on the full sample and locally around the cutoff point using different sample windows h, i.e., in the subsample identified by the set $S_{\bar{s},h} \equiv \{\bar{s} - h < s < \bar{s} + h\}$. Furthermore, regression (4.70) also provides the correct standard errors for ATE, provided that the rate of convergence of the bandwidth to zero, as N goes to infinity, is "sufficiently" high and is assumed to be higher than the usual rate 1/5 (see footnote 2). Indeed, if a rate of 1/5 is assumed, a bias would arise also asymptotically. For the bias to disappear asymptotically, we need that the bias goes to zero faster than the variance and, for this to happen, we have to assume a rate of convergence δ such that $1/5 < \delta < 2/5$, where 2/5 is the fastest rate of convergence for nonparametric estimators (Stone 1982). This assumption is known as "undersmoothing."

Interestingly, regression (4.70) has a powerful graphical representation (as illustrated by Fig. 4.4) showing that, for sharp RDD, ATE is equal to the discontinuity in the outcome at the threshold (assuming in this case a linear form of the potential outcomes as function of s).

One limitation of estimating ATE by (4.70) lies in the linear assumption: when potential outcomes are nonlinear functions of s, then bias due to functional misspecification can arise. For robustness purposes, one can generalize (4.70) using: (1) a local polynomial regression or (2) a kernel local polynomial regression, as long as a bandwidth h has been properly specified. Figure 4.5 provides a

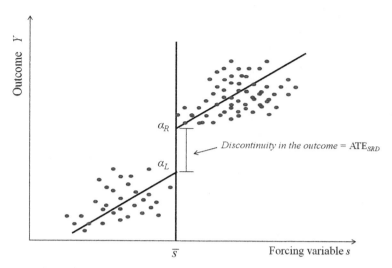

Fig. 4.4 Sharp RDD. ATE = discontinuity in the outcome. Linear form of the potential outcomes as function of s

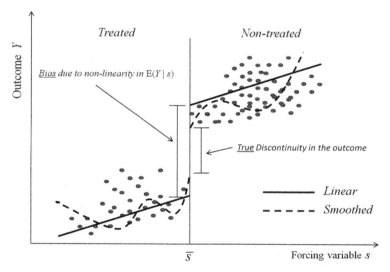

Fig. 4.5 Discontinuity in the outcome for sharp RDD: linear bias of ATE estimation due to functional misspecification of the potential outcomes

graphical representation of the potential bias due to functional misspecification in the sharp RDD case.

In the case in which a local polynomial regression is implemented, (4.70) becomes:

$$Y_i = \alpha_L + \text{ATE} \cdot D_i + \sum_{p=1}^{P} \delta_{L,\,p}(s_i - \bar{s})^P + D_i \sum_{p=1}^{P} (\delta_{R,\,p} - \delta_{L,\,p}) \cdot (s_i - \bar{s})^P + \varepsilon$$

$$i \in \{\bar{s} - h < s_i < \bar{s} + h\}$$

$$(4.71)$$

where P is the degree of the polynomial function and h the bandwidth. One could also fit a weighted local regression function on either side of the discontinuity point, by using a kernel local polynomial regression:

$$\operatorname*{Min}_{\alpha_L,\,\delta_{L,1}} \left\{ \sum_{i:\ x_i < x_0} K\left(\frac{s_i - \bar{s}}{h}\right) \cdot \left[Y_i - \alpha_L - \delta_{L,1}(s_i - \bar{s}) - \cdots - \delta_{L,\,p}(s_i - \bar{s})^P \right]^2 \right\}$$

$$\operatorname*{Min}_{\alpha_R,\,\delta_{R,1}} \left\{ \sum_{i:\ x_i \geq x_0} K\left(\frac{s_i - \bar{s}}{h}\right) \cdot \left[Y_i - \alpha_R - \delta_{R,1}(s_i - \bar{s}) - \cdots - \delta_{R,\,p}(s_i - \bar{s})^P \right]^2 \right\}$$

$$(4.72)$$

where $K(\cdot)$ is a prespecified kernel function. Observe that, in this case, all the observations on the left and on the right of the cutoff are used in the estimation, although the final number of observations considered depends on the specific kernel function adopted, as well as on h. Estimation of ATE in the case of (4.72) proceeds by estimating a regression like (4.71), weighting observations through a specific kernel function. In general, and coherently with the semi-experimental nature of RDD, kernel functions give more (less) weight to observations whose value of s is closer to (farther from) the threshold.

4.3.2 Fuzzy RDD

In the fuzzy RDD, the probability of receiving the treatment does not change from zero to one at the threshold, as in the deterministic case of sharp RDD. Even if eligibility for treatment depends on a cutoff rule, not all the eligible individuals may obtain the treatment because imperfect compliance at the threshold is assumed. In this sense, the statistical setting of fuzzy RDD presents strong similarities with the randomization under imperfect compliance presented in Sect. 4.2.1.

Fuzzy RDD allows for a milder jump in the probability of assignment to treatment at the threshold. To see this, we can assume—with no loss of generality—a linear probability model in the left and right side of the threshold as:

$$p(D_i = 1 \mid s_i = \bar{s}) = \mu_L + \pi_L(s_i - \bar{s}) \qquad (4.73)$$

$$p(D_i = 1 \mid s_i = \bar{s}) = \mu_R + \pi_R(s_i - \bar{s}) \tag{4.74}$$

As in the sharp case, in order to work more compactly, we can estimate both previous regressions in a single pooled one by writing:

$$p(D_i = 1 \mid s_i - \bar{s}) = \mu_L + (\mu_R - \mu_L) \cdot T_i + \pi_L(s_i - \bar{s}) + (\pi_R - \pi_L) \cdot T_i \cdot (s_i - \bar{s}) \tag{4.75}$$

where $T_i = 1[s_i \geq \bar{s}]$. Observe that in the fuzzy RDD, "T_i can be different from D_i" because of imperfect compliance, while in the sharp RDD we have that T_i is equal to D_i. In this sense, T_i plays the same role as that played by z_i in the LATE setting presented in Sect. 4.2. Finally, observe that since D is a binary variable, we also have:

$$D_i = p(D_i = 1 \mid s_i - \bar{s}) + \eta_i \tag{4.76}$$

where η_i is a genuine error term independent of s:

$$E(D_i \mid s_i - \bar{s}) = p(D_i = 1 \mid s_i - \bar{s}) + E(\eta_i \mid s_i - \bar{s}) = p(D_i = 1 \mid s_i - \bar{s}) \tag{4.77}$$

It can be proved that the estimation of the causal effect of D on Y in the case of fuzzy RDD is equivalent to the following LATE:

$$\text{ATE}_{\text{FRD}} = E(Y_{1i} - Y_{0i} \mid \text{unit is a complier} \cap s = \bar{s}) \tag{4.78}$$

where, in this setting, compliers are those units i following this rule:

1. When $T_i = 1$, then $D_i = 1$
2. When $T_i = 0$, then $D_i = 0$

thus compliers are units having $T_i = D_i$. As previously argued, we cannot identify these units by observation, since for each unit i we observe either (1) or (2), but never both. We can conclude that the identification and estimation of the average treatment effect for fuzzy RDD strictly follows that of LATE. Thus, it envisages a Wald estimator form of the treatment effect based on an IV estimation of Y on D, with T playing the role of the instrumental variable for D in a neighborhood of the threshold (Hahn et al. 2001). In this sense, fuzzy RDD leads to an estimation procedure very close to that of other methods suitable under selection on unobservables, with the advantage that in this case extensions to a nonparametric environment are relatively easier to implement (Imbens and Lemieux 2008).

In order to identify the ATE in the case of fuzzy RDD, we have to rely on a less restrictive assumption than IA:

Assumption 4.6 Identification of ATE for fuzzy RDD ($IA_{\text{Fuzzy-RDD}}$):

$$(Y_1--Y_0) \perp D \mid s$$

that is, the selection-into-treatment is independent of the participation gain, given s. In fact, under this assumption, considering again $Y = Y_0 + D\,(Y_1 - Y_0)$, we can show that:

$$E(Y \mid s) = E(Y_0 \mid s) + E(D(Y_1 - Y_0) \mid s) = E(Y_0 \mid s) + E(D \mid s) \cdot E(Y_1 - Y_0) \mid s)$$
$$= E(Y_0 \mid s) + E(D \mid s) \cdot ATE(s)$$

that is:

$$E(Y \mid s) = E(Y_0 \mid s) + E(D \mid s) \cdot ATE(s) \tag{4.79}$$

As in the case of sharp RDD, taking the limit from the left and from the right produces:

$$\lim_{s \downarrow \bar{s}} E(Y \mid S = s) = \lim_{s \downarrow \bar{s}} E(Y_0 \mid S = s) + \lim_{s \downarrow \bar{s}} E(D \mid S = s) \cdot \lim_{s \downarrow \bar{s}} ATE(s) \tag{4.80}$$

$$\lim_{s \uparrow \bar{s}} E(Y \mid S = s) = \lim_{s \uparrow \bar{s}} E(Y_0 \mid S = s) + \lim_{s \uparrow \bar{s}} E(D \mid S = s) \cdot \lim_{s \uparrow \bar{s}} ATE(s) \tag{4.81}$$

and by taking (4.80) minus (4.81) we obtain:

$$ATE_{\text{FRD}} = \frac{\lim\limits_{s \downarrow \bar{s}} E(Y \mid S = s) - \lim\limits_{s \uparrow \bar{s}} E(Y \mid S = s)}{\lim\limits_{s \downarrow \bar{s}} E(D \mid S = s) - \lim\limits_{s \uparrow \bar{s}} E(D \mid S = s)}$$
$$= \frac{\lim\limits_{s \downarrow \bar{s}} E(Y \mid S = s) - \lim\limits_{s \uparrow \bar{s}} E(Y \mid S = s)}{\lim\limits_{s \downarrow \bar{s}} p(D = 1 \mid S = s) - \lim\limits_{s \uparrow \bar{s}} p(D = 1 \mid S = s)} \tag{4.82}$$

which formally shows that the ATE in fuzzy RDD is in fact a Wald estimator. Observe that formula (4.82) generalizes the formula for ATE obtained for sharp RDD, as in the sharp case:

$$\begin{cases} \lim\limits_{s \downarrow \bar{s}} p(w = 1 \mid S = s) = 1 \\ \lim\limits_{s \uparrow \bar{s}} p(w = 1 \mid S = s) = 0 \end{cases} \Rightarrow \lim\limits_{s \downarrow \bar{s}} p(D = 1 \mid S = s) - \lim\limits_{s \uparrow \bar{s}} p(D = 1 \mid S = s) = 1$$

meaning that in sharp RDD the denominator in (4.82) is equal to 1 (i.e., *sharp jump*). Formula (4.82) states therefore that a comparison of treated and untreated units around the threshold is a biased estimator, when the forcing variable does not discriminate sharply between treated, and untreated (i.e., in the absence of perfect compliance). This means that around the threshold individuals can be different for a different propensity to be treated: this confounding effect needs to be taken into account and the denominator in (4.82) properly clears out this effect.

Formula (4.82) correctly allows to estimate this effect both parametrically and nonparametrically. This formula is equal to "the ratio between the discontinuity of the outcome and the discontinuity of the probability to be treated at the threshold." A consistent estimator is the sample analog:

$$\widehat{\text{ATE}}_{FRD} = \frac{\hat{E}(Y \mid S = s)^+ - \hat{E}(Y \mid S = s)^-}{\hat{p}(D = 1 \mid S = s)^+ - \hat{p}(D = 1 \mid S = s)^-} \qquad (4.83)$$

provided that both the numerator and the denominator are consistent estimators of the two discontinuities. A consistent estimation procedure for implementing (4.83) may therefore be the following:

1. Estimate the numerator: calculate the average of the outcome Y on the sample on the right and on the left of the cutoff, given a certain sample window, and take the difference
2. Estimate the denominator: calculate the frequency of treated individuals on the left and on the right of the cutoff, given a certain sample window, and take the difference
3. Form the ratio between the numerator and the denominator to obtain:

$$\widehat{\text{ATE}}_{FRD} = \frac{\bar{Y}_R - \bar{Y}_L}{\bar{D}_R - \bar{D}_L} \qquad (4.84)$$

where the standard error can be computed via bootstrap.

Since formula (4.83) is a special case of the Wald estimator, a simple IV regression of Y on D using T as instrument for D, around the threshold, allows for correct inference, including the analytical standard error.

An alternative to the previous approach is to use a more parametric approach based on a linear specification of $\hat{E}(Y \mid S = s)$ and $\hat{p}(D = 1 \mid S = s)$, which can be implemented as follows:

1. Estimate consistently the discontinuity in the outcome at the threshold as the difference between the two intercepts of the right and left regression, which can be obtained as the coefficient of T_i in an OLS of this regression:

$$Y_i = \alpha_L + (\alpha_R - \alpha_L) \cdot T_i + \delta_L(s_i - \bar{s}) + (\delta_R - \delta_L) \cdot T_i \cdot (s_i - \bar{s}) + \varepsilon_i \qquad (4.85)$$

2. Estimate consistently the discontinuity in the probability at the threshold as the difference between the two intercepts of the right and left regression, which can be obtained as the coefficient of T_i in an OLS of this regression:

$$D_i = \mu_L + (\mu_R - \mu_L) \cdot T_i + \delta_L(s_i - \bar{s}) + (\pi_R - \pi_L) \cdot T_i \cdot (s_i - \bar{s}) + \eta_i \qquad (4.86)$$

3. Obtain a consistent estimation of ATE as:

$$\widehat{\mathrm{ATE}}_{\mathrm{FRD}} = \frac{\widehat{\alpha}_R - \widehat{\alpha}_L}{\widehat{\mu}_R - \widehat{\mu}_L} \qquad (4.87)$$

Observe that (4.85) and (4.86) can also be seen as the reduced forms associated with a two-equation structural system in which Y and D are endogenous and T exogenous; formula (4.87) can therefore be obtained by the IV estimation of ATE of the following regression (Hahn et al. 2001):

$$Y_i = \alpha_L + \mathrm{ATE_{FRD}} \cdot D_i + \delta_L(s_i - \bar{s}) + (\delta_R - \delta_L) \cdot T_i \cdot (s_i - \bar{s}) + \varepsilon_i \qquad (4.88)$$

using T_i as instrument for D. In practice, one can first derive the *fitted values of D* (D_{fv}) from the OLS of:

$$D_i = \mu_L + (\mu_R - \mu_L) \cdot T_i + \pi_L(s_i - \bar{s}) + (\pi_R - \pi_L) \cdot T_i \cdot (s_i - \bar{s}) + \eta_i \qquad (4.89)$$

and then run an OLS regression of (4.88) using D_{fv} instead of D. In this manner, we apply a Direct-2SLS estimation (see Chap. 3, Sect. 3.2.2.1), thus providing standard errors for all the parameters, including ATE.

Rather than using a local linear model for the probability of treatment, one can use a local logit or probit model such as:

$$\begin{aligned} p(D = 1 \mid s)^+ &= G[\theta_L + \gamma_L(s - \bar{s})] \quad \text{if} \quad s < \bar{s} \\ p(D = 1 \mid s)^- &= G[\theta_R + \gamma_R(s - \bar{s})] \quad \text{if} \quad s \geq \bar{s} \end{aligned} \qquad (4.90)$$

so that:

$$\widehat{\mathrm{ATE}}_{\mathrm{FRD}} = \frac{\widehat{\alpha}_R - \widehat{\alpha}_L}{G\left(\widehat{\theta}_R\right) - G\left(\widehat{\theta}_L\right)} \qquad (4.91)$$

where $G(\cdot)$ is the normal (probit) or logistic (logit) c.d.f. This approach corresponds to the Probit/Logit-OLS procedure presented in Chap. 3.

Finally, one can estimate the ATE for fuzzy RDD by an IV local polynomial regression, namely:

$$Y_i = \alpha_L + \mathrm{ATE} \cdot D_i + \sum_{p=1}^{P} \delta_{L,p}(s_i - \bar{s})^p + T_i \sum_{p=1}^{P} (\delta_{R,p} - \delta_{L,p}) \cdot (s_i - \bar{s})^p + \varepsilon$$

$$D_i = \mu_L + (\mu_R - \mu_L) \cdot T_i + \sum_{p=1}^{P} \pi_{L,p}(s_i - \bar{s})^p + T_i \sum_{p=1}^{P} (\mu_{R,p} - \mu_{L,p}) \cdot (s_i - \bar{s})^p + \eta$$

$$\qquad (4.92)$$

using T_i as instrument for D with $i \in \{\bar{s} - h < s_i < \bar{s} + h\}$. Thus, a kernel local polynomial regression can be employed also for fuzzy RDD.

4.3.3   The Choice of the Bandwidth and Polynomial Order

In the next subsections, we discuss methods for choosing correctly the bandwidth for an RDD nonparametric estimation, as well as the order of the polynomial when a local polynomial regression is used.

4.3.3.1   Computing Optimal Bandwidth

While it is straightforward to estimate previous regressions within a given window of width h around the cutoff point, a more difficult question is how to select such a bandwidth (Fan and Gijbels 1996). In general, choosing a bandwidth estimation involves finding an optimal balance between estimation *precision* and estimation *bias*:

- On the one hand, a larger bandwidth yields more precise estimates as a larger number of observations can be used in the estimation phase (higher efficiency)
- On the other hand, when a larger bandwidth is used, estimation is less likely to be accurate, for we are considering observations that are increasingly far from the threshold (higher bias).

Figure 4.6 displays the trade-off between estimation efficiency and correctness as function of the bandwidth h. It is easy to see that there exists a decreasing pattern between efficiency and unbiasedness. Points A and B are two extreme situations in which: a larger h allows for a larger efficiency with lower correctness (point B), and

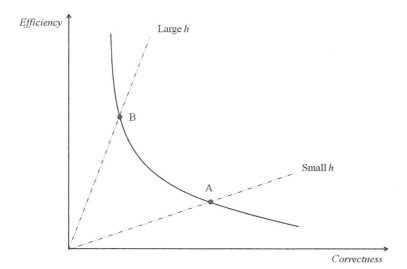

Fig. 4.6 Trade-off between estimation efficiency and correctness as function of the bandwidth h in nonparametric regression

a smaller h allows for a larger correctness accompanied with a smaller efficiency (point A).

The choice of the bandwidth h therefore seeks to balance efficiency and correctness. In the nonparametric statistics literature, two kinds of approaches have been proposed to choose the bandwidth: (1) plug-in estimation and (2) cross-validation (Pagan and Ullah 1999; Härdle 1991).

Before presenting these methods in the RDD contexts, it is first necessary to define the notion of "optimal" bandwidth for local nonparametric regressions. Given a generic regression function $m(x_0)$ evaluated at x_0 and given a nonparametric estimation $\widehat{m}(x_0)$ of such a function, we define the optimal bandwidth as the one minimizing the mean integrated square error (MISE) of $\widehat{m}(x_0)$, i.e.:

$$h^* = \mathrm{argmin}\left\{ \int \mathrm{MSE}[\widehat{m}(x_0)]f(x_0)dx_0 \right\} \qquad (4.93)$$

where MSE is the mean square error defined as:

$$\mathrm{MSE}[\widehat{m}(x_0)] = \mathrm{E}[\widehat{m}(x_0) - m(x_0)]^2 \qquad (4.94)$$

The MSE is in turn equal to:

$$\mathrm{MSE}[\widehat{m}(x_0)] = \mathrm{Var}\{\widehat{m}(x_0)\} + \{\mathrm{E}[\widehat{m}(x_0)] - m(x_0)\}^2 \qquad (4.95)$$

i.e., the variance of the nonparametric estimator of $m(x_0)$ plus its squared bias. In general, the optimal bandwidth is that which allows for the same asymptotic rate of convergence of the variance and the squared bias as the sample size goes to infinity. Thus, at least asymptotically, choosing a bandwidth different from the optimal one implies either increasing the rate of convergence to zero of the bias at the expenses of the rate of convergence of the efficiency ($h < h^*$ or *undersmoothing*) or increasing the rate of convergence to zero of the variance at the expenses of the rate of convergence of the bias ($h > h^*$, or *oversmoothing*).

Estimating the optimal bandwidth is not straightforward, since it is function of unknown quantities that have to in turn be estimated nonparametrically, thus requiring estimation of nested bandwidths. This produces a cyclicality which is computational burdensome and imprecise. Furthermore, in the context of RDD, we have to estimate two regressions around one single point, thus boundary problems also arise.

Recently, methods for estimating optimal bandwidths for RDD have been provided in the case of local linear regression. We distinguish between plug-in and cross-validation approaches.

Plug-in approach In the case of sharp RDD, assuming an estimation of ATE based on a local linear regression as in (4.70), Imbens and Kalyanaraman (2012) have suggested estimating h^* by minimizing the following MSE over h:

$$h^* = \text{argmin } E\left[\widehat{ATE}_{SRD} - ATE_{SRD}\right]^2$$

$$= \text{argmin } E[(\hat{a}_R - a_R) - (\hat{a}_L - a_L)]^2 \tag{4.96}$$

Using a mean square error approximation of previous formula and adopting a number of convenient assumptions (including "regularization"), the authors illustrate that the two-side unique estimation of the optimal bandwidth takes on the following form:

$$\hat{h}^*_{\text{Sharp-RDD}} = C_K \cdot \left(\frac{\hat{\sigma}_R^2(\bar{s}) - \hat{\sigma}_L^2(\bar{s})}{\hat{f}(\bar{s})[\hat{m}''_R(\bar{s}) - \hat{m}''_L(\bar{s})]^2 + \hat{r}_R + \hat{r}_L}\right)^{\frac{1}{5}} \cdot N^{-\frac{1}{5}} \tag{4.97}$$

where $\hat{\sigma}_j^2(\bar{s})$ is an estimation of $\text{Var}_j(Y \mid s = \bar{s})$; $\hat{m}''_j(\bar{s})$ is an estimation of the second derivative (curvature) of the regression curve; $\hat{f}(\bar{s})$ is an estimation of the density function of s at the threshold; $\hat{r}_j$ is an estimation of $\text{Var}\left[\hat{m}''_j(\bar{s})\right]$, with $j = R, L$. Computing (4.97) requires estimating all previous quantities that are unknown, which need to be nonparametrically estimated. Imbens and Kalyanaraman (2012), however, provide a consistent procedure to estimate the optimal bandwidth, involving the following steps:

1. Estimate the sample variance of the forcing variable and call it V_s^2. Use the so-called Silverman rule-of-thumb to estimate a pilot bandwidth h_1 using uniform kernel thus obtaining:

$$h_1 = 1 \cdot 84 \cdot V_s \cdot N^{-1/5} \tag{4.98}$$

2. Using h_1 as bandwidth, estimate $\hat{\sigma}_R^2(\bar{s})$ and $\hat{\sigma}_L^2(\bar{s})$ using sample equivalents and $\hat{f}(\bar{s})$ by a kernel approach;
3. Estimate $\hat{m}''_R(\bar{s})$ and $\hat{m}''_L(\bar{s})$ in the following manner: first, fit globally a third-order polynomial regression of this type:

$$Y_i = \gamma_0 + \gamma_1 \cdot 1[s_i \geq \bar{s}] + \gamma_2 \cdot (s_i - \bar{s}) + \gamma_3 \cdot (s_i - \bar{s})^2 + \gamma_4 \cdot (s_i - \bar{s})^3 + error \tag{4.99}$$

and estimate the third derivative of this function as $\hat{m}'''(s) = 6 \cdot \hat{\gamma}_4$. Calculate two pilot bandwidths as:

$$h_{2,R} = 3 \cdot 56 \cdot \left(\frac{\hat{\sigma}_R^2(\bar{s})}{\hat{f}(\bar{s})[\hat{m}'''(\bar{s})]^2}\right)^{1/7} \cdot N_R^{-1/7} \tag{4.100}$$

$$h_{2,L} = 3 \cdot 56 \cdot \left(\frac{\hat{\sigma}_L^2(\bar{s})}{\hat{f}(\bar{s})[\hat{m}'''(\bar{s})]^2} \right)^{1/7} \cdot N_L^{-1/7} \qquad (4.101)$$

where N_R and N_L are the number of observations in the right and left of the threshold. Given these pilot bandwidths, fit using OLS a local quadratic regression of Y on S on the right and left separately, using only those observations falling in the interval defined by $h_{2,R}$ and $h_{2,L}$, respectively. For the RHS, for example, this involves estimating:

$$Y_i = \lambda_0 + \lambda_1 \cdot 1[s_i \geq \bar{s}]\lambda_2 \cdot (s_i - \bar{s}) + \lambda_3 \cdot (s_i - \bar{s})^2 + error$$
$$i \in \{\bar{s} < s_i < \bar{s} + h_{2,R}\} \qquad (4.102)$$

thus estimating the curvature as $\hat{m}_R''(\bar{s}) = 2 \cdot \hat{\lambda}_3$, and similarly on the left side;
4. Finally, calculate the regularization terms as follows:

$$\hat{r}_R = \frac{2160 \cdot \hat{\sigma}_R^2(\bar{s})}{N_{2,R} \cdot h_{2,R}^4} \quad \text{and} \quad \hat{r}_L = \frac{2160 \cdot \hat{\sigma}_L^2(\bar{s})}{N_{2,L} \cdot h_{2,L}^4}$$

and set $C_K = 3 \cdot 4375$, thus providing the final ingredients required to feasibly calculate the optimal bandwidth as expressed in formula (4.97).

This procedure leads to a consistent estimation of the optimal bandwidth in the case of sharp RDD (Imbens and Kalyanaraman 2012, Theorem 4.1).

As for the estimation of the optimal bandwidth in the case of fuzzy RDD, the authors provide a formula and an estimation procedure very close to that previously illustrated for sharp RDD. In the case of fuzzy RDD, the proposed formula takes the following form:

$$\hat{h}_{\text{Fuzzy-RDD}}^* = C_K \cdot$$

$$\left(\frac{\left(\hat{\sigma}_{Y,R}^2(\bar{s}) + \hat{\sigma}_{Y,L}^2(\bar{s})\right) + \widehat{\text{ATE}}_{\text{FRD}}^2 \left(\hat{\sigma}_{D,R}^2(\bar{s}) + \hat{\sigma}_{D,L}^2(\bar{s})\right) - 2\widehat{\text{ATE}}_{\text{FRD}}\left(\hat{\sigma}_{YD,R}(\bar{s}) + \hat{\sigma}_{YD,L}(\bar{s})\right)}{\hat{f}(\bar{s})\left[\hat{m}_{Y,R}''(\bar{s}) - \hat{m}_{Y,L}''(\bar{s})\right]^2 - \widehat{\text{ATE}}_{\text{FRD}}\left[\hat{m}_{D,R}''(\bar{s}) - \hat{m}_{D,L}''(\bar{s})\right] + \hat{r}_{Y,R} + \hat{r}_{Y,L} + \widehat{\text{ATE}}_{\text{FRD}}[\hat{r}_{D,R} + \hat{r}_{D,L}]} \right)^{\frac{1}{5}}$$
$$\cdot N^{-\frac{1}{5}}$$

$$(4.103)$$

and estimation follows the same algorithm illustrated for the sharp RDD case, with the exception of the presence of the covariances between Y and D and few other terms that are to be additionally estimated. Of course, estimating such a formula is computationally more intensive and generally less precise because of the presence of a higher number of unknown terms. Fortunately, Imbens and Kalyanaraman find that in general such a formula provides bandwidths that are close to those based on the optimal bandwidth for estimation of only the numerator of the fuzzy RDD estimator. In other words, it is possible to use the algorithm provided for sharp

RDD, thus ignoring the fact that the Regression-discontinuity-design is fuzzy (Imbens and Kalyanaraman 2012, p. 14).

Cross-validation approach Ludwig and Miller (2007) and Imbens and Lemieux (2008) have proposed a cross-validation approach to select the optimal bandwidth in a local linear regression setting for RDD. Cross-validation is a general computational technique used for estimating the optimal bandwidth for nonparametric regressions when plug-in approaches may be problematic (Härdle and Marron 1985). Cross-validation is based on the "leave-one-out" procedure, in which a regression function is estimated by leaving out one observation at the time. In our RDD context, the cross-validation procedure requires the following steps:

1. Fix a given bandwidth h;
2. Consider an observation i. In order to assess the goodness of fit associated to the fixed h, perform a linear regression of Y on s by leaving out observation i. If s_i falls on the left of the cutoff, then estimate the regression only on those s belonging to $\{s_i - h; s_i\}$. If s_i falls on the right of the cutoff on the other hand, then estimate the regression only on those s belonging to $\{s_i; s_i + h\}$;
3. Estimate the predicted value of previous regression calculated at $s = s_i$ and call it $\widehat{Y}_{-i}(s_i)$;
4. Repeat steps 2 and 3 for each observation and finally compute the following quadratic loss function:

$$\mathrm{CV}_Y(h) = \frac{1}{N} \sum_{i=1}^{N} \left(\widehat{Y}_{-i} - \widehat{Y}_{-i}(s_i) \right)^2 \qquad (4.104)$$

which is the cross-validation criterion and is clearly a function of h;
5. The optimal bandwidth is the one which minimizes (4.104) over a grid of chosen h and such a minimum is found numerically.

In order to increase the precision of the bandwidth's estimate, Imbens and Lemieux (2008) suggest a cross-validation criterion with *trimming*, using specific quantiles of the distribution of s. On the left of the cutoff, one could, for example, use only observations having a value of s falling on the right of the median of s in that part. On the right of the cutoff, instead, one could use only observations having a value of s falling on the left of the median of s in that part. Of course, it is also possible to use a larger rule than the 50 % cutoff observations on both sides by choosing other quantiles.

In the case of fuzzy RDD, an identical cross-validation criterion can be used for estimating the conditional probabilities in the denominator of the fuzzy RDD estimand. In practice, Imbens and Lemieux (2008) suggest to use only one bandwidth, chosen as the smallest between $\mathrm{CV}_Y(h)$ and $\mathrm{CV}_D(h)$.

Finally, observe that the plug-in and the cross-validation approaches, although asymptotically equivalent, can lead to different estimations of the optimal bandwidth in finite samples.

4.3.3.2 Optimal Bandwidth for Local Polynomial Regression

The previous discussion regarding the choice of the bandwidth referred to the case of a local linear regression. When a local polynomial is fitted, one can however rely on the so-called rule-of-thumb (ROT) method of bandwidth selection based on a plug-in approach. Although not yet specifically derived for RDD, we know that for a generic function $m(s) = E(Y \mid s)$ to be estimated nonparametrically, the ROT is the asymptotically optimal constant bandwidth as it minimizes the conditional weighted mean integrated squared error. Following (Fan and Gijbels 1996), the ROT is estimated by:

$$
\widehat{h}_{\text{ROT, pol}} = C_{K,P} \cdot \left(\frac{\widehat{\sigma}^2 \int w_0(s)ds}{N \int \left(\widehat{m}^{(P+1)}(s) \right)^2 w_0(s)\widehat{f}(s)ds} \right)^{\frac{1}{2P+3}}
\tag{4.105}
$$

where: $C_{K,P}$ is a constant depending on the kernel function used and the degree P of the polynomial; $\widehat{\sigma}^2$ is the residual variance assumed to be constant over s; $w_0(s)$ is an indicator function on the interval $[min(s) + 0.05 \cdot range(s); max(s) - 0.05 \cdot range(s)]$ with $min(s), max(s)$, and $range(s)$ indicating the minimum, maximum, and the range of s, respectively; $\widehat{m}^{(P+1)}$ is an estimation of the $(P+1)$th derivative of $m(s)$ and $\widehat{f}(s)$ an estimation of the density of s.

In order to obtain an estimation of the constant residual variance and of the $(P+1)$th derivative of $m(s)$, a global polynomial fit in s of order $(P+3)$ is appropriate, thus estimating $\widehat{\sigma}^2$ by the standardized residual sum of squares of such regression.

Heuristically, one could estimate (4.105) either on the right or on the left of the cutoff, thus obtaining two different bandwidths on the two sides. One could then choose the same bandwidth on both sides by taking, for instance, an average of the two bandwidths or the lowest of them. Although this approach gives useful guidance for selecting the bandwidth, it is not specific to RDD, given the additional complication of finding an optimal bandwidth at a discontinuous point of s. It can however be used as an acceptable approximation. It goes without saying that checking robustness by providing a comparison of results for this and other possible choices of the bandwidth is highly recommended.

4.3.3.3 Choosing the Polynomial Order

Previous procedures detect the optimal bandwidth when a local linear regression is interpolated. When a local polynomial regression is used instead, a comparable optimal rule is not available and it becomes more important to decide in the first instance the order of the polynomial, and then calculate the RDD causal effect for different choices of the bandwidth (Lee and Lemieux 2009).

To detect the order of polynomial, one could use the traditional Akaike information criterion by comparing the value of such index for models with different polynomial order; the Akaike index takes the form:

$$\text{AIC} \cong N \cdot \ln\left(\frac{\text{RSS}}{N}\right) + 2(P+1) \tag{4.106}$$

where RSS is the residual sum of squares of the estimated regression and P the order of the polynomial. The specification with the smallest AIC should be selected.

The problem with this measure is that it is based on a global parametric regression, while in RDD we have stressed the role played by locality and non-parametric approach. Thus, in order to take into account this aspect, an alternative test for choosing the order of the polynomial has been proposed. The idea behind this test is that of choosing the order by rendering the explicative power of local information useless as explanation of the variance of the outcome Y. In practice, this is done by including K bin dummies B_k, for k going from 2 to $K-1$, into the polynomial regression thus fitting:

$$Y_i = \alpha_L + \text{ATE} \cdot D_i + \sum_{p=1}^{P} \delta_{L,p}(s_i - \bar{s})^p$$

$$+ D_i \sum_{p=1}^{P} \left(\delta_{R,p} - \delta_{L,p}\right) \cdot (s_i - \bar{s})^p + \sum_{k=2}^{K-1} \phi_k B_{k,i} + \varepsilon \tag{4.107}$$

and then testing the null hypothesis that $\phi_2 = \phi_3 = \cdots = \phi_{K-1} = 0$; one should choose a P corresponding to the polynomial specification leading to accept such hypothesis; one should continue to add higher order terms until it is rejected.

Of course, the choice of the number of bins to be included will depend on the choice of the bandwidth h and should follow such a procedure:

1. For a given bandwidth h, fix the number of bins equal to $K = K_L + K_R$, where K_L is the number of bins on the left and K_R the one on the right of the threshold;
2. Define the k-th bin as the interval $(b_k; b_{k+1}]$ for k going from 1 to K, where:

$$b_k = \bar{s} - (K_0 - k + 1) \cdot h \tag{4.108}$$

3. For each observation i, construct the generic dummy $B_{k,i}$ as:

$$B_{k,i} = \begin{cases} 1 & \text{if} \quad i \in (b_k; b_{k+1}] \\ 0 & \text{otherwise} \end{cases} \qquad (4.109)$$

with k going from 1 to K.

It is worth stressing that in regression (4.107), two bin dummies are excluded because of collinearity.

A further benefit of such an approach is that it is also useful to detect discontinuity in the conditional expectation of the outcome different from that in the threshold. To see how, assume we have built only two bins, so that regression (4.107) becomes:

$$E(Y_i \mid s_i; D_i; B_{2,i}) = f(s_i; D_i) + \phi_2 B_{2,i} \qquad (4.110)$$

where $f(s_i; D_i)$ is the polynomial. Using (4.110), we see that

$$\phi_2 = E(Y_i \mid s_i; D_i; B_{2,i} = 1) - E(Y_i \mid s_i; D_i; B_{2,i} = 0) \qquad (4.111)$$

thus, as long as $\phi_2 \neq 0$, a discontinuity in the conditional mean of the outcome arises. Such a discontinuity can jeopardize the RDD continuity assumption; thus, since testing $\phi_2 = \phi_3 = \cdots = \phi_{K-1} = 0$ is equivalent to test whether $\phi_{K-1} - \phi_{K-1} = 0$, accepting such an hypothesis is necessary to assure RDD reliability.

For practical purposes, Lee and Lemieux (2009, p. 48) suggest to use: higher order polynomials when the bandwidth is large (i.e., equal or more than 0.50); lower order polynomials for bandwidths ranging between 0.05 and 0.50; finally, zero order polynomials for bandwidths lower than 0.05. Note that the choice of zero order polynomial coincides with the comparison of the two means as expressed by (4.63).

4.3.4 Accounting for Additional Covariates

Although the identification assumptions behind a reliable use of RDD do not involve any exploitation of the additional covariates $\mathbf{x}$, usually present in standard datasets, using such additional information may be worthwhile.

Firstly, additional covariates can be used to test whether, around the threshold, conditions for a quasi-randomized experiment are correctly in place. In general, one should not find any statistically significant discontinuities of $\mathbf{x}$ at the threshold. If they are in fact found, we could erroneously attribute the effect to the treatment when, on the contrary, the effect could have been driven by discontinuities in the covariates. This is the typical "observable confounders' effect" we met several times in previous chapters. We will come back on this point more in detail in the next section.

Secondly, as long as discontinuities in **x** can be excluded, it may be wise to add the variables **x** in previous RDD regressions in order to eliminate some minor biases arising from the use of a too large bandwidth, including observations far from the threshold. In such a situation, conditioning on **x** would provide a good account of units' observable differences either to the left or to the right of the threshold.

Thirdly, as also happens in pure randomized settings, including covariates which have some nonnegligible explicative power on the outcome, generally increases the precision of the estimations by reducing standard errors. Furthermore, they may also increase the R^2 of the regression, thus providing a more compelling fit of the model.

4.3.5 Testing RDD Reliability

It is essential, when applying RDD, to carry out a series of tests to assess the RDD reliability. This allows to evaluate whether the assumptions under which RDD should return correct inference are actually met in practice. In what follows, we provide a number of tests that, taken altogether, should help practitioners when running RDD analysis on real datasets.

Testing quasi-randomness at the threshold

In order to assess whether the "natural experiment" approximation at the threshold characterizing RDD is appropriate, the calculation of difference-in-means (DIM) estimators for the covariates **x** is recommended, comparing units' characteristics on the left and right of the threshold. If no significant differences are found, then the assumption of randomness in a neighborhood of the cutoff can be accepted. In other words, a sort of "balancing property," very similar to the one defined for Matching methods in Chap. 3, has to be tested. If the threshold is well defined, then the mean of the **x**-variables on the right and left of the cutoff point should be approximately the same. If not, the threshold is not a good demarcating point and the idea to replicate a natural experiment around that point should be questioned.

Testing "non-manipulation" of the forcing variable

To be reliable, RDD requires that the forcing variable is not manipulated by individuals. Manipulation means that individuals may strategically modify the value of the variable s in order to take advantage of changing position around the cutoff. When this is the case, one cannot trust the idea that s is purely exogenous as it becomes, on the contrary, a variable determined by individuals and thus inherently endogenous.

For example, Article 18 of the Italian labour legislation ("workers' statute") establishes that Italian companies with more than 15 employees must reinstate unfairly dismissed workers, provided that the Italian courts decide whether or not dismissals are justified. As judges usually tend to be sympathetic with workers, thus deciding to reinstate workers most of the time, there is an ongoing debate in Italy around the suitability of such a rule. Since companies with less than 15 employees are not subject to Article 18, the "15 threshold" might be a good candidate for a cutoff point to assess, by means of an RDD, whether Article 18 produces or not adverse effects on company activity. Yet, since companies can control, at least to some relevant extent, the number of employees, the idea that around the 15 threshold a natural experiment takes place is somewhat questionable. Companies may, for example, not extend their workforce beyond the threshold in order to avoid Article 18 constrains. Many other examples of this kind are set out in the literature.

McCrary (2008) has suggested testing the presence of such manipulation by assessing the continuity of the density of the forcing variable at the threshold. Although the presence of a discontinuity should not be immediately interpreted as representing some form of manipulation, when the discontinuity is relevant, some doubts about pure randomization at the cutoff may be cast. Figure 4.7 displays two different shapes of the density function of the forcing variable, with panel (a) representing a continuity at the threshold (non-manipulation case) and panel (b) a strong discontinuity (possible manipulation).

Note that in such graphical representations, it is recommended not to use kernel density estimates, rather histograms with different numbers of bins.

Testing the continuity of the outcome conditional expectation

We have seen that continuity of the conditional expectation of the potential outcomes at the cutoff is necessary in order to identify ATE in an RDD setting. As suggested by Imbens and Lemieux (2008), one possible way to test whether such condition holds in our data is to estimate the jump of the conditional expectation of Y at points of the forcing variable different from that of the threshold. On both the left and right side of the cutoff, one can consider a specific quantile of the (left and right) distribution of s such as, for example, the median. One can then run an RDD using formula (4.70) by substituting $\bar{s}$ with $q_{s,\tau,L}$ (in the left) and $q_{s,\tau,L}$ (in the right), which indicate the value of the specific quantile τ in the two sides, respectively. For instance, τ is equal to 0.5 for the median. If we accept the null hypothesis of a no

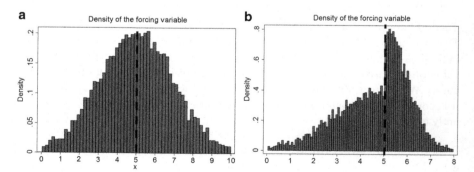

Fig. 4.7 Density function of the forcing variable. Panel (**a**) sets out a continuity at the threshold (non-manipulation case), whereas panel (**b**) shows a strong discontinuity suggesting some manipulation on the part of the individuals

jump on both the left and right side, we can conclude fairly reliably that the continuity of the conditional expectation of the outcome is confirmed and RDD results trustable.

Testing the sensitivity of results to different bandwidths and polynomial orders
As argued above, the choice of the bandwidth and that of the polynomial order can remarkably affect the results of an RDD. Although the literature has suggested ways to find optimal bandwidths and polynomial order, it is worthwhile conducting a sensitivity analysis presenting results for a range of bandwidths and various polynomial orders. Such a sensitivity test is important to guarantee transparence in the results and, possibly, inconsistencies of the dataset (due, for instance, to the presence of outliers).

4.3.6 A Protocol for Practical Implementation of RDD

As a final step, following Imbens and Lemieux (2008) and Lee and Lemieux (2009), it seems useful to summarize previous discussions by providing some guidelines for implementing RDD empirically.

A plausible protocol for implementing sharp RDD may be the following:

1. *Visualizing outcome discontinuity.* To this end, plot two overlapping histograms of the outcome variable, one for values of Y on the left and one for values of Y on the right of the cutoff by varying the number of bins. See whether there is evidence of a significant difference of such distributions.
2. *Testing balancing at the threshold.* Once the discontinuity at the threshold has been detected, look at whether, in a neighborhood of the threshold, the characteristics $\mathbf{x}$ of individuals placed on the left and on the right of the cutoff are sufficiently similar. If not, randomization may be questionable and RDD possibly invalidated. If yes, local randomization can be accepted and one can proceed to step 3.
3. *Testing non-manipulation of the forcing variable.* To assess whether the forcing variable is properly exogenous, plot its density and see whether a discontinuity at the threshold is visible. If yes, RDD may not be reliable; if not, proceed to step 4.
4. *Estimating ATE by sharp RDD.* If step 1, 2, and 3 have been satisfied, consider a given bandwidth as, for instance, the optimal one provided in (4.97), and use a local linear regression to calculate ATE by (4.70), with standard errors obtained using robust OLS. For the sake of comparison, calculate ATE as the difference of the outcome means in the left and in the right of the cutoff using a standard t-test.
5. *Checking robustness.* First, look at the possible presence of discontinuities in the covariates $\mathbf{x}$, by using the quantile approach proposed by Imbens and Lemieux (2008) presented in the previous section. If discontinuities are present, then argue why (or why not) RDD results should be questionable. Second, try various additional RDD estimation by varying the bandwidth and the polynomial order

of the basic local regression. Third, add covariates to previous regressions to see what happens to results. Finally, assess whether results are similar or significantly different.

A similar protocol for implementing fuzzy RDD may encompass:

1. *Visual analysis of outcome and treatment discontinuity.* Plot two overlapping histograms of the outcome variable and two overlapping histograms of the probability of treatment, one for values of Y and $p(D = 1)$ on the left and one for values of Y and $p(D = 1)$ on the right of the threshold by varying the number of bins. See whether there is evidence of a significant difference of such distributions.
2. *Testing balancing at the threshold.* Follow the same procedure outlined in step 2 for sharp RDD.
3. *Testing non-manipulation of the forcing variable.* Follow the same procedure outlined in step 3 for sharp RDD.
4. *Estimating ATE by fuzzy RDD.* If previous steps have been successfully implemented, consider a given bandwidth as, for instance, the fuzzy optimal one in (4.103), and use a local linear regression to calculate ATE by (4.88)–(4.89), standard errors being obtained by robust 2SLS, using the T variable as instrument for treatment. Just for the sake of comparison, calculate ATE as the ratio between the difference of the outcome means and the difference in the probability of treatment in the left and in the right of the cutoff obtaining standard errors by bootstrap.
5. *Checking robustness.* Follow the procedure outlined in point 5 for the practical implementation of sharp RDD.

Of course, the guidelines presented above are to be considered tentative and the minimal protocol to follow, as other relevant steps will depend on the specific context of the application in hand.

4.4 Application and Implementation

This section is dedicated to the application and implementation of LATE and RDD. We begin with LATE first to go on with RDD. Both the sharp and the fuzzy cases are considered.

4.4.1 An Application of LATE

In this section we present an application of LATE to both real and simulated data. In the first case, we consider an exercise using the same data as Angrist and Evans (1998). In the second case, we simulated a specific data generating process (DGP) for LATE in order to check the reliability of the Stata code developed in the application on real data.

4.4.1.1 LATE Estimation with Real Data

We consider the dataset CHILDREN.DTA containing a subset of data from the paper by Angrist and Evans (1998) where the authors investigate the effect of childbearing on female labor market participation (labor supply). The dataset comes from the 1980 Census Public Use Micro Samples (PUMS) and considers a sample of married women aged within 21 and 35 having at least two children. In order to capture childbearing the authors assume a binary covariate having a value equal to one for additional childbearing (more than two children), and zero otherwise.

In order to deal with a potential omitted-variables bias that OLS would produce, Angrist and Evans (1998) suggest estimating the relationship between childbearing and labor participation of women by a LATE estimator using as an instrument a binary variable accounting for "sibling sex composition," indicating whether the first two children are of the same sex or not. The choice of this variable as instrument rests on the assumption that when parents have already had two children of the same sex, they will be more prone to have a third children than in the case in which the gender of the first two kids is different. On the one hand, having a mixed pair of children can be taken as a random event, thus being independent of potential outcomes or other characteristics of women; on the other hand, this is a variable expected to be correlated with having had more than two kids. Sibling sex composition, therefore, seems a good candidate as instrument for childbearing.

As the outcome variable for this example, we consider the variable "*weeksm*," indicating the number of weeks worked by women; as treatment variable, we consider the dummy "*morethan2*," having a value one if the woman has had more than two children and zero otherwise; as instrument, we use the variable "*samesex*," taking value one if the first two kids are same sex and zero otherwise.

We set out this application by declaring a series of global macros:

```
. set more off
. global Y weeksm   // outcome
. cap drop morethan2
. gen morethan2=(kidcount>2)
. global D morethan2 // treatment
. global z samesex   // instrument
```

As a first step, we calculate LATE by hand, to then observe that the obtained value is equivalent to a 2SLS of Y on D, using z as instrument for D. To begin with, we calculate the DIM estimator of ATE by running this OLS regression:

```
. reg $Y $D
      Source |       SS          df       MS                    Number of obs  =    254654
-------------+------------------------------------             F(  1,254652)  =   3696.02
       Model |   1742078.14       1   1742078.14               Prob > F       =    0.0000
    Residual |   120027337254652     471.338679                R-squared      =    0.0143
-------------+------------------------------------             Adj R-squared  =    0.0143
       Total |   121769415254653     478.177816                Root MSE       =     21.71

      weeksm1 |     Coef.    Std. Err.      t     P>|t|    [95% Conf.  Interval]
-------------+----------------------------------------------------------------------------
    morethan2 |  -5.386996    .0886093    -60.79   0.000    -5.560667   -5.213324
        _cons |   21.06843    .0546629    385.42   0.000    20.96129    21.17557
```

We find out an ATE equal to -5.38, which we assume to be biased as some selection on unobservables is assumed. In such a situation, we can estimate the value of LATE by using formula (4.22) as follows (observe that no use of the covariates is needed at this stage):

- Compute an estimate of $E(Y \mid z = 1)$ and put it into a scalar:

```
. qui sum $Y if $z == 1
. scalar mean_y_z1 = r(mean)
```

- Compute an estimate of $E(Y \mid z = 0)$ and put it into a scalar:

```
. qui sum $Y if $z == 0
. scalar mean_y_z0 = r(mean)
```

- Compute an estimate of $p(D = 1 \mid z = 1)$ and put it into a scalar:

```
. count if $D == 1 & $z == 1
. scalar num_d_z1 = r(N)
. count if $z==1
. scalar num_z1 = r(N)
. scalar p_1_1 = num_d_z1/num_z1
```

- Compute an estimate of $p(D = 1 \mid z = 0)$ and put it into a scalar:

```
. count if $D == 1 & $z == 0
. scalar num_d_z0 = r(N)
. count if $z==0
. scalar num_z0 = r(N)
. scalar p_1_0 = num_d_z0/num_z0
```

• Compute the value of LATE and put it into a scalar:

```
. scalar late = (mean_y_z1-mean_y_z0)/(p_1_1-p_1_0)
```

We can finally look at the value of LATE typing:

```
. di late
-6.3136852
```

showing that LATE is equal to -6.313. Such a value can also be obtained by a 2SLS estimation as follows:

```
. ivreg $Y ($D = $z)
Instrumental variables (2SLS) regression
      Source |       SS       df       MS              Number of obs =   254654
-------------+------------------------------           F(  1,254652) =    24.54
       Model |  1690526.44        1  1690526.44        Prob > F      =   0.0000
    Residual |  120078889254652  471.541119            R-squared     =   0.0139
-------------+------------------------------           Adj R-squared =   0.0139
       Total |  121769415254653  478.177816            Root MSE      =   21.715

------------------------------------------------------------------------------
     weeksm1 |      Coef.   Std. Err.      t    P>|t|     [95% Conf. Interval]
-------------+----------------------------------------------------------------
    morethan2 |  -6.313685   1.274604    -4.95   0.000    -8.811875   -3.815496
       _cons |   21.42109   .4869726    43.99   0.000     20.46664    22.37555
------------------------------------------------------------------------------
Instrumented:  morethan2
Instruments:   samesex
------------------------------------------------------------------------------
```

confirming what was expected. Observe that our results indicate a positive bias of around 14.6 % in the OLS estimation.

We can move on to estimate LATE($\mathbf{x}$) using the Abadie-kappas in order to estimate (4.26) and the so-called LARF. A set of exogenous covariates $\mathbf{x}$ is now needed. Following the authors, we consider the following set: "*agem*," age of the mother at 1980 census; "*agefstm*," age of the mother when she gave birth to the first child; "*boy1st*," dummy taking one if the first child was a boy; "*boy2nd*," taking value one if the second child was a boy; "*black*," dummy equal to one if the mother is black; "*hispan*," equal to one if the mother is Hispanic; and, finally, "*othrace*," taking value one if the mother belongs to other ethnic group.

To begin with, these covariates are placed into the global macro xvars:

```
. global xvars agem agefstm boy1st boy2nd black hispan othrace
```

We calculate the Abadie-kappas as follows:

- Start by computing $E(z \mid Y, D = 1, \mathbf{x})$:

```
. probit $z $Y $xvars if $D==1
. predict p_z1 , p   // that is equal to E(z|Y,D=1,x)
```

- Compute $E(z \mid Y, D = 0, \mathbf{x})$:

```
. probit $z $Y $xvars if $D==0
. predict p_z0 , p   // that is equal to E(z|Y,D=0,x)
```

- Compute $p(z = 1 \mid \mathbf{x})$:

```
. probit $z $xvars
. predict p_z , p   // that is equal to p(z=1|x)
```

- Compute $E(k \mid Y, D, \mathbf{x})$

```
. gen Ek = 1- $D*(1-p_z1)/(1-p_z) - (1-$D)*p_z0/p_z
```

- Eliminate values of $E(k \mid Y, D, \mathbf{x})$ not included within $[0; 1]$:

```
. replace Ek=1 if Ek>=1 & Ek!=.
. replace Ek=0 if Ek<=0 & Ek!=.
```

- Compute the Weighted least squares (WLS) using $E(k \mid Y, D, \mathbf{x})$ as weights:

```
regress $Y $D $xvars [pweight=Ek]
```

```
----------------------------------------------------------------------
Linear regression                          Number of obs =    252248
                                           F(  8,252239) =   1975.86
                                           Prob > F      =    0.0000
                                           R-squared     =    0.0748
                                           Root MSE      =    20.773
----------------------------------------------------------------------
```

weeksm1	Coef.	Robust Std. Err.	t	P>|t|	[95% Conf. Interval]	
morethan2	-5.435849	.090615	-59.99	0.000	-5.613452	-5.258246
agem1	1.411412	.0147141	95.92	0.000	1.382573	1.440251
agefstm	-1.481689	.0181049	-81.84	0.000	-1.517174	-1.446204
boy1st	-.4159261	.0902139	-4.61	0.000	-.592743	-.2391092
boy2nd	-.499382	.0901446	-5.54	0.000	-.6760631	-.3227009
black	10.51577	.2205934	47.67	0.000	10.08341	10.94812

```
       hispan |    .136516    .1939291     0.70   0.481     -.2435798     .5166118
      othrace |    2.99749    .2269159    13.21   0.000      2.552741     3.442239
        _cons |   7.531347    .4402346    17.11   0.000      6.668499     8.394195
     -----------------------------------------------------------------------------
```

The value of LATE is now found to be approximately -5.43 and is still significant. We might however be interested in estimating LARF for $D = 1$ and $D = 0$. For $D = 1$, we want to obtain an estimate of:

$$E(Y \mid D = 1, D_1 > D_0) = E_{\mathbf{x}}\{E(Y \mid \mathbf{x}, D = 1, D_1 > D_0)\}$$

which can be obtained in Stata using the `margins` command as follows[3]:

```
. margins , at($D=1) atmeans
-----------------------------------------|-------------------------------------
Adjusted predictions                             Number of obs    =     252248
Model VCE      : Robust
Expression     : Linear prediction, predict()
at             : morethan2      =           1
                 agem1          =    30.83818  (mean)
                 agefstm        =    20.57244  (mean)
                 boy1st         =    .4338817  (mean)
                 boy2nd         =    .4310196  (mean)
                 black          =    .0388756  (mean)
                 hispan         =    .0643707  (mean)
                 othrace        =    .0511755  (mean)
-------------------------------------------------------------------------------
             |            Delta-method
             |    Margin   Std. Err.      t    P>|t|     [95% Conf. Interval]
-------------+-----------------------------------------------------------------
       _cons |   15.31421   .0669219   228.84   0.000     15.18305     15.44538
-------------------------------------------------------------------------------
```

The result obtained suggests that, among the compliers' subgroup, the average of Y (number of weeks worked) for those compliers who are treated (i.e., $D = 1$)— once observable confounders are neutralized—is equal to 15.31; observe that it is roughly the same as the unconditional average outcome of all treated we obtain by typing:

---

[3] Observe that variables' mean at which predictions are calculated using `margins` are in this case weighted means; for instance, for variable "*agem1*" this weighted mean can be got by typing: `sum agem1 [iweight=Ek]` returning exactly 30.83818.

```
. sum $Y if $D==1
    Variable |        Obs        Mean    Std. Dev.        Min         Max
-------------+-----------------------------------------------------------
     weeksm1 |      96912     15.68143    20.76991          0          52
```

Similarly, we can get an estimate of LARF for $D = 0$, i.e.:

$$E(Y \mid D = 0, D_1 > D_0) = E_{\mathbf{x}}\{E(Y \mid \mathbf{x}, D = 0, D_1 > D_0)\}$$

by typing:

```
. margins , at($D=0) atmeans
--------------------------------------------------------------------------
Adjusted predictions                            Number of obs   =     252248
Model VCE     : Robust
Expression    : Linear prediction, predict()
at            : morethan2      =          0
                agem1          =    30.83818  (mean)
                agefstm        =    20.57244  (mean)
                boy1st         =    .4338817  (mean)
                boy2nd         =    .4310196  (mean)
                black          =    .0388756  (mean)
                hispan         =    .0643707  (mean)
                othrace        =    .0511755  (mean)
--------------------------------------------------------------------------
             |            Delta-method
             |    Margin   Std. Err.      t    P>|t|    [95% Conf. Interval]
-------------+------------------------------------------------------------
       _cons |  20.75006   .0610766  339.74   0.000     20.63036    20.86977
--------------------------------------------------------------------------
```

illustrating that, among the compliers' subgroup, the average of Y for those compliers that are untreated (i.e., $D = 0$)—when observable confounders are neutralized—is equal to 20.75. Note that it is slightly lower than the unconditional average outcome of all untreated obtained by typing:

```
. sum $Y if $D==0
    Variable |        Obs        Mean    Std. Dev.        Min         Max
-------------+-----------------------------------------------------------
     weeksm1 |     157742     21.06843    22.26841          0          52
```

Moreover, we can see that:

$$\text{LATE} = E(Y \mid D = 1, D_1 > D_0) - E(Y \mid D = 0, D_1 > D_0)$$

since it is immediate to see that: $(15.31 - 20.75) = -5.43$

We can also calculate the predictions used by `margins` to calculate previous means. In other words, we are interested in computing both $E(Y \mid \mathbf{x}, D = 1, D_1 > D_0)$ and $E(Y \mid \mathbf{x}, D = 0, D_1 > D_0)$. In estimating previous quantities, we proceed as follows:

- Estimate $E(Y \mid \mathbf{x}, D = 1, D_1 > D_0)$ calling it `y_1est` by typing:

```
. cap drop y_1est
. qui regress $Y $xvars [pweight=Ek] if $D==1
. predict y_1est
. sum y_1est [iweight=Ek]
    Variable |     Obs      Weight       Mean   Std. Dev.       Min        Max
-------------+----------------------------------------------------------------
      y_1est |  252248  17613.8365   15.30617    4.80354   2.605387   36.65147
```

- Estimate $E(Y \mid \mathbf{x}, D = 0, D_1 > D_0)$ calling it `y_0est` by typing:

```
. cap drop y_0est
. qui regress $Y $xvars [pweight=Ek] if $D==0
. predict y_0est
. sum y_0est [iweight=Ek]
    Variable |     Obs      Weight       Mean   Std. Dev.       Min        Max
-------------+----------------------------------------------------------------
      y_0est |  252248  17613.8365   20.73786   5.747229   5.344197   45.69891
```

Observe that: $15.30 - 20.73 = -5.43 = \text{LATE}$

- Obtain a joint density plot of the estimations by typing:

```
. graph twoway ///
(kdensity y_1est [aweight=Ek] , lpattern (solid))   ///
(kdensity y_0est [aweight=Ek] , lpattern(dash)) , ///
title("Outcome response distr. for compliers by treatment" , size(med)) ///
xtitle(E(Y|x,D;compliers)) ///
legend(label(1 "D=1: treated compliers") label(2 "D=0: untreated compliers"))
///
note(Note: A linear form of the potential outcomes is assumed)
```

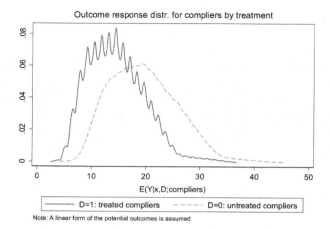

The above graph shows that treated women compliers have a lower tendency to supply work than untreated compliers. Furthermore, this difference can be interpreted in a causal sense, as the difference in means of the two distributions returns exactly the LATE equal to -5.43.

Finally, we can plot directly the distribution of LATE($\mathbf{x}$) as follows:

```
. cap drop late_x
. gen late_x = y_1est - y_0est
. tw (kdensity late_x) [aweight=Ek] , title(Distribution of LATE(x)) xtitle(LATE(x))
```

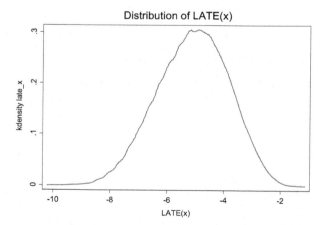

The density of LATE($\mathbf{x}$) has a clear bell-shaped form centered in LATE that is equal to the mean of such distribution.

4.4.1.2   LATE Estimation with Simulated Data

In this sub-section, we generate a simulated dataset. The usefulness of working with a simulation is twofold. On the one hand, it is a good exercise itself obliging us to determine the data generating process behind a quasi-randomized experiment (i.e., experiment with imperfect compliance). On the other hand, it allows us to compare data results with simulated results, thus providing a useful tool to determine whether our generating process and formulas are correct. The Stata code for the data generating process (DGP) of LATE is as follows:

```
* Data generating process for LATE
. clear
. set seed 10101
. set obs 5000
. gen z = uniform()>.5  // assign the instrument randomly
. sort z
. gen D1=rnormal()>0  // generate D1
. gen D0=5+5*rnormal()>0 // generate D0
. tostring D1 D0 , replace
. gen group=D1+D0
. encode group , generate(group2)
. la def gr_lab 1 never_taker 2 defier 3 complier 4 always_taker
. la values group2 gr_lab
. drop if group2==2
. destring D0 D1 , replace
. gen D=D0+z*(D1-D0)
. gen x=rnormal(0,1)
. gen y1 = 20 + 3*x + (rchi2(1)-1)
. gen y0 = 10 + 6*x + 5*rnormal(0,1)
*LATE=E(y1-y0)=(20-10)+(6-3)E(x)=10+3*0=10
. gen te=y1-y0 // treatment effect
. sum te
. gen y=y0+D0*(y1-y0)+z*(D1-D0)*(y1-y0)
```

In this DGP, LATE is fixed equal to 9.76. This is obtained by typing:

```
* LATE in the DGP
. sum te if group2==3
. scalar LATE_dgp=r(mean)
. di LATE_dgp
9.7633642
```

For the sake of comparison, we calculate LATE by hand using the Wald estimator formula as follows:

```
* E(y|z=1)
. qui reg y if z==1
. scalar yz1=_b[_cons]
* E(y|z=0)
. qui reg y if z==0
. scalar yz0=_b[_cons]
* E(D|z=1)
. qui reg D if z==1
. scalar Dz1=_b[_cons]
* E(D|z=0)
. qui reg D if z==0
. scalar Dz0=_b[_cons]
* Wald estimator
. scalar wald=(yz1-yz0)/(Dz1-Dz0)
. di wald
9.8477456
```

The compliers can be characterized by counting their number and characteristics, by treatment status. In our DGP, it is immediate to see that the number of compliers is equal to:

```
. count if group2==3
404
```

We can estimate this value by using the formula provided in the theoretical part of this chapter, that is:

$$N \cdot p(D_1 > D_0) = N[p(D = 1 \mid z = 1) - p(D = 1 \mid z = 0)]$$

obtained in Stata by writing:

```
. scalar Num_compl=_N*(Dz1-Dz0)
. di Num_compl
397.43418
```

showing, as expected, that we do a slight sample error of around 1.7 % ($=|(404 - 397)/404| \times 100$) when we use previous formula.

In order to characterize compliers, we can apply the formula:

$$E(x \mid D_1 > D_0) = E(k \cdot x)/E(k)$$

where first we need to compute k; to that aim, we write:

```
*compute p_xz=p(z=1|x)
. probit z x
. cap drop p_zx
. predict p_zx , p
. cap drop k
. gen k = 1-D*(1-z)/(1-p_zx)-(1-D)*z/p_zx
*compute E(k)
. sum k
. scalar sc_Ek=r(mean)
. di sc_Ek
*compute kx=k·x
. cap drop kx
. gen kx=k*x
. sum kx
. scalar sc_Ekx=r(mean)
```

Given k, we can compute the mean of x in the compliers' subgroup as follows:

```
*Compute E(x|D1>D0)=E(k·x)/E(k)
. scalar sc_ExD1D0=sc_Ekx/sc_Ek
. di sc_ExD1D0
.09138501
```

where a mean equal to 0.091 is obtained. The true value obtained by our DGP is:

```
* Calculate E(x|D1>D0)=E(x|compliers) as from simulation
. sum x if group2==3
    Variable |        Obs        Mean    Std. Dev.        Min         Max
-------------+--------------------------------------------------------------
           x |        404    .0855207     1.003132   -2.946875    2.853899
```

The value obtained, 0.085, is only slightly lower than the estimated value. If we run the DGP using a larger sample size (as, for instance $N = 200{,}000$), we can see that the simulated and estimated values are reasonably similar.

We can now go on to estimate LATE($\mathbf{x}$) using the Abadie-kappas to estimate (4.26), the so-called LARF. To this end, we first calculate the Abadie-kappas as we did with real data as follows:

```
*start by computing E(z | Y, D=1, x):
. probit z y x if D==1
. predict p_z1 , p  // that is equal to E(z|Y,D=1,x)
*compute E(z | Y, D=0, x):
. probit z y x if D==0
. predict p_z0 , p  // that is equal to E(z|Y,D=0,x)
*compute p(z=1 | x):
. probit z x
. predict p_z , p  // that is equal to p(z=1|x)
*compute E(k | Y, D, x)
. gen Ek = 1- D*(1-p_z1)/(1-p_z)-(1-D)*p_z0/p_z
*eliminate values of E(k | Y, D, x) not included within [0;1]:
. replace Ek=1 if Ek>=1 & Ek!=.
. replace Ek=0 if Ek<=0 & Ek!=.
*compute the weighted least squares (WLS) using E(k|Y,D,x) as weights:
. regress y D x [pweight=Ek]
--------------------------------------------------------------------------
Linear regression                              Number of obs =     2909
                                               F( 2,  2906) = 1715.83
                                               Prob > F      =  0.0000
                                               R-squared     =  0.7279
                                               Root MSE      =   3.979
--------------------------------------------------------------------------
             |               Robust
           y |     Coef.   Std. Err.      t    P>|t|    [95% Conf. Interval]
-------------+------------------------------------------------------------
           D |   9.15505   .2166926    42.25   0.000    8.730163   9.579936
           x |    4.5947   .1187562    38.69   0.000    4.361845   4.827554
       _cons |    10.315   .2132976    48.36   0.000    9.896768   10.73323
--------------------------------------------------------------------------
```

The value of LATE is now around 9.15, that is a bit lower than the true value 9.76. We might also be interested in estimating LARF for $D = 1$ and $D = 0$. For $D = 1$ and $D = 0$, we want to get an estimate of $E(Y \mid D = 1, D_1 > D_0)$ and $E(Y \mid D = 0, D_1 > D_0)$, respectively, which can be obtained in Stata using the `margins` command as follows:

```
. margins , at(D=1) atmeans
--------------------------------------------------------------------------
Adjusted predictions                           Number of obs  =     2909
Model VCE    : Robust
Expression   : Linear prediction, predict()
at           : D         =           1
               x         =    .0924395 (mean)
```

```
                  --------------------------------------------------------------------------------
                  |              Delta-method
                  |      Margin   Std. Err.      t    P>|t|     [95% Conf. Interval]
        ----------+---------------------------------------------------------------------
            _cons |   19.89478   .0364695   545.52   0.000     19.82327    19.96629
                  --------------------------------------------------------------------------------

. margins , at(D=0) atmeans

                  --------------------------------------------------------------------------------
Adjusted predictions                              Number of obs   =        2909
Model VCE       : Robust
Expression      : Linear prediction, predict()
at              : D                =              0
                  x                =       .0924395 (mean)

                  --------------------------------------------------------------------------------
                  |              Delta-method
                  |      Margin   Std. Err.      t    P>|t|     [95% Conf. Interval]
        ----------+---------------------------------------------------------------------
            _cons |   10.73973   .2135455    50.29   0.000     10.32101    11.15845
                  --------------------------------------------------------------------------------
```

We can see that $\text{LATE} = E(Y \mid D = 1, D_1 > D_0) - E(Y \mid D = 0, D_1 > D_0) = 9.15$.

We can also calculate the predictions used by `margins` to calculate previous means. In other words, we are interested in computing both:

$$E(Y \mid \mathbf{x}, D = 1, D_1 > D_0) \quad \text{and} \quad E(Y \mid \mathbf{x}, D = 0, D_1 > D_0)$$

In the simulated DGP, the true values of these quantities are computed as follows:

```
* calculate now E(y|x,D=1,D1>D0) in the DGP:
. cap drop y_1dgp
. gen y_1dgp= 20+3*x if D==1 & group2==3
* calculate now E(y|x,D=0,D1>D0) in the DGP:
. cap drop y_0dgp
. gen y_0dgp= 10+6*x if D==0 & group2==3
```

and a graph can be plotted as:

```
. graph twoway ///
(kdensity y_1dgp , lpattern (solid)) ///
(kdensity y_0dgp , lpattern(dash)) , ///
title("Outcome response distr. for compliers by treatment in DGP" , size(med))
///
```

```
xtitle(E(Y|x,D;compliers)) ///
legend(label(1 "D=1: treated compliers") label(2 "D=0: untreated compliers"))
///
note(Note: A linear form of the potential outcomes is assumed)
```

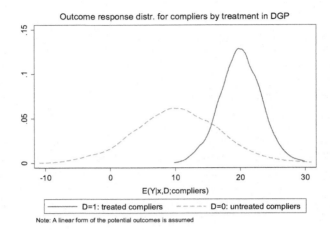

Note: A linear form of the potential outcomes is assumed

In the estimation phase previous quantities are instead computed as follows:

```
. qui regress y x [pweight=Ek] if D==1
. predict y_1est
. qui regress y x [pweight=Ek] if D==0
. predict y_0est
```

so that a graph can be plotted as:

```
. graph twoway ///
(kdensity y_1est [aweight=Ek], lpattern (solid)) ///
(kdensity y_0est [aweight=Ek], lpattern(dash)) , ///
title("Outcome response distr. for compliers by treatment in estimation" ,
size(med)) ///
xtitle(E(Y|x,D;compliers)) ///
legend(label(1 "D=1: treated compliers") label(2 "D=0: untreated compliers"))
///
note(Note: A linear form of the potential outcomes is assumed)
```

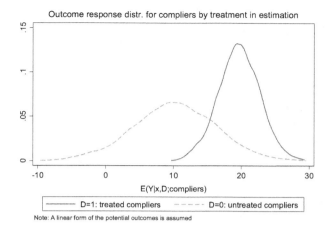

Outcome response distr. for compliers by treatment in estimation

E(Y|x,D;compliers)

———— D=1: treated compliers   ----- D=0: untreated compliers

Note: A linear form of the potential outcomes is assumed

The two graphs look very similar, thus offering support for the correctness of our estimation procedure for compliers' characterization.

4.4.2   An Application of RDD by Simulation

The next subsections present two simulative experiments for sharp RDD and fuzzy RDD, respectively. The virtue of such a simulation approach lies in being able to write down the correct data generating process of each RDD type. Thus, it allows an in-depth inspection of the assumption, properties, and expected results relative to this quasi-experimental technique. Of course, the Stata codes presented can be easily used in real datasets.

4.4.2.1   Simulating Sharp RDD

In this application we generate by simulation a sharp RDD setting producing a forcing variable s with a cutoff at $\bar{s} = 10$. Recall that, in the sharp RDD, the treatment D is a deterministic function of s. The outcome Y is modeled as a cubic function of s to allow for some nonlinearity in the response of Y to s. Given such a simulative setting, the objectives of this application are: (1) to estimate ATE using standard polynomial regression approach and graph the result; (2) to estimate ATE using a nonparametric local polynomial regression and graph the result; (3) to write a simple program to obtain the bootstrapped standard error of ATE in case (2); and (4) to replicate these results using the user-written Stata command rd.

The first step is that of generating a sharp RDD (observe that the treatment D is here indicated by the variable "w"):

```
. clear all
. set scheme s1mono
. set obs 1000        // generate N=1000
. set seed 1010       // set the simulation seed to get same results
. gen s = 10 +5 * invnorm(uniform())
. global s_star = 10
. gen x=s-$s_star  // define x as (s-s*)
. gen w=1 if s > $s_star // define w=treatment
. replace w=0 if s <= $s_star
. gen y1 = 600+6.5*x-2*x^2+0.001*x^3 + 300*invnorm(uniform()) // generate y1
. gen y0 = 200+6.5*x-0.20*x^2+0.01*x^3+ 300*invnorm(uniform()) // generate y0
. gen y=y0+w*(y1-y0) // generate the observable outcome by POM
```

Given such a data generating process, we saw that ATE is equal to the difference between the intercept of "*y1*" and that of "*y0*," that is $600 - 200 = 400$. As the simulated value for ATE is 400, we take this value as benchmark for the next analysis. Firstly, we visualize the outcome discontinuity at the cutoff. To that end, we plot two overlapping histograms of the outcome variable, one for values of Y on the left and the other for values of Y on the right of the cutoff by typing:

```
. twoway ///
hist y if s>$s_star, barw(60) bcolor(gray)  ///
|| ///
hist y if s<$s_star , barw(60) bcolor(black) ///
legend(order(1 "Right side" 2 "Left side") pos(11) col(1) ring(0)) ///
xtitle() ytitle(Frequency) ylabel()
```

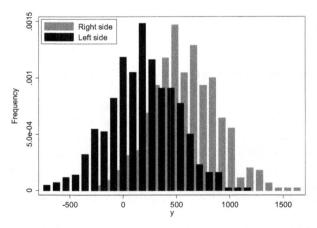

This plot shows evidence of a significant difference in such distributions, leading one to suspect that a relevant jump of the outcome at the threshold is present.

We then illustrate that, by construction, manipulation in the forcing variable is excluded plotting its density as follows:

```
. hist s , xline(10)
```

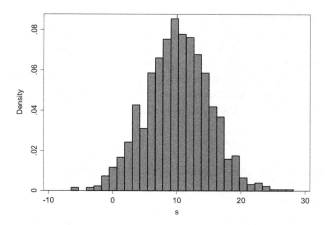

Given this result (namely, non-manipulation), we can go on to apply sharp RDD in the linear case using formula (4.70) and in the polynomial regression case using formula (4.71). We set out by using a full parametric model interpolated globally over all observations, so that no bandwidth has to be declared. Note that we adopt a third degree polynomial, whose terms are calculated as follows:

```
. gen wx=w*x
. gen wx2=w*x^2
. gen wx3=w*x^3
. gen x2=x^2
. gen x3=x^3
```

Thus, we have all the ingredients necessary to estimate ATE in the first instance by a linear regression:

```
. reg y w x wx // linear regression

      Source |       SS       df       MS              Number of obs =    1000
-------------+------------------------------           F(  3,   996) =  144.39
       Model |  41978638.2      3  13992879.4          Prob > F      =  0.0000
    Residual |  96521388.4    996  96909.0245          R-squared     =  0.3031
-------------+------------------------------           Adj R-squared =  0.3010
       Total |   138500027    999  138638.665          Root MSE      =   311.3

------------------------------------------------------------------------------
           y |      Coef.   Std. Err.      t    P>|t|     [95% Conf. Interval]
-------------+----------------------------------------------------------------
           w |   417.6347   32.37368    12.90   0.000     354.1063    481.1632
```

x	13.70573	4.682043	2.93	0.003	4.517933	22.89353
wx	-31.77256	6.53887	-4.86	0.000	-44.6041	-18.94102
_cons	235.5256	22.89783	10.29	0.000	190.592	280.4591

The obtained results provide us with an estimation of ATE (i.e., the coefficient of "w") equal to 417, which is highly significant too. Such a value is slightly biased in that the true value of ATE is equal to 400: a (small) bias of around 4.25 %, calculated as $|(400 - 417)/400| \cdot 100$, appears. We conclude that the linear approximation is a little imprecise with a small, but evident, overestimation of the true causal effect. A graphical analysis may at this point be useful too. We save the fitted values of previous linear regression by typing:

```
. predict y_hat_1 , xb // global linear fit
```

We can therefore plot the sharp RDD graph for the linear fit by typing:

```
. graph twoway ///
    (scatter y s if s>=$s_star , clstyle(p1)) ///
    (scatter y s if s<=$s_star , clstyle(p1)) ///
    (scatter y_hat_1 s if s>=$s_star , msymbol(o)) ///
    (scatter y_hat_1 s if s<=$s_star , msymbol(o)) ///
    , xline($s_star, lpattern(dash))  ///
  title("Sharp-RDD - Parametric linear regression") ///
    legend( label(1 "Right Actual Data") label(2 "Left Actual Data") ///
  label(3 "Right Prediction") label(4 "Left Prediction"))
```

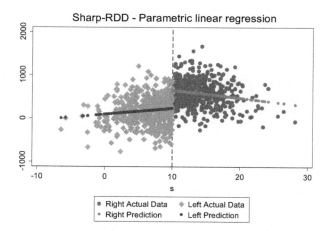

This graph clearly suggests the presence of a jump at the threshold, although the global linear approximation results in a rather unsatisfying estimation.

In an attempt to increase estimation precision, we subsequently estimate ATE by a global third degree polynomial regression and save the fitted values as follows:

```
. reg y w x x2 x3 wx wx2 wx3  // global polynomial regression

      Source |       SS        df       MS              Number of obs =    1000
-------------+------------------------------           F(  7,   992) =   64.01
       Model |  43094373.3        7  6156339.05         Prob > F      =  0.0000
    Residual |  95405653.3      992  96175.0537         R-squared     =  0.3112
-------------+------------------------------           Adj R-squared =  0.3063
       Total |   138500027      999  138638.665         Root MSE      =  310.12

------------------------------------------------------------------------------
           y |      Coef.   Std. Err.      t    P>|t|     [95% Conf. Interval]
-------------+----------------------------------------------------------------
           w |   399.6854    54.4856     7.34   0.000     292.7652    506.6057
           x |  -14.40288   26.97959    -0.53   0.594    -67.34651    38.54074
          x2 |  -2.833962    4.92639    -0.58   0.565     -12.5013    6.833381
          x3 |  -.0177433   .2431435    -0.07   0.942     -.494878    .4593914
          wx |    33.2883   37.41278     0.89   0.374    -40.12898    106.7056
         wx2 |  -1.101202   6.589222    -0.17   0.867    -14.03162    11.82921
         wx3 |   .0810121    .313127     0.26   0.796    -.5334552    .6954794
       _cons |   191.4839   37.43172     5.12   0.000     118.0295    264.9384
------------------------------------------------------------------------------

. predict y_hat , xb  // polynomial fit
```

The previous Stata output table illustrates an estimation of ATE equal to 399, which is highly significant. This value of the ATE proves to be almost exactly equal to the true value 400. As we did with the linear fit, we plot the sharp RDD graph for this third degree polynomial by typing:

```
. graph twoway ///
   (scatter y s if s>=$s_star , clstyle(p1)) ///
   (scatter y s if s<=$s_star , clstyle(p1)) ///
   (scatter y_hat s if s>=$s_star , msymbol(o)) ///
   (scatter y_hat s if s<=$s_star , msymbol(o)) ///
   , xline($s_star, lpattern(dash))  ///
   title("Sharp-RDD - Parametric Polynomial Regression") ///
     legend( label(1 "Right Actual Data") label(2 "Left Actual Data") ///
   label(3 "Right Prediction") label(4 "Left Prediction"))
```

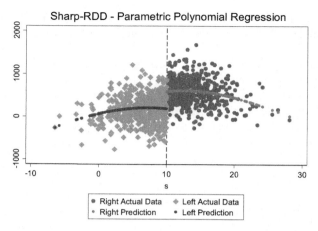

where, again, the significance of the jump at the cutoff is clearly visible.

We can now proceed to estimate the ATE using a local polynomial regression (i.e., a nonparametric approach) and graphing the results. To this end, we apply a smoothing approach using the Stata command lpoly. Before proceeding, it is useful to look at the help file of this command:

```
. help lpoly
Title

     [R] lpoly -- Kernel-weighted local polynomial smoothing
Syntax

          lpoly yvar xvar [if] [in] [weight] [, options]
------------------------------------------------------------------------------

    options     description
------------------------------------------------------------------------------

Main
  kernel(kernel)                specify kernel function; default is kernel(epanechnikov)
  bwidth(#|varname)             specify kernel bandwidth
  degree(#)                     specify degree of the polynomial smooth; default is
                                degree(0)
generate([newvar_x]newvar_s)    store the grid in newvar_x and smoothed points in
                                newvar_s
  n(#)                          obtain the smooth at # points; default is min(N,50)
  at(varname)                   obtain the smooth at the values specified by varname
  nograph                       suppress graph
  noscatter                     suppress scatterplot only
SE/CI
  ci                            plot confidence bands
  level(#)                      set confidence level; default is level(95)
  se(newvar)                    store standard errors in newvar
  pwidth(#)                     specify pilot bandwidth for standard error calculation
  var(#|varname)                specify estimates of residual variance
------------------------------------------------------------------------------
```

The main options for `lpoly` are reported above. For our purposes, the most relevant are: the one for the choice of the bandwidth, i.e., `bwidth()`; the one for the choice of the kernel, i.e., `kernel()`; the one specifying the degree of the polynomial smooth, i.e., `degree(#)`. As for the choice of the bandwidth, if not differently specified, `lpoly` uses by default the rule-of-thumb (ROT) formula of (4.105). As clearly discussed, this adopts a plug-in approach using all the observations present in the dataset. With regard to the choice of the kernel function, `lpoly` uses, by default, the Epanechnikov kernel, although many other options are possible as it is listed below:

```
--------------------------------------------------------------------------------
    kernel                          description
--------------------------------------------------------------------------------
    epanechnikov                    Epanechnikov kernel function; the default
    epan2                           alternative Epanechnikov kernel function
    biweight                        biweight kernel function
    cosine                          cosine trace kernel function
    gaussian                        Gaussian kernel function
    parzen                          Parzen kernel function
    rectangle                       rectangle kernel function
    triangle                        triangle kernel function
--------------------------------------------------------------------------------
```

Moreover, `lpoly` also allows for considering a local varying bandwidth that can be specified by the user as `bwidth(varname)`, along with an explicit smoothing grid using the `at()` option.

In this exercise, we fix a bandwidth equal to 5, we consider the forcing variable as the grid, we call the left-side smoothing estimates "$f0$" and the right-side estimates as "$f1$," and we assume a third degree local polynomial:

```
. global bendw 5  // Fix the bandwidth
. capture drop f0 f1
* Left (smoothed) estimates are called "f0".
* The grid is "s".
* The bandwight is 5.
* The polynomial degree is 3.
. lpoly y s if s<$s_star, gen(f0) at(s) k(tri) bw($bendw) deg(3)  nogr

* Right (smoothed) estimates are called "f1".
* The grid is "s".
* The bandwight is 5.
* The polynomial degree is 3.
. lpoly y s if s>=$s_star, gen(f1) at(s) k(tri) bw($bendw) deg(3) nogr
```

Finally, we graph the results:

```
. graph twoway ///
    (scatter y s if s>=$s_star , clstyle(p1)) ///
    (scatter y s if s<=$s_star , clstyle(p1)) ///
    (scatter f0 s if s<$s_star, msize(medsmall) msymbol(o))  ///
    (scatter f1 s if s>=$s_star, msize(medsmall) msymbol(o))  ///
    , xline($s_star, lpattern(dash))  ///
    title("Sharp RDD - Local polynomial regression (LPR)") ///
        legend(label(1 "Right actual data") label(2 "Left actual data") ///
            label(3 "Right LPR prediction") label(4 "Left LPR prediction")) ///
    note(Bandwidth = $bendw)
```

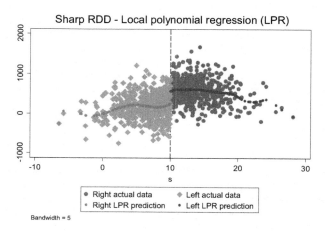

We can now also calculate the ATE in this framework. The trick here is to put the grid equal to a constant variable $z = \bar{s}$ returning a single value for "*f1*" and "*f0*" equal to the difference in the two curves in $z = \bar{s}$ (namely, in the threshold) that we know to be exactly the ATE:

```
. cap drop f0 f1
. gen z=$s_star
. qui lpoly y s if s<$s_star, gen(f0) at(z) k(tri) bw($bendw) deg(3) nogr
. qui lpoly y s if s>=$s_star, gen(f1) at(z)  k(tri) bw($bendw) deg(3) nogr
. scalar ate=f1[1]-f0[1]
. display ate
. 306.80612
```

We see that the value of the ATE in this case is around 307, resulting in a bias of around 23 % given by:

```
. di (400-307)/400*100
23.25
```

indicating that the nonparametric approach has in this case reduced the estimate precision, given that our DGP is perfectly interpolated by a cubic function over all observations. Unlike the parametric case, however, the previous nonparametric approach does not provide the standard error of the ATE estimate, so that the usual test of significance cannot be implemented. Nevertheless, we can in this case write a simple Stata program to recover the bootstrapped standard error for ATE. We call such a program `rdd_s`; observe that this is not a Stata ADO program, but just a program returning the estimate of ATE and taking as arguments the degree of the polynomial degree (`deg`) and the type of kernel function (`ker`):

```
* Program "rdd_s"
. capture program drop rdd_s
. prog rdd_s, rclass
  version 13
  args deg ker band cut
  cap drop f0 f1z
  gen z='cut'
  qui lpoly y s if s<'cut', gen(f0) at(z) k('ker') bw('band') deg('deg') nogr
  qui lpoly y s if s>='cut', gen(f1) at(z) k('ker') bw('band') deg('deg') nogr
  return scalar ate=f1[1]-f0[1]
  end
```

In order to get the estimation of ATE using, for instance, a three-degree polynomial and a triangular kernel, we can type:

```
. rdd_s 3 tri 5 10
. return list
scalars:
             r(ate) = 306.8061226179061
```

This returns an ATE equal to around 307 as obtained above. It is now possible to bootstrap the ATE's standard error in a straightforward way as follows:

```
. bootstrap r(ate), reps(50) seed(101): rdd_s 3 tri
------------------------------------------------------------------------------
Bootstrap results                               Number of obs     =       1000
                                                Replications      =         50
       command:  rdd_s 3 tri
        _bs_1:  r(ate)
------------------------------------------------------------------------------
            |   Observed   Bootstrap                         Normal-based
            |    Coef.     Std. Err.      z    P>|z|     [95% Conf. Interval]
-------------+----------------------------------------------------------------
      _bs_1 |   306.8061   93.06776    3.30   0.001     124.3967    489.2156
------------------------------------------------------------------------------
```

From this result, we can conclude—as expected—that the previous ATE estimation is still statistically significant.

Now, we can replicate the previous results using the rd.ado user-written Stata command (Nichols 2007). The syntax of this command, along with its main options, is displayed below (more information can be obtained by typing help rd):

```
-------------------------------------------------------------------------------
Description
-------------------------------------------------------------------------------
rd implements a set of regression-discontinuity estimation methods. rd estimates
    local linear or kernel regression models on both sides of the cut-off, using
    a triangle kernel. Estimates are sensitive to the choice of bandwidth, so by
    default several estimates are constructed using different bandwidths. In
    practice, rd uses kernel-weighted suest (or ivreg if suest fails) to estimate
    the local linear regressions and reports analytic SE based on the
    regressions.
-------------------------------------------------------------------------------
Syntax
        rd outcomevar [treatmentvar] assignmentvar [if] [in] [weight] [, options]
Note: there should be two or three variables specified after the rd command; if
two are specified, a sharp RD design is assumed, where the treatment variable
jumps from zero to one at the cut-off. If no variables are specified after the
rd command, the estimates table is displayed.
-------------------------------------------------------------------------------
Main options
-------------------------------------------------------------------------------
mbw(numlist): specifies a list of multiples for bandwidths, in percentage terms.
    The default is "100 50 200" (i.e. half and twice the requested bandwidth) and
    100 is always included in the list, regardless of whether it is specified.

z0(real): specifies the cut-off Z0 in assignmentvar Z.

x(varlist): requests estimates of jumps in control variables varlist.

ddens: requests a computation of a discontinuity in the density of Z. This is
    computed in a relatively ad hoc way, and should be redone using McCrary's
    test described at: http://www.econ.berkeley.edu/~jmccrary/DCdensity/.

s(stubname): requests that estimates be saved as new variables beginning with
    stubname.

graph: requests that local linear regression graphs for each bandwidth be
    produced.

bdep: requests a graph of estimates versus bendwidths.

bwidth(real): allows specification of a bandwidth for local linear regressions.
    The default is to use the estimated optimal bandwidth for a "sharp" design as
```

given by Imbens and Kalyanaraman (2012). The optimal bandwidth minimizes MSE,
or squared bias plus variance, where a smaller bandwidth tends to produce
lower bias and higher variance. Note that the optimal bandwidth will often
tend to be larger for a fuzzy design, due to the additional variance that
arises from the estimation of the jump in the conditional mean of treatment.

kernel(rectangle): requests the use of a rectangle (uniform) kernel. The default
   is a triangle (edge) kernel.

covar(varlist): adds covariates to Local Wald Estimation.

The rd command considers only local linear regressions, thus excluding the
possibility to fit local polynomial regressions as we did using rdd_s. One important advantage, however, is that—by default—rd considers bandwidth as the
optimal one provided by Imbens and Kalyanaraman (2012) expressed in (4.97).
Users can also choose to set different bandwidths.

First of all, we show that rd provides the same results as the program rdd_s,
provided that in rdd_s we consider a polynomial of degree one (i.e., a local linear
regression) and in rd the same bandwidth. If we run program rdd_s with a
polynomial degree option equal to one, we get an ATE equal to:

```
. rdd_s 1 tri
. return list
scalars:
            r(ate) =  379.8166986980401
```

which is the same as the one obtained by typing :

```
. rd y s , z0($s_star) bw($bendw)

Two variables specified; treatment is
assumed to jump from zero to one at Z=10.

 Assignment variable Z is s
 Treatment variable X_T unspecified
 Outcome variable y is y

Estimating for bandwidth 5
Estimating for bandwidth 2.5
Estimating for bandwidth 10
-----------------------------------------------------------------------------
        y |    Coef.   Std. Err.     z    P>|z|    [95% Conf. Interval]
----------+------------------------------------------------------------------
    lwald |  379.8167   49.66377   7.65   0.000    282.4775    477.1559
  lwald50 |  343.0671   66.97426   5.12   0.000    211.7999    474.3342
 lwald200 |  410.6234   37.5783   10.93   0.000    336.9713    484.2755
-----------------------------------------------------------------------------
```

The result for the bandwidth equal to 5 is 379.81, that is rather close to the true
ATE value. rd also provides by default results for proportionally smaller and larger
bandwidths as displayed in the results' table above. One can also declare a series of
proportional bandwidths separated by a specific step and then plot the various ATE
estimates versus bandwidths using the following command:

```
. rd y s , z0($s_star) bw($bendw) mbw(10(10)200) bdep

Estimating for bandwidth 5
Estimating for bandwidth .5
Estimating for bandwidth 1
Estimating for bandwidth 1.5
Estimating for bandwidth 2
Estimating for bandwidth 2.5
Estimating for bandwidth 3
Estimating for bandwidth 3.5
Estimating for bandwidth 4
Estimating for bandwidth 4.5
Estimating for bandwidth 5.5
Estimating for bandwidth 6
Estimating for bandwidth 6.5
Estimating for bandwidth 7
Estimating for bandwidth 7.5
Estimating for bandwidth 8
Estimating for bandwidth 8.5
Estimating for bandwidth 9
Estimating for bandwidth 9.5
Estimating for bandwidth 10
```

y	Coef.	Std. Err.	z	P>|z|	[95% Conf. Interval]	
lwald	379.8167	49.66377	7.65	0.000	282.4775	477.1559
lwald10	213.1167	136.7133	1.56	0.119	-54.83646	481.0698
lwald20	307.2441	96.9611	3.17	0.002	117.2039	497.2844
lwald30	318.5954	82.2223	3.87	0.000	157.4426	479.7481
lwald40	335.6237	73.66202	4.56	0.000	191.2488	479.9986
lwald50	343.0671	66.97426	5.12	0.000	211.7999	474.3342
lwald60	350.7385	61.32289	5.72	0.000	230.5479	470.9292
lwald70	358.5919	57.70817	6.21	0.000	245.4859	471.6978
lwald80	369.8862	54.58116	6.78	0.000	262.9091	476.8633
lwald90	376.8164	51.8844	7.26	0.000	275.1249	478.508
lwald110	384.7128	47.83083	8.04	0.000	290.9661	478.4595
lwald120	389.6336	46.09231	8.45	0.000	299.2943	479.9728
lwald130	394.7869	44.29958	8.91	0.000	307.9614	481.6125
lwald140	401.0488	42.76487	9.38	0.000	317.2312	484.8664

```
   lwald150 |    405.1497    41.47248     9.77   0.000       323.8651      486.4343
   lwald160 |     407.381    40.40292    10.08   0.000       328.1927      486.5692
   lwald170 |     408.767    39.51606    10.34   0.000        331.317      486.2171
   lwald180 |    410.2129    38.75568    10.58   0.000       334.2531      486.1726
   lwald190 |       410.7    38.12595    10.77   0.000       335.9745      485.4255
   lwald200 |    410.6234     37.5783    10.93   0.000       336.9713      484.2755
---------------------------------------------------------------------------------
```

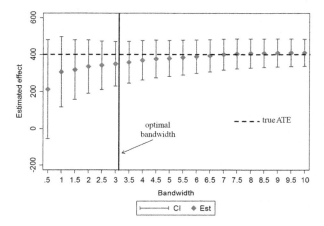

The graph obtained is particularly explicative in showing that, as soon as the bandwidth increases, estimation becomes more precise. Observe, moreover, that the optimal bandwidth can be obtained by default by writing:

```
. rd y s , z0($s_star)

Estimating for bandwidth 3.193236072866368
Estimating for bandwidth 1.596618036433184
Estimating for bandwidth 6.386472145732736
---------------------------------------------------------------------------------
          y |      Coef.   Std. Err.      z    P>|z|     [95% Conf. Interval]
------------+--------------------------------------------------------------------
      lwald |   352.2594    59.74646     5.90   0.000      235.1585      469.3603
    lwald50 |   324.9141    80.21817     4.05   0.000      167.6893      482.1388
   lwald200 |   393.4936    44.70381     8.80   0.000      305.8757      481.1114
---------------------------------------------------------------------------------
```

where it is visible that the optimal (default) bandwidth is equal to 3.16. Note that for this bandwidth, the estimated value of the ATE is 352 that is quite far from the true value, 400, with a bias of around 12 %. The fact we still obtain a bias with an optimal bandwidth in large samples is not surprising. As argued in the theoretical part of this chapter, the asymptotic normal distribution of nonparametric estimates presents an asymptotic nonzero bias with convergence occurring at rate $N^{-0.4}$. In this case, however, since our DGP assumes a global parametric regression, it is not surprising that precision increases as soon as the bandwidth increases.

4.4.2.2 Fuzzy RDD

For fuzzy RDD, we follow in the footsteps of the previous example but this time, for the sake of simplicity, we generate a forcing variable with a cutoff at 0. Recall that in the fuzzy RDD, the treatment variable is a stochastic (rather than deterministic) function of s. Moreover, we assume, as in the case of sharp RDD, potential outcomes to be nonlinear functions of s. In this exercise, once a fuzzy RDD data generating mechanism has been produced, the objective will be that of: (1) estimating ATE using a global parametric regression approach and graph the results; (2) estimating ATE using a nonparametric local linear regression and graph the results; (3) writing a simple Stata program to obtain the bootstrapped standard error for ATE in case (2); (4) replicating results using the rd Stata command.

We set out by producing the following fuzzy RDD setting, similar to that of Yang (2013): the forcing variable is drawn from a uniform distribution in the interval $[-1; 1]$. This implies that the variable s has mean equal to 0 and variance equal to 1/3. As the threshold is at zero, we assume at that point a discontinuity in the probability of getting treated. The binary treatment variable is thus defined through the following index function:

$$D_i = 1[-0.5 + T_i + s_i + u_i \geq 0]$$
$$T_i = 1[s_i \geq 0]$$
$$u_i \sim N(0; 1)$$

where T_i is equal to 1 if unit i is located in the right and 0 if located in the left of the zero cutoff. The previous DGP generates a discontinuity in the probability of treatment at the cutoff equal to 0.383. In fact, we immediately see that:

$$\lim_{s \downarrow \bar{s}} p(D = 1 \mid S = s) - \lim_{s \uparrow \bar{s}} p(D = 1 \mid S = s) = \Phi(0.5) - \Phi(-0.5) = 0.383$$

with $\Phi(\cdot)$ representing the Normal cumulative distribution function. Finally, we assume the following form of the potential outcomes:

$$Y_1 = 2 + f(s) + v$$
$$Y_0 = 1 + f(s) + v$$
$$f(s) = s + s^2 + 3s^3$$
$$v \sim N(0; 1)$$

This DGP for the potential outcomes results in this form of the observable outcome Y:

$$Y = Y_0 + D(Y_1 - Y_0) = 1 + D + f(s) + v$$

Since:

$$E(Y \mid s) = 1 + E(D \mid s) + f(s) = 1 + p(D = 1 \mid s) + f(s)$$

we have that:

$$\lim_{s \downarrow \bar{s}} E(Y \mid S = s) - \lim_{s \uparrow \bar{s}} E(Y \mid S = s) = [1 + \Phi(0.5)] - [1 + \Phi(-0.5)]$$

$$= \Phi(0.5) - \Phi(-0.5) = 0.383$$

showing that the Wald estimator of such a DGP is equal to 1. In other words:

$$\frac{\lim_{s \downarrow \bar{s}} E(Y \mid S = s) - \lim_{s \uparrow \bar{s}} E(Y \mid S = s)}{\lim_{s \downarrow \bar{s}} p(D = 1 \mid S = s) - \lim_{s \uparrow \bar{s}} p(D = 1 \mid S = s)} = \frac{0.383}{0.383} = 1$$

We now implement such a DGP in Stata as follows:

```
. clear all
. set seed 10101
. set scheme s1mono
. set obs 1000 // Generate N=1000
. gen s = -1+2*runiform()
. gen T=(s>=0)
* Generate w (binary treatment variable)
. gen v = rnormal(0,1)
. gen w = (-0.5+T+s+v>=0)
. gen y1 = 2 + s + s^2 + 3*s^3 + invnorm(uniform())
. gen y0 = 1 + s + s^2 + 3*s^3 + invnorm(uniform())
. gen y = y0 + w*(y1-y0)
```

We show that, in this DGP, the actual value of ATE is equal to 1 by performing an Instrumental-variables regression of Y on D using T as instrument:

```
. gen s2 = s^2
. gen s3 = s^3
. reg w T s s2 s3
. ivreg y (w=T) s s2 s3
```

```
Instrumental variables (2SLS) regression
```

Source	SS	df	MS		Number of obs =	1000
					F(4, 995) =	1088.22
Model	4513.46408	4	1128.36602		Prob > F =	0.0000
Residual	995.058127	995	1.00005842		R-squared =	0.8194
					Adj R-squared =	0.8186
Total	5508.52221	999	5.51403625		Root MSE =	1

y	Coef.	Std. Err.	t	P>|t|	[95% Conf.	Interval]
w	.9988115	.451382	2.21	0.027	.1130416	1.884581
s	1.006081	.4235583	2.38	0.018	.1749108	1.837251
s2	.8569674	.1030806	8.31	0.000	.6546871	1.059248
s3	3.051368	.3222467	9.47	0.000	2.419007	3.683729
_cons	1.035791	.225424	4.59	0.000	.5934302	1.478152

```
Instrumented:  w
Instruments:   s s2 s3 T
```

which reports an ATE equal to 0.998, very close to 1, as expected.

We can go on by estimating nonparametrically the outcome discontinuity, using a local third degree polynomial and then drawing the corresponding graph:

```
* Outcome discontinuity
. global s_star 0
. global bendw 5  // Fix the bandwidth
. capture drop f0 f1
* Left estimates are called "f0".
* The grid is "s".
* The bandwight is 5.
* The polynomial degree is 3.
. lpoly y s if s<$s_star, gen(f0) at(s) k(tri) bw($bendw) deg(3)  nogr
* Right estimates are called "f1".
* The grid is "s".
* The bandwight is 5.
* The polynomial degree is 3.
. lpoly y s if s>=$s_star, gen(f1) at(s) k(tri) bw($bendw) deg(3) nogr
* Make the graph:
. graph twoway ///
    (scatter y s if s>=$s_star , clstyle(p1)) ///
    (scatter y s if s<=$s_star , clstyle(p1)) ///
    (scatter f0 s if s<$s_star, msize(medsmall) msymbol(o))  ///
```

```
(scatter f1 s if s>=$s_star, msize(medsmall) msymbol(o))   ///
, xline($s_star, lpattern(dash))   ///
title("Fuzzy-RDD - Outcome Non-parametric Local Linear Regression" ,
size(medlarge)) ///
    legend(label(1 "Right Actual Data") label(2 "Left Actual Data") ///
        label(3 "Right LLR Prediction") label(4 "Left LLR Prediction")) ///
note(Bandwidth = $bendw)
```

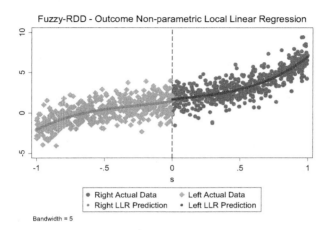

Fuzzy-RDD - Outcome Non-parametric Local Linear Regression

Bandwidth = 5

Likewise, we can do the same for the probability discontinuity:

```
* Probability discontonuity
. global s_star 0
. global bendw 5  // Fix the bandwidth
. capture drop f0 f1
* Left estimates are called "g0".
* The grid is "s".
* The bandwight is 5.
* The polynomial degree is 3.
. lpoly w s if s<$s_star, gen(g0) at(s) k(tri) bw($bendw) deg(3)   nogr
* Right estimates are called "g1".
* The grid is "s".
* The bandwight is 5.
* The polynomial degree is 3.
. lpoly w s if s>=$s_star, gen(g1) at(s) k(tri) bw($bendw) deg(3) nogr
* Graph:
. graph twoway ///
    (scatter w s if s>=$s_star & w==1 , clstyle(p1)) ///
    (scatter w s if s<=$s_star & w==0, clstyle(p1)) ///
    (scatter g0 s if s<$s_star, msize(medsmall) msymbol(o))   ///
```

```
(scatter g1 s if s>=$s_star, msize(medsmall) msymbol(o))   ///
, xline($s_star, lpattern(dash))   ///
title("Fuzzy-RDD - Probability Non-parametric Local Linear Regression") ///
    legend(label(1 "Right Actual Data") label(2 "Left Actual Data") ///
        label(3 "Right LLR Prediction") label(4 "Left LLR Prediction")) ///
note(Bandwidth = $bendw)
```

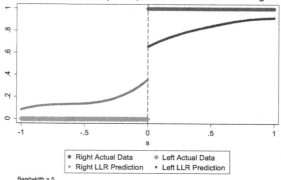

Fuzzy-RDD - Probability Non-parametric Local Linear Regression

Finally, we write a simple program to obtain the bootstrapped standard error for ATE in the nonparametric case. We call this program rdd_f, taking as arguments the degree of the polynomial (deg), the type of kernel function (ker), the bandwidth (band), and the cutoff (cut):

```
* Program "rdd_f"
capture program drop rdd_f
prog rdd_f, rclass
version 13
args deg ker band cut
* Outcome discontinuity
cap drop z f0 f1
gen z='cut'
cap drop f0 f1
qui lpoly y s if s<'cut', gen(f0) at(z) k('ker') bw('band') deg('deg') nogr
qui lpoly y s if s>='cut', gen(f1) at(z) k('ker') bw('band') deg('deg') nogr
scalar disc_y=f1[1]-f0[1]
* Probability discontinuity
cap drop g0 g1
qui lpoly w s if s<'cut', gen(g0) at(z) k('ker') bw('band') deg('deg') nogr
qui lpoly w s if s>='cut', gen(g1) at(z) k('ker') bw('band') deg('deg') nogr
scalar disc_w=g1[1]-g0[1]
return scalar ate=disc_y/disc_w
end
```

```
. rdd_f 3 tri 5 0
. return list
scalars:
                r(ate) =  .681765296755097
```

It is now possible to bootstrap the standard error for ATE in a straightforward way:

```
. bootstrap r(ate), reps(10): rdd_f 3 tri 5 0

--------------------------------------------------------------------------------
Bootstrap results                           Number of obs      =        1000
                                            Replications       =          10
        command:  rdd_f 3 tri 5 0
          _bs_1:  r(ate)
--------------------------------------------------------------------------------
             |   Observed   Bootstrap                         Normal-based
             |     Coef.    Std. Err.     z    P>|z|     [95% Conf. Interval]
-------------+------------------------------------------------------------------
       _bs_1 |   .6817653   1.082933   0.63   0.529    -1.440745    2.804275
--------------------------------------------------------------------------------
```

Finally, as in the sharp RDD case, we replicate results using the `rd` Stata command. For the sake of comparison, however, we have to consider a polynomial of degree 1, as `rd` implements a local linear approach:

```
. rdd_f 1 tri 5 0
. return list

scalars:
                r(ate) =  -1.747380009730471
```

that is equivalent to running:

```
. rd y w s , z0(0) bw(5)

Estimating for bandwidth 5
Estimating for bandwidth 2.5
Estimating for bandwidth 10
--------------------------------------------------------------------------------
           y |     Coef.    Std. Err.     z    P>|z|     [95% Conf. Interval]
-------------+------------------------------------------------------------------
       numer |  -.7499524   .1483967   -5.05  0.000    -1.040805   -.4591003
       denom |   .4291868   .0534704    8.03  0.000     .3243868    .5339868
       lwald |   -1.74738   .4720134   -3.70  0.000    -2.672509   -.8222507
     numer50 |  -.6751287   .1489964   -4.53  0.000    -.9671563   -.3831011
```

```
denom50  |    .4246377    .0542582     7.83   0.000      .3182935     .5309819
lwald50  |   -1.589893    .4671927    -3.40   0.001     -2.505574    -.6742127
numer200 |   -.7828516    .1482526    -5.28   0.000     -1.073421    -.4922819
denom200 |    .4311897    .0531644     8.11   0.000      .3269893      .53539
lwald200 |   -1.815562    .4743201    -3.83   0.000     -2.745212    -.8859117
-----------------------------------------------------------------------------
```

We can see that, according to the previous results, the Wald estimator obtained using `rd` is equal to -1.747, the same as the one obtained using `rdd_f`. Such a value seems however really far from the true value of ATE, which we saw to be equal to 1. This result is caused by an incorrect choice of the bandwidth, so that we need to reestimate the model using the optimal bandwidth as follows:

```
. rd y w s , z0(0)

Estimating for bandwidth .4713549912056355
Estimating for bandwidth .2356774956028178
Estimating for bandwidth .942709982411271

-----------------------------------------------------------------------------
        y |     Coef.   Std. Err.      z    P>|z|     [95% Conf. Interval]
----------+------------------------------------------------------------------
    numer |   .2267855    .2365194    0.96   0.338    -.2367841     .6903551
    denom |   .3243078    .0919351    3.53   0.000     .1441183     .5044973
    lwald |    .699291    .6594338    1.06   0.289    -.5931755     1.991757
  numer50 |   .2075673    .3331399    0.62   0.533     -.445375     .8605096
  denom50 |   .2442051    .1298294    1.88   0.060    -.0102558      .498666
  lwald50 |   .8499711    1.219224    0.70   0.486    -1.539664     3.239606
 numer200 |  -.1048066    .1662147   -0.63   0.528    -.4305815     .2209682
 denom200 |   .3901452    .0639885    6.10   0.000       .26473     .5155603
 lwald200 |   -.268635    .4467665   -0.60   0.548    -1.144281     .6070113
-----------------------------------------------------------------------------
```

The value of ATE with optimal bandwidth (equal to 0.471) is now equal to 0.7, while is much closer to 1, it is not exactly one. The bias which occurs depends on the fact that, in the case of nonparametric regressions, even asymptotically, the bias does not disappear although it tends to become smaller when N is rather large. Moreover, recall that the rate of convergence of nonparametric methods is $N^{-0.4}$, that is slower than that of parametric approaches. It is interesting to see that when the bandwidth is chosen as half of the optimal one (see the value for `lwald50` in the previous table), then we have a reduction of the bias which moves from $(1 - 0.699) = 0.301$ to $(1 - 0.849) = 0.151$. This is the case of undersmoothing, which occurs with a choice of the bandwidth (0.235) lower than the optimal one (0.471). Of course, undersmoothing has a price, since it returns a larger estimated standard error (1.219) compared to the one obtained under optimal smoothing (0.659).

Finally, in what follows, we write a Stata code to calculate the value of the Wald estimator for different sample sizes. We put the attained results into a matrix A with six rows and two columns:

```
. mat def A=J(6,2,.)
. local k=1
foreach i of numlist 1000 10000 50000 100000 200000 300000  {
. clear
. set seed 10101
. set obs `i'
. gen s = -1+2*runiform()
. gen T=(s>=0)
* Generate w (binary treatment variable)
. gen v = rnormal(0,1)
. gen w = (-0.5+T+s+v>=0)
. gen y1 = 2 + s + s^2 + 3*s^3 + invnorm(uniform())
. gen y0 = 1 + s + s^2 + 3*s^3 + invnorm(uniform())
. gen y = y0 + w*(y1-y0)
. qui rd y w s , z0(0)
. matrix A[`k',1]=_b[lwald]
. matrix A[`k',2]=`i'
. local k=`k'+1
}
. matrix colnames A = Wald_est Sample_size
. mat list A

A[6,2]
        Wald_est  Sample_size
r1      .69929098        1000
r2      1.0268281       10000
r3      .98720917       50000
r4      .82719328      100000
r5      1.0884702      200000
r6      .99637508      300000
```

As expected, we clearly see that—when using optimal bandwidth—and as long as N becomes sufficiently large, the Wald estimator converges to 1. Finally, after regenerating the simulation with $N = 10,000$, as we did at the outset of this section, we can draw the Wald estimator for different bandwidths as follows:

```
. rd y w s , z0(0) mbw(10(10)100) bdep

Estimating for bandwidth .4713549912056355
Estimating for bandwidth .0471354991205636
Estimating for bandwidth .0942709982411271
Estimating for bandwidth .1414064973616906
```

```
Estimating for bandwidth .1885419964822542
Estimating for bandwidth .2356774956028178
Estimating for bandwidth .2828129947233813
Estimating for bandwidth .3299484938439448
Estimating for bandwidth .3770839929645085
Estimating for bandwidth .424219492085072
```

y	Coef.	Std. Err.	z	P>|z|	[95% Conf.	Interval]
numer	.2267855	.2365194	0.96	0.338	-.2367841	.6903551
denom	.3243078	.0919351	3.53	0.000	.1441183	.5044973
lwald	.699291	.6594338	1.06	0.289	-.5931755	1.991757
numer10	-.9352515	.500547	-1.87	0.062	-1.916306	.0458026
denom10	.1389788	.2854189	0.49	0.626	-.420432	.6983896
lwald10	-6.729454	15.31744	-0.44	0.660	-36.75109	23.29219
numer20	-.3321133	.4564705	-0.73	0.467	-1.226779	.5625524
denom20	.1718275	.1987912	0.86	0.387	-.2177961	.561451
lwald20	-1.93283	4.102229	-0.47	0.638	-9.973051	6.10739
numer30	-.1312488	.4242862	-0.31	0.757	-.9628345	.7003369
denom30	.126333	.1716659	0.74	0.462	-.210126	.4627921
lwald30	-1.038911	4.159927	-0.25	0.803	-9.192218	7.114396
numer40	.0881357	.3747688	0.24	0.814	-.6463976	.822669
denom40	.1784971	.1472767	1.21	0.226	-.1101599	.467154
lwald40	.4937656	1.948472	0.25	0.800	-3.325169	4.3127
numer50	.2075673	.3331399	0.62	0.533	-.445375	.8605096
denom50	.2442051	.1298294	1.88	0.060	-.0102558	.498666
lwald50	.8499711	1.219224	0.70	0.486	-1.539664	3.239606
numer60	.1859986	.3084208	0.60	0.546	-.418495	.7904922
denom60	.2625558	.1198433	2.19	0.028	.0276673	.4974443
lwald60	.7084156	1.061916	0.67	0.505	-1.372901	2.789732
numer70	.1985204	.2853907	0.70	0.487	-.3608351	.7578759
denom70	.2687388	.1102866	2.44	0.015	.052581	.4848966
lwald70	.7387114	.9581545	0.77	0.441	-1.139237	2.61666
numer80	.2127692	.2653003	0.80	0.423	-.3072099	.7327483
denom80	.289658	.102578	2.82	0.005	.0886087	.4907073
lwald80	.7345531	.8263895	0.89	0.374	-.8851404	2.354247
numer90	.2260461	.2495957	0.91	0.365	-.2631524	.7152446
denom90	.3120691	.0968244	3.22	0.001	.1222967	.5018414
lwald90	.7243465	.721625	1.00	0.315	-.6900126	2.138706

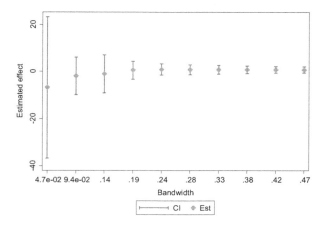

The results obtained seem to confirm that a moderate undersmoothing reduces the bias, although with a slighter increase in the variance of the estimator.

References

Abadie, A. (2003). Semiparametric instrumental variable estimation of treatment response models. *Journal of Econometrics, 113*, 231–263. doi:10.1016/S0304-4076(02)00201-4.

Abadie, A., Angrist, J., & Imbens, G. (2002). Instrumental variables estimates of the effect of subsidized training on the quantiles of trainee earnings. *Econometrica, 70*, 91–117. doi:10.1111/1468-0262.00270.

Angrist, J. D. (1990). Lifetime earnings and the Vietnam era draft lottery: Evidence from social security administrative records. *American Economic Review, 80*, 313–336.

Angrist, J. D., & Evans, W. N. (1998). Children and their parents' labor supply: Evidence from exogenous variation in family size. *American Economic Review, 88*, 450–477.

Angrist, J. D., & Imbens, G. W. (1995). Two-stage least squares estimation of average causal effects in models with variable treatment intensity. *Journal of the American Statistical Association, 90*, 431–442. doi:10.1080/01621459.1995.10476535.

Angrist, J. D., & Lavy, V. (1999). Using Maimonides' rule to estimate the effect of class size on scholastic achievement. *Quarterly Journal of Economics, 114*, 533–575.

Angrist, J. D., & Pischke, J.-S. (2008). *Mostly harmless econometrics: An empiricist's companion.* Princeton, NJ: Princeton University Press.

Bloom, H. S. (1984). Accounting for no-shows in experimental evaluation designs. *Evaluation Review, 8*, 225–246. doi:10.1177/0193841X8400800205.

Cook, T. D. (2008). "Waiting for life to arrive": A history of the regression-discontinuity design in psychology, statistics and economics. *Journal of Econometrics, 142*, 636–654. doi:10.1016/j.jeconom.2007.05.002.

Fan, J., & Gijbels, I. (1996). *Local polynomial modelling and its applications: Monographs on statistics and applied probability* (Vol. 66). Boca Raton, FL: CRC Press.

Hahn, J., Todd, P., & Van der Klaauw, W. (2001). Identification and estimation of treatment effects with a regression-discontinuity design. *Econometrica, 69*, 201–209. doi:10.1111/1468-0262.00183.

Härdle, W. (1991). *Applied nonparametric regression.* Cambridge: Cambridge University Press.

Härdle, W., & Marron, J. S. (1985). Optimal bandwidth selection in nonparametric regression function estimation. *Annals of Statistics, 13*, 1465–1481.

Imbens, G. W., & Angrist, J. D. (1994). Identification and estimation of local average treatment effects. *Econometrica, 62*, 467–475. doi:10.2307/2951620.

Imbens, G., & Kalyanaraman, K. (2012). Optimal bandwidth choice for the regression discontinuity estimator. *Review of Economic Studies, 79*, 933–959.

Imbens, G. W., & Lemieux, T. (2008). Regression discontinuity designs: A guide to practice. *Journal of Econometrics, 142*, 615–635. doi:10.1016/j.jeconom.2007.05.001.

Lee, D. S., & Lemieux, T. (2009). *Regression discontinuity designs in economics* (NBER Working Paper No. 14723). National Bureau of Economic Research, Inc.

Lee, D. S., Moretti, E., & Butler, M. J. (2004). Do voters affect or elect policies? Evidence from the U. S. House. *Quarterly Journal of Economics, 119*, 807–859.

Ludwig, J., & Miller, D. L. (2007). Does head start improve children's life chances? Evidence from a regression discontinuity design. *Quarterly Journal of Economics, 122*, 159–208. doi:10.1162/qjec.122.1.159.

McCrary, J. (2008). Manipulation of the running variable in the regression discontinuity design: A density test. *Journal of Econometrics, 142*, 698–714.

Nichols, A. (2007). Causal inference with observational data: Regression discontinuity and related methods in Stata (North American Stata Users' Group Meetings 2007 No. 2). Stata Users Group.

Pagan, A., & Ullah, A. (1999). *Nonparametric econometrics*. Cambridge: Cambridge University Press.

Porter, J. (2003). Estimation in the regression discontinuity model. Dep. Econ. Univ. Wis. Mimeo.

Stone, C. J. (1982). Optimal global rates of convergence for nonparametric regression. *Annals of Statistics, 10*, 1040–1053.

Thistlethwaite, D. L., & Campbell, D. T. (1960). Regression-discontinuity analysis: An alternative to the ex post facto experiment. *Journal of Education & Psychology, 51*, 309–317. doi:10.1037/h0044319.

Van Der Klaauw, W. (2002). Estimating the effect of financial aid offers on college enrollment: A regression-discontinuity approach. *International Economic Review, 43*, 1249–1287. doi:10.1111/1468-2354.t01-1-00055.

Van Der Klaauw, W. (2008). Regression-discontinuity analysis: A survey of recent developments in economics. *Labour, 22*, 219–245. doi:10.1111/j.1467-9914.2008.00419.x.

Wald, A. (1940). The fitting of straight lines if both variables are subject to error. *Annals of Mathematical Statistics, 11*, 284–300. doi:10.1214/aoms/1177731868.

Wooldridge, J. M. (2010). *Econometric analysis of cross section and panel data*. Cambridge, MA: MIT Press.

Yang, M. (2013). Treatment effect analyses through orthogonality conditions implied by a fuzzy regression discontinuity design, with two empirical studies. Dep. Econ. Rauch Bus. Cent. Lehigh Univ., Bethlehem, PA.

CPSIA information can be obtained at www.ICGtesting.com
Printed in the USA
LVOW04*0848250515

439718LV00004B/128/P

9 783662 464045